Lecture Notes in Computer Science 16117

Founding Editors

Gerhard Goos
Juris Hartmanis

The series Lecture Notes in Computer Science (LNCS), including its subseries Lecture Notes in Artificial Intelligence (LNAI) and Lecture Notes in Bioinformatics (LNBI), has established itself as a medium for the publication of new developments in computer science and information technology research, teaching, and education.

LNCS enjoys close cooperation with the computer science R & D community, the series counts many renowned academics among its volume editors and paper authors, and collaborates with prestigious societies. Its mission is to serve this international community by providing an invaluable service, mainly focused on the publication of conference and workshop proceedings and postproceedings. LNCS commenced publication in 1973.

Santiago Escobar · Laura Titolo

Editors

Logic-Based Program Synthesis and Transformation

35th International Symposium, LOPSTR 2025
Rende, Italy, September 9–10, 2025
Proceedings

 Springer

Editors
Santiago Escobar ⓘ
Universitat Politècnica de València
Valencia, Spain

Laura Titolo ⓘ
Code Metal
Boston, MA, USA

ISSN 0302-9743   ISSN 1611-3349 (electronic) ,
Lecture Notes in Computer Science
ISBN 978-3-032-04847-9   ISBN 978-3-032-04848-6 (eBook)
https://doi.org/10.1007/978-3-032-04848-6

This Springer imprint is published by the registered company Springer Nature Switzerland AG
The registered company address is: Gewerbestrasse 11, 6330 Cham, Switzerland

If disposing of this product, please recycle the paper.

Preface

This volume contains the papers selected for presentation at LOPSTR 2025, the 35th International Symposium on Logic-Based Program Synthesis and Transformation, held in Rende, Italy, September 9-10, 2025. The symposium was held in conjunction with PPDP 2025, the 27th International Symposium on Principles and Practice of Declarative Programming, and ICLP 2025, the 41st International Conference on Logic Programming. Details about the organisation of LOPSTR 2025 can be found at https://lopstr.github.io/2025/.

The LOPSTR series of symposia aim to stimulate and promote research and collaboration on logic-based program development, interpreted broadly and covering the entire software life cycle. LOPSTR has held a prominent place in this area for more than three decades, ever since the inaugural meeting in Manchester, in 1991. Information about the previous symposia can be found at https://lopstr.webs.upv.es/.

In response to the call for papers, 21 submissions were received, 17 regular papers and 4 short papers.

They were written by 36 authors from Austria, Brazil, France, Georgia, Germany, Greece, Italy, Japan, Spain, UK, and USA. After a screening for all conflicts of interest, the submissions went through a single-blind review process, each paper receiving three independent reviews. This was followed by an online discussion among the members of the program committee. Based on the final discussion, 9 regular papers and 3 short papers were selected for presentation.

The symposium featured two distinguished invited speakers: Robbert Krebbers, Radboud University Nijmegen, The Netherlands, and José Meseguer, University of Illinois Urbana-Champaign, IL, USA. Robbert was kindly sponsored by the Association for Logic Programming and was a shared invited speaker with PPDP 2025. We would like to extend our thanks to all who submitted a paper, for their interest in LOPSTR, and to the invited speakers, for agreeing to come and make highly valued contributions to the symposium. Sincere thanks are also due to the program committee and external reviewers for their careful work. It has been a pleasure to work with the ICLP general chair, Francesco Ricca, and with the PPDP 2025 chairs Małgorzata Biernacka and Carlos Olarte. We also thank the Chair of the LOPSTR Steering Committee, Maurizio Proietti. Finally, we thank the Springer staff for their guidance and collaboration in preparing the current volume.

July 2025   Santiago Escobar
                                                               Laura Titolo

Organization

Program Committee

Elvira Albert	Complutense University of Madrid, Spain
Roberto Amadini	University of Bologna, Italy
João Barbosa	University of Porto, Portugal
Juliana Bowles	University of St. Andrews, UK
Włodek Drabent	IPI PAN Warszawa, Poland
Catherine Dubois	ENSIIE-Samovar, France
Santiago Escobar (Co-chair)	Universitat Politècnica de València, Spain
Fabio Fioravanti	University of Chieti-Pescara, Italy
Mário Florido	University of Porto, Portugal
Gopal Gupta	University of Texas at Dallas, USA
Michael Hanus	CAU Kiel, Germany
Bishoksan Kafle	University of Melbourne, Australia
Temur Kutsia	Johannes Kepler University Linz, Austria
Salvador Lucas	Universitat Politècnica de València, Spain
Fred Mesnard	Université de La Réunion, France
Julia Sapiña	Universitat Politècnica de València, Spain
Harald Søndergaard	University of Melbourne, Australia
Theresa Swift	Johns Hopkins Applied Physics Lab, USA
Laura Titolo (Co-chair)	Code Metal, USA
Wim Vanhoof	Université de Namur, Belgium
Alicia Villanueva	Universitat Politècnica de València, Spain

Additional Reviewers

Dasgupta, Sopam
Ehling, Georg
Hernández-Cerezo, Alejandro
Hermant, Olivier
Pau, Cleo
Rodríguez-Núñez, Clara
Tudor, Alexis
Varanasi, Sarat Chandra

Contents

Symbolic Computation and Verification Methods in Maude

José Meseguer$^{(\boxtimes)}$

University of Illinois at Urbana-Champaign, Urbana, IL 61801, USA
meseguer@illinois.edu

Abstract. Maude and its formal tools support ten different symbolic computation features. This paper focuses on one of them, *narrowing of constrained patterns*, as well as its combination with *inductive theorem proving* in a novel style of *deductive model checking*, to illustrate how Maude's symbolic features can be used to model check modal logic properties of infinite-state systems specificed as rewrite theories in Maude.

Keywords: Rewriting Logic · Maude · Symbolic Methods · Constrained Narrowing · Modal Logic · Model Checking · Inductive Theorem Proving

1 Introduction

Rewriting logic and Maude are first briefly explained, and a summary of Maude's symbolic features is given. Different property logics for specifying formal requirements of concurrent systems are considered, as well as various model checking and theorem proving method for verifying such properties. A unifying thread is then chosen: how to model check modal logic properties of concurrent systems specified as rewrite theories in Maude in three different ways: (i) by explicit-state model checking; (ii) by narrowing-based model checking; and (iii) by *deductive* model checking, which combines narrowing and inductive theorem proving.

1.1 Rewriting Logic and Maude

Rewriting logic [27,29] is a simple computational logic to specify, program and verify *concurrent systems*. A *rewrite theory* is a triple $\mathcal{R} = (\Sigma, E, R)$ with (Σ, E) an *equational theory* with typed function symbols Σ and equations E, and R a set of *rewrite rules* of the form:

$$l \to r \ \text{if} \ \phi$$

with l, r Σ-terms and ϕ a conjunction of Σ-equations.

$\mathcal{R} = (\Sigma, E, R)$ has an *initial model* $\mathbb{T}_{\mathcal{R}}$, which defines a *mathematical model* of the concurrent system specified by $\mathcal{R}$. Its *concurrent states* are elements of the initial algebra $\mathbb{T}_{\Sigma/E}$. Its *local concurrent transitions* are specified by the rewrite rules R.

S. Escobar and I. Titolo (Eds.): LOPSTR 2025, LNCS 10117, pp. 1–21, 2026.
https://doi.org/10.1007/978-3-032-04848-6_1

Maude [12,16] is a *declarative programming language* based on rewriting logic. A Maude program is a *rewrite theory* meeting suitable executability conditions and specified with syntax mod (Σ, E, R) endm. Let us see an example, namely, the following QLOCK mutual exclusion protocol proposed by K. Futatsugi.

```
mod QLOCK is protecting NAT-PRESBURGER .
  sorts NeMSet MSet NeList List State .
  subsorts Nat < NeList < List .          subsorts Nat < NeMSet < MSet .
  op mt : -> MSet [ctor] .                          *** empty multiset
  op _ _ : MSet MSet -> MSet [assoc comm id: mt] .
  op _ _ : NeMSet NeMSet -> NeMSet [ctor assoc comm id: mt] .
  op nil : -> List [ctor] .                         *** empty list
  op _;_ : List List -> List [assoc id: nil] .
  op _;_ : NeList NeList -> NeList [ctor assoc id: nil] .
  op <_|_|_|_> : MSet MSet MSet List -> State [ctor] .
  var i j : Nat . vars U W C : MSet .  var Q Q' Q" : List .

  rl [r2w] : < U i | W | C | Q > => < U | W i | C | Q ; i > .
  rl [w2c] : < U | W i | C | i ; Q > => < U | W | C i | i ; Q > .
  rl [c2r] : < U | W | C i | i ; Q > => < U i | W | C | Q >  .
endm
```

QLOCK is a rewrite theory $\mathcal{R} = (\Sigma, E, R)$ importing the NAT-PRESBURGER equational theory of natural numbers with addition and equality and order predicates. QLOCK's types (called sorts) are declared with the sorts declaration and their subtype inclusions by subsorts declarations. The typed function symbols in Σ added to those of NAT-PRESBURGER are declared with op declarations. All operator syntax is *user-definable*. Note that there are as many "underbar" place holders in each operator as arguments. For example, list concatenation is declared with syntax _;_ and multiset union with (empty) syntax _ _ (i.e., juxtaposition). Constants like mt and nil are function symbols with no arguments. QLOCK's equations E are *equational axioms* of *associativity* (A), *commutativity* (C), or *unit element* (U), which are not written out explicitly, but are instead declared with the respective keywords assoc comm and id:. For example, the assoc declaration _;_ states the axiom $(Q\,;\,Q')\,;\,Q'' = Q\,;\,(Q'\,;\,Q'')$. Declared this way, these equational axioms can be applied by Maude in a *built-in* way when applying QLOCK's transition rules R, which are declared with the rl keyword and are labelled [r2w], [w2c] and [c2r]. These rules are applied *modulo* the declared axioms. Processes in QLOCK are abstractly modeled as natural numbers. The states of QLOCK have the general form < U | W | C | Q >, where U are the processes in the *reception* area, W the processes in the *waiting* area, and C the processes in the *critical section*, and where Q is a list of process names awaiting to enter (or in) the critical section. The meaning of the rules [r2w] (reception to waiting), [w2c] (waiting to critical) and [c2r] (critical to reception) is self-explanatory and formalizes the protocol's semantics.

Note that, since rewriting happens *modulo* the declared axioms, we can, for example, have a [w2c] transition of the form:

< mt | 1 0 | mt | 1 ; 0 > → < mt | 0 | 1 | 1 ; 0 >

because these axioms ensure 0 1 = 1 0 and mt 1 = 1.

1.2 Symbolic Reasoning Features of Maude

Besides *execution by rewriting* modulo axioms B, with B any combination of associativity (A) and/or commutativity (C) and/or unit element (U) axioms, Maude and its formal tools provide *symbolic reasoning features* such as:

1. B-**Generalization** (modulo any $B \subseteq \{A, C, U\}$) [4,5].
2. B-**Unification** and B-**Matching** (modulo any $B \subseteq \{A, C, U\}$) [13,19].
3. $E \cup B$-**Unification** for any *convergent* $(\Sigma, E \cup B)$, which is *finitary* iff $(\Sigma, E \cup B)$ has the *finite variant property* (FVP) [13,21].
4. **Domain-Specific SMT-Solving** through CVC4 [15] and Yices [39] interfaces [13].
5. **Theory-Generic SMT-Solving** for: (i) FVP theories $(\Sigma, E \cup B)$ under natural requirements about their constructors [31,34] and (ii) equational theories of the form (Σ, B) with B C and/or C axioms [30].
6. **Symbolic Reachability Analysis by Rewriting Modulo SMT** [36].
7. **Symbolic Reachability Analysis by Narrowing Modulo SMT** [25].
8. **Narrowing-Based Symbolic Reachability Analysis** of topmost system modules **mod** $(\Sigma, E \cup B, R)$ **endm** [13,32].
9. B-**Homeomorphic Embedding** (modulo any $B \subseteq \{A, C\}$) [2].
10. **Partial Evaluation** of *convergent* Maude *functional modules* (equational theories) fmod $(\Sigma, E \cup B)$ endfm [3].

For a gentle introduction with examples to the use of many of these symbolic reasoning features in Maude I refer the reader to [33].

1.3 Formal Verification of Maude Programs

Formal properties of Maude programs specified in *property logics* such as:

1. **Inductive Equational Logic**, e.g., [35],
2. **Modal Logic** [9],
3. **Temporal Logics** LTL [11], LTL$^+$ [14] and LTLR [8], and
4. **Constructor-Based Reachability Logic** [37],

can be *formally verified* by either:

– **Theorem Proving**, or
– **Model Checking**, including:
   1. *Explicit-state* model checking,
   2. *Rewriting modulo SMT symbolic* model checking,
   3. *Narrowing-based symbolic* model checking, and
   4. A combination of *Constrained narrowing-based symbolic* model checking and *inductive theorem proving*.

Maude and its environment of formal tools supports program verification of properties in all of these logics by all of the above methods.

1.4   Outline of This Paper

It is beyond the scope of this paper to illustrate the use of *all* symbolic features for *all* property logics using *all* theorem proving or model checking methods. I will focus on the verification of **Modal Logic** properties of a rewrite theory $\mathcal{R}$ in Maude by the following **Model Checking** methods:

1. *Explicit-state* model checking,
2. *Narrowing-based symbolic* model checking, and
3. *Constrained Narrowing-based symbolic* model checking in combination with *Inductive Theorem Proving.*

In all these cases, we model check a modal logic property φ for a Maude program mod $\mathcal{R} = (\Sigma, E, R)$ endm from a set I of *initial states* under the (to be explained) *reachability modal satisfaction relation*:

$$\mathcal{R}, I \models_* \varphi.$$

2   Modal Logic

Modal Logic is parametric on a set of *state predicate symbols* $p \in \Pi$ and has formulas φ defined by the grammar:

$$p \mid \top \mid \bot \mid \neg\varphi \mid \varphi \vee \varphi \mid \varphi \wedge \varphi \mid \Box\varphi \mid \Diamond\varphi$$

The meaning of such formulas is interpreted on Π-*Kripke structures*, which are triples $\mathcal{Q} = (Q, \to_{\mathcal{Q}}, \_{\mathcal{Q}})$, where Q is the set of *states*, $\to_{\mathcal{Q}} \subseteq Q \times Q$ is the *transition relation*, and

$$\_{\mathcal{Q}} : \Pi \ni p \mapsto p_{\mathcal{Q}} \in \mathcal{P}(Q)$$

is the function *interpreting* each state predicate symbol $p \in \Pi$ as a *subset* of Q.

Given a set $I \subseteq Q$ of *initial states* the *satisfaction relation*, $\mathcal{Q}, I \models \varphi$ has an easy inductive definition. In what follows I will focus on modal formulas of the form either $\Box B$ or $\Diamond B$, where B is a *Boolean combination* of state predicates in Π.

2.1   The Reachability Interpretation of Modal Logic

Given $\mathcal{Q} = (Q, \to_{\mathcal{Q}}, \_{\mathcal{Q}})$, $\mathcal{Q}^*$ denotes the Kripke structure $\mathcal{Q}^* = (Q, \to_{\mathcal{Q}}^*, \_{\mathcal{Q}})$, with $\to_{\mathcal{Q}}^*$ the *reflexive-transitive closure* of $\to_{\mathcal{Q}}$. For $I \subseteq Q$ and modal formula φ the *reachability satisfaction relation* $\mathcal{Q}, I \models_* \varphi$ is defined by the equivalence:

$$\mathcal{Q}, I \models_* \varphi \Leftrightarrow \mathcal{Q}^*, I \models \varphi$$

For $I \subseteq Q$ and formulas $\Box B$, resp. $\Diamond B$, with B a Boolean combination of Π-predicates, the reachability satisfaction relation $\models_*$ is defined by the equivalences:

$$\mathcal{Q}, I \models_* \Box B \Leftrightarrow \mathcal{Q}^*[I] \subset B_{\mathcal{Q}} \Leftrightarrow \forall q \in I, (q \to_{\mathcal{Q}}^* q') \Rightarrow q' \in B_{\mathcal{Q}}$$

with $\mathcal{Q}^*[I] = \rightarrow_{\mathcal{Q}}^* [I]$ the *states reachable* from I. $B_{\mathcal{Q}}$ is then called an *invariant* from initial states I.

$$\mathcal{Q}, I \models_* \Diamond B \;\Leftrightarrow\; \mathcal{Q}^*[I] \cap B_{\mathcal{Q}} \neq \emptyset \;\Leftrightarrow\; \exists q \in I, \; \exists q' \in B_{\mathcal{Q}} \; s.t. \; q \rightarrow_{\mathcal{Q}}^* q'$$

$\Diamond B_{\mathcal{Q}}$ is called a *reachability property* from I. $B_{\mathcal{Q}}$ interprets Boolean combinations of state predicates in the expected way: $\neg B_{\mathcal{Q}} = Q \backslash B_{\mathcal{Q}}$, $(B \vee B')_{\mathcal{Q}} = B_{\mathcal{Q}} \cup B'_{\mathcal{Q}}$, and $(B \wedge B')_{\mathcal{Q}} = B_{\mathcal{Q}} \cap B'_{\mathcal{Q}}$.

2.2   An Expressive Modal Logic for Rewrite Theories

Given a rewrite theory $\mathcal{R} = (\Sigma, E, R)$ we can choose as a sort of *states* a sort St that is closed under $\rightarrow_{R/E}$-transitions, where, by definition, $\rightarrow_{R/E}$ is the composed relation,

$$=_E; \rightarrow_R; =_E$$

This defines a *transition system* $\mathcal{R}_{St} = (\mathbb{T}_{\Sigma,E,St}, \rightarrow_{R/E})$, where $\mathbb{T}_{\Sigma,E,St}$ denotes the set of elements of the initial algebra $\mathbb{T}_{\Sigma,E}$ that have sort St.

To verify modal logic properties of $\mathcal{R}$ from initial states $I \subseteq \mathbb{T}_{\Sigma,E,St}$ the transition system $\mathcal{R}_{St}$ is not enough: we need a Π-*Kripke structure* $\mathcal{R}_{St} = (\mathbb{T}_{\Sigma,E,St}, \rightarrow_{R/E}, \_\mathcal{R}_{St})$.

The million-dollar question is: which state predicates Π and with which interpretation function $\_\mathcal{R}_{St}$? The more *expressive* the interpretation of state predicates $p \in \Pi$ can be, the more sophisticated the modal properties φ that can be verified will be.

A very expressive and general set Π of state predicates that can make the transition system $\mathcal{R}_{St} = (\mathbb{T}_{\Sigma,E,St}, \rightarrow_{R/E})$ into a Kripke structure is given by the (infinite) set $\Pi = CCPatts_{St}$ of *constrained constructor patterns* of sort St. This assumes that we have identified a subsignature $\Omega \subseteq \Sigma$ of *constructor symbols*, i.e., a subsignature Ω such the for each $[u] \in \mathbb{T}_{\Sigma,E}$ there is a ground constructor term $v \in \mathbb{T}_{\Omega}$ such that $[u] = [v]$. For example, for the natural numbers in Peano notation, $\Omega = \{0, s\}$, with $s : Nat \rightarrow Nat$ the successor function is a constructor subsignature of $\Sigma = \{0, s, \_ + \_, \_ * \_\}$, where addition and multiplication have been defined by the usual recursive equations.

Choosing as Π the infinite set $CCPatts_{St}$ of constrained patterns $u \mid \phi$ with $u \in \mathbb{T}_{\Omega}(X)_{St}$ an Ω-term of sort St with variables in an infinite set X of variables of all sorts, and ϕ a conjunction of Σ-equations. The *state predicate interpretation function* has the form: $u \mid \phi \mapsto [\![u \mid \phi]\!]$, where, by definition,

$$[\![u \mid \phi]\!] =_{def} \{[v] \in \mathbb{T}_{\Sigma,E,St} \mid \exists \rho \in [vars(u \mid \phi) \rightarrow \mathbb{T}_{\Omega}] \; s.t. \; [v] =_E [u\rho] \wedge E \vdash \phi\rho\}.$$

I.e., all states $[u\rho]$ that are *ground instances* of u and *satisfy* the constraint $\phi\rho$.

3   Explicit-State Model Checking

Given a Maude program mod $\mathcal{R} = (\Sigma, E \cup B, R)$ endm with sort of states St we can model check modal logic properties in the $CCPatts_{St}$-Kripke structure $\mathcal{R}_{St} = (\mathbb{T}_{\Sigma, E \cup B, St}, \rightarrow_{R/E \cup B}, [\![\_]\!])$ for $I = \{[u_1], \ldots [u_n]\}$ a *finite* set of initial states, provided $\mathcal{R}$ satisfies the following *executability conditions*: (i) the oriented equations $\vec{E}$ are *ground convergent* modulo B [17]; (ii) rules R are *ground coherent* with $\vec{E}$ modulo B [17]; and (iii) Ω is a constructor subsignature s.t. $\forall u, v \in \mathbb{T}_{\Omega}$, $u =_{E \cup B} v$ iff $u =_B v$.

Theorem 1. $\mathcal{R}_{St}, \{[u_1], \ldots [u_n]\} \models_* \Diamond(v_1 \mid \phi_1 \vee \ldots v_m \mid \phi_m)$ *holds under these conditions, where* $vars(\phi_j) \subseteq vars(u_j)$, $1 \leq j \leq m$, *iff: there exist* i, j, $1 \leq i \leq n$, $1 \leq j \leq m$, *s.t. Maude's breadth first search command:*

$$\textit{search } u_i \texttt{ =>* } v_j \textit{ s.t. } \phi_j \textit{ .}$$

finds at least one solution.

Let us see an example.

3.1   Explicit-State Model Checking of QLOCK

Consider the QLOCK mutual exclusion protocol with initial state the term $\langle\, 0\ 1\ (1+1) \mid mt \mid mt \mid nil\, \rangle$, from which want to verify the reachability property:

$$\Diamond(\langle\, U \mid W \mid C \mid Q\, \rangle \mid C = mt \wedge Q = (1+1)\,;\, 1\,;\, 0)$$

This property holds because we have:

```
Maude> search < 0 1 (1 + 1) | mt | mt | nil > =>* < U | W | C | Q >
                           s.t. C = mt /\ Q = (1 + 1) ; 1 ; 0 .

Solution 1 (state 23)
states: 24  rewrites: 29 in 0ms cpu (0ms real) (55238 rewrites/second)
U --> mt
W --> 0 1 1 + 1
C --> mt
Q --> (1 + 1) ; 1 ; 0

No more solutions.
```

It follows easily from the definition of $\models_*$ that we have the equivalence, $\Box B \Leftrightarrow \neg\Diamond\neg B$ and in particular the equivalence, $\Box\neg B \Leftrightarrow \neg\Diamond B$. Therefore we have the equivalence:

$$\mathcal{R}_{St}, I \models_* \Box\neg(v_1 \mid \phi_1 \vee \ldots v_m \mid \phi_m) \Leftrightarrow \mathcal{R}_{St}, I \not\models_* \Diamond(v_1 \mid \phi_1 \vee \ldots v_m \mid \phi_m)$$

Therefore, we can *prove* an invariant $\Box\neg(v_1 \mid \phi_1 \vee \ldots v_m \mid \phi_m)$ from I by *disproving* $\mathcal{R}_{St}, I \models_* \Diamond(v_1 \mid \phi_1 \vee \ldots v_m \mid \phi_m)$, which by Theorem 1 we can do for I finite by failure of $|I|$ search commands. Let us see an example.

The *mutual exclusion* property of `QLOCK` can be stated as the invariant:

$$\square\neg(\langle\, U \mid W \mid i\, j\, C \mid Q \,\rangle)$$

which we can prove from the initial state $\langle\, 0\, 1\, (1+1) \mid mt \mid mt \mid nil \,\rangle$ by giving the `search` command:

```
Maude> search < 0 1 (1 + 1) | mt | mt | nil > =>* < U | W | i j C | Q > .
```

```
No solution.
```

Model checking invariants or reachability properties by using `search` always terminates if the set of *reachable states* from the chosen initial state is *finite*. Otherwise, the search may never terminate. When either: (i) the set I of initial states is *infinite* or (ii) the set of states reachable from some initial state is *infinite*; or (iii) both, we can use *narrowing-based symbolic model checking methods*, to which I turn next.

4 Narrowing-Based Symbolic Model Checking

Narrowing-based model checking is a style of infinite-state symbolic model checking that can verify modal logic properties of rewrite theories from infinite sets of initial states. Technically, completeness of the model checking algorithm requires such theories to be *topmost*.

4.1 Topmost Rewrite Theories

The *CCPatts$_{St}$*-Kripke structures $\mathcal{R}_{St} = (\mathbb{T}_{\Sigma,E\cup B,St}, \rightarrow_{R/E\cup B}, [\![\_]\!])$ to be symbolically model checked will be associated to rewrite theories $\mathcal{R} = (\Sigma, E \cup B, R)$ such that:

1. $(\Sigma, E\cup B)$ is ground convergent and $(\Omega, E_\Omega \cup B_\Omega) \subseteq (\Sigma, E\cup B)$ is a *constructor subspecification* with $(\Omega, E_\Omega \cup B_\Omega)$ FVP s.t. $\mathbb{T}_{\Sigma,E\cup B}|_\Omega \cong \mathbb{T}_{\Omega/E_\Omega\cup B_\Omega}$.
2. There is a transition-closed sort St such that if $c(u_1,\ldots,u_n) \in \mathbb{T}_\Omega(X)_{St}$ then no u_i has sort St, $1 \leq i \leq n$.
3. The rules R are of the form $l \rightarrow r$ *if* ϕ, with $l, r \in \mathbb{T}_\Omega(X)_{St}\backslash X$, and ϕ a conjunction of Σ-equalities.

Call $\mathcal{R}$ satisfying (1)–(3) a *topmost* rewrite theory with top sort St. The topmost requirement ensures *completeness* of narrowing-based symbolic model checking. In practice this does not overly restrict the rewrite theories that can be model check, because many rewrite theories are *bisimilar* to (and can be easily transformed into) topmost ones. For example, all Actor-based systems [1], which in practice include all network protocols and all distributed protocols, can be specified by rewrite theories [28] that are bisimilar to topmost rewrite theories.

4.2   The Constrained Narrowing Relation

Exploiting the fact that in a topmost rewrite theory $\mathcal{R} = (\Sigma, E \cup B, R)$ we have an isomorphism $\mathbb{T}_{\Sigma, E \cup B}|_\Omega \cong \mathbb{T}_{\Omega/E_\Omega \cup B_\Omega}$, its associated Kripke structure $\mathcal{R}_{St}$ can be defined as $\mathcal{R}_{St} = (\mathbb{T}_{\Omega/E_\Omega \cup B_\Omega, St}, \rightarrow_{R/E_\Omega \cup B_\Omega}, [\![\_]\!])$, where for any $[u], [v] \in \mathbb{T}_{\Omega/E_\Omega \cup B_\Omega, St}$ $[u] \rightarrow_{R/E_\Omega \cup B_\Omega} [v]$ holds iff there exists a ground Ω-substitution ρ and a rule $l \rightarrow r$ if ϕ in R such that $[u] = [l\rho]$, $[v] = [r\rho]$ and $E \cup B \vdash \phi\rho$.

To symbolically model check modal properties of $\mathcal{R}_{St}$ we will use the following *constrained narrowing relation*:

$$u \mid \varphi \overset{\alpha}{\leadsto}_{R/E_\Omega \cup B_\Omega} v \mid \psi$$

which holds between two constrained patterns $u \mid \varphi$ and $v \mid \psi$ with $u, v \in \mathbb{T}(X)_{\Omega, St}$ iff there exist: (i) a rule $l \rightarrow r$ if ϕ in R (renamed to not share variables with $u \mid \varphi$); and (ii) a unifier $\alpha \in \mathit{Unif}_{E_\Omega \cup B_\Omega}(l = u)$ such that $v \mid \psi = (r \mid \varphi \wedge \phi)\alpha$.

4.3   The Lifting Lemma and Narrowing-Based Model Checking

The key property about the constrained narrowing relation $\overset{\alpha}{\leadsto}_{R/E_\Omega \cup B_\Omega}$ is that it can *symbolically cover* all transitions in $\mathcal{R}_{St}$. This is expressed by the following:

Lemma 1. *(Lifting Lemma). For $\mathcal{R}$ topmost, if $[w] \in [\![u \mid \varphi]\!]$ and $[w] \rightarrow_{R/E_\Omega \cup B_\Omega} [w']$ with, say, rule $l \rightarrow r$ if ϕ in R, then there is a constrained narrowing step $u \mid \varphi \overset{\alpha}{\leadsto}_{R/E_\Omega \cup B_\Omega} v \mid \psi$ with the same rule such that $[w'] \in [\![v \mid \psi]\!]$.*

The Lifting Lemma gives us as a corollary the following narrowing-based symbolic model checking method to verify modal reachability properties:

Theorem 2. *For $\mathcal{R}$ topmost, $\mathcal{R}_{St}, [\![u_1 \mid \varphi_1 \vee \ldots \vee u_n \mid \varphi_n]\!] \models_* \Diamond(v_1 \mid \psi_1 \vee \ldots v_m \mid \psi_m)$ holds, iff: there exist i, j, $1 \leq i \leq n$, $1 \leq j \leq m$, a constrained narrowing sequence $u_i \mid \varphi_i \overset{\alpha}{\leadsto}^*_{R/E_\Omega \cup B_\Omega} u' \mid \varphi'$ (with α the composed substitution), a unifier $\beta \in \mathit{Unif}_{E_\Omega \cup B_\Omega}(u' = v_j)$, and a ground substitution ρ s.t. $E \cup B \vdash (\varphi' \wedge \psi_j)\beta\rho$.*

Recall that the equivalence, $\Box \neg B \Leftrightarrow \neg \Diamond B$ gives us the equivalence:

$$\mathcal{R}_{St}, [\![u_1 \mid \varphi_1 \vee \ldots \vee u_n \mid \varphi_n]\!] \models_* \Box \neg(v_1 \mid \phi_1 \vee \ldots v_m \mid \phi_m) \Leftrightarrow$$

$$\mathcal{R}_{St}, [\![u_1 \mid \varphi_1 \vee \ldots \vee u_n \mid \varphi_n]\!] \not\models_* \Diamond(v_1 \mid \phi_1 \vee \ldots v_m \mid \phi_m)$$

Therefore, for $\mathcal{R}$ topmost an *invariant* $\Box \neg(v_1 \mid \phi_1 \vee \ldots v_m \mid \phi_m)$ from initial states $[\![u_1 \mid \varphi_1 \vee \ldots \vee u_n \mid \varphi_n]\!]$ holds iff for all i, j, $1 \leq i \leq n$, $1 \leq j \leq m$, there is no constrained narrowing sequence $u_i \mid \varphi_i \overset{\alpha}{\leadsto}^*_{R/E_\Omega \cup B_\Omega} u' \mid \varphi'$, no unifier $\beta \in \mathit{Unif}_{E_\Omega \cup B_\Omega}(u' = v_j)$, and no ground substitution ρ such that $E \cup B \vdash (\varphi' \wedge \psi_j)\beta\rho$.

5   The Folding Narrowing Search Algorithm

Narrowing-based model checking uses constrained narrowing to explore all reachable states from initial states $[\![u_1 \mid \varphi_1 \vee \ldots \vee u_n \mid \varphi_n]\!]$ by exploring all $\leadsto_{R/E_\Omega \cup B_\Omega}$-reachable *symbolically states* of the form $v \mid \psi$.

The problem, however, is that the set of $\leadsto_{R/E_\Omega \cup B_\Omega}$-reachable symbolic states may easily be *infinite*. Symbolic *state space reduction* techniques are needed to hopefully obtain a *finite* set of $\leadsto_{R/E_\Omega \cup B_\Omega}$-reachable states. The notion of *constrained pattern subsumption* provides an effective state space reduction method.

Pattern $u \mid \varphi$ is B_Ω-*subsumed* by pattern $v \mid \psi$, denoted $u \mid \varphi \sqsubseteq_{B_\Omega} v \mid \psi$, iff there exists a substitution γ such that: (i) $u =_{B_\Omega} v\gamma$, and (ii) $\mathbb{T}_{\Sigma,E\cup B} \models \varphi \Rightarrow (\psi)\gamma$, i.e., $\varphi \Rightarrow (\psi)\gamma$ is an *inductive theorem* true in the initial algebra $\mathbb{T}_{\Sigma,E\cup B}$.

The key idea is that $u \mid \varphi \sqsubseteq_{B_\Omega} v \mid \psi \Rightarrow [\![u \mid \varphi]\!] \subseteq [\![v \mid \psi]\!]$. Therefore, state $u \mid \varphi$ is *redundant* and can be dropped. This is what *folding narrowing search* does to drastically reduce (hopefully from infinite to finite) the number of state.

A problem with the relation $u \mid \varphi \sqsubseteq_{B_\Omega} v \mid \psi$ is that in general it is *undecidable*, because the check $\mathbb{T}_{\Sigma/E\cup B} \models \varphi \Rightarrow (\psi)\gamma$ requires inductive theorem proving. We can *under-approximate* the relation $u \mid \varphi \sqsubseteq_{B_\Omega} v \mid \psi$ by the decidable relation $u \mid \varphi \sqsubseteq^\sigma_{B_\Omega} v \mid \psi$, where σ is a *terminating strategy* in an inductive theorem prover. So, what we prove is: $(\Sigma, E \cup B) \vdash^\sigma_{ind} \varphi \Rightarrow (\psi)\gamma$, where $\vdash_{ind}$ is the inference system of our chosen inductive theorem prover and σ is our chosen terminating strategy. Likewise, we try to check that a conjunction ϕ of equalities is *satisfiable* in $\mathbb{T}_{\Sigma/E\cup B}$ by proving $(\Sigma, E \cup B) \vdash^\sigma_{ind} \exists \phi$.

Let me introduce some notation. $\mathcal{R}[\![u_1 \mid \varphi_1 \vee \ldots \vee u_n \mid \varphi_n]\!]$ denotes all the states $\rightarrow_{R/E_\Omega \cup B_\Omega}$-*reachable* in one step from $[\![u_1 \mid \varphi_1 \vee \ldots \vee u_n \mid \varphi_n]\!]$. Likewise, $\mathcal{R}^{\leq d}[\![u_1 \mid \varphi_1 \vee \ldots \vee u_n \mid \varphi_n]\!]$ denotes all the states $\rightarrow_{R/E_\Omega \cup B_\Omega}$-*reachable* in d or fewer steps (including 0 steps) from $[\![u_1 \mid \varphi_1 \vee \ldots \vee u_n \mid \varphi_n]\!]$. Finally, $\mathcal{R}^*[\![u_1 \mid \varphi_1 \vee \ldots \vee u_n \mid \varphi_n]\!]$ denotes the set of all $\rightarrow_{R/E_\Omega \cup B_\Omega}$-*reachable* states from $[\![u_1 \mid \varphi_1 \vee \ldots \vee u_n \mid \varphi_n]\!]$.

Let me now describe the *folding narrowing search* algorithm. This algorithm model checks $\mathcal{R}_{St}, [\![u_1 \mid \varphi_1 \vee \ldots \vee u_n \mid \varphi_n]\!] \models_* \Diamond(v_1 \mid \psi_1 \vee \ldots v_m \mid \psi_m)$ for $\mathcal{R}$ topmost.

For each depth $d \in \mathbb{N}$ the algorithm iteratively computes pattern disjunctions P_d and F_d, with $F_d \sqsubseteq^\sigma_{B_\Omega} P_d$ and s.t. $\mathcal{R}^*[\![u_1 \mid \varphi_1 \vee \ldots \vee u_n \mid \varphi_n]\!] = [\![P_d]\!]$. The algorithm (searching for one solution) *terminates* if a d is reached s.t. either: (i) $[\![F_d]\!] \cap [\![v_1 \mid \psi_1 \vee \ldots v_m \mid \psi_m]\!] \neq \emptyset$ can be proved by finding: $u' \mid \varphi'$ in F_d, $j, 1 \leq j \leq m$, and $\beta \in Uinf_{E_\Omega, B_\Omega}(u' = v_j)$ (W.L.O.G. can assume $vars(u') \cap vars(v_j) = \emptyset$) s.t. $(\Sigma, E \cup B) \vdash^\sigma_{ind} \exists(\varphi' \wedge \psi_j)\beta$, i.e., a *solution* is found, or (ii) $F_d = \bot$, i.e., *a fixpoint was reached* and *no solution* was found[1] using $\vdash^{\sigma}_{ind}$. Otherwise, the search *loops forever*.

Pattern disjunctions $P_d(u_1 \mid \varphi_1 \vee \ldots \vee u_n \mid \varphi_n)$ and $F_d(u_1 \mid \varphi_1 \vee \ldots \vee u_n \mid \varphi_n)$ are computed inductively for increasing depth $d \in \mathbb{N}$ as follows:

- $P_0 = F_0 = u_1 \mid \varphi_1 \vee \ldots \vee u_n \mid \varphi_n$.
- $P_{d+1} = P_d \vee F_{d+1}$, where for $F_d = u'_1 \mid \varphi'_1 \vee \ldots \vee u'_k \mid \varphi'_k$

$$F_{d+1} = \bigvee \{(w \mid \phi) \mid \exists i,\ 1 \leq i \leq k,\ s.t., u'_1 \leadsto_{R/E_{\Omega} \cup B_{\Omega}} w \mid \phi \ \wedge \ w \mid \phi \not\sqsubseteq^{\sigma}_B P_d\}.$$

where the notation $\bigvee$ generalizes the pattern disjunction operation $\vee$ to any finite set of patterns. That is, F_{d+1} *excludes* all $w \mid \phi$ such that $w \mid \phi \sqsubseteq^{\sigma}_B P_d$, i.e., that can be *folded* into P_d. Call F_d the *frontier* of P_d, $d \in \mathbb{N}$.

Theorem 3. *(Fixpoint Theorem).* If $F_{d+1} = \bot$, then

$$\mathcal{R}^* [\![u_1 \mid \varphi_1 \vee \ldots \vee u_n \mid \varphi_n]\!] = [\![P_d]\!].$$

6   Unconstrained Folding Narrowing Search in Maude

We can view a *constructor pattern* u as the special case of a *constrained constructor pattern* $u \mid \top$. Then, if the rules R in the topmost rewrite theory $\mathcal{R}$ are *unconditional* and the reachability properties we want to model check have the simpler form:

$$\mathcal{R}_{St}, [\![u_1 \vee \ldots \vee u_n]\!] \models_* \Diamond(v_1 \vee \ldots \vee v_m)$$

no constraints are ever encountered and the folding narrowing search algorithm becomes considerably simpler because: (i) the subsumption relation $u \sqsubseteq_{B_{\Omega}} v$ becomes *decidable* by B_{Ω}-matching for B_{Ω} any combination of A and/or C and/or U axioms, and (ii) deciding whether we have reached a target pattern v_j from a pattern w in P_d becomes *decidable* since $[\![v_j]\!] \cap [\![w]\!] \neq \emptyset$ iff (assuming W.L.O.G. that w and v_j share no variables) $Unif_{B_{\Omega} \cup B_{\Omega}}(v_j \stackrel{?}{=} v) \neq \emptyset$.

Maude supports narrowing-based model checking of reachability properties and invariants for unconstrained pattern disjunctions and unconditional rules through its {fold} vu-narrow search command. Let us see an example.

6.1   A Fair Readers and Writers (R&W) Protocol

The following R&W *fair* protocol does not starve readers or writers:

---

[1] Since $\exists(\varphi' \wedge \psi_j)\beta$ may hold without being provable with $\vdash^{\sigma}_{ind}$, if $\vdash^{\sigma}_{ind}$ cannot prove $\exists(\varphi' \wedge \psi_j)\beta$ it must be inductively proved or disproved offline for completeness.

```
mod R&W-FAIR is sorts NzNat Nat Conf .  subsorts NzNat < Nat .
  op 0 : -> Nat [ctor] .
  op 1 : -> NzNat [ctor] .
  op _+_ : Nat Nat -> Nat [ctor assoc comm id: 0] .
  op _+_ : NzNat Nat -> NzNat [ctor assoc comm id: 0] .
  op <_,_>[_|_] : Nat Nat Nat Nat -> Conf .  *** state with "turnstile"
  op $ : -> [Conf] .                          *** unreachable state
  op init : NzNat -> Conf .
  vars N N1 N2 N3 N4 M M1 M2 K K1 K2 I J : Nat . vars N' N1' N2' N3' M' : NzNat .
  eq init(N') = < 0,0 >[ 0 | N'] .
  rl [w-in]  : < 0,0 >[ 0 | N] => < 0,1 >[0 | N] [narrowing] .
  rl [w-out] : < 0,1 >[ 0 | N] => < 0,0 >[N | 0] [narrowing] .
  rl [r-in]  : < N,0 >[M + 1 | K] => < N + 1,0 >[M | K] [narrowing] .
  rl [r-out] : < N + 1,0 >[M | K] => < N,0 >[M | K + 1] [narrowing] .
endm
```

The unreachable state $ is added to check whether a *fixpoint* can be reached by folding narrowing from some disjunction of initial patterns. For the initial pattern < 0,0 >[0 | N + 1] folding search for $ seems not to terminate. One way to reach a fixpoint is to begin with a disjunction of patterns that subsumes the above pattern < 0,0 >[0 | N + 1] and is hopefully *closed under transitions*. One way of making such a guess is to reach a fixpoint for the simplest ground instance of < 0,0 >[0 | N + 1], namely, < 0,0 >[0 | 1] using the search command: search < 0,0 >[0 | 1] =>* $. Inspecting the search graph we obtain the following transition-closed disjunction of ground patterns:

< 0, 0 >[0 | 1] $\vee$ < 0, 1 >[0 | 1] $\vee$ < 0, 0 >[1 | 0] $\vee$ < 1, 0 >[0 | 0]

This suggests guessing that the following pattern disjunction is transition-closed:

< I,0 >[J | N + 1] $\vee$ < 0, 1 >[0 | N1 + 1] $\vee$ < M,0 >[N2 + 1 | K] $\vee$
< N3 + 1,0 >[M1 | K1]

Since, by the Fixpoint Theorem 3, a pattern disjunction D is transition-closed (called an *inductive invariant*) if $F_1(D) = \bot$, and Maude implements the (unconstrained) folding narrowing search by the {fold} vu-narrow command, which can be customized by giving a *depth bound*, we can settle this issue by giving the following two Maude commands:

```
Maude> {fold} vu-narrow  < I,0 >[ J | N + 1] \/ < 0, 1 >[0 | N1 + 1] \/
                    < M,0 >[N2 + 1 | K] \/ < N3 + 1,0 >[M1 | K1]  =>1 $ .

No solution.

Maude> show frontier states .
*** frontier is empty ***
```

which show that our guessed pattern disjunction is transition-closed. Note, further, that our original initial state pattern < 0,0 >[0 | N + 1] is *subsumed* by the first pattern in the disjunction using the substitution $\{I \mapsto 0, J \mapsto 0\}$.

We can now verify that R&W-FAIR satisfies the *mutual exclusion* of readers and writers invariant by showing that its complement is unreachable from (and therefore disjoint from) our inductive invariant by giving the command:

```
Maude> {fold} vu-narrow  < I,0 >[ J | N + 1] \/ < 0, 1 >[0 | N1 + 1] \/
                          < M,0 >[N2 + 1 | K] \/ < N3 + 1,0 >[M1 | K1] =>*
                          < 1 + m:Nat , 1 + i:Nat >[j:Nat | k:Nat] .
```

```
No solution.
```

Likewise, we can verify that R&W-FAIR satisfies the (at most) *one-writer* invariant by showing that its complement is unreachable from (and therefore disjoint from) our inductive invariant by giving the command:

```
Maude> {fold} vu-narrow  < I,0 >[ J | N + 1] \/ < 0, 1 >[0 | N1 + 1] \/
                          < M,0 >[N2 + 1 | K] \/ < N3 + 1,0 >[M1 | K1] =>*
                          < m:Nat, 1 + 1 + i:Nat >[j:Nat | k:Nat] .
```

```
No solution.
```

7   Deductive Model Checking in DM-Check

By *deductive model checking* I mean a method that combines model checking and theorem proving to verify properties of infinite-state systems. Such a method may have two modes: (i) an *automated* mode supported by an algorithm; and (ii) an *interactive* mode, where only some subtasks are automated.

Folding narrowing search is an automated deductive model checking method that uses an inductive theorem prover's strategy as an oracle. However, there is a need for having also an *interactive* mode due to the following *limitations*:

1. An inductive theorem proving strategy σ may not discharge many proof obligations, which may require user interaction and proving *auxiliary lemmas*.
2. The pattern subsumption relation $u \mid \varphi \sqsubseteq_{B_\Omega}^{\sigma} v \mid \psi$ is only a *sufficient condition* for the set containment $[\![u \mid \varphi]\!] \subseteq [\![v \mid \psi]\!]$, and is further limited by the proof strategy σ. To prove such set containments we often need: (i) methods to reason about *semantic equivalence* between constrained patterns; and (ii) interactive inductive theorem proving assisting such reasoning.

7.1   The DM-Check Tool

The **DM-Check** tool [6] combines folding narrowing search and Maude's **NuITP** inductive theorem prover [18]. It can prove inductive invariants (the check invariant command) and provides *interactive reasoning features* to:

1. Add *auxiliary lemmas* (with add lemma).
2. Reason about *subsumption* (with subsumed by) and compute *intersections* (with intersect) of (disjunctions of) constrained patterns.
3. Reason about *semantic equivalence* between (disjunctions of) constrained patterns (with case), and delegates to **NuITP** equational proof obligations.

7.2   Reasoning About QLOCK in DM-Check

Let us see **DM-Check** in action by means of the QLOCK example. A big limitation of *explicit-state* model checking is that we could only verify mutual exclusion of QLOCK for *finite sets* of initial states. But in fact QLOCK is *parametric* on the *infinite* set of initial states specified by the following constrained pattern, with S of sort NeMSet:

$$< S \mid mt \mid mt \mid nil > \mid set(S) = tt$$

As we did for unconstrained patterns for R&W-FAIR, we can guess the following *inductive invariant* (i.e., transition-closed invariant) from the initial state pattern < S | mt | mt | nil > | set(S) = tt:

```
< U | W | mt | Q > | non-mt(U W) = tt /\ set(U W) = tt /\ 12ms(Q) = W
\/
< U' | W' | i | i ; Q' > | non-mt(U' W' i) = tt /\ set(U' W' i) = tt /\
                                                  12ms(i ; Q') = W' i .
```

where the functions appearing in the constrains are defined by the equations:

```
eq non-mt(mt) = ff [variant] .
eq non-mt(S) = tt [variant] .

eq set(mt) = tt .
eq set(n) = tt .
eq set(S S U) = ff .
ceq set(n U) = tt if n in U = ff /\ set(U) = tt .

eq 12ms(nil) = mt .
eq 12ms(n ; L) = n 12ms(L) .
```

The attribute [variant] for the equations defining non-mt specify that these equations satisfy the *finite variant property* (FVP) [21]. As we shall see, this can be exploited, since systems of equations involving FVP symbols have a finite number of solutions that can be computed by variant unification [21].

This conjectured inductive invariant can be verified by **DM-Check** by checking that $F_1 = \bot$ by folding narrowing in one step using its check invariant command:

```
DM-Check> check invariant ((< U:MSet | W:MSet | mt | Q:List >) |
  (non-mt(U:MSet W:MSet) = tt) /\ (set(U:MSet W:MSet) = tt) /\
  (12ms(Q:List) = W:MSet))
  \/
  ((< V:MSet | T:MSet | i:Nat | i:Nat ; Q':List >) |
  (non-mt(V:MSet T:MSet i:Nat) = tt) /\
  (set(V:MSet T:MSet i:Nat) = tt) /\ (12ms(i:Nat ; Q':List) = T:MSet i:Nat)) .

Invariant satisfied.
```

This inductive invariant satisfies the *mutual exclusion property*, since for all its states their critical section component is either mt or a single process i.

We still need to check that our inductive invariant is actually an invariant *from* the initial state pattern < S | mt | mt | nil > | set(S) = tt. This is a *subsumption check* supported by **DM-Check**'s check subsumed by command:

```
DM-Check> check ((< S:NeMSet | mt | mt | nil >) | (set(S:NeMSet) = tt))
subsumed by
((< U:MSet | W:MSet | mt | Q:List >) | (non-mt(U:MSet W:MSet) = tt) /\
 (set(U:MSet W:MSet) = tt) /\ (l2ms(Q:List) = W:MSet))
\/
((< V:MSet | T:MSet | i:Nat | i:Nat ; Q':List >) |
 (non-mt(V:MSet T:MSet i:Nat) = tt) /\
 (set(V:MSet T:MSet i:Nat) = tt) /\ (l2ms(i:Nat ; Q':List) = T:MSet i:Nat)) .

   Subsumption satisfied.
```

Any mutex algorithm worth its salt should be deadlock-free. Let us show that our inductive invariant from < S | mt | mt | nil > | set(S) = tt is *deadlock free*, i.e., that all its states are *enabled* to perform some *transition* in QLOCK. The set of all *transition-enabled states* has a very simple expression as the disjunction of lefthand side patterns:

```
< U1:MSet n1:Nat | W1:MSet | C1:MSet | Q1:List > | true \/
< U2:MSet | W2:MSet n2:Nat | C2:MSet | n2:Nat ; Q2:List >| true \/
< U3:MSet | W3:MSet | C3:MSet n3:Nat | n3:Nat ; Q3:List > | true
```

Deadlock freedom can then be proved with the following subsumption command:

```
DM-Check> check ((< U:MSet | W:MSet | mt | Q:List >) |
 (non-mt(U:MSet W:MSet) = tt) /\
 (set(U:MSet W:MSet) = tt) /\ (l2ms(Q:List) = W:MSet))
\/
((< V:MSet | T:MSet | i:Nat | i:Nat ; Q':List >) |
 (non-mt(V:MSet T:MSet i:Nat) = tt) /\
 (set(V:MSet T:MSet i:Nat) = tt) /\ (l2ms(i:Nat ; Q':List) = T:MSet i:Nat))
subsumed by
((< U1:MSet n1:Nat | W1:MSet | C1:MSet | Q1:List >) | true)
\/ ((< U2:MSet | W2:MSet n2:Nat | C2:MSet | n2:Nat ; Q2:List >) | true)
\/ ((< U3:MSet | W3:MSet | C3:MSet n3:Nat | n3:Nat ; Q3:List >) | true) .

   Constrained terms on the left that could not be subsumed:

Term 4:
   < U:MSet | W:MSet | mt | Q:List >
Matching: no matching found
Constraint 4:
   (non-mt(U:MSet W:MSet) = tt) /\ (set(U:MSet W:MSet) = tt) /\
    l2ms(Q:List) = W:MSet
```

Subsumption is only a *sufficient condition* for set-theoretic containment. The subsumption check failed for the first pattern in the inductive invariant:

```
< U | W | mt | Q > | non-mt(U W) = tt ∧ set(U W) = tt ∧ 12ms(Q) = W
```

because it is *too general* to show that all its ground instances are *transition-enabled*. However, this pattern is *semantically equivalent* to (has the same ground instances as) a disjunction of constrained patterns that is subsumed by the left-hand side patterns. This can be shown using the following *equivalence-preserving* pattern transformations:

1. **Case.** Decomposes a variable $x : s'$ in $u \mid \varphi$ into constructor terms (with fresh variables) of sort s' in a *generator set* for sort s'. For example, $\{0, s(n)\}$ is a generator set for the sort *Nat* of Peano natural numbers, because any such number is a constructor instance of either 0 or $s(n)$.
2. **Variant Unify.** Unifies FVP equations φ_1 in a constrained pattern $u \mid (\varphi_1 \wedge \varphi_2)$ (we assume _ $\wedge$ _ *AC*).
3. **Narrowing.** Narrows a subterm $f(u_1, \ldots, u_n)$ in the constraint φ, such that the $u_1, \ldots, u_n$ are constructor terms and f is a defined function, by narrowing $f(u_1, \ldots, u_n)$ with each of the equations defining f.
4. **Variable Abstraction.** Abstracts a subterm w of sort s in the constraint φ by a fresh $x : s$. In this way, we get a semantic equivalence between the original constrained pattern $u \mid \varphi[w]_p$ and the resulting constrained pattern $u \mid \varphi[x : s]_p \wedge x : s = w$.
5. **Substitution.** Replaces $u \mid \varphi \wedge x : s = v$ by $(u \mid \varphi)\{x : s \mapsto v\}$ if $v \in \mathbb{T}_\Omega(X)_s$.

Currently, only transformation (1) is supported by **DM-Check** (with `case`). Transformations (2)–(5) can be applied with the help of Maude's symbolic features, even in the absence of a **DM-Check** implementation. Let us see how using these pattern transformations we can show that `QLOCK` is deadlock-free. Since `non-mt` is FVP, we can use **Variant Unify** to unify away the equation `non-mt(U W) = tt` using Maude's `filtered variant unify` command:

```
Maude> filtered variant unify non-mt(U:MSet W:MSet) =? tt .

Unifier 1          Unifier 2          Unifier 3
U --> #1:NeMSet    U --> mt           U --> #1:NeMSet
W --> mt           W --> #1:NeMSet    W --> #2:NeMSet

No more unifiers.
Advisory: Filtering was complete.
```

Thus, our pattern becomes equivalent to the 3-pattern disjunction:

```
< U:NeMSet | mt | mt | Q1:List > | set(U:NeMSet mt = tt ∧
12ms(Q1:List) = mt
∨
< mt | W:NeMSet | mt | Q2:List > | set(mt W:NeMSet) = tt ∧
12ms(Q2:List) = W:NeMSet
∨
< V:NeMSet | T:NeMSet | mt | Q3:List > | set(V:NeMSet T:NeMSet) = tt ∧
12ms(Q3:List) = T:NeMSet
```

We can now use **Case** with $\{m : Nat, (k : Nat\ S : NeMSet)\}$ as generator set for sort *NeMSet* to make this 3-pattern disjunction semantically equivalent to the 5-pattern disjunction:

```
< n1:Nat | mt | mt | Q1:List > | set(n1:Nat mt) = tt ∧ l2ms(Q1:List) = mt
∨
< U:NeMSet n2:Nat | mt | mt | Q2:List > | set(U:NeMSet n2:Nat mt) = tt ∧
l2ms(Q2:List) = mt
∨
< mt | W:NeMSet | mt | Q3:List > | set(mt W:NeMSet) = tt ∧
l2ms(Q3:List) = W:NeMSet
∨
< n5:Nat | T:NeMSet | mt | Q4:List > | set(n5:Nat T:NeMSet) = tt ∧
l2ms(Q4:List) = T:NeMSet
∨
< V:NeMSet n6:Nat | T1:NeMSet | mt | Q5:List > |
set(V:NeMSet n6:Nat T1:NeMSet) = tt ∧ l2ms(Q5:List) = T1:NeMSet
```

We can try again to check whether this 5-pattern disjunction is subsumed by the disjunction of lefthand side patterns:

```
DM-Check> check ((< n1:Nat | mt | mt | Q1:List >) | (set(n1:Nat mt) = tt) ∧
  (l2ms(Q1:List) = mt))
  ∨
  ((< U:NeMSet n2:Nat | mt | mt | Q2:List >) | (set(U:NeMSet n2:Nat mt) = tt) ∧
  (l2ms(Q2:List) = mt))
  ∨
  ((< mt | W:NeMSet | mt | Q3:List >) | (set(mt W:NeMSet) = tt) ∧
  (l2ms(Q3:List) = W:NeMSet))
  ∨
  ((< n5:Nat | T:NeMSet | mt | Q4:List >) | (set(n5:Nat T:NeMSet) = tt) ∧
  (l2ms(Q4:List) = T:NeMSet))
  ∨
  ((< V:NeMSet n6:Nat  | T1:NeMSet | mt | Q5:List >) |
  (set(V:NeMSet n6:Nat T1:NeMSet) = tt) ∧ (l2ms(Q5:List) = T1:NeMSet))
  subsumed by
  ((< U1:MSet n1:Nat | W1:MSet | C1:MSet | Q'1:List >) | true)
  ∨
  ((< U2:MSet | W2:MSet n2:Nat | C2:MSet | n2:Nat ; Q'2:List >) | true)
  ∨
  ((< U3:MSet | W3:MSet | C3:MSet n3:Nat | n3:Nat ; Q'3:List >) | true) .

     Constrained terms on the left that could not be subsumed:

Term 6:
  < mt | W:NeMSet | mt | Q3:List >
Matching: no matching found
Constraint 6:
  (set(mt W:NeMSet) = tt) ∧ l2ms(Q3:List) = W:NeMSet
```

That is, the only pattern not yet shown deadlock-free is:

```
< mt | W:NeMSet | mt | Q3:List > | set(mt W:NeMSet) = tt ∧
l2ms(Q3:List) = W:NeMSet
```

To show that this pattern is deadlock-free because it is semantically subsumed by the lefthand side pattern:

```
< U2:MSet | W2:MSet n2:Nat | C2:MSet | n2:Nat ; Q'2:List >) | true
```

we can first use **Narrowing** applied to the expression 12ms(Q3:List) in the constraint, which in this way becomes equivalent to the pattern disjunction:

```
< mt | W:NeMSet | mt | nil > | set(mt W:NeMSet) = tt ∧ mt = W:NeMSet
∨ < mt | W:NeMSet | mt | n:Nat ; L:List > | set(mt W:NeMSet) = tt ∧
n:Nat 12ms(L:List) = W:NeMSet
```

where the first pattern can be shown empty by using **Variant Unify**:

```
Maude> variant unify in QLOCK : mt =? W:NeMSet .

No unifiers.
```

So, we are left with the second pattern, which using **Variable Abstraction** on the term 12ms(L:List) with fresh variable U:MSet becomes semantically equivalent to the pattern:

```
< mt | W:NeMSet | mt | n:Nat ; L:List > | set(mt W:NeMSet) = tt ∧
n:Nat U:MSet = W:NeMSet ∧ U:MSet = 12ms(L:List)
```

which using **Substitution** for the equation n:Nat U:MSet = W:NeMSet becomes equivalent to the pattern:

```
< mt | n:Nat U:MSet | mt | n:Nat ; L:List > | set(mt n:Nat U:MSet) = tt ∧
U:MSet = 12ms(L:List)
```

which can now be subsumed by the lefthand side of rule [w2c]:

```
DM-Check> check ((< mt | n:Nat U:MSet | mt | n:Nat ; L:List >) |
(set(mt n:Nat U:MSet) = tt) ∧ (U:MSet = 12ms(L:List)))
subsumed by
((< U2:MSet | W2:MSet n2:Nat | C2:MSet | n2:Nat ; Q'2:List >) | true) .

    Subsumption satisfied.
```

This finishes the proof of deadlock freedom for QLOCK.

8   Conclusion and Related Work

8.1   Conclusion

After briefly summarizing ten different ways in which Maude and its formal tools support symbolic reasoning I have focused on one particular symbolic reasoning method, namely, *constrained narrowing* to illustrate how formal verification of properties of a concurrent system expressed as Modal Logic formulas can be verified automatically by: (i) explicit-state model checking using Maude's search command; and (ii) for infinite-state systems by *folding narrowing search* in Maude. I have then illustrated a third possibility, namely, (iii) a form of *deductive model checking* that combines folding narrowing of constrained patterns with inductive theorem proving in two different modes: one automatic and another interactive, and have shown how the **DM-Check** tool supports the interactive mode with the help of Maude's **NuITP**.

The choice of Modal logic as a property specification logic is not exclusive. For example, unconstrained narrowing-based infinite-state model checking of LTL properties of Maude programs has been supported since 2013 [7]. Indeed, LTL, LTL$^+$ and LTLR seem all attractive property specification logics where the constrained narrowing and deductive model checking methods presented here should also be quite useful.

8.2   Related Work

Regarding related work on *narrowing*, as I pointed out in [33], narrowing emerged from efforts to make resolution theorem provers reason efficiently about equality. It was introduced by Slagle [38] as an efficient kind of *paramodulation*; it was further elaborated by Lankford as a component of a resolution-with-equality strategy assuming convergent equations [24]. Hullot further advanced the narrowing ideas, proposed his *basic narrowing* strategy, and explored under some restrictions the notion of narrowing modulo axioms B for a convergent theory $(\Sigma, E \cup B)$ in [22]. A more systematic generalization to this case was carried out by J.-P. Jouannaud, C. Kirchner and H. Kirchner in [23], assuming a B-unification algorithm. The generalization to narrowing with convergent order-sorted *conditional* equational theories modulo B was carried out in [10]. Finally, the *folding narrowing strategy* for a convergent theory $(\Sigma, E \cup B)$ was developed in [21], is efficiently supported in Maude [13], and provides a *finitary* variant unification algorithm for FVP theories whose usefulness has been illustrated by the **Variant Unify** method to reason about equivalence between constrained patterns in the deductive model checking of QLOCK.

In all the above work, the rewrite rules used for narrowing were always *equations or conditional equations*. To the best of my knowledge, the first proposal for using narrowing, not with equations for equational reasoning, but with transition rules for *symbolic reachability analysis* of concurrent systems was [26]. Since [26], formal analysis of *cryptographic protocols* has been an important application area for narrowing based model checking. The Maude-NPA narrowing-based model checker [20] has been used to analyze many cryptographic protocols by narrowing modulo FVP equational theories. The generalization to narrowing reachability analysis for constrained patterns with conditional rewrite rules, which this paper extends in several ways, was presented in [32]. Finally, the ideas on narrowing-based deductive model checking were first presented in [6].

Acknowledgments. I thank the LOPSTR organizers for giving me the opportunity of presenting these ideas at LOPSTR 2025. I am very grateful to all my fellow members of the Maude team, and in particular to Steven Eker and Santiago Escobar, for all the Maude advances that have made variant unification and narrowing-based symbolic model checking possible. I am also very grateful my fellow members of the DM-Check team, Kyungming Bae, Santiago Escobar, Raúl López-Rueda and Julia Sapiña, and those of the NuITP team, Francisco Durán, Santiago Escobar and Julia Sapiña, for respectively making possible the DM-Check tool and Maude's NuITP on which Deductive Model Checking is based.

Disclosure of Interests. The author has no competing interests to declare that are relevant to the content of this article.

References

1. Agha, G.: Actors. MIT Press, Cambridge (1986)
2. Alpuente, M., Cuenca-Ortega, A., Escobar, S., Meseguer, J.: Order-sorted homeomorphic embedding modulo combinations of associativity and/or commutativity axioms. Fundam. Informaticae **177**(3–4), 297–329 (2020)
3. Alpuente, M., Cuenca-Ortega, A., Escobar, S., Meseguer, J.: A partial evaluation framework for order-sorted equational programs modulo axioms. J. Log. Algebraic Methods Program. **110** (2020)
4. Alpuente, M., Escobar, S., Espert, J., Meseguer, J.: A modular order-sorted equational generalization algorithm. Inf. Comput. **235**, 98–136 (2014)
5. Alpuente, M., Escobar, S., Meseguer, J., Sapiña, J.: Order-sorted equational generalization algorithm revisited. Ann. Math. Artif. Intell. **90**(5), 499–522 (2022)
6. Bae, K., Escobar, S., López-Rueda, R., Meseguer, J., Sapiña, J.: Verifying invariants by deductive model checking. In: Rewriting Logic and Its Applications – WRLA 2024. Lecture Notes in Computer Science, vol. 14953, pp. 3–21. Springer, Cham (2024)
7. Bae, K., Escobar, S., Meseguer, J.: Abstract logical model checking of infinite-state systems using narrowing. In: Rewriting Techniques and Applications (RTA 2013). LIPIcs, vol. 21, pp. 81–96. Schloss Dagstuhl–Leibniz-Zentrum fuer Informatik (2013)
8. Bae, K., Meseguer, J.: Model checking linear temporal logic of rewriting formulas under localized fairness. Sci. Comput. Program. **99**, 193–234 (2015)
9. van Benthem, J.: Modal Logic for Open Minds. Center for the Study of Language and Information. Stanford University (2010)
10. Cholewa, A., Escobar, S., Meseguer, J.: Constrained narrowing for conditional equational theories modulo axioms. Sci. Comput. Program. **112**, 24–57 (2015)
11. Clarke, E.M., Grumberg, O., Peled, D.A.: Model Checking. MIT Press, Cambridge (2001)
12. Clavel, M., et al.: All About Maude – A High-Performance Logical Framework. Springer LNCS, vol. 4350 (2007)
13. Clavel, M., et al.: Maude Manual (Version 3.1) (2020). http://maude.cs.uiuc.edu
14. Clavel, M., et al.: Maude Manual (Version 3.5.1) (2025). https://maude.cs.illinois.edu/manual.pdf
15. CVC4: https://cvc4.github.io

16. Durán, F., et al.: Programming and symbolic computation in Maude. J. Log. Algebraic Methods Program. **110** (2020)
17. Durán, F., Meseguer, J.: On the Church-Rosser and coherence properties of conditional order-sorted rewrite theories. J. Algebraic Logic Program. **81**, 816–850 (2012)
18. Durán, F.J., Escobar, S., Meseguer, J., Sapiña, J.: NuITP: an inductive theorem prover for equational program verification. In: Bruni, A., Momigliano, A., Pradella, M., Rossi, M., Cheney, J. (eds.) Proceedings of the 26th International Symposium on Principles and Practice of Declarative Programming, PPDP 2024, Milano, Italy, September 9-11, 2024, pp. 6:1–6:11. ACM (2024). https://doi.org/10.1145/3678232.3678236
19. Eker, S.: Associative unification in Maude. J. Logical Algebraic Methods Program. **126**, 100747 (2022)
20. Escobar, S., Meadows, C., Meseguer, J.: Maude-NPA: cryptographic protocol analysis modulo equational properties. In: Aldini, A., Barthe, G., Gorrieri, R. (eds.) FOSAD 2007-2009. LNCS, vol. 5705, pp. 1–50. Springer, Heidelberg (2009). https://doi.org/10.1007/978-3-642-03829-7_1
21. Escobar, S., Sasse, R., Meseguer, J.: Folding variant narrowing and optimal variant termination. J. Algebraic Logic Program. **81**, 898–928 (2012)
22. Hullot, J.-M.: Canonical forms and unification. In: Bibel, W., Kowalski, R. (eds.) CADE 1980. LNCS, vol. 87, pp. 318–334. Springer, Heidelberg (1980). https://doi.org/10.1007/3-540-10009-1_25
23. Jouannaud, J.-P., Kirchner, C., Kirchner, H.: Incremental construction of unification algorithms in equational theories. In: Diaz, J. (ed.) ICALP 1983. LNCS, vol. 154, pp. 361–373. Springer, Heidelberg (1983). https://doi.org/10.1007/BFb0036921
24. Lankford, D.S.: Canonical inference. Technical report ATP-32, Southwestn Univ. (1975)
25. López-Rueda, R., Escobar, S., Sapiña, J.: An efficient canonical narrowing implementation with irreducibility and SMT constraints for generic symbolic protocol analysis. J. Log. Algebraic Methods Program. **135**, 100895 (2023)
26. Meseguer, J., Thati, P.: Symbolic reachability analysis using narrowing and its application to the verification of cryptographic protocols. J. Higher-Order Symbolic Comput. **20**(1–2), 123–160 (2007)
27. Meseguer, J.: Conditional rewriting logic as a unified model of concurrency. Theoret. Comput. Sci. **96**(1), 73–155 (1992)
28. Meseguer, J.: A logical theory of concurrent objects and its realization in the Maude language. In: Agha, G., Wegner, P., Yonezawa, A. (eds.) Research Directions in Concurrent Object-Oriented Programming, pp. 314–390. MIT Press (1993)
29. Meseguer, J.: Twenty years of rewriting logic. J. Algebraic Logic Program. **81**, 721–781 (2012)
30. Meseguer, J.: Order-sorted rewriting and congruence closure. In: Jacobs, B., Löding, C. (eds.) FoSSaCS 2016. LNCS, vol. 9634, pp. 493–509. Springer, Heidelberg (2016). https://doi.org/10.1007/978-3-662-49630-5_29
31. Meseguer, J.: Variant-based satisfiability in initial algebras. Sci. Comput. Program. **154**, 3–41 (2018)
32. Meseguer, J.: Generalized rewrite theories, coherence completion, and symbolic methods. J. Log. Algebraic Methods Program. **110** (2020)
33. Meseguer, J.: Symbolic computation in Maude: some tapas. In: LOPSTR 2020. LNCS, vol. 12561, pp. 3–36. Springer, Cham (2021). https://doi.org/10.1007/978-3-030-68446-4_1

34. Meseguer, J.: Variants and satisfiability in the infinitary unification wonderland. J. Log. Algebraic Methods Program. **134**, 100877 (2023)
35. Meseguer, J.: Inductive reasoning with equality predicates, contextual rewriting and variant-based simplification. J. Log. Algebraic Methods Program. **144**, 101036 (2025)
36. Rocha, C., Meseguer, J., Muñoz, C.A.: Rewriting modulo SMT and open system analysis. J. Logic Algebraic Methods Program. **86**, 269–297 (2017)
37. Skeirik, S., Stefanescu, A., Meseguer, J.: A constructor-based reachability logic for rewrite theories. Fundam. Inform. **173**(4), 315–382 (2020)
38. Slagle, J.R.: Automated theorem-proving for theories with simplifiers commutativity, and associativity. J. ACM **21**(4), 622–642 (1974)
39. Yices. https://yices.csl.sri.com

Verifying Smart Contracts in Yul via Transformation to CHC by Interpreter Specialization

Elvira Albert[1] , Emanuele De Angelis[2] , Fabio Fioravanti[3] ,
Alejandro Hernández-Cerezo[1(✉)] , and Giulia Matricardi[3(✉)]

[1] Complutense University of Madrid, Madrid, Spain
elvira@fdi.ucm.es, aleher06@ucm.es
[2] IASI-CNR, Rome, Italy
emanuele.deangelis@iasi.cnr.it
[3] DEc, University 'G. d'Annunzio', Chieti-Pescara, Italy
{fabio.fioravanti,giulia.matricardi}@unich.it

Abstract. Yul is an intermediate representation that lies in between the
(high-level) source code and the (low-level) bytecode languages for
Ethereum smart contracts. Although it was proposed to favour the development of verification and optimization techniques, there exists no verifier that can be applied on Yul code directly yet. In this paper, we present
a transformational approach to verifying Yul code by transforming it into
an equivalent set of Constrained Horn Clauses (CHCs), leading, to the
best of our knowledge, to the first approach to directly verify Yul code.
Our transformational approach applies the first Futamura projection,
i.e., specializes a Yul interpreter written in CHC with respect tothe Yul
code to be verified. The verification of the transformed CHC code can
rely on existing tools for CHC verification, namely we have used Z3 with
the SPACER engine on our case studies.

1 Introduction and Motivation

Ethereum smart contracts and their verification have become rather active
research topics both because of the novel features introduced by the languages
used in the blockchain context (e.g., their gas model [25] opens new opportunities
for optimization), and also because of the vulnerability of smart contracts (due
to their immutability and public nature together with the fact that they often
hold and manipulate financial assets their verification is crucial). Existing verification approaches have been developed either at the level of the source-code or
at the *low-level bytecode* –named Ethereum Virtual Machine code– (abbreviated
as EVM [25]). At the source-level, being Solidity [23] the most popular programming language that targets EVM bytecode, there are several Solidity verifiers
[4,13,22,24]. At the EVM bytecode level, there are fewer verification tools, but
still very popular [2,9,19]. While both types of approaches are useful, there is
a significant gap in between them: approaches that operate on the source level
may overlook information generated during compilation, whereas approaches

S. Escobar and L. Titolo (Eds.): LOPSTR 2025, LNCS 16117, pp. 22–39, 2026.
https://doi.org/10.1007/978-3-032-04848-6_2

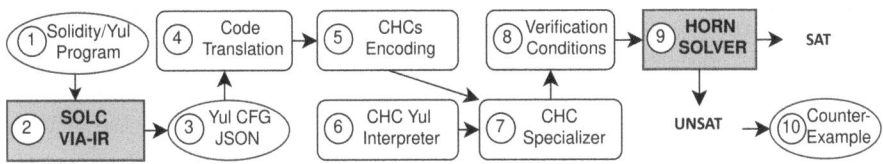

Fig. 1. Overview of the Verification Framework. Grey boxes represent external tools used in the framework, rounded boxes represent our internal components, and ellipses denote the input or output generated by external tools.

that work directly on EVM bytecode offer limited guidance for generating counterexamples or fixing issues at the source level.

Yul [16] has been proposed recently as an intermediate language which lies in between the source-level Solidity code and the low-level EVM bytecode. Yul provides a simple syntax and semantics designed to be easily translated into bytecode, while remaining suitable for manual inspection, formal verification, and optimization. Unlike the EVM, Yul provides high-level syntax to avoid stack operations for variable management and low-level jumps in the control flow. In contrast to Solidity, Yul can be obtained in a Control Flow Graph (CFG) and Single Static Assignment (SSA) form (abbreviated as SSA-CFG in what follows) with explicit opcodes for the computation of expressions. One of the main purposes of Yul has been to help in the development of verification and optimization techniques. While Yul-optimization has been the focus of important efforts within the Solidity compiler team, to the best of our knowledge, there exists no verification tool yet applicable to Yul directly.

Motivated by the maturity of CHC verifiers [8] (such as Eldarica [12] and Spacer [15]) and the success of the interpretative approach to transform code from one language to another, we propose a verification framework from Yul to CHC based on the first Futamura projection [10] as depicted in Fig. 1. As we will see, the input is a program that can be given in Solidity form which, importantly, can contain Yul assembly code ①. From there, using the Solidity compiler ②, we obtain a CFG representation in SSA-form of the Yul code ③. The next step is to encode as CHC clauses such Yul code ⑤ using our own code translator ④. We have implemented, as main contributions of the paper, a CHC interpreter of Yul ⑥ and an extension of an existing CHC specializer ⑦ that applies the first Futamura projection to generate a set of CHCs ⑧, representing the verification conditions (VCs) for checking that all the assertions included in the source code ① are met, thereby reducing this verification problem to a satisfiability problem for CHCs: all the assertions in ① are met *iff* the CHCs in ⑧ are satisfiable. Then, the satisfiability is proved, if at all possible (in general, the problem is undecidable), by using an off-the-shelf CHC solver ⑨. If proved unsatisfiable, a counter-example can be generated as well ⑩.

This paper is organized as follows. Section 2 introduces the Yul language and the CHC interpreter, as well as the CHC encoding of the Yul program under analysis. The main challenges when developing the interpreter, that will be discussed in the paper, concern the handling of the different types of memory used by Ethereum smart contracts and the semantics of EVM operations. Section 3 describes the specializer for CHCs that uses unfold/fold transformation rules whose application is guided by a strategy dedicated to generating VCs, known as the *VCG strategy* [20]. In Sect. 4 we apply our approach to two case studies that show the relevance of our work. The first example presents a contract fully implemented in Solidity; the second, on the other hand, is a contract that incorporates blocks of Yul code, showing how our methodology can also successfully deal with low-level code.

2   The Yul Language and CHC Interpreter

Motivation. Fig. 2a presents a simple example of a Solidity program that includes a fragment written in Yul, inside the `assembly` block. The program defines a single contract, `Operation`, which implements the function `Positive- Difference`. This function computes the absolute difference `diff` between two non-zero, distinct positive integers, `x` and `y`. First, a `require` statement is used to enforce that x>0, y>0 and x≠y. From these preconditions, it follows that subtracting the smaller value from the larger can neither underflow nor produce zero, thus making the assertion `diff>0` at line 19 (L19 for short) valid. However, when analyzed using the model-checker built into Solidity's compiler (`solc`), SolCMC [4], a spurious counterexample is generated: `x=1, y=2, diff=0`. SolCMC issues a warning about potential false positives when Yul code is involved, which explains the inconsistency. Let us note that this version of the contract is more efficient than one written entirely in Solidity because, in the pure Solidity version, the compiler `solc` introduces additional, unnecessary checks, resulting in larger bytecode. Such efficiency gains motivates the introduction of Yul code within Solidity programs.

2.1   Introduction to Yul and Its SSA-CFG Form

To support reasoning about both Solidity and Yul code, our approach operates on the Yul SSA-CFG representation shown in the example at Fig. 2b. In this representation, the control flow is modeled using conditional and unconditional jump instructions, simplifying the CHC generation for program verification. Yul programs are typically divided into two parts: one for deploying the smart contract to the blockchain (`Operation`, line 1-or L1 for brevity), and another representing the deployed contract itself (`Operation_deployed`, L5). Each part includes a list of basic blocks representing their respective main entry point, `blocks` (L2, L6), along with a list of functions, `functions` (L7). This structure enables us to identify `require` and `assert` statements from the original Solidity code: functions related to these checks are named accordingly (e.g., `assert_helper` in L17 is the function that enforces the `diff>0` assertion). Both the main blocks and helper functions contain basic blocks comprising all necessary Yul operations. Each Yul operation receives a set of input values (`in`) and produces one or more

```
1  contract Operation {
2
3    function positiveDifference(uint256 x, uint256 y)
4    public pure returns (uint256) {
5      require(x > 0 && y > 0 && x != y,
6        "Inputs must be non-zero and different");
7      uint256 diff;
8
9      assembly {
10       switch gt(x, y)
11       case 0 {
12         diff := sub(x, y)
13       }
14       default {
15         diff := sub(y, x)
16       }
17     }
18
19     assert(diff > 0);
20     return diff;
21   }
22 }
```

(a) Solidity Program, with a Yul fragment

```
1  {"Operation": {
2    "blocks": [...],
3    "functions": {...},
4    "subObjects": {
5      "Operation_deployed": {
6        "blocks": [...],
7        "functions": {
8          "fun_positiveDifference": {
9            "arguments": ["v0","v1"],
10           "entry": "Block0",
11           "blocks": [{
12             {"in": ["0x00","v27"],
13              "out": ["v28"], "op": "gt"},
14             {"in": ["v28"], "out": [],
15              "op": "assert_helper"}
16           }]},
17         "assert_helper": {
18           "arguments": ["v0"], "entry": "Block0",
19           "blocks": [
20             {"id": "Block0", "instructions":
21              [{"in": ["v0"], "out": ["v1"],
22               "op": "iszero"}],
23              "exit": {
24                "cond": "v1",
25                "type": "ConditionalJump",
26                "targets": ["Block2","Block1"]
27              }},
28             {"id": "Block2", "instructions": []},
29             {"id": "Block1", "instructions":
30              [{"in": [], "out": [],
31               "op": "panic_error_0x01"}]}]},
32         "panic_error_0x01": {
33           "arguments": [], "entry": "Block0",
34           "blocks": [...,
35             {"in": ["0x01","0x04"], "out": [],
36              "op": "mstore"},
37             {"in": ["0x24","0x00"], "out": [],
38              "op": "revert"}]}}}}}
```

(b) Yul CFG Representation

```
1  % State
2  globals([]).
3  memory([0x00, 0x04, 0x40]).
4  %Function Declarations
5  fun(init_contract, [],
6      [var(v6), var(v2), var(v4),
7       var(v3), var(v5), var(v0)],
8      'init_contract_Block0_1').
9
10 fun(assert_helper,
11     [var(v0)], [var(v1)],
12     'assert_helper_Block0_1').
13
14 fun(fun_PositiveDifference,
15     [var(v0), var(v1)],
16     [var(v27), ..., var(v28)],
17     'fun_PositiveDifference_45_Block0_1').
18
19 fun(panic_error_0x01, [], [],
20     'panic_error_0x01_Block0_1').
21 % For fun_PositiveDifference
22 at('fun_PositiveDifference_45_Block5_4',
23    asgn(var(v28),
24    expr(gt([num(0x00), var(v27)])))).
25
26 nextlab('fun_PositiveDifference_45_Block5_4',
27    'fun_PositiveDifference_45_Block5_5').
28
29 at('fun_PositiveDifference_45_Block5_5',
30    fun_call(assert_helper,
31            [var(v28)], [])).
32
33 nextlab('fun_PositiveDifference_45_Block5_5',
34    'fun_PositiveDifference_45_ret').
35
36 at('fun_PositiveDifference_45_ret',
37    ret([])).
38 % For assert_helper
39 at('assert_helper_Block0_1',
40    asgn(var(v1),
41    expr(iszero([var(v0)])))).
42
43 nextlab('assert_helper_Block0_1',
44    'assert_helper_Block0_jump').
45
46 at('assert_helper_Block0_jump',
47    cj(var(v1), 'assert_helper_ret',
48    'assert_helper_Block1_1')).
49
50 at('assert_helper_ret', ret([])).
51
52 at('assert_helper_Block1_1',
53    fun_call(panic_error_0x01, [], [])).
54 % For panic_error_0x01
55 at('panic_error_0x01_Block0_2',
56    mstore([num(0x01), mem(0x04)])).
57
58 nextlab('panic_error_0x01_Block0_2',
59    'panic_error_0x01_Block0_3').
60
61 at('panic_error_0x01_Block0_3',
62    revert([num(0x24), mem(0x00)])).
```

(c) Fragment of the CHC clauses, in
Prolog format, generated from (b)

Fig. 2. Diagram showing the different representations of the source program in our framework. For (b) and (c), only a fragment of the translation is shown.

outputs (out). These Yul operations can be either: (1) the application of an EVM opcode to some arguments, identifying the resulting value (if any) as a variable; or (2) a jump to a function included in functions. For instance, in the function fun_positiveDifference (L8), the gt opcode is applied in L12-L13 to determine whether the positive difference (stored in variable v27) is zero. This variable is then passed as an argument to the assert_helper function (L14-L15), which checks whether the argument is zero (L21-L22) and performs a conditional jump based on the result (L23-L27). If the value is not zero, it calls the panic_error_0x01 function (L32), which reverts the execution (L37-L38). Before the revert, a MSTORE operation is executed (L35-L36), storing the value 0x01 in the *Memory* region. To fully understand the effect of these operations, we now describe the main features of the EVM. The EVM is a stack machine that contains 256-bit words, and that manages data through different types of storage areas[1], each with specific purposes and duration.

- *Storage*: the contract's persistent memory where data that must survive between calls and transactions is saved. This region is managed through SSTORE and SLOAD opcodes.
- *Memory*: a volatile area that exists only for the duration of the current call. It is used for temporary operations such as internal calculations or preparing return data. It can be manipulated through MSTORE and MLOAD opcodes, among other operations.
- *Stack*: a volatile area used to store operands and intermediate results during arithmetic and logical operations. The Yul language does not model the stack directly but rather introduces *local variables* (*Locals*) which are managed through the operational stack.

In addition to the previous areas, the EVM can access information about the blockchain state or the current transaction through several opcodes. For instance, opcode CALLER returns the address of the caller of the current function, CALLDATASIZE returns the byte size of the calldata (the data sent as part of the transaction) or NUMBER returns the current block number. In our CHC interpreter we model the *Storage*, *Memory* and *Locals*, as well as the EVM environmental data.

2.2   Translating the Yul Program to CHC

In this section we present the component ④ of the verification framework shown in Fig. 1, which is responsible for translating the Yul SSA-CFG ③ into CHCs. A CHC (or simply, a *clause*) is a universally quantified formula of the form $H \leftarrow c \wedge L$. The conclusion (or *head*) H is either an atomic formula (atom, for short) or *false*. The premise (or *body*) $c \wedge L$ is a conjunction of a constraint c, and a (possibly empty) conjunction L of atoms. A fact is a clause of the form $H \leftarrow c$.

---

[1] We skip the *transient storage* area, which has been introduced recently in the Cancun hardfork [1], as it does not introduce new challenges.

```
<Program>  ::= <Globals> <Function>* <Clause>*
<Globals>  ::= globals([<GlobalElement>*])
<Function> ::= fun(<FuncName>, <VarList>, <VarList>, <Lab>).
<Clause>   ::= at(<Lab>,<Cmd>) | nextlab(<Lab>,<Lab>)
<Cmd>      ::= <BuiltIn> | <Asgn> | <Jumps> | <FuncCall> | <Ret> | ...
```

Fig. 3. Syntax of CHCs for encoding Yul programs

Let D be the usual interpretation for the symbols of theory *LIA*. A set S of CHCs is said to be D-satisfiable if it has a least D-model. The notion of a CHC we use in this paper is essentially the same[2] as the notion of a clause in Constraint Logic Programming (CLP) [14], whose concrete syntax will be used to present the CHC encodings and showcase the verification framework at work. Preliminaries. Constrained Horn clauses (CHCs) constitute a class of first order logic formulas where the Horn clause syntax is extended by allowing the use of formulas of an arbitrary, possibly non-Horn, constraint theory. In this paper, we consider CHCs whose constraints are linear integer arithmetic (*LIA*) expressions.

Figure 3 depicts a fragment of the grammar for CHC facts encoding Yul programs. Commands (<Cmd>) can be built-in operations of Yul (e.g., add, sub) (<BuiltIn>), assignments (<Asgn>), conditional or unconditional jumps (<Jumps>), function calls (<FuncCall>), or the <Ret> instruction, which indicates the final instruction of a function and can return zero or more elements. We adopt the same variable identifiers v that appear in the Yul SSA-CFG, including constants. For reasons of efficiency and readability, in the translation, these variables occur in terms wrapped using different functors, each indicating the memory region accessed: off(v) for the *Storage*; mem(v) for the *Memory*; var(v) for variables for the *Locals*. Function definitions are represented by facts of the form

fun(FuncName, Args, LocalVars, EntryLabel).

where FuncName is the function name, Args is the list of variables passed as arguments to the function, LocalVars contains the local scope variables used for internal operations, and EntryLabel defines the point from which to begin execution (i.e. the label of the first command of the function body). For example, function assert_helper in Fig. 2c, lines L10-L12, is passed variable v0 and uses the local variable v1. Its entry label is the command labeled by assert_helper_Block0_1 at line L39.

The at and nextlab predicates are used to represent the labeled commands of the program, and the flow of control, respectively. The at(Lab,Cmd) atom is used to associate a label Lab to a command Cmd. For instance, the command in the previous example, at lines L39-L41, is associated with the asgn command by the following CHC fact:

at(assert_helper_Block0_1, asgn(var(v1), expr(iszero([var(v0)])))).

---

[2] The term CHC is often used in the verification context [6], where the focus is on the construction of models for CHCs. The term CLP also refers to the notion of execution based on its operational semantics.

The nextlab(L,L1) atom is used to specify the links between two labels: L1 indicates the label of the command that is written, in the Yul program, immediately after the command with label L. For example, nextlab(assert_helper_Block0_1,assert_helper_Block0_jump) at lines L43-L44 connects the label of a block with that of a conditional jump command.

```
{"entries": ["Block6",
             "Block7"],
 "id": "Block5",
 "instructions": [
    {"in": ["v23","v24"],
     "op":"PhiFunction",
     "out":["v25"]},
    ...]}
```

Fig. 4. ϕ-function in Block5 of fun_positiveDifference

Another relevant aspect to address in the CHC encoding is the representation of ϕ-functions. In SSA form, these expressions assign fresh variables to values modified along different paths in the CFG, ensuring every variable in the program is defined exactly once. They appear at joint nodes in the CFG and have the form $x_0 \leftarrow \phi(x_1 : B_1, \ldots, x_n : B_n)$, where $x_1, \ldots, x_n$ are values from the predecessor blocks $B_1, \ldots, B_n$ renamed in the joint block, and x_0 represents the resulting value. switch, if/else, and for statements in Yul introduce ϕ-functions to handle modifications to the same variable across different paths. Figure 4 shows a ϕ-function in Block5 of Operation_Deployed. Here, the field in lists the x_i values, and entries map each x_i to their corresponding predecessor block B_i. The variable v25 represents the value of diff, with its value depending on the branch taken in the switch statement (L10 in Fig. 2a): v23 corresponds to x-y when x > y (L11-L13), and v24 to y-x (L14-L16). The translation of a ϕ-function resembles a standard technique used in eliminating ϕ-nodes during the generation of executable code, known as the *SSA destruction phase* [21]. For each ϕ-node preceded by block B_i, the variable x_0 is assigned the value of x_i immediately after executing B_i, ensuring x_0 holds the correct value based on the branch taken. This approach preserves the both original control flow and variable definitions without any loss of information. In the previous example, the following predicates are generated:

```
at(Block6_2, goto(Block5_1_5)).
at(Block7_2, goto(Block5_1_6)).
at(Block5_1_5, asgn(var(v25), expr(phiFunction([var(v23)])))).
nextlab(Block5_1_5, Block5_2).
at(Block5_1_6, asgn(var(v25), expr(phiFunction([var(v24)])))).
nextlab(Block5_1_6, Block5_2).
```

Label Block5_1 is split into two different labels: Block5_1_5 and Block5_1_6, which indicate the corresponding predecessor: Block6_2 and Block7_2, respectively. In both cases, v25 is assigned the appropriate value, and both paths continue to label Block5_2.

Table 1. Rules for assignment, SSTORE, function call, and conditional jump.

Name	Code	Explanation

asgn	`tr(cf(cmd(L, asgn(X, expr(E))), Env),`
	`   cf(cmd(L1, C), Env1)) :-`
	`      eval(E, Env, V), update(Env, X, V, Env1),`
	`      nextlab(L, L1), at(L1, C).`
		Encodes the transition (a single execution step) for an assignment command. It evaluates expression E, and uses the resulting value to update X in context. Finally it advances to the next command.

sstore	`tr(cf(cmd(L,sstore(V0,var(V1))),Env), Cf1) :-`
	`   lookup_local(V1, Env, K2),`
	`   tr(cf(cmd(L, sstore(V0, K2)), Env), Cf1).`
	
	`tr(cf(cmd(L, sstore(V0, off(V1))), Env),`
	`   cf(cmd(L1, C), Env1)) :-`
	`      eval_arg(V0, Env, X0),`
	`      update(Env, off(V1), X0, Env1),`
	`      nextlab(L, L1), at(L1, C).`
		Encodes the SSTORE command. In the first clause, lookup_local is used to retrieve the concrete key corresponding to var(V1) into which the value is to be stored and recursively invokes the sstore rule. In the second clause, eval_arg calculates the value to be written and updates the environment.

fun_call	`tr(cf(cmd(L, fun_call(F, InList, OutList)),`
	`       Env), Cf3) :-`
	`   fun_call_prologue(F,InList,Env, Cf1),`
	`   reach(Cf1, Cf2),`
	`   fun_call_epilogue(L,OutList,Cf2, Cf3).`
		The function call rule initially invokes the prologue, which evaluates the arguments and constructs the configuration for the first label of the function (entry point). The reach(Cf1, Cf2) atom encodes reachability from the entry point of the function to one of its exit points. The exit points are computed by epilogue, which distinguishes two alternatives: regular termination and abnormal termination (error configuration). For regular termination we can have three cases: return of values (evaluation and assignment of the output, advancement of the label), revert and commit (corresponding to the return opcode).

jumpi	`tr(cf(cmd(L, jumpi(V0, L1, L2)), Env),`
	`   cf(cmd(L1,C), Env)) :-`
	`      eval_arg(V0,Env,X0), X0 = 0, at(L1,C).`
	
	`tr(cf(cmd(L, jumpi(V0, L1, L2)), Env),`
	`   cf(cmd(L2,C), Env)) :-`
	`      eval_arg(V0,Env,X0), X0 =\= 0, at(L2,C).`
		Encodes the conditional jump command: the variable V0 is evaluated for the jump and one of the two possible destinations is chosen according to that value (0 or 1).

2.3   CHC Interpreter of the Yul Language

In our CHC interpreter for Yul programs (component ⑥), the operational semantics is defined by a predicate `tr`, which represents the transition relation that leads from a *configuration*, a program execution state, to a new configuration, when a Yul command is executed. Configurations are represented as terms of the form: `cf(cmd(Lab, Cmd), (D, M, S))` where `Lab` is a program label and `Cmd` is the command with that label. The `(D,M,S)` tuple is used to represent the storage areas of our program as described in Sect. 2.1, where:

- D represents the area that includes both the execution context data and the *Storage*, providing globally accessible variables at every point in the code;
- M represents the *Memory* area;
- S represents the set of local variables in the *Locals*: they can only be accessed within the context of the function in which they are declared.

In Table 1 a selection of the most representative rules in our interpreter is shown and Table 2 describes some auxiliary predicates used in the former transition rules. Some predicates, such as `eval`, which is used for evaluating arithmetic

Table 2. Auxiliary Rules.

Name	Code	Explanation
	`eval(E, Env, V)`	Represents the evaluation of an expression E in the environment Env, yielding the value V

eval	`eval(add([V0,V1],Env,V2)) :-`
	`    eval_arg(V0, Env, Y0),`
	`    eval_arg(V1, Env, X0),`
	`    V2 = X0 + Y0`
		The **eval** rule for addition. Similar rules are defined for other arithmetic and bitwise operations (**mul**, **div**, **and**, **or**, **not**, **shl**, **shr**, ...) for a total of 86 clauses.

update	`update(Env, X, V, Env1)`	update(Env, X, V, Env1) holds if Env1 is obtained from the environment Env by assigning the value V to the program variable X
nextlab	`nextlab(L, L1)`	Holds if L1 is the label immediately following L
at	`at(L1, C)`	Holds if Cmd is the corresponding command
eval_arg	`eval_arg(X, Env, V)`	Retrieves the value V of X in the corresponding component of the environment Env according to the scope of X

expressions, do not explicitly modify the configuration, but base their evaluation on the current configuration and the results they produce indirectly affect the new configuration (e.g., the result of an arithmetic operation will be used to update the environment). Note that, since we consider a multistep semantics [5], the `tr` clause for the function call is defined in terms of configuration reachability.

```
reach(Cf,Cf).
reach(Cf1,Cf3) :- tr(Cf1,Cf2), reach(Cf2,Cf3).
```

We have that `reach(Cf1,Cf3)` holds if `Cf3` can be reached from `Cf1` by zero or more steps (i.e. the `reach` predicate is the reflexive and transitive closure of the `tr` predicate).

3 Verification Conditions Generation by CHC Specialization

In this work we focus on the problem of checking whether all the assertions included in a Yul program p are met, and we propose an automatic verification method that reduces it to a satisfiability problem for CHCs.

Let us consider the following clause

```
false :- initConf(Cf1), reach(Cf1,Cf2), errorConf(Cf2).        (Q)
```

where: (i) `Cf1` represents an *initial configuration*, that is, the state of the EVM where the smart contract has been successfully deployed on the blockchain, (ii) `reach` represents the interpreter I for Yul programs presented in Sect. 2.3, and (iii) `Cf2` represents an *error configuration*, that is, a call to the function `panic_error_0x01` resulting from a violation of the condition included in an assertion of the Yul program under analysis. Now, checking whether the assertions in a Yul program p are met reduces to checking the satisfiability of CHCs as follows. Given a set P of CHC facts encoding p (see Sect. 2.2), the Yul interpreter I (see Sect. 2.3), and the clause Q, we have that all the assertions included in p are met if and only if the set of CHCs $P \cup I \cup \{Q\}$ is satisfiable.

State-of-the-art CHC solvers struggle at checking satisfiability of CHCs that contain complex terms, such as lists, that occur in the Yul interpreter to represent commands and environments. Thus, we apply the satisfiability-preserving unfold / fold CHC transformation rules to specialize it and remove the level of interpretation which is present in I. The specialization process realizes the *first Futamura projection* and produces a set VC of CHCs, called *verification conditions* (or *VCs*, for short), such that VC is satisfiable if and only if $P \cup I \cup \{Q\}$ is satisfiable. Moreover, since the generated VCs contain variables and constants only (see Fig. 6), CHC solvers can check their satisfiability more easily.

During CHC specialization we apply the following transformation rules: *unfolding, definition introduction*, and *folding*, according to the *Verification Condition Generation* strategy (*VCG*), similarly to what has been done for C programs in [5]. The rules and the strategy are described in the following subsections.

3.1   The CHC Transformation Rules

Let us first recall the definition of the transformation rules used by the specializer (component ⑦ in Fig. 1).

Unfolding. The *unfolding* rule replaces an atom in the body of a clause with its definition, and is conceptually similar to inlining in imperative programming.

Let `C` be a clause of the form `H :- c,L,A,R`, where `H` and `A` are atoms, `L` and `R` are (possibly empty) conjunctions of atoms, and `c` is a constraint. Given a set `P` of CHCs, by unfolding atom `A` in the body of `C` we replace `C` by the set of clauses obtained by applying one resolution step rooted in `A` with respect to the clauses in `P` whose head unifies with `A`. We denote by $Unf(C, A)$ the set of CHCs obtained by unfolding.

The application of the unfolding rule in the VCG strategy is guided by an annotation function that tells us whether or not a clause should be unfolded with respect to an atom in its body. This annotation guarantees that the number of applications of the unfolding rule is finite.

Definition Introduction. A new predicate `newr` is introduced by the clause: `newr(X) :- reach(cf1,cf2)`, where `X` is a tuple of all variables occurring in the terms `cf1` and `cf2` representing configurations. Clauses introduced by the *definition introduction* rule are called *definitions*.

Folding. The *folding* rule is a special case of an inverse of the unfolding rule. Let C be a clause H :- e,L,B,R and let D be a definition newr(X) :- A such that for some renaming substitution θ, $D\theta$ is of the form newr(Y) :- B. Then C is folded with respect to B by using D, thereby deriving the new clause H :- e,L,newr(Y),R.

Notably, this version of the folding rule is less general than that in [5], but has simpler applicability conditions and is suitable for VC generation.

3.2   The VCG Strategy

The transformation rules are applied according to the VCG strategy shown in Fig. 5. It takes as input the set $P \cup I \cup \{Q\}$ and produces as output the equisatisfiable set *VC* of verification conditions ⑧ shown in Fig. 1. The strategy keeps a set *Is* of CHCs to be specialized and a set *Ds* of definition clauses.

$Ds := \emptyset$; $VC := \emptyset$; $Is := \{Q\}$;

while there exists a clause C in *Is* with an atom in its body

(*unfold*) Let A be the leftmost atom occurring in the body of C.

  $Us := Unf(C, A)$;

  while there exists a clause D in *Us* whose body contains an unfoldable atom B

    $Us := (Us \setminus \{D\}) \cup Unf(D, B)$;

(*define and fold*)   Let *Us* be the clauses obtained by unfolding.

  while there exists a clause E in *Us* of the form: H :- e, L, reach(cf1,cf2), R

    Let F be the clause obtained by folding reach(cf1,cf2) in E
    using a suitable definition D.

    $VC := VC \cup \{F\}$;

    if (a variant of) D is not in *Ds* **then**

      $Ds := Ds \cup \{D\}$; $Is := Is \cup \{D\}$;

Fig. 5. The VCG strategy

The strategy terminates when all clauses in *Is* have been processed, and no new definitions are introduced.

Correctness of the VCG Strategy. We say that VCG strategy is correct in the sense that the CHCs it produces as output are equisatisfiable with respect to those provided as input. This is a direct consequence of the correctness of the transformation rules with respect to the least model semantics [5]. In particular, if the VCG strategy terminates on the input set of CHCs $P \cup I \cup \{Q\}$ thereby producing the output *VC*, then $P \cup I \cup \{Q\}$ is satisfiable iff *VC* is satisfiable.

Termination of the VCG Strategy. The unfolding annotation for VCG marks as unfoldable all atoms except those of the form reach(cf(cmd(L, Cmd),_Env), _Cf2) where L is the label of the entry point of a function or Cmd encodes the conditional jump command (jumpi). Thus, possibly recursive function calls and conditional jumps (used for encoding loops) are unfolded in a controlled manner and the (*unfold*) phase of VCG is guaranteed to terminate. Moreover, the (*define and fold*) phase is guaranteed to terminate because only a finite number of new definitions is introduced. Indeed, the definition introduction rule introduces new clauses of the form `new(X) :- reach(cf1,cf2)`, where X is the tuple of variables occurring in `cf1` and `cf2`. The new definitions abstract away the constraints representing the actual parameters provided to functions and the expressions occurring in conditional jumps, and therefore can be used to fold all atoms representing different calls to the same function or the same loop head. Consequently, the maximum number of definitions that can be introduced by the VCG is equal to the sum of the number of functions and conditional jumps occurring in the program. Thus, the VCG strategy terminates.

For the sake of efficiency, when there is no risk of non-termination, we call some atoms instead of fully unfolding them.

Each step of the verification pipeline shown in Fig. 1 is fully automatic, except for the task of specifying the initial configuration, that is, the label of the first instruction of the function under analysis and its call context. The interpreter and the specializer, which have been implemented as a module of the VeriMAP system [7], are available at https://github.com/chc-lab/yul-chc.

3.3   Example Application of the VCG Strategy

Let us show the application of the VCG strategy on the property we are studying for contract `Operation` in Fig. 2. After some iterations, the VCG strategy reaches the conditional jump (`jumpi`) encoding the `switch` statement shown in Fig. 2a at L10, and therefore introduces the following definition `D_jumpi`

```
jumpi(A,B,...,U,...) :- reach(
  cf( cmd(..., jumpi(var(v24), case0, default)),                    (1)
    ([('msg.value',A),...],[(0,B),...],[...,(v24,U),...]])),       (2)
  cf( cmd(panic_error_0x01,abort),...)) ).                         (3)
```

The term at line (1) encodes the configuration whose command is the conditional jump (`jumpi`). According to the value of `var(v24)`, it either jumps to the command at label `case0` or to the command at label `default`. The term at line (2) encodes the environment mapping storage and memory locations, as well as local variables, to their values (e.g., `(v24,U)` maps the local variable `v24` to its value represented by the logic variable U). Finally, the term at line (3) encodes the *error configuration* whose command is `abort` and whose label is `panic_error_0x01` (the final environment is omitted). The error configuration has been introduced in the interpreter for verification purposes and, in the rest of this section, we will use `errCf` to denote it.

Then, the VCG strategy proceeds by unfolding the atom `reach(cf(...),` `errCf)` occurring in the definition of the predicate `jumpi`. After some unfolding steps, we obtain the following two clauses.

```
jumpi(A,B,...,U,...) :- U=0, reach(cfCase0,errCf).
jumpi(A,B,...,U,...) :- U=1, reach(cfDefault,errCf).
```

where U is a logic variable whose value is 0 if gt(x,y), and 1 otherwise, and cfCase0 and cfDefault are configurations representing the two alternative branches of the switch command. In particular, the command occurring in cfCase0 is asgn(var(v26),expr(sub([var(v1),var(v0)]))), encoding the Yul statement diff := sub(x,y) at L12 of Fig. 2a. Similarly, the command occurring in cfDefault is asgn(var(v26),expr(sub([var(v1),var(v0)]))), encoding the Yul statement diff := sub(y,x) at L14 of Fig. 2a. The unfolding process stops when no clause contains atoms that are annotated as unfoldable. One of the clauses obtained by unfolding is a clause, say U_jumpi_1, of the form:

```
jumpi(A,B,...,U,...) :- U=0, G1=F-E, ...,
   reach(cf(cmd(...,fun_call(cleanup_t_rational_0_by_1,...),...),
        cf(cmd(...,ret([var(v4)])),...))  ),
   reach(cf(cmd(assert,asgn(var(v1),expr(iszero([var(v0)])))),...),
        errCf)).
```

Recall that, for function calls, the fun_call_epilogue predicate of the interpreter considers two alternatives: the regular termination of the function and its abnormal termination leading to the error configuration. Indeed, clause U_jumpi_1 contains two reach atoms. The first one represents the regular termination of cleanup_t_rational_0_by_1, producing as result v4, whereas the second atom represents the abnormal termination of the helper function assert. Note that assert is responsible for the evaluation of the condition diff > 0 at line 9 of Fig. 2a: if the condition does not hold, it calls the auxiliary function panic_error_0x01 leading to the error configuration errCf. Now, the VCG strategy introduces two additional definitions :

```
cleanup_t_rational_0_by_1(...) :-
   reach(cf(cmd(...,fun_call(cleanup_t_rational_0_by_1,...),...),
        cf(cmd(...,ret([var(v4)])),...))  ).
assert_ERR(...) :-
   reach(cf(cmd(assert,asgn(var(v1),expr(iszero([var(v0)])))),...),
        errCf)).
```

and uses the new definitions to fold U_jumpi_1 as follows:

```
jumpi(A,B,...,U,...) :- U=0, G1=F-E, ...,
                 cleanup_t_rational_0_by_1(...), assert_ERR(...).
```

The VCG strategy continues by performing the (define and fold) step on the other clauses obtained from the (unfold) step. The complete specialization of the definition D_jumpi is shown in Fig. 6. On the left side, we show the CHCs for case 0, with the constraints U=0 (gt(x,y) holds) and G1=F-E (diff := sub(x, y)). As already mentioned, clauses at line 1 and 6 represent the regular termination of cleanup_t_rational_0_by_1 and the abnormal termination of the helper function assert, respectively, and differ only for the constraints obtained by the evaluation of comparison statements included in the

```
1    jumpi(A,B,E,F,U,...,E1,F1,G1) :-              14   jumpi(...) :-
2        U=0, G1=F-E, G1>E1, F1=1, ...,            15       U=1, G1=E-F, G1>E1, F1=1, ...,
3        cleanup_t_rational_0_by_1(...),           16       cleanup_t_rational_0_by_1(...),
4        assert_ERR(...).                          17       assert_ERR(...).
5                                                  18
6    jumpi(...) :-                                 19   jumpi(...) :-
7        U=0, G1=F-E, G1=<E1, F1=0, ...,           20       U=1, G1=E-F, G1=<E1, F1=0, ...,
8        cleanup_t_rational_0_by_1(...),           21       cleanup_t_rational_0_by_1(...),
9        assert_ERR(...).                          22       assert_ERR(...).
10                                                 23
11   jumpi(...) :-                                 24   jumpi(...) :-
12       U=0, G1=F-E, ...,                         25       U=1, G1=E-F, ...,
13       cleanup_t_rational_0_by_1_ERR(...).       26       cleanup_t_rational_0_by_1_ERR(...).
```

Fig. 6. CHCs obtained from the specialization of `jumpi` presented in Sect. 3.3, corresponding to the `switch` statement in the Yul code.

function `positiveDefinition`. The clause at line 11 represents the abnormal termination of `cleanup_t_rational_0_by_1`. On the right side, we show similar CHCs for the `default` case, with the constraints U=1 ($gt(x,y)$ does not hold) and F1=E-F ($diff := sub(y, x)$).

4   Case Studies

Let us show the relevance of our work on two case studies. The first, `Auction`, analyzes a smart contract extracted from the article [18], while the second, `Splitter`, examines a modified version of the `PaymentSplitter` [17] from the popular OpenZeppelin smart contract, which includes inline assembly. For each case study, we start with an initial configuration `Cf1` and show that no execution path can lead to an error configuration `Cf2`.

The `Auction` contract in Fig. 7 implements a simple auction in Solidity: bidders send Ether, from which a net bid (`new_bid`) is calculated, which must exceed the current stored one. If there is a previous winner, the contract checks that the balance (`cash`) is sufficient to repay it, makes the transfer, and updates the status. Here, `require(new_bid > bid)` acts as a precondition, verifying that the incoming bid is indeed higher than the current bid before continuing. Only if this condition is met, the flow continues. The block `if(winner != address(0))` determines whether it is a bid following the first bid: only in this case is the previous winner refunded. `assert(bid <= cash)` is a post-condition and at the same time a contract invariant, which guarantees that the internal state (`cash`) is always sufficient to cover the amount to be returned (`bid`). If by a logical error the state is inconsistent (e.g. `cash < bid`),

```
contract Auction {
  uint public bid = 0;
  uint public cash = 0;
  address payable public winner;

  constructor() {
      winner = payable(address(0));
  }

  function offer() public payable {
      uint new_bid = msg.value - 1015 wei;
      require(new_bid > bid);

      if (winner != payable(address(0))) {
          assert(bid <= cash);
          winner.transfer(bid);
          cash -= bid;
      }

      bid = new_bid;
      cash += msg.value;
      winner = payable(msg.sender);
  }
}
```

Fig. 7. Auction contract

the assert will fail and cause irreversible revert, signaling a critical bug. In this way, `require` protects the input conditions, while `assert` ensures that the financial correctness invariant of the contract remains valid once the internal transactions are executed. For this specific example, the initial configuration used in clause Q of Sect. 3 is defined as follows:

```
Cf1 = cf(cmd(external_fun_offer_85_Block0_3,
               fun_call(fun_offer_85, [], [])), Env1)
```

which corresponds to the initial configuration where, in the post-deployment environment (`Env1`), a call is made to the `fun_offer_85` function (the function under consideration which contains the `assert`). An equivalent version of this same contract, in which some operations were replaced by bytecode, was subjected to the same verification process: the results obtained exactly match those of the original Solidity contract, confirming the unique ability of our approach to handle contracts in both source code and bytecode.

```
function releasable(address account)
  public view returns (uint256) {
    require(msg.sender == account);
    require(account == payee0
            | account == payee1
            | account == payee2);
    require(totalShares > 0);
    require(amountp0 >= released0
        && amountp1 >= released1
        && amountp2 >= released2);

    uint256 sumPend; uint256 yours;

    assembly {
      for { let i := 0 } lt(i, 3)
        { i := add(i, 1) } {
        let payee := sload(i)
        let amount := sload(add(6, i))
        let rel := sload(add(9, i))
        let pend := sub(amount, rel)
        sumPend := add(sumPend, pend)
        if eq(payee, account)
            { yours := pend }
      }
    }
    assert(address(this).balance
           >= sumPend);
    return yours;
}
```

Fig. 8. Releasable function

The `Splitter` contract (see the full contract in the repository) allows funds to be split between three predetermined addresses, each with a fixed payee quota defined at the time of creation. Each time one of the three `payees` sends ETH to the contract, the `receive` function checks that the sender's address matches one of the stakeholders and that the amount deposited is exactly equal to its `share`, accumulating the total amount deposited for each stakeholder. To check how much remains to be withdrawn, each payee may invoke the `releasable` function (Fig. 8) which, in `assembly`, iterates over the three addresses, calculates the difference between the `amount` paid in and the amount already `released` for each, and identifies the amount due. To ensure the integrity of the state, a final `assert` in the releasable function ensures that the balance of the contract is at least equal to the sum of all outstanding amounts, preventing inconsistent conditions. The `release` function then allows the payee to withdraw a validated amount: it checks, via `require`, the origin of the call, the contract balance, the positive amount and compliance with the limit calculated by releasable, and then updates the released counters and transfers ETH with call. For this specific example we define:

```
Cf1 = cf(cmd(external_fun_releasable_259_Block2_3,
               fun_call(fun_releasable_259, [var(v0)], [])),Env1)
```

where v0 is the variable representing the value passed as input to the function. Our verifier confirms that the property holds as expected. As with contract `Operation` in Fig. 2, the version of this contract written entirely in Solidity is less optimized than the one including Yul code, making the Yul-based version more desirable for deployment and more used in practice by smart contract developers. However, as we have noted before, there is no other tool that can verify Yul code.

5   Conclusions, Related and Future Work

We have proposed a transformational approach to the verification of Ethereum smart contracts which consists in transforming their intermediate Yul representation into an equivalent CHC program which can be directly used as input to off-the-shelf CHC verifiers (like Eldarica [12] or Spacer [15]). Our work is based on the interpretative approach to compilation [6,10] which has been successfully applied to transform low-level code into higher-level representation (e.g., transforming Java bytecode to CHC [11]) and to transform from one high-level code to another (e.g., transforming C to CHC [5] and other imperative programs [20]). The advantages of the interpretative approach include, among others, faster development time as –assuming that a specializer is available (as it was in our case)– one just needs to implement the Yul interpreter in CHC, as well as higher reliability in the correctness of the implementation as –assuming that the specializer is a trusted component– one just needs to ensure the correctness of the interpreter implementation.

On the one hand, compared to existing verifiers for Ethereum smart contracts [4,13,22,24], we are behind their capabilities as some of them are being developed already for a number of years and are able to prove complex properties such as callback freeness [3]. Our work is a first step towards the direction of building a strong verifier able to prove complex properties as well. On the other hand, our work is covering an important gap in the verification of Ethereum smart contracts as there is no other tool able to directly analyze Yul code yet. However, Yul is being proposed by the Ethereum community as the target language for high-level optimization and analysis stages so that all target platforms equally can benefit from progress at the Yul level. Hence our work has the potential of providing such benefits to all target platforms as well.

Finally, while our work is based on the VCG approach in [5] for C programs, they differ in some significant aspects. First, the interpreter has to take into account the Yul syntax and semantics as well as the EVM memory model, which contains blockchain-specific components, and the management of the different ways in which the execution of a Yul function can terminate (ret, commit, revert, error). There are important differences as well between the VCG strategy for Yul and C: (1) the unfolding annotation for C programs considers as non-unfoldable the entry points of functions and conditional jumps, as well as the junction points of conditional jumps. However, for Yul, the junction points are not directly recognizable thus in the current version of the strategy we do not consider them;

(2) the VCG strategy for Yul requires extending the unfolding annotation to keep track of atoms that are associated with the contract deployment phase on the blockchain; (3) the VCG strategy for C programs makes use of additional annotations that help to reduce the number of new predicate definitions as well as the number of their arguments. For instance, the VCG strategy can be configured to use annotations that keep track of (i) the absence of side-effects for functions thus reducing the number of variables for predicates, and (ii) to the impossibility for auxiliary functions of reaching an error configuration thus reducing non-determinism and the number of clauses. This fine tuning of the VCG strategy for C programs was instrumental to achieve the optimal time and space complexity presented in [5]. For Yul, we aim to extend the strategy to get similar results in the near future. Besides, although we have implemented all components of the overall verification framework, namely the translator from Yul to CHCs, the Yul interpreter and the adaptations required in the specializer, we have not automated the overall process yet. Our current work is focused on implementing the full pipeline that connects all components as well as making a thorough experimental evaluation using real contracts.

Acknowledgments. This work was partially funded by: the Spanish MCI, Comunidad de Madrid, AEI and FEDER (EU) projects PID2021-122830OB-C41 and TEC-2024/COM-235, the Italian PNRR MUR project PE0000013-FAIR and the MUR PRIN 2022 Project DOMAIN (2022TSYYKJ, CUP B53D23013220006, PNRR M4.C2.1.1) funded by the European Union - NextGenerationEU. Emanuele De Angelis and Fabio Fioravanti are members of the INdAM-GNCS research group.

References

1. Akhunov, A., Salem, M.: EIP-1153: Transient storage opcodes (2018). https://eips.ethereum.org/EIPS/eip-1153. Ethereum Improvement Proposals, no. 1153
2. Albert, E., Correas, J., Gordillo, P., Román-Díez, G., Rubio, A.: SAFEVM: a safety verifier for Ethereum smart contracts. In: Proceedings of the 28th ACM SIGSOFT International Symposium on Software Testing and Analysis, pp. 386–389 (2019)
3. Albert, E., Grossman, S., Rinetzky, N., Rodríguez-Núñez, C., Rubio, A., Sagiv, M.: Relaxed effective callback freedom: a parametric correctness condition for sequential modules with callbacks. IEEE Trans. Dependable Secur. Comput. **20**(3), 2256–2273 (2023)
4. Alt, L., Blicha, M., Hyvärinen, A.E.J., Sharygina, N.: SolCMC: solidity compiler's model checker. In: Computer Aided Verification (CAV), vol. 13371 of LNCS, pp. 325–338. Springer, Heidelberg (2022)
5. De Angelis, E., Fioravanti, F., Pettorossi, A., Proietti, M.: Semantics-based generation of verification conditions via program specialization. Sci. Comput. Program. **147**, 78–108 (2017)
6. De Angelis, E., Fioravanti, F., Gallagher, J.P., Hermenegildo, M.V., Pettorossi, A., Proietti, M.: Analysis and transformation of constrained horn clauses for program verification. Theory Pract. Log. Program. **22**(6), 974–1042 (2022)

7. De Angelis, E., Fioravanti, F., Pettorossi, A., Proietti, M.: VeriMAP: a tool for verifying programs through transformations. In: Ábrahám, E., Havelund, K. (eds.) TACAS 2014. LNCS, vol. 8413, pp. 568–574. Springer, Heidelberg (2014). https://doi.org/10.1007/978-3-642-54862-8_47
8. De Angelis, E., Krishnan, H.G.V.: Competition of solvers for constrained horn clauses (CHC-COMP 2023). In: TOOLympics Challenge 2023, pp. 38–51. Springer, Cham (2023)
9. Dxo, M.S., Paraskevopoulou, Z., Lundfall, M., Brockman, M.: Hevm, a fast symbolic execution framework for EVM bytecode. In: Computer Aided Verification (CAV), vol. 14681 of LNCS, pp. 453–465. Springer, Heidelberg (2024)
10. Futamura, Y.: Partial evaluation of computation process - an approach to a compiler-compiler. High. Order Symb. Comput. **12**(4), 381–391 (1999)
11. Gómez-Zamalloa, M., Albert, E., Puebla, G.: Decompilation of java bytecode to prolog by partial evaluation. Inf. Softw. Technol. **51**(10), 1409–1427 (2009)
12. Hojjat, H., Rümmer, P.: The ELDARICA horn solver. In: Formal Methods in Computer Aided Design, pp. 1–7. IEEE (2018)
13. Jackson, D., Nandi, C., Sagiv, M.: Certora Technology White Paper (2022). https://docs.certora.com/en/latest/docs/whitepaper/index.html
14. Jaffar, J., Maher, M.J.: Constraint logic programming: a survey. J. Logic Program. **19–20**, 503–581 (1994)
15. Komuravelli, A., Gurfinkel, A., Chaki, S.: SMT-based model checking for recursive programs. In: Biere, A., Bloem, R. (eds.) CAV 2014. LNCS, vol. 8559, pp. 17–34. Springer, Cham (2014). https://doi.org/10.1007/978-3-319-08867-9_2
16. Koutavas, V., Lin, Y.Y., Tzevelekos, N.: An operational semantics for yul. In: Software Engineering and Formal Methods, pp. 328–346. Springer, Heidelberg (2024)
17. OpenZeppelin. PaymentSplitter Contract. https://docs.openzeppelin.com/contracts/4.x/api/finance#PaymentSplitter
18. Otoni, R., Marescotti, M., Alt, L., Eugster, P., Hyvärinen, A., Sharygina, N.: A solicitous approach to smart contract verification. ACM Trans. Priv. Secur. **26**(2), 1–28 (2023)
19. Park, D., Zhang, Y., Saxena, M., Daian, P., Rosu, G.: A formal verification tool for Ethereum VM bytecode. In: ACM Joint Meeting on European Software Engineering Conf. and Symposium on the Foundations of Software Engineering, pp. 912–915. ACM (2018)
20. Peralta, J.C., Gallagher, J.P., Sağlam, H.: Analysis of imperative programs through analysis of constraint logic programs. In: Levi, G. (ed.) SAS 1998. LNCS, vol. 1503, pp. 246–261. Springer, Heidelberg (1998). https://doi.org/10.1007/3-540-49727-7_15
21. Rastello, F., Bouchez-Tichadou, F. (eds.): SSA-based Compiler Design. Springer, Heidelberg (2022)
22. So, S., Lee, M., Park, J., Lee, H., Oh, H.: VERISMART: a highly precise safety verifier for ethereum smart contracts. In: 2020 IEEE Symposium on Security and Privacy (SP), pp. 1678–1694 (2020)
23. Solidity Team. Solidity Documentation. Release 0.8.30 (2025). https://docs.soliditylang.org/_/downloads/en/v0.8.30/pdf/
24. Wesley, S., Christakis, M., Navas, J.A., Trefler, R., Wüstholz, V., Gurfinkel, A.: Verifying SOLIDITY smart contracts via communication abstraction in SMARTACE. In: Finkbeiner, B., Wies, T. (eds.) VMCAI 2022. LNCS, vol. 13182, pp. 425–449. Springer, Cham (2022). https://doi.org/10.1007/978-3-030-94583-1_21
25. Wood, G., et al.: Ethereum: a secure decentralised generalised transaction ledger. Ethereum Proj. Yellow Paper **151**(2014), 1–32 (2014)

Implementing a Many-Valued Semantics for Logic Programs with Ordered Disjunction Using ASP

Angelos Charalambidis[1]([✉]), Georgios Nikolaou[2], and Antonis Troumpoukis[3]

[1] Harokopio University of Athens, Athens, Greece
acharal@hua.gr
[2] National and Kapodistrian University of Athens, Athens, Greece
sdi2000153@di.uoa.gr
[3] National Centre of Scientific Research "Demokritos", Agia Paraskevi, Greece
antru@iit.demokritos.gr

Abstract. Logic Programs with Ordered Disjunction (LPODs) are a well-known extension of logic programming used to express qualitative preferences via the operator of ordered disjunction. However, the semantics originally proposed for LPODs can yield counterintuitive preferred solutions in some cases. An alternative logical semantics for LPODs addresses these cases by introducing an additional truth value representing the failure to satisfy a preference. In this paper we present an implementation of this alternative many-valued semantics. We propose a transformation of an LPOD into an ASP program and reformulate the task of finding the many-valued preferred models as an answer set optimization task. Notably, our approach can be extended to also support standard disjunction for expressing preferences of equal importance. Finally, we compare our system with existing systems implementing the original semantics. The experimental results suggest that the alternative semantics are not only feasible to implement but also comparable in performance.

Keywords: Logic Programs with Ordered Disjunction · Answer Set Programming · Many-Valued Logic

1 Introduction

Logic Programs with Ordered Disjunction (LPODs) [4] were introduced as a powerful extension of traditional logic programming to express qualitative preferences. LPODs introduce a new disjunctive connective $\times$, called ordered disjunction, which allows for the expression of preferences in the head of program rules. The head of an LPOD rule is a formula $C_1 \times \cdots \times C_n$ intuitively understood as: "*I prefer C_1; however, if C_1 is impossible, I can accept C_2; $\cdots$; if all of $C_1, \ldots, C_{n-1}$ are impossible, I can accept C_n*". In other words, this operator

S. Escobar and L. Titolo (Eds.): LOPSTR 2025, LNCS 16117, pp. 40–56, 2026.
https://doi.org/10.1007/978-3-032-04848-6_3

enables the expression of alternatives of decreasing degrees of preference where the most preferred outcome is listed first, followed by less preferred alternatives.

The meaning of LPODs was originally defined [4,6] using the answer set semantics, through a two-phase process. In the first phase, candidate answer sets of an LPOD are generated, using a variation of the standard definition of answer sets. In the second phase, these answer sets are "filtered" to identify the "most preferred" answer sets and this decision involves computing the "degree of satisfaction" for every program rule. The meaning of LPODs is defined as the subset of their answer sets which satisfies in the best possible way the preferences in the head of program rules.

Despite its strengths, the original semantics of LPODs has been found to produce some counterintuitive preferred solutions in some cases [2,9]. To demonstrate one of the reported counterintuitive behaviors, consider the following program.

```
1  mbz × bmw.
2  gas × ev ← mbz.
3  f ← gas,not f.
```

The intuitive meaning is: "*I prefer buying a Mercedes to a BMW. If a Mercedes is available, I prefer a gas model to an electric one. However, a gas model is not available*". This program under the original semantics has two preferred answer sets: one where both mbz and ev are true, and another where mbz is false and bmw is true. It seems reasonable though that the first model is more preferred since the first rule specifies an unconditional preference, whereas the second rule describes a secondary preference that depends on the choice made in the first. In addition to this example, other cases have been reported [2,9] where the original semantics may exhibit undesirable behavior. This issue appears to stem from the sensitivity to the degree of satisfaction of the program's rules.

This shortcoming has motivated further research into improving the semantics of LPODs, leading to the development of a many-valued logical semantics that addresses the reported issues [9]. This semantics is fundamentally different from the original one as it does not rely on the notion of degrees of satisfaction. Instead, an additional false value is used to indicate that a preference fails only if it is impossible to be satisfied. The most preferred answer sets are those that minimize the number of atoms assigned this additional value. One of the merits of the new semantics is that it is purely logical, allowing for well-known properties, such as strong equivalence of logic programs, to be described in purely logical terms [8]. Despite these theoretical merits, no implementation has yet been proposed, and the practical feasibility of this approach remains unclear.

This paper proposes an implementation of the alternative many-valued semantics for LPODs. We show that the many-valued semantics can be translated to standard Answer Set Programming (ASP) in a way that any answer set of the translated program can be mapped back to an answer set of the original LPOD. Although the answer sets of the logic program are two-valued, the additional false value required by the many-valued semantics can be recovered by introducing auxiliary predicates. Identifying the preferred answer sets is then formulated as an optimization problem.

The second contribution of this paper is the implementation of a class of disjunctive LPODs (DLPODs) i.e., programs that allow both ordered and standard disjunction in the head of the rules. This extension is meaningful in practice, as standard disjunction can be used to expresses preferences of equal importance. Our proposed ASP encoding generalizes naturally to DLPODs, and, to the best of our knowledge, this is the first system that supports this broader class of programs.

Finally, we have realized these concepts in a working system. This system utilizes clingo [10] as the ASP solver and asprin [5] for identifying the optimal answer sets. We evaluated the performance of our system and compared it against systems that implement the original semantics. The results indicate that the alternative semantics are not merely of theoretical interest, but can also be implemented efficiently in practice.

The rest of the paper is structured as follows. Section 2 introduces the syntax and semantics of LPODs. Section 3 details the transformation of LPODs to ASP and Sect. 4 extends it to DLPODs. Section 5 reviews related work. Section 6 presents experiments and compares our implementation with existing LPOD systems. Finally, Sect. 7 outlines future directions for research.

2   Logic Programs with Ordered Disjunction

Let Σ be a nonempty, countably infinite, set of propositional atoms. Every element of Σ is a well-formed formula. If ϕ_1 and ϕ_2 are well-formed formulas then $not\ \phi_1$, $\phi_1 \wedge \phi_2$, $\phi_1 \vee \phi_2$, $\phi_1 \times \phi_2$ are also well-formed formulas. The operators "$\wedge$", "$\vee$" and "$\times$" are left associative and we will omit parentheses whenever possible. A logic program with ordered disjunction (LPOD) is a set of formulas of a special kind specified in the following definition.

Definition 1. *An LPOD is a set of rules of the form*

$$C_1 \times \cdots \times C_n \leftarrow A_1 \wedge \ldots \wedge A_m \wedge not\ A_{m+1} \wedge \ldots \wedge not\ A_k$$

where $n \geq 1$, $k \geq 0$ and C_i, A_j are atoms.

If P is an LPOD, then $At(P) \subseteq \Sigma$ denotes the set of atoms occurring in P. The formula $C_1 \times \cdots \times C_n$ is referred to as the *head* of the rule and $A_1 \wedge \ldots \wedge A_m \wedge not\ A_{m+1} \wedge \ldots \wedge not\ A_k$ as the *body* of the rule.

We refer to a rule as a *fact* when $k = 0$ and we will also omit $\leftarrow$. If $m = k$ then the rule is *positive* and if also $m = 1$ then the rule is *simple*. We will call a rule *regular* if its head is a propositional atom and *ordered disjunctive* if $n > 1$. An LPOD is a regular logic program when every rule is regular.

We will follow the common ASP practice and write a body B of a rule as $A_1, \ldots, A_m, not\ A_{m+1}, \ldots, not\ A_k$ instead of $A_1 \wedge \cdots \wedge A_m \wedge not\ A_{m+1} \wedge \ldots \wedge not\ A_k$. We will also write $\leftarrow B$ as abbreviation for $f \leftarrow B, not\ f$ for some f not appearing in the rest of the program. We will refer to this rule as a *constraint*, expressing that "it is not allowed for B to be true". We will also write $\{h\} \leftarrow B$ as an abbreviation of the rules $h \leftarrow B, not\ \bar{h}$ and $\bar{h} \leftarrow B, not\ h$ where $\bar{h}$ is an atom not appearing in the rest of the program. This represents a *conditional choice rule*, expressing that "if B holds, then h may be included in the answer set".

In order to define the semantics of LPODs we follow the development of [9]. We start with the set $V = \{F, F^*, T\}$ of truth values which are ordered as $F < F^* < T$. Given two truth values v_1, v_2, we write $v_1 \leq v_2$ if and only if either $v_1 < v_2$ or $v_1 = v_2$. Notice that V is a complete lattice. We use min and max to refer to minimum and maximum element, respectively, of a set of elements in V.

The intuitive reading of the value F^* is "impossible to make true in order to satisfy a preference". To understand the need for F^*, consider again the intuitive meaning of $C_1 \times C_2$: we prefer C_2 *only if it is impossible for us to get C_1*. Impossible here means that if we try to make C_1 true, then the interpretation will become inconsistent. Therefore, we seem to need two types of false, namely F and F^*: F means *"false by default"* while F^* means *"impossible to make true"*.

Before defining the interpretation of well-formed formulas we assume that there exist constants that are also well-formed formulas for the truth values, namely the constants F, F^* and T. This assumption helps for the definition of the answer sets.

Definition 2. *An interpretation I is a function from Σ to the set V. We can extend I to apply to formulas, as follows:*

$$
\begin{aligned}
I(F) &= F \\
I(F^*) &= F^* \\
I(T) &= T \\
I(not\ \phi) &= \begin{cases} F, \text{ if } I(\phi) = T \\ T, \text{ if } I(\phi) = F \text{ or } I(\phi) = F^* \end{cases} \\
I(\phi_1 \wedge \phi_2) &= \min\{I(\phi_1), I(\phi_2)\} \\
I(\phi_1 \vee \phi_2) &= \max\{I(\phi_1), I(\phi_2)\} \\
I(\phi_1 \times \phi_2) &= \begin{cases} I(\phi_2), \text{ if } I(\phi_1) = F^* \\ I(\phi_1), \text{ otherwise} \end{cases}
\end{aligned}
$$

It is easy to see that indeed the meanings of "$\wedge$", "$\vee$" and "$\times$" are associative and therefore we can write $I(\phi_1 \wedge \cdots \wedge \phi_n)$, $I(\phi_1 \vee \cdots \vee \phi_n)$, and $I(\phi_1 \times \cdots \times \phi_n)$ unambiguously. Moreover, given atoms $C_1, \ldots, C_n$ we will often write $I(C_1, \ldots, C_n)$ instead of $I(C_1 \wedge \cdots \wedge C_n)$.

The ordering $<$ (respectively, $\leq$) on truth values extends in the standard way on interpretations: given interpretations I_1, I_2 we write $I_1 < I_2$ (respectively, $I_1 \leq I_2$), if for all atom $A \in \Sigma$, $I_1(A) < I_2(A)$ (respectively, $I_1(A) \leq I_2(A)$).

Definition 3. *Let P be an LPOD and I be an interpretation of P. Then, I is a model of P if for every rule $C_1 \times \cdots \times C_n \leftarrow A_1, \ldots, A_m, not\ A_{m+1}, \ldots, not\ A_k$ of P, it holds that $I(C_1 \times \cdots \times C_n) \geq I(A_1, \ldots, A_m, not\ A_{m+1}, \ldots, not\ A_k)$.*

The most preferred answer sets of an LPOD are generated using a two-step procedure. In the first step, a subset of the models of the program is selected that constitute the *answer sets* of the given LPOD. This is done using a reduct-based procedure similar to regular ASP. In the second step, a subset of the answer sets is selected using a minimization procedure that examines the set of atoms that have the value F^* in each answer set. The notion of the reduct of an LPOD is formally defined in the following definition. The following definition formally introduces the notion of the reduct of an LPOD.

Definition 4. *Let P be an LPOD. The $\times$-reduct of a rule R of P of the form:*

$$C_1 \times \cdots \times C_n \leftarrow A_1, \ldots, A_m, not\ A_{m+1}, \ldots, not\ A_k$$

with respect to an interpretation I, is denoted by $R_\times^I$ and is defined as follows:

- *If $I(A_i) = T$ for some i, $m + 1 \leq i \leq k$, then $R_\times^I$ is the empty set.*
- *If $I(A_i) \neq T$ for all i, $m + 1 \leq i \leq k$, then $R_\times^I$ is the set that contains the rules:*

$$C_1 \quad \leftarrow F^*, A_1, \ldots, A_m$$
$$\vdots$$
$$C_{r-1} \leftarrow F^*, A_1, \ldots, A_m$$
$$C_r \quad \leftarrow A_1, \ldots, A_m$$

where r is the least index such that $I(C_1) = \cdots = I(C_{r-1}) = F^*$ and either $r = n$ or $I(C_r) \neq F^*$.

The $\times$-reduct of P with respect to I is denoted by $P_\times^I$ and is the union of the reducts $R_\times^I$ for all R in P.

Note that the $\times$-reduct is a positive regular program. The main difference with the reduct of a regular program is the inclusion of clauses of the form $C_i \leftarrow F^*, A_1, \ldots, A_m$ which allow for F^* to be assigned to C_i when $I(A_j) = T$ for all $j \in \{1, \ldots, m\}$.

Definition 5. *Let P be an LPOD and M an interpretation of P. We say that M is an answer set of P if it is a $\leq$-minimal model of $P_\times^M$.*

If the program is regular, i.e., it has no ordered disjunctive rules, the $\times$-reduct coincides with the standard reduct of a regular ASP program [11]. Moreover, the answer sets of Definition 5 coincide with the standard notion of answer sets for such programs [11]. As a consequence, if the program is regular then the answer sets are two-valued, that is, they do not have atoms that are assigned the F^* value.

Example 1. Consider again the program given in the introduction.

```
1   mbz × bmw.
2   gas × ev ← mbz.
3   f ← gas,not f.
```

Let $I_1 = \{(\text{mbz}, T), (\text{bmw}, F), (\text{gas}, F), (\text{ev}, T), (\text{f}, F)\}$ be an interpretation of P. The program $P_\times^{I_1}$ is the following.

```
1  mbz.
2  gas ← mbz.
3  f ← gas.
```

It is easy to see that I_1 is not a model of $P_\times^{I_1}$ and therefore not an answer set of P. On the other hand, consider $I_2 = \{(\mathtt{mbz}, T), (\mathtt{bmw}, F), (\mathtt{gas}, F^*), (\mathtt{ev}, T), (\mathtt{f}, F^*)\}$. The corresponding program $P_\times^{I_2}$ is the following.

```
1  mbz.
2  gas ← F*,mbz.
3  ev ← mbz.
4  f ← F*,gas.
```

Indeed, I_2 is a $\leq$-minimal model of $P_\times^{I_2}$ and therefore an answer set of P. Actually, using the same reasoning it is easy to verify that P has also another answer set I_3 where $I_3 = \{(\mathtt{mbz}, F^*), (\mathtt{bmw}, T), (\mathtt{gas}, F^*), (\mathtt{ev}, F^*), (\mathtt{f}, F^*)\}$.

We now need to define a preference relation over the answer sets of a program. Intuitively, we prefer those answer sets that maximize the prospect of satisfying our top choices in ordered disjunctions. This can be achieved by minimizing with respect to F^* values. More formally, we define the following ordering.

Definition 6. *Let P be an LPOD and let M_1, M_2 be answer sets of P. Let M_1^* and M_2^* be the sets of atoms in M_1 and M_2 respectively that have the value F^*. We say that M_1 is preferred to M_2, written $M_1 \sqsubset M_2$, if $M_1^* \subset M_2^*$.*

Definition 7. *An answer set of an LPOD P is called most preferred if it is minimal among all the answer sets of P with respect to the $\sqsubset$ relation.*

The intuition behind the definition of $\sqsubset$ is that we prefer those answer sets that minimize the need for F^* values. In other words, an answer set will be most preferred if all the literals that get the value F^*, do this because there is no other option: these literals *must be false* in order for the program to have a model.

Example 2. Continuing with Example 1, $I_2^* = \{\mathtt{gas}, \mathtt{f}\}$ and $I_3^* = \{\mathtt{mbz}, \mathtt{gas}, \mathtt{ev}, \mathtt{f}\}$ and therefore I_2 is most preferred than I_3. It is worth noting that the original semantics of LPODs yields both answer sets I_2 and I_3 as preferred.

3 Encoding LPOD Semantics to ASP

In this section we present an encoding of a given LPOD into a regular logic program. Conceptually, the answer sets of the resulting logic program will align with the answer sets of the original LPOD. Given that the answer sets of the logic program are two-valued, and the fact that atoms that are assigned the F^* play a crucial role for the selection of the preferred models, we will use additional predicates to compute F^* values.

The encoding of an LPOD P is the union of two regular logic programs $\varepsilon(P) \cup \varphi(P)$. The program $\varepsilon(P)$ evaluates whether an atom in the LPOD is true or false and $\varphi(P)$ ascertains whether an atom that is false is actually F^*. In particular, we apply a three-step transformation on P. First, we transform P into a normal form. Then, we eliminate the ordered disjunctive rules, and finally we produce auxiliary predicates to compute the F^* values.

In the first step of our transformation, we translate arbitrary LPODs into LPODs in normal form. Specifically, an LPOD in normal form consists of a set of regular rules (i.e., without ordered disjunctive heads) and a set of ordered disjunctive rules that must be simple (i.e., either facts or the body is a single positive atom). If the body of the rule is not already in a normal form, we introduce an auxiliary propositional atom to represent the body and then add a corresponding regular rule. The following definition formalizes this process.

Definition 8. *Let P be an LPOD. Then, $\sigma(P)$ is an LPOD that contains exactly:*

– *For every rule R of P, if it is either regular or simple then R is in $\sigma(P)$.*
– *For every rule R of P that is non-regular and non-simple and is of the form*

$$C_1 \times \cdots \times C_n \leftarrow A_1, \ldots, A_m, not\, A_{m+1}, \ldots, not\, A_k$$

$\sigma(P)$ contains the rules:

$$C_1 \times \cdots \times C_n \leftarrow B^R \tag{1}$$
$$B^R \leftarrow A_1, \ldots, A_m, not\, A_{m+1}, \ldots, not\, A_k \tag{2}$$

where B^R is a new propositional atom not in $At(P)$.

An LPOD P is in normal form if $P = \sigma(P)$. The following proposition suggests that it suffices to consider the normal form of LPODs.

Proposition 1. *Let P be an LPOD. Then, the most preferred answer sets of $\sigma(P)$ coincide with the most preferred answer sets of P if we restrict them to the atoms in $At(P)$.*

The second step of our transformation eliminates the ordered disjunctions from a LPOD yielding a regular program. The resulting program essentially checks which atoms of an ordered disjunction are true in an answer set of the LPOD. This is achieved by transforming each ordered disjunctive rule into a set of ASP choice rules. The following definition introduces the aforementioned transformation.

Definition 9. *Let P be an LPOD in normal form. Then, $\varepsilon(P)$ is a regular program that contains exactly:*

– *For every ordered disjunctive fact $C_1 \times \cdots \times C_n$, $\varepsilon(P)$ contains the rules:*

$$\{C_i\} \leftarrow not\, C_1, \ldots, not\, C_{i-1} \qquad for\ i \in \{1, \ldots, n\} \tag{3}$$
$$\leftarrow not\, C_1, \ldots, not\, C_n \tag{4}$$

- *For every ordered disjunctive rule R of P of the form $C_1 \times \cdots \times C_n \leftarrow B$, $\varepsilon(P)$ contains the rules:*

$$\{C_i\} \leftarrow B, \text{not } C_1, \ldots, \text{not } C_{i-1} \qquad \text{for } i \in \{1, \ldots, n\} \qquad (5)$$
$$\leftarrow B, \text{not } C_1, \ldots, \text{not } C_n \qquad\qquad (6)$$

- *For every other rule R of P, R is in $\varepsilon(P)$.*

Intuitively, the rules for each atom C_i generated by (5), expresses the fact that C_i can be "chosen" if the body of the rule holds and none of the preceding atoms C_j, $j < i$ are chosen. On the other hand, the corresponding rule generated by (6) expresses the constraint that if the body is true then at least one of C_i must also be true. This transformation is similar to the one introduced in [7] for the LPODs under the original semantics.

Example 3. Consider again the LPOD P given in the introduction which is already in normal form. The program $\varepsilon(P)$ is the following.

```
1   {mbz}.                    % Transformation of Rule 1:
2   {bmw} ← not mbz.          % i.e., mbz × bmw.
3   ← not mbz,not bmw.
4   {gas} ← mbz.              % Transformation of Rule 2:
5   {ev} ← mbz,not gas.       % i.e., gas × ev ← mbz.
6   ← mbz,not gas,not ev.
7   f ← gas,not f.            % Rule 3 remains the same.
```

It is easy to verify that it has two answer sets, $\{\text{bmw}\}$ and $\{\text{mbz}, \text{ev}\}$.

Notice that the answer sets of the transformed program are not directly comparable to the answer sets of the LPOD since it is only two-valued. The following definition offers a method to convert a many-valued interpretation into a set by including only the atoms with assigned value T.

Definition 10. *Let I be an interpretation of an LPOD P. We define*

$$collapse(I) = \{A \in At(P) \mid I(A) = T\}$$

The following proposition suggests that if we collapse any answer set of the LPOD P then it is an answer set of $\varepsilon(P)$.

Proposition 2. *Let P be an LPOD in normal form and M be an answer set of P. Then, $collapse(M)$ is an answer set of $\varepsilon(P)$.*

The converse is also true. We can reconstruct M from an LPOD P and an answer set N of $\varepsilon(P)$. The key idea is to define the set $S \subseteq At(P)$ that contains the atoms that are assigned a value greater or equal to F^*.

Definition 11. *Let I and S be subsets of $At(P)$. We define $collapse_S^{-1}(I)$ as*

$$collapse_S^{-1}(I)(A) = \begin{cases} F & \text{if } A \notin I \text{ and } A \notin S \\ F^* & \text{if } A \notin I \text{ and } A \in S \\ T & \text{if } A \in I \end{cases}$$

We are interested in N and S such that $collapse_S^{-1}(N)$ is a model of P. If N be an answer set of $\varepsilon(P)$ then $collapse_S^{-1}(N)$ is a model of P iff the following property holds:

$$S \supseteq \{C_j \mid \quad (C_1 \times \cdots \times C_n \leftarrow A_1, \ldots, A_m, not\ A_{m+1}, \ldots not\ A_k) \in P,$$
$$\{A_1, \ldots, A_m\} \subseteq S \cup N, \quad \{C_1, \ldots, C_j, A_{m+1}, \ldots, A_k\} \cap N = \emptyset\}$$

Moreover, if S is minimal then $collapse_S^{-1}(N)$ is an answer set of P. We denote $\mathcal{F}_P(N)$ the set of all minimal S with that property.

Proposition 3. *Let P be an LPOD in normal form and N an answer set of $\varepsilon(P)$ and $S \in \mathcal{F}_P(N)$. Then, $collapse_S^{-1}(N)$ is an answer set of P.*

The final step of our transformation determines which atoms must receive the F^* value by deriving them through an auxiliary ASP program. This can be achieved by encoding the set S by introducing two special atoms $isF^*(A)$ and $isTF^*(A)$ for each $A \in At(P)$. If M is an answer set of an LPOD P, then $isF^*(A)$ holds if $M(A) = F^*$ and $isTF^*(A)$ holds if $M(A) \geq F^*$. In the following, we define the program that contains the rules for $isF^*(A)$ and $isTF^*(A)$ and we assume that $isF^*(A)$ and $isTF^*(A)$ do not occur as atoms in P.

Definition 12. *Let P be an LPOD in normal form. Then, $\varphi(P)$ is a program that contains exactly the following rules:*

- *For every ordered disjunctive fact $C_1 \times \cdots \times C_n$, $\varphi(P)$ contains:*

$$isTF^*(C_i) \leftarrow isF^*(C_1), \ldots, isF^*(C_{i-1}) \qquad for\ i \in \{1, \ldots, n\} \qquad (7)$$

- *For every simple ordered disjunctive rule $C_1 \times \cdots \times C_n \leftarrow B$, $\varphi(P)$ contains:*

$$isTF^*(C_i) \leftarrow isTF^*(B), isF^*(C_1), \ldots, isF^*(C_{i-1})\ for\ i \in \{1, \ldots, n\} \quad (8)$$

- *For every regular rule $H \leftarrow A_1, \ldots, A_m, not\ A_{m+1}, \ldots, not\ A_k$, $\varphi(P)$ contains:*

$$isTF^*(H) \leftarrow isTF^*(A_1), \ldots, isTF^*(A_n), not\ A_{m+1}, \ldots, not\ A_k \qquad (9)$$

- *For every atom $A \in At(P)$, $\varphi(P)$ contains:*

$$isF^*(A) \leftarrow isTF^*(A), not\ A \qquad (10)$$

The rules (7–9) define the predicate $isTF^*(A)$ for the different kinds of rules, and encode the definition of the set S. Rule (10) defines the predicate $isF^*(A)$ by checking that A is false and also $isTF^*(A)$ holds.

Definition 13. *Let P be an LPOD. The encoding of P is the regular program $\varepsilon(P') \cup \varphi(P')$ where $P' = \sigma(P)$.*

Proposition 4. *Let P be an LPOD in normal form and M be an answer set of P. There exists an answer set N of $\varepsilon(P) \cup \varphi(P)$ such that $collapse_S^{-1}(N) = M$ where $S = \{A \mid isTF^*(A) \in N\}$.*

Example 4. The program $\varphi(P)$ for the LPOD P presented in the introduction is the following.

```
1   isTF*(mbz).                              % isTF* for mbz × bmw.
2   isTF*(bmw) ← isF*(mbz).
3   isTF*(gas) ← isTF*(mbz).                 % isTF* for gas × ev ← mbz.
4   isTF*(ev)  ← isTF*(mbz),isF*(gas).
5   isTF*(f)   ← isTF*(gas),not f.           % isTF* for f ← gas,not f.
6   isF*(mbz)  ← isTF*(mbz),not mbz.         % isF* definitions
7   isF*(bmw)  ← isTF*(bmw),not bmw.
8   isF*(gas)  ← isTF*(gas),not gas.
9   isF*(ev)   ← isTF*(ev),not ev.
10  isF*(f)    ← isTF*(f),not f.
```

If we combine $\varphi(P)$ and $\varepsilon(P)$ listed in Example 3 we will get the encoding of P. It is easy to see that the answer sets of $\varepsilon(P) \cup \varphi(P)$ are

$$\{mbz, ev, isF^*(gas), isF^*(f), isTF^*(mbz), isTF^*(ev), isTF^*(gas), isTF^*(f)\}$$
$$\{bmw, isF^*(mbz), isF^*(gas), isF^*(ev), isF^*(f),$$
$$isTF^*(bmw), isTF^*(mbz), isTF^*(ev), isTF^*(gas), isTF^*(f)\}$$

which indeed correspond to the answer sets of Example 1.

Finding the most preferred answer sets can be expressed as an optimization problem over the answer sets of $\varepsilon(P) \cup \varphi(P)$ on predicate isF^*. According to Definition 7, we are interested in answer sets that minimize the set isF^*. More details about how we implement this task in our case can be found in Sect. 6.

4 Disjunctive LPODs

In this section, we extend our encoding to include programs that allow both ordered and standard disjunctions in the head. The case of disjunctive LPODs (DLPODs) was initially considered by [12] and re-examined by [7]. Here, we consider a class of DLPODs, which has also been examined in [9]. This class allows formulas with standard disjunction to occur inside an ordered disjunction to express indifference between alternatives. However, arbitrary combinations of ordered and standard disjunction are not allowed.

Definition 14. *A disjunctive LPOD (DLPOD) is a set of rules of the form:*

$$D_1 \times \cdots \times D_n \leftarrow A_1, \ldots, A_m, not\ A_{m+1}, \ldots, not\ A_k$$

where D_i is a formula of the form $C_i^1 \vee \cdots \vee C_i^{r_i}$ and $C_i^l \in \Sigma$, $i \in \{1, \ldots, n\}$, $l \in \{1, \ldots, r_i\}$ and $A_j \in \Sigma$, $j \in \{1, \ldots, k\}$.

Intuitively, the heads of the program rules denote a hierarchy of preferences imposed by the × operator; in each level of this hierarchy, we may have atoms that have equal preference (this is expressed by standard disjunction). Note that a DLPOD is an LPOD if for every rule and $i \in \{1, \ldots, n\}$, D_i is an atom. Moreover, it is a disjunctive logic program (DLP) when $n = 1$. We will call the rule *disjunctive* if its head is a standard disjunction.

Example 5. Consider the following DLPOD that expresses the preferred car brands depending on the fuel type.

```
1   mbz × (bmw ∨ audi) ← gas.
2   ford ∨ toyota ← not gas.
3   f ← not f,gas.
```

The intuitive meaning is: "*If gas is available, I prefer to buy a Mercedes. If that is not possible, I would be satisfied with either a BMW or an Audi. On the other hand, if gas is not available, I equally prefer buying a Ford or a Toyota. However, gas is not available*".

The semantics of DLPODs can be defined analogously to LPODs. The primary distinction lies in the definition of the ×-reduct, which, in the case of DLPODs, results in a disjunctive positive program. As with LPODs, a (three-valued) interpretation M is an answer set of a DLPOD if it is a minimal model of its ×-reduct, and the most preferred answer sets are those that minimize the use of the F^* value. The interested reader should refer to [9] for more details.

In the remainder of the section we will extend our transformation presented in Sect. 3 in order to accommodate DLPODs. It should be noted that our goal is not to eliminate all disjunctive rules, but only the ordered disjunctive ones; therefore, the resulting program of our transformation is a standard disjunctive logic program rather than a regular program. Again, the transformation comprises 3 steps: normalization, ordered disjunction elimination, and failure ascertainment.

The normalization step of a DLPOD P is more involved and includes an additional step that handles the disjunctions that occur in the head of an ordered disjunctive rule. More specifically, every D_i that is a disjunction, i.e., of the form $C_i^1 \vee \cdots \vee C_i^n$, and occurs in an ordered disjunctive rule R, is replaced with an auxiliary atom D_i^R and additional rules that express the equivalence $C_i^1 \vee \cdots \vee C_i^n \leftrightarrow D_i^R$. This ensures that if a rule is ordered disjunctive, then its heads must be an ordered disjunction of atoms. We will refer to this additional step as $\delta(P)$. To calculate the normal form of P, we first translate P to $\delta(P)$ and then we normalize the result to $\sigma(\delta(P))$. The transformation $\sigma(P)$ (Definition 8) can be redefined to work unchanged on DLPODs instead of LPODs if we assume that the disjunctive rules are non-regular. Slightly abusing notation, we let $\sigma(P)$ denote the transformation applied to a DLPOD P.

Definition 15. *Let P be a DLPOD. Then, $\delta(P)$ is a DLPOD that contains exactly the following rules:*

– *For every ordered disjunctive rule R in P of the form:*

$$D_1 \times \cdots \times D_n \leftarrow A_1, \ldots, A_m, not\ A_{m+1}, \ldots, not\ A_k$$

with $J = \{j \mid D_j$ is of the form $C_j^1 \vee \cdots \vee C_j^{r_j}, r_j > 1\}$, $\delta(P)$ contains:

$$D_1' \times \cdots \times D_n' \leftarrow A_1, \ldots, A_m, not\ A_{m+1}, \ldots, not\ A_k \tag{11}$$

$$C_j^1 \vee \cdots \vee C_j^{r_j} \leftarrow D_j^R \qquad for\ j \in J \tag{12}$$

$$D_j^R \leftarrow C_j^i \qquad for\ j \in J\ and\ i \in \{1, \ldots, r_j\} \tag{13}$$

where D_j^R, for $j \in J$, are new propositional atoms that do not occur in P and $D_j' = D_j^R$ if $j \in J$ and $D_j' = D_j$ otherwise.
– *For every other rule R in P, $\delta(P)$ contains R.*

A DLPOD P is in normal form if $P = \sigma(\delta(P))$. It is easy to see that a DLPOD P of normal form consists of three distinct sets of rules: a set of regular rules, a set of simple ordered disjunctive rules and a set of simple disjunctive rules. We will denote these sets as P^r, P^o and P^d respectively.

Example 6. Consider again the DLPOD P in Example 5. The program $\sigma(\delta(P))$ is the following:

```
1   mbz × cr1 ← br1.          % mbz × (bmw ∨ audi) ← gas.
2   br1 ← gas.
3   bmw ∨ audi ← cr1.
4   cr1 ← bmw.
5   cr1 ← audi.
6   ford ∨ toyota ← not gas.  % ford ∨ toyota ← not gas.
7   f ← not f, gas.           % f ← not f, gas.
```

Note that the disjunction bmw ∨ audi in the first rule of P has been replaced with a new atom cr1. Moreover, the first rule of P is not simple and therefore its body has been replaced with an atom br1. On the other hand, notice that the second rule of P has not been altered because it contains only standard disjunctions.

Proposition 5. *Let P be a DLPOD. Then, the most preferred answer sets of $\delta(P)$ coincide with the most preferred answer sets of P if we restrict them to the atoms in $At(P)$.*

The ordered disjunction elimination is exactly the same with $\varepsilon(P)$ but requires P to be a DLPOD in normal form. Essentially, the disjunctive rules are retained in $\varepsilon(P)$. On the other hand, we need to extend $\varphi(P)$ to include rules to also infer $isTF^*(A)$ from the disjunctive rules of P.

Definition 16. *Let P be a DLPOD in normal form. The program $\varphi^*(P)$ contains exactly all the rules of $\varphi(P^r \cup P^o)$ and for every rule $R \in P^d$ of the form $C_1 \vee \cdots \vee C_n \leftarrow B$ it contains the rule:*

$$isTF^*(C_1) \vee \cdots \vee isTF^*(C_n) \leftarrow isTF^*(B) \tag{14}$$

Definition 17. *Let P be a DLPOD. The encoding of P is the disjunctive logic program $\varepsilon(P') \cup \varphi^*(P')$ where $P' = \sigma(\delta(P))$.*

The following propositions are the corresponding generalizations of Propositions 2 and 4 for DLPODs.

Proposition 6. *Let P be a DLPOD in normal form and M be an answer set of P. Then, collapse(M) is an answer set of $\varepsilon(P)$.*

Proposition 7. *Let P be a DLPOD in normal form and M be an answer set of P. There exists an answer set N of $\varepsilon(P) \cup \varphi^*(P)$ such that collapse$_S^{-1}(N) = M$ where $S = \{A \mid isTF^*(A) \in N\}$.*

5 Related Work

In this section, we review related work on the implementation of LPODs. Although the many-valued semantics has not been implemented, several approaches exist for implementing the original LPOD semantics. Aside from this key difference from our work, none of the existing approaches implement DLPODs.

The system psmodels [3] extends smodels and utilizes two regular logic programs: a generator program to produce candidate answer sets and a tester program to check if a candidate is maximally preferred. The generator program encodes all split programs to a single ASP program by incorporating an explicit choice over the options in the ordered disjunction. These two programs operate in an interleaved manner, similar to the operation of asprin. The generator produces a candidate answer set and the tester tests whether there exists an answer set that is more preferred than the one produced by the generator.

Similar to psmodels, Cabalar [7] uses also a generator and a tester program to find the maximally preferred answer sets but uses a different encoding for generating candidate answer sets. The encoding of [7] is similar to the one presented in this work. A notable difference, however, with the present work is that it includes different auxiliary predicates to keep track of the choices of the ordered disjunction.

Lee and Yang [14] proposed translating to an ASP program using an assumption logic program. Unlike [3] and [7], their method is a one-pass reduction where all candidate answer sets are encoded to a single answer of the encoded ASP program. This enables the preference to be expressed in the ASP encoding and therefore alleviates the need for repetitive calls to the ASP solver. However, solving a single instance becomes more complicated since the ASP encoding uses weak constraints to express consistency of the candidate answer sets.

Lastly, the implementation most similar to ours is that of lpod2asprin [13]. It generates candidate answer sets using the encoding of [7]. Since choices are not tracked explicitly in this encoding the degrees of satisfaction for each rule are computed using aggregates. This implementation uses also asprin to find the optimal answer sets by defining a custom preference on the computed aggregates. A difference with our system is that the preference used in this work is based on the predicate isF^* as we will see in Sect. 6.

6   Implementation and Experiments

The result of our proposed transformation presented in Sects. 3 and 4 is a standard ASP program. Thus, the computation of answer sets for an LPOD (or DLPOD) can be performed using standard ASP solvers, such as clingo [10] or DLV [1,15]. However, determining the most preferred answer sets requires additional effort, that is, to find the answer sets where the extension of isF^* is minimal. To address this, we have implemented a solution by formulating the problem as a preference optimization task. We use the system asprin [5] which is designed to express custom user-defined preference relations and can search for the best answer sets that satisfy those preferences. In our implementation, the preference relation is defined as the subset relation over the predicate isF^* and we seek answer sets where the extension of isF^* is minimal. The following code shows the configuration of asprin for this task.

```
1  #preference(p, subset) { isF*(X) }.
2  #optimize(p).
```

During the optimization process, asprin successively tests whether the current answer set is preferred over previously found answer sets based on the defined subset relation over isF^*. The ideas have been realized in a system[1] which automatically generates the encodings described in Sects. 3 and 4.

We present experiments and comparisons with other LPOD systems. Specifically, we compare our implementation with psmodels [3], which is a variant of smodels [16], and with lpod2asprin [13], which is based on the same underlying solvers, clingo [10] and asprin [5]. It is important to note that our system implements a fundamentally different semantics from the aforementioned systems: it is the first to implement the three-valued semantics of LPODs. As a result, while performance comparisons are informative, the systems are not directly comparable in terms of output, as they implement different semantics. Our main goal is to assess whether the three-valued logical semantics and its implementation offer a practical and efficient alternative to existing approaches.

To the best of our knowledge, there does not exist any standard benchmark for evaluating the performance of LPOD solvers. Therefore, for our experiments, we randomly generate programs of various sizes and characteristics. The sizes of these LPODs differ in terms of the number of atoms and rules. A specified percentage of the rules are ordered disjunctive, and the number of disjuncts in the heads of ordered disjunctive rules (MaxD) are varied. Furthermore, a percentage of the alternatives in the ordered disjunctive rules are intentionally chosen to be unsatisfiable. This influences the number of candidate answer sets and the number of preferred answer sets which indicate the complexity of each program. We report these numbers for each program in Table 1. While the number of candidate answer sets coincide for all the systems, the number of preferred answer sets may differ since the systems implement different semantics. The preferred answer sets depicted in Table 1 are the ones obtained by our system.

---

[1] https://www.github.com/acharal/lpod.

Table 1. Execution time (in seconds) comparison between three LPOD systems (psmodels, lpod2asprin, and ours) across nine programs with varying characteristics.

#	Size Atoms/Rules	Ord. Disj Rules/MaxD	Answer Sets Candidates	Preferred	Execution Time (sec) psmodels	lpod2asprin	Ours
P1	13/5	2/8	1	1	0.001	0.066	0.056
P2	231/5	2/200	1	1	0.005	0.355	4.576
P3	405/250	135/4	4	1	0.002	34.588	33.159
P4	299/200	134/3	210	1	0.039	7.475	7.040
P5	36/18	18/2	512	512	0.044	43.612	3.151
P6	41/82	61/34	9603	1	174.12	0.528	0.510
P7	36/27	18/2	2×10^4	512	2.988	78.256	5.124
P8	39/20	19/2	5×10^5	19	95.86	0.822	0.303
P9	41/21	20/2	10×1^6	20	209.68	1.022	0.334

Table 1 displays the characteristics of each test along with the execution times (in seconds) for each system. The experiments were conducted on a Linux machine equipped with an 8-core CPU clocked at 3.8 GHz and 16 GB of RAM. For the experiments, we used version 3.1.1 of asprin, version 5.4.0 of clingo, and version 2.26a of psmodels. All executions with psmodels and lpod2asprin were performed under the inclusion preference relation.

For programs with fewer candidate answer sets, psmodels clearly outperforms both lpod2asprin and our implementation, taking only a few milliseconds to find the preferred answer set (see, for example, P1, P2, P3, P4). This advantage likely stems from the specific optimizations within smodels tailored for LPODs, in contrast to the other two systems which depend on more general-purpose solvers. However, as the number of candidate answer sets increases, such as in the case of P6, the performance of psmodels declines. This decrease is presumably due to the need for generating several suboptimal models and subsequently many calls to the tester for validating the minimality of each produced model. In contrast, the performance of our implementation and lpod2asprin remains unaffected, likely due to the multi-shot answer set solving technique employed by asprin.

Our implementation is comparable with lpod2asprin in several tests. However, lpod2asprin tends to perform better when there exist ordered disjunctive rules with many options. For example, the maximum ordered disjunction in P2 involves most atoms in the program. The performance of our implementation seems to be impacted by the number of additional rules needed for computing the value F^*. Conversely, our implementation performs better on P5 and P7, programs that have many candidate and preferred answers sets. One factor that we believe affects lpod2asprin's performance is the more complex processing needed to calculate the degrees of satisfaction which is needed because of the semantics.

7 Conclusions and Future Work

The present work proposes a first implementation of an alternative many-valued semantics of propositional LPODs and also of a class of disjunctive LPODs. We have shown that it is possible to encode this semantics to ASP and thus enabled the use of mature ASP solvers and optimizers. Moreover, the experimental results suggest that the alternative semantics are at least as efficient to compute as the original semantics with the existing implementations.

An important area of future investigation is to consider variables in the LPOD rules. Even though the semantics of [9] handles propositional LPODs (and DLPODs) it is conceivable that the semantics of LPODs with variables can be defined using the ground instantiation of the program. It would be interesting to explore whether the ideas of the encoding can be applied directly to the first-order setting, i.e., translating first-order LPODs to first-order ASP programs.

Acknowledgments. This work is funded by a research project which is implemented in the framework of H.F.R.I call "Basic research Financing (Horizontal support of all Sciences)" under the National Recovery and Resilience Plan "Greece 2.0" funded by the European Union - NextGenerationEU (H.F.R.I. Project Number: 16166).

References

1. Alviano, M., Calimeri, F., Dodaro, C., Fuscà, D., Leone, N., Perri, S., Ricca, F., Veltri, P., Zangari, J.: The ASP system DLV2. In: Balduccini, M., Janhunen, T. (eds.) LPNMR 2017. LNCS (LNAI), vol. 10377, pp. 215–221. Springer, Cham (2017). https://doi.org/10.1007/978-3-319-61660-5_19

2. Balduccini, M., Mellarkod, V.S.: Cr-prolog with ordered disjunction. In: Answer Set Programming, Advances in Theory and Implementation, Proceedings of the 2nd International ASP'03 Workshop, Messina, Italy, 26–28 September 2003. CEUR Workshop Proceedings, vol. 78. CEUR-WS.org (2003)

3. Brewka, G., Niemelä, I., Syrjänen, T.: Implementing ordered disjunction using answer set solvers for normal programs. In: Flesca, S., Greco, S., Ianni, G., Leone, N. (eds.) JELIA 2002. LNCS (LNAI), vol. 2424, pp. 444–456. Springer, Heidelberg (2002). https://doi.org/10.1007/3-540-45757-7_37

4. Brewka, G.: Logic programming with ordered disjunction. In: AAAI'02, pp. 100–105. AAAI Press/The MIT Press (2002)

5. Brewka, G., Delgrande, J., Romero, J., Schaub, T.: asprin: Customizing answer set preferences without a headache. In: AAAI, vol. 29, no. 1 (2015)

6. Brewka, G., Niemela, I., Syrjanen, T.: Logic programs with ordered disjunction. Comput. Intell. **20**(2), 335–357 (2004)

7. Cabalar, P.: A logical characterisation of ordered disjunction. AI Commun. **24**(2), 165–175 (2011)

8. Charalambidis, A., Nomikos, C., Rondogiannis, P.: Strong equivalence of logic programs with ordered disjunction: a logical perspective. Theory Pract. Log. Program. **22**(5), 708–722 (2022)

9. Charalambidis, A., Rondogiannis, P., Troumpoukis, A.: A logical characterization of the preferred models of logic programs with ordered disjunction. Theory Pract. Log. Program. **21**(5), 629–645 (2021)

10. Gebser, M., Kaminski, R., Kaufmann, B., Schaub, T.: Multi-shot ASP solving with clingo. Theory Pract. Log. Program. **19**(1), 27–82 (2019)

11. Gelfond, M., Lifschitz, V.: Classical negation in logic programs and disjunctive databases. New Gener. Comput. **9**(3/4), 365–386 (1991)

12. Kärger, P., Lopes, N., Olmedilla, D., Polleres, A.: Towards logic programs with ordered and unordered disjunction. In: ASPOCP2008, ICLP 2008, pp. 46–60 (2008)

13. Lee, J., Yang, Z.: Computing logic programs with ordered disjunction using asprin. In: KR 2018, pp. 57–61. AAAI Press (2018)

14. Lee, J., Yang, Z.: Translating LPOD and CR-Prolog2 into standard answer set programs. Theory Pract. Log. Program. **18**(3–4), 589–606 (2018)

15. Leone, N., et al.: The DLV system for knowledge representation and reasoning. ACM Trans. Comput. Log. **7**(3), 499–562 (2006)

16. Syrjänen, T., Niemelä, I.: The smodels system. In: Eiter, T., Faber, W., Truszczyński, M. (eds.) LPNMR 2001. LNCS (LNAI), vol. 2173, pp. 434–438. Springer, Heidelberg (2001). https://doi.org/10.1007/3-540-45402-0_38

Extending the FSyntax/Hiord Approach with Imperative Notation

Paula Corral[1,2], Jose F. Morales[1,2(✉)], Pedro Lopez-Garcia[2,3], and Manuel V. Hermenegildo[1,2]

[1] Universidad Politécnica de Madrid (UPM), Madrid, Spain
`{josefrancisco.morales,manuel.hermenegildo}@upm.es`
[2] IMDEA Software Institute, Madrid, Spain
`{paula.corral,josef.morales,pedro.lopez,manuel.hermenegildo}@imdea.org`
[3] Spanish Council for Scientific Research (CSIC), Madrid, Spain

Abstract. State variables, loops, and other features of imperative programming languages can bring coding simplification for certain programming idioms that are more cumbersome to express recursively. Because of this, some logic programming systems have incorporated various imperative constructs. `FSyntax` is a syntactic approach to supporting functional notation in `Prolog` systems which is based on the use of the syntax and term expansion facilities of the language. `Hiord` is also a syntactic approach to supporting higher-order in `Prolog`, building on `call/n`, and adding other features such as anonymous predicates. Both are used extensively, for example, in the `Ciao Prolog` system. In this paper, we propose a number of imperative-style constructs based on extending `FSyntax` and `Hiord`. These extensions are designed to combine nicely with the basic functional notation and the higher-order facilities, as well as with other extensions, such as constraints. In contrast to other proposals, our approach provides a set of primitives and a higher-level mechanism that, together, allow users to easily extend the language with features such as array notation, state variables, loops, etc. We illustrate the approach by defining a set of such features and using them to translate idiomatically in imperative style a large collection of small but interesting programs from the Euler Project, for which imperative-style implementations are available in multiple languages. We also show that the approach offers competitive performance.

Keywords: Imperative Constructs in Declarative Languages · Syntactic Extensions · Logic and Functional Programming · Higher Order · Prolog

1 Introduction

Declarative programming allows for the efficient development of complex software systems while also helping in achieving correctness and safety. However,

Partially funded by MICIU projects CEX2024-001471-M *María de Maeztu*, and TED2021-132464B-I00 *PRODIGY*, as well as by the Tezos foundation. We also thank J. Fruhman, H. Kjellerstrand, W.W. Rong, B. Zhou, and N.F. Zhou for making their code for the Euler programs available. Finally, we would like to thank the anonymous reviewers for their very valuable and constructive feedback.

S. Escobar and L. Titolo (Eds.): LOPSTR 2025, LNCS 16117, pp. 57–74, 2026.
https://doi.org/10.1007/978-3-032-04848-6_4

```
:- module(_, _, [functional]).                                    run ▶

primes(Limit) := ~sift(~integers(2, Limit)).

integers(Low, High) := ( Low =< High ? [Low | ~integers(Low+1, High)] | [] ).

sift([])        := [].
sift([I| Is])   := [I | ~sift( ~remove(Is, I))].

remove([])       := [].
remove([I| Is], P) := ( I mod P =\= 0 ? [I | ~remove(Is, P)] | ~remove(Is, P) ).
```

Fig. 1. Classical declarative example for computing primes in Prolog + FSyntax.

for certain problems, it can sometimes be easier or more convenient for the programmer to use syntactic constructs and features borrowed from other programming paradigms. For example, FSyntax [5] is a syntactic approach to supporting functional notation in Prolog systems which is based on the use of the syntax and term expansion facilities of the language. Hiord [3] is also a syntactic approach to supporting higher-order in Prolog, building on call/n. Together they bring in the syntactic convenience of functional and higher-order constructs and both are used extensively in the Ciao Prolog system [10]. In this paper our focus is instead (or, more precisely, in addition to) on convenient syntactic constructs from imperative programming. For example, state variables and loops are important features of imperative programming languages that can bring coding simplification for certain algorithms that are more cumbersome to express using recursion and single assignment. Also, descriptions of algorithms in papers and textbooks are most often presented using imperative pseudocode, containing loops and other imperative constructs. Such algorithms can be implemented in logic languages using recursion, frequently rather elegantly, but this encoding can also in some cases be awkward and/or blur the correspondence with the original algorithm description.

Consider, for example, the *Sieve of Eratosthenes* algorithm for computing primes (we will refer to it simply as Eratosthenes' algorithm). It is a classic example in both functional and logic programming, where it is typically presented in an elegant recursive form. Figure 1 shows a version of this classic encoding, using the FSyntax package in Ciao Prolog.[1] Note that FSyntax allows tilde-annotated predicates to be written in function application style, e.g., Z = ~p(~sort(X)) is expanded to sort(X,Y), p(Y,Z).

This program is relatively simple, and arguably illustrates the elegance of declarative programming. Unfortunately, this classic encoding does *not* implement Eratosthenes' algorithm, but rather a naive algorithm known as *trial division* (see O'Neill [14]). If we want to implement the actual algorithm by Eratosthenes, we can perhaps turn to the Wikipedia, which provides a description of the algorithm in imperative pseudocode, shown in Fig. 2. This algorithm can be

---

[1] This is the classical eager version. For completeness, a lazy version (from [5]) is shown in Fig. 7, which is essentially the same as in lazy functional languages.

```
input: integer N > 1
output: list of prime numbers from 2 to N

A = array with index from 2 to N with all the values set to True

for i = 2,3, ..., sqrt(N) do
    if A[i] == True
        for j = i*i, i*i + i, i*i + 2i, ... below or equal to N do
            A[j] = False

return list with all k where A[k] is True
```

Fig. 2. Eratosthenes' algorithm in pseudocode (based on Wikipedia).

```
:- module(_, _).                                                      run ▶
:- use_module(library(logarrays)).

primes(N,Res) :-
    new_array(A), % Initialize an extendable array
    To is floor(sqrt(N)), % Just need to go to sq root of n
    completegieve(2,To,N,A,CompleteSieve), % Complete the sieve
    % Create a list with the primes
    take_primes(2,N,CompleteSieve,Res).

complete_sieve(Curr,To,_N,Sieve,RSieve):-
    Curr > To, !, RSieve = Sieve.
complete_sieve(Curr,To,N,Sieve,RSieve) :- % If it is marked (0) it is not prime
    aref(Curr,Sieve,_El), !,
    NewCurr is Curr + 1,
    complete_sieve(NewCurr,To,N,Sieve,RSieve).
complete_sieve(Curr,To,N,Sieve,RSieve) :- % Gets here if it is not marked (0)
    From is Curr * Curr,
    set_multiples(From,Curr,N,Sieve,Sieve1), % Mark with 0 multiples of a prime
    NewCurr is Curr + 1,
    complete_sieve(NewCurr,To,N,Sieve1,RSieve).

set_multiples(Curr,_Step,To,Sieve,RSieve) :-
    Curr > To, !, RSieve = Sieve.
set_multiples(Curr,Step,To,Sieve,RSieve) :-
    aset(Curr,Sieve,0,Sieve1),
    NewCurr is Curr + Step,
    set_multiples(NewCurr,Step,To,Sieve1,RSieve).

take_primes(Curr,N,_Sieve,Res) :-
    Curr > N, !, Res = [].
take_primes(Curr,N,Sieve,Res) :- % If it is marked (0) it is not prime
    aref(Curr,Sieve,_El), !,
    NewCurr is Curr + 1,
    take_primes(NewCurr,N,Sieve,Res).
take_primes(Curr,N,Sieve,Res) :- % Not marked (0): add it to Res
    Res = [Curr| Rest],
    NewCurr is Curr + 1,
    take_primes(NewCurr,N,Sieve,Rest).
```

Fig. 3. Eratosthenes, direct Prolog coding, using expandable, logarithmic arrays.

coded in standard Prolog (see, e.g., Fig. 3), but the result is not very compact and can feel a bit awkward. A version coded using again **FSyntax** is shown in Fig. 4. In these two cases we have used the **logarrays** library of expandable, logarithmic arrays. Other array implementations provide different performance/flexibility trade-offs. For example, a version using (arbitrary arity) terms and **arg/3**

```
:- module(_, _, [functional]).                                    run ▶
:- use_module(library(logarrays)).

primes(N) := Res :-
    complete_sieve(2,~floor(sqrt(N)),N,~new_array,CompleteSieve),
    take_primes(2,N,CompleteSieve,Res).

complete_sieve(Curr,To,N,Sieve) :=
    ( Curr > To                    ? Sieve
    | aref(Curr,Sieve,_El) ? ~complete_sieve(Curr+1,To,N,Sieve)
    | ~complete_sieve(Curr+1,To,N,~set_multiples(Curr*Curr,Curr,N,Sieve)) ).

set_multiples(Curr,Step,To,Sieve) :=
    ( Curr > To ?  Sieve
    | aset(Curr,Sieve,0,Sieve1) ? ~set_multiples(Curr+Step,Step,To,Sieve1) ).

take_primes(Curr,N,Sieve) :=
    ( Curr > N                     ? []
    | aref(Curr,Sieve,_El) ? ~take_primes(Curr+1,N,Sieve)
    | [Curr| ~take_primes(Curr+1,N,Sieve)] ).
```

Fig. 4. Eratosthenes' algorithm in Prolog + FSyntax.

```
:- module(_, _, [functional]).                                    run ▶

primes(N) := Res :-
    A = ~functor(~,a,N),
    complete_sieve(2,~floor(sqrt(N)),N,A),
    take_primes(2,N,A,Res).

complete_sieve(Curr,To,N,Sieve) :-
    Curr > To -> true
    ; arg(Curr,Sieve,El), nonvar(El) -> complete_sieve(Curr+1,To,N,Sieve)
    ; set_multiples(Curr*Curr,Curr,N,Sieve), complete_sieve(Curr+1,To,N,Sieve).

set_multiples(Curr,Step,To,Sieve) :-
    ( Curr > To -> true
    ; arg(Curr,Sieve,0), set_multiples(Curr+Step,Step,To,Sieve) ).

take_primes(Curr,N,Sieve) :=
    ( Curr > N                     ? []
    | arg(Curr,Sieve,El), nonvar(El) ? ~take_primes(Curr+1,N,Sieve)
    |                                  [Curr | ~take_primes(Curr+1,N,Sieve)] ).
```

Fig. 5. Eratosthenes' algorithm in Prolog, using FSyntax, and terms for arrays.

for the arrays is shown in Fig. 5. The performance of this version, in the default bytecode grade, is comparable to that of the equivalent Python version, shown in Fig. 6.

The versions of Figs. 4 and 5 are arguably more compact and elegant than that of Fig. 3, but they still suffer from some of the previously mentioned issues. In particular, the correspondence with the original pseudocode is not obvious, at least to the untrained eye.[2] This brings us back to the idea that there are cases where incorporating syntactic features from imperative programming can bring programmer convenience and in general potentially also contribute to the wider

---

[2] Note that coding the actual Eratosthenes algorithm in a lazy functional language is not trivial, as shown by O'Neill [14], and suffers from the same issues.

```python
import math

def primes(n):
    # Initialize the array with n+1 values to access until index n
    a = [True] * (n+1)

    # The loop goes until the square root of n
    to = math.floor(math.sqrt(n))

    # We cross out the non primes
    for i in range(2,to+1):
        if a[i]: # If a[i] is prime we cross out its multiples
            for j in range(i*i,n+1,i):
                a[j] = False

    # We take the primes from the sieve and put them into a list
    result = []
    for k in range(2,n+1):
        if a[k]:
            result.append(k)

    return result
```

Fig. 6. Eratosthenes' algorithm, in Python.

```prolog
:- module(_, _, [fsyntax, lazy]).                                    run ▶

:- use_module(library(lazy/lazy_lib), [take/3, nums_from/2]).

:- lazy fun_eval cut/1.
cut([])       := [].
cut([H | T]) := [H | ~cut(~cut_(T, H))].

:- lazy fun_eval cut_/2.
cut_([], _ )       := [].
cut_([H2 | T], H1) := R :-
    R = ( H2 mod H1 > 0 ? [H2 | ~cut_(T, H1)] | ~cut_(T, H1) ).

:- lazy fun_eval primes/0.
primes := ~cut(~nums_from(2)).

test_primes(N) := ~take(N, ~ primes)
```

Fig. 7. Classical declarative example for computing primes (trial division): *lazy* version, using `FSyntax`. Note that N here is the *number* of primes computed.

adoption of declarative languages. Also, depending on their semantics, the use of loops and other imperative constructs can sometimes help static analyzers by providing implicit information such as determinacy, non-failure, modes, types, and bounds on the number of times the loops are executed, which can be useful, e.g., for cost and complexity analysis.

Motivated by this, and building on the `FSyntax` and `Hiord` functional notation and higher-order facilities, we develop a set of primitives and a higher-level mechanism that together allow users to easily and selectively extend the language with imperative features. This generalization of `FSyntax`, which we call `xsyntax`, also allows more fine-grained control of the different extension components, so that they can be activated and deactivated selectively at a finer granularity level:

e.g., being able to use state variables without enabling functional notation. We also propose within `xsyntax` a `notation` facility, a convenience built over the expansion mechanisms of [2] that allows easily defining replacements for given term patterns.

Related Work: Regarding the declarative representation of state, Definite Clause Grammars (DCGs), can be used to represent, thanks to their implicit arguments, both the previous and next state of a variable. DCGs can be extended to track multiple variables by encapsulating them in a single structure, but this can be difficult to manage. To address this, extended DCGs were introduced by Peter Van Roy [15], which allow simultaneous updates to multiple variables. However, EDGCs are still a comparatively less intuitive method for state management. A more direct approach is offered by languages like `Picat` [21,22], which uses the `:=` operator for updating state variables. Mercury uses the `!` notation to denote state variables and automatically expands variables into two to represent the state before and after a state change [9]. In addition to state variables, logic programming systems often support some form of mutable variables and/or the `setarg/3` primitive, which allows destructive updates to term arguments. This is typically used for localized updates to large data structures—such as array assignments– rather than for tracking the state of individual variables. However, this kind of destructive assignment is at odds with the declarative nature of logic programming, as it complicates the semantics significantly. Also monads, originally from functional programming, offer a structured way to manage state changes while preserving declarative semantics, somewhat related to DCGs. For example the functional-logic language Curry [8] uses monads to handle effects like I/O. The addition of monadic abstractions to Prolog via higher-order extensions and syntactic transformations has received some attention [12]. However, monads are arguably a less natural solution in logic programming.

A number of multiparadigm programming languages exist that integrate features from logic-, functional-, constraint-, or imperative programming. Alma-0 [1] was one of the first approaches, where imperativeness (as an extension of Modula-2) played a very prominent role, whereas newer proposals start as us from a declarative programming foundation. Some of these proposals are entirely new languages, rather than extensions of Prolog, in contrast to our approach. For example, `Picat`, in addition to the previously mentioned state variables, also incorporates two types of loops and array access notation [22]. MiniZinc [13,18] is a popular modeling language for combinatorial problems. It provides a loop construct which can be used to place constraints that depend on the loop bounds in a natural and regular way.

Returning to approaches based on extending Prolog with new syntactic constructs, as in our proposal, apart from the already mentioned `Hiord` and `FSyntax` extensions in `Ciao Prolog`, for instance `ECLiPSe` introduces *logical loops* as a language extension [17], and array notation, although it does not include state variable support. SICStus [4] has traditionally supported `setarg/3` and later incorporated *mutables*. XSB [19] also supports `setarg/3` and has an array facility. SWI [20] has global variables (also supported by Yap [16]) and some other extensions. François Fages has developed a mathematical modeling library for Prolog [6], inspired by MiniZinc. This library brings constraint modeling capabilities to Prolog with a mathematical focus. It includes the forall loop notation, which, like MiniZinc, is limited to verifying that a constraint holds across all iterations and does not support state variables. To the best of our knowledge, none of the current Prolog-based systems integrate all of the features that we address herein or use the compositional approach proposed.

2   Core Primitives and Their Translations

This section introduces and describes the primitives and translations used in our approach, without committing yet to a specific syntax, as the building blocks that later will be used to define specific notations in user programs. In order to combine imperative constructs with other expansions, our approach introduces a generalization of FSyntax, called xsyntax that coordinates the expansion of all the primitives above, and performs a controlled fine-grained expansion of notations. A design objective is to be able to use one extension, like state variables, without necessarily having to use another, like functional notation.

The following sections describe all the primitives and their translations. We begin with closures, anonymous predicates that *capture* variables from their environment; follow with state variables, abstractions of logical mutable updates using threaded variables; and finally address loop constructs, code that iterates while a condition is met.

2.1   Higher-Order and Closures

The Hiord extension (hiord package) enables higher-order untyped logic programming, allowing the declaration of anonymous predicates and closures in term positions. A closure is simply a predicate that captures variables from its surrounding environment. As an instrumental part of this work, we have reworked and enhanced the Hiord closures in two ways, referring to this extended version as hiordx. In particular, we have extended the declaration of captured variables, so that, in addition to specifying which variables are shared (already possible in Hiord), we can also declare non-shared variables, as follows:

$$P = \{[ShVars] \rightarrow \text{''}(A_1, \ldots, A_n) :- Body\} \tag{1}$$

$$P = \{-[NonShVars] \rightarrow \text{''}(A_1, \ldots, A_n) :- Body\} \tag{2}$$

$$P = \{\text{''}(A_1, \ldots, A_n) :- Body\} \tag{3}$$

The closure syntax (1) specifies *positive* sharing, where none of the parent environment variables are captured, except those listed as shared variables (*ShVars*). In contrast, syntax (2) specifies *negative* sharing, where all parent environment variables are captured, except those listed as non-shared variables (*NonShVars*). Finally, syntax (3) specifies *default* sharing, that is equivalent to the negative sharing of all variables from the terms in head arguments, which is a useful convention in practice. Other enhancements of **hiordx** with respect to **Hiord** concern performance. In particular, the translation generates auxiliary predicates as needed, rather than higher-order callable terms, so that no run-time overhead is incurred from declaring anonymous predicates.

Translation of Closures: Syntactic closures, which can appear in arbitrary term positions (in curly braces), are first translated to an internal literal representation by **xsyntax**.[3] This internal representation is then handled by another translation step, which we will refer as **xcontrol**, to compute the actual shared variables required in the closure, resulting only in a positive sharing list. Note that although positive sharing can be easily implemented as a goal-local translation step, negative or default sharing requires keeping track of variable lifetimes. This can be complex in the presence of other closures or control structures. Our implementation reuses the same lifetime tracking algorithm that computes shared variables in if-then-elses, disjunctions, and negated goals in the compiler, which annotates for each variable if it appears in more than one scope.

We have also included two new optimizations beyond those in the original **Hiord** implementation:

- Once the translation process has left only positive sharing closures given by the literal ($P = \{[ShVars] \rightarrow$ ''$(A_1, \ldots, A_n)$:- $Body\}$), these are expanded as $P = $ **auxpred**($ShVars$), with **auxpred** a fresh different name, and a new clause '**auxpred**($ShVars, A_1, \ldots, A_n$) :- $Body$.',[4] so that P can be called as usual with **call/n**.
- In some cases, the (auxiliary) predicate referenced by a closure may be known statically when using **call/n**. In general, this requires global program analysis, but in certain cases (such as those for loops we will see) the propagation is quite simple. In those cases, the compiler can completely translate the code into static calls, without needing to create a closure term or perform a dynamic call.

The use of negative and default sharing closures to manage variable scopes is essential to simplify the introduction of the loop control structures. Moreover, the optimization of closure compilation, in addition to having value on its own, also makes the implementation of efficient loop constructs easier.

2.2   State Variables

State variables provide a means to model state transitions in a purely declarative fashion, representing and managing mutable state by explicitly threading state values through predicates as additional input and output arguments. As mentioned in the introduction, this concept is closely related to Definite Clause

---

[3] This also ensures that other expansions, such as functional notation, are performed at the correct step.

[4] For clarity of presentation, the actual translation shuffles arguments at call time (using a dedicated internal functor for closures) to preserve first-argument indexing, which is assumed for predictable performance in Ciao.

Grammars (DCGs) in Prolog and has been generalized as Extended DCGs to allow tracking multiple states. However, in this work we adopt a more convenient syntax based on the state variables of Mercury [9].

We now briefly introduce the syntax and semantics of such state variables. Given a state variable (S) passed as an argument (denoted as !S, e.g., p(!S)), each predicate receives the *current version* of the variable as input (a logical variable) and returns an *updated version* as output (e.g., p(S_0, S_n), where n is the last version number of the variable in the clause body). Similarly, each body literal can refer to the current version of the state variable (e.g., p(S) as p(S_k), where k is the current version of the variable), or call a predicate that performs an update (e.g., p(!S) as p(S_k, S_{k+1})). The sequence of variable versions represents the sequence of updates for that variable. Usually, an assignment operator is provided as a special literal that just performs an update (e.g., S := V as S_{k+1} = V).

Similar to the treatment of closures, the user-level syntax for state variables is delegated to the **xsyntax** package, which is customized to transform high-level constructs into a set of intermediate primitives. These primitives are processed later by the **xcontrol** translation phase, responsible for managing versions of state variable across control structures.

Syntactic Lowering: As mentioned before, this first phase is performed by **xsyntax**, which specializes in expanding terms to give them a meaning. It defines the syntax for representing and modifying state and performs the following transformations:

- The syntax !X as an argument of a structure is expanded as a pair of arguments $X_\circ$, $X_\bullet$ (read as "before X" and "after X") that represents the initial version and updated versions of the state variable, respectively.
- The goal X :=V , denoting an imperative assignment of state variable X to value V (which itself can be a logical variable), is translated into the form $X_\bullet$ = V. That is, the unification of the updated version of X with V.

Translation of State Variables: The translation of state variables is performed as part of the **xcontrol** phase. We introduce some notation to describe this process. Let Γ be a state variable environment mapping each state variable to a (logical) variable representing its current state; $\Gamma(S)$ obtains the value (logical variable) for S in the environment; $\Gamma[S \mapsto V]$ obtains a new environment where the value for S is updated to V. The environment is initialized with all the state variables in the clause (including variables in the head and other state variables appearing in the body). We define a translation for terms and goals $\mathsf{T}[\![t]\!](\Gamma) = (t', \Gamma')$, where t is a term or goal, t' is its translated form, Γ is the initial environment, and Γ' is the resulting environment. This translation is then applied to the clause body. Note that at this point other notations (such as functional notation) have already been expanded by **xsyntax**.

The translation of terms or literals (except conjunctions and disjunctions and other control structures) is as follows:

$$\mathsf{T}[\![t]\!](\Gamma) = (t', \Gamma') \quad \text{where:}$$
$$\Gamma' = \Gamma[X \mapsto \textit{new-fresh-var} \mid X_\bullet \text{ occurs in } t]$$
$$t' = t \text{ with all } X_\circ \text{ replaced by } \Gamma(X), \text{ and all } X_\bullet \text{ replaced by } \Gamma'(X)$$

The translation of control structures is as follows. Conjunctions are translated by sequentially threading the environments:

$$\mathsf{T}[\![G_1, \; G_2]\!](\Gamma) = ((G_1', \; G_2'), \; \Gamma_2)$$
$$\text{where } (G_1', \Gamma_1) = \mathsf{T}[\![G_1]\!](\Gamma),$$
$$(G_2', \Gamma_2) = \mathsf{T}[\![G_2]\!](\Gamma_1)$$

Treatment of disjunctions is more involved. The translation processes each branch individually, applying updates based on the environment at the disjunction point. After translating both branches, their resulting environments are unified. Specifically, if a state variable is updated in both branches, it unifies the two resulting states. If the state variable is updated in only one branch, it adds a new clause to the other branch that unifies the current state of the first branch with the environment at the disjunction point:

$$\mathsf{T}[\![G_1 \; ; \; G_2]\!](\Gamma_0) = ((G_1', U \; ; \; G_2', U), \; \Gamma')$$
$$\text{where } (G_1', \Gamma_1) = \mathsf{T}[\![G_1]\!](\Gamma_0),$$
$$(G_2', \Gamma_2) = \mathsf{T}[\![G_2]\!](\Gamma_0),$$
$$(U, \Gamma') = \mathsf{Join}(\Gamma_1, \Gamma_2, \Gamma_0)$$

The join operator $\mathsf{Join}(\Gamma_1, \Gamma_2, \Gamma_0) = (U, \Gamma')$ is defined as follows. For each variable X, $\Gamma_i(X) = x_i$, and:

- If $x_1 = x_2$: set $\Gamma'(X) = x_1$ and emit no unification.
- If $x_1 \neq x_2$: introduce fresh x', set $\Gamma'(X) = x'$, and emit unifications $x' = x_1$, $x' = x_2$.
- U is the conjunction of all such unifications.

2.3 Loops

In declarative languages, loops are not primitive constructs; instead, they must be encoded using recursion. The purpose of loop syntax is to provide a more natural and expressive way of modeling iteration, often involving mutable state variables that evolve across iterations. In this section we define a general-purpose logical loop construct as a building block (purely internal, and not exposed to the user), without committing to any fixed concrete syntax. As for previous primitives, the concrete user-level syntax will be handled by an **xsyntax** expansion, but for the case of loops, this will be described in more detail in Sect. 3.

Primitive Loop Construct: A loop '`$loop`'(`Vars, Init, Cond, Goal`) consists of the following components:

– A set of *iteration variables*, scoped to each iteration.
– An *initialization goal*, evaluated once before the loop starts.
– A *condition*, tested at the beginning of each iteration.
– A *body goal*, executed if the condition holds, also must prepare state for the next iteration.

Operationally, the loop executes the initialization first, and then repeatedly: it checks the condition, and if true, executes the body, prepares the state for the next iteration, and loops again. When the condition fails, the loop terminates. This corresponds to the recursive schema:

$$«begin» \text{ :- } Init, «body».$$
$$«body» \text{ :- } (Cond \text{ -> } Goal, «body» \text{ ; } true).$$

Note that the use of "->" in the schema implicitly introduces a *cut*. We additionally support pairs of conditions with the syntax *posneg(PosCond, NegCond)*, that is then expanded into the following pure recursive schema.

$$«begin» \text{ :- } Init, «body».$$
$$«body» \text{ :- } (NegCond \text{ ; } PosCond, Goal, «body»).$$

Note that such a recursive schema without cut is more convenient for some use cases, such as when using breadth-first and other search strategies, program analyses or transformations, running "backwards" (supporting several modes), etc.

Translation of Loops: Translation of loops requires identifying all the state variables involved during iterations. This is performed in the **xcontrol** step as part of the variable lifetime analysis. Loop constructs are annotated as:

$$\textbf{\$shloop(Vars, StLoopVars, Init, Cond, Goal)}$$

where `StLoopVars` is the set of state variables $(S_1, ..., S_n)$ potentially updated within the loop.

The final loop form is finally translated to nested closures, where each closure introduces its own scope and versioned state variables. These closures are then statically compiled into plain predicates (similary for the pure recursive schema):

```
Begin = {
  ''(!S1, ..., !Sn) :-
    Init,
    Body = {
      -[Vars] -> ''(!S1, ..., !Sn) :-
        ( Cond -> Goal, Body(!S1, ..., !Sn) ; true )
    },
    Body(!S1, ..., !Sn)
},
Begin(!S1, ..., !Sn).
```

Each closure introduces new versions of the state variables through the transformation rules described in Sect. 2.2. Since each iteration forms a distinct scope, proper versioning and unification of state is required to maintain correctness. The use of negative-sharing in *Body* ensures that the marked iteration variables are independent through recursive invocations.

Once transformed into this canonical form, the `hiordx` translation (see Sect. 2.1) eliminates the closures via specialization, resulting in efficient (as handwritten recursions), statically compiled code that faithfully implements the loop semantics in a declarative setting.

3   Defining a Concrete Imperative Syntax

As mentioned before, in our proposal, we make an explicit separation between the higher-level syntactic constructs and the core primitives (such as closures, state variables, and loops) necessary to define such constructs in a coherent and composable way that fits in a logic programming setting. Following this idea, this section presents an example concrete proposal for imperative syntax, built on top of the previous primitives, and the `xsyntax` expansions.

More Flexible Notation: FSyntax allows customization of expansions using the `fun_eval` declaration. For example, `:- fun_eval arith(true)` enables the evaluation of arithmetic functors (in a module or module context) as Prolog arithmetic functions (`p(A+B)` expands to `X is A+B, p(X)`), or `:- fun_eval append/3` enables functional expansion of, e.g., `p(append([1],[2]))` to `append([1],[2],X), p(X)` without having to explicitly annotate the expansion (i.e., without the ~ in `p(~append([1],[2]))`). In `xsyntax` we offer a richer customization. First, it is possible to select different arithmetic evaluations. For example, `:- fun_eval arith(clpfd)` expands `p(A+B)` as `X #= A+B, p(X)`, which is convenient for constraint modeling, running imperative code backwards, etc. Another notable addition is the possibility of defining notation patterns with `:- notation(Pattern, T)`, where all occurrences that match `Pattern` are replaced by `T` (the "notation" name is intended to evoke the process of introducing notation in mathematical text). For example, `:- notation(X ∈ Ls, member(X,Ls))` expands `X ∈ [1,2,3]` to `member(X, [1,2,3])`. Note that these declarations are just user-definable notational aids which do not change the underlying semantics of Prolog. They are a user-friendly convenience built over the more traditional (and also more powerful) term expansion mechanisms –in particular, those of [2]. This notation facility will be useful in what follows to easily map the higher-level imperative constructs to the lower level primitives.

Array Notation: Arrays are a fundamental data structure in programming, especially in imperative languages. They also offer a natural way to represent mathematical objects such as vectors, matrices, or functions over finite domains, which are useful in modeling constraints or mathematical problems. We use the previously introduced notation declarations to define custom syntax for accessing array elements and to overload the assignment operator for element updates, analogous to function update in mathematical logic:[5]

```
:- notation(Arr[I], ~get_elem(Arr,I)).
:- notation(Arr[I]:=Val, (Arr := ~replace_elem(Arr,I,Val))).
```

The notation above maps access and updates to `get_elem/3` and `replace_elem/4` predicates. If defined as *multifile* (e.g., as described in [7]), these predicates can act as a bridge interface between several array-like data structures. To test this we implement a package for array-like syntax and interface (including other useful operations like `array_length/2`). We provide this unified interface with non-destructive arrays with logarithmic access (`library(array_log)`), functor-based arrays with O(n) update operations, destructive mutable arrays using `setarg/3`, as well as linked lists with nth-element accessor and update operations.

While Loops: We can define a *while* loop simply by setting an empty initialization and iterating *Goal* while the condition *Cond* holds:

```
:- notation(while (Cond) { Goal },
            '$loop'([], true, Cond, Goal)).
```

For Loops with Iterators: Similarly to *while* loops, it is possible to define *for* loops that iterate over elements extracted from an *iterable* object. As with arrays, we define a simple interface to iterable objects (terms) as *multifile* predicates, as follows:

- `iter_cond(Curr,X)`: obtains the iterator value `X` for the current state `Curr`; fails if there are no more values.
- `iter_next(Curr, Curr2)`: transitions from `Curr` to next state `Curr2`.

For example, we can define iterators over lists or integer ranges as follows:

```
iter_cond([X|_], X).
iter_next([_|Xs], Xs).

iter_cond(range_iter(B, _Step, X), X) :- X=<B.
iter_next(range_iter(B,Step,Curr), range_iter(B,Step,Curr2)) :-
    Curr2 is Curr+Step.
```

We can then use a notation declaration to define a *for* loop over an iterable as follows:

```
:- notation(for (I in Iter) { Goal },
            '$loop'([I],
                    Curr := Iter,
                    iter_cond(Curr, I),
                    (Goal, Curr := ~iter_next(Curr)))).
```

---

[5] Note that the same approach can be used to offer notation for access and update of other indexed data structures like dictionaries.

```
:- module(_, _, [functional,loops,arrays]).                              run ▶

:- use_module(library(arrays/arrays_log)).

primes(N) := Res :-
    % Initialize the array with n+1 values to access until index n
    A = ~new_array_log,
    for (I in 2 .. N){A [I] := true },
    % We cross out the non primes
    for (I in 2 .. ~floor(sqrt(N))) { % Loop goes until square root of N
        if (A[I] == true) { % If a[i] is prime we cross out its multiples
            for (J in I*I .. I .. N) { A[J] := false }
        }
    },
    % We take the primes from the sieve and put them into a list
    Res = ResTail,
    for (K in 2 .. N) {
        if (A[K] == true) { accum(!ResTail,K) }
    },
    ResTail = [].

accum(!R, X) :- R = [X| Tail], R := Tail.
```

Fig. 8. Eratosthenes algorithm, in Prolog + the developed syntax.

This represents generic code that would work for any data that implements the iterator interface. In particular, it is also convenient to define shorter syntax for some iterators (or alternatively, just map **Begin..End** as a notation for range_iter(Begin,1,End)):

```
:- notation(for (I in Begin..End) { Goal },
            for (I in range_iter(End, 1, Begin)) { Goal }).
```

Additionally, for efficiency, unfolded iterators can be provided using auxiliary notations that factorize definitions (note that the same effect can also be achieved through partial evaluation). As an example, this is the result for this range iteration:

```
:- notation(for (I in Begin..End) { Goal },
            '$loop'([I],
                    Curr := Begin,
                    Curr =< End,
                    (Goal, Curr := Curr + 1))).
```

Back to Eratosthenes: Figure 8 presents an encoding of the Sieve of Eratosthenes algorithm using a number of the extensions developed. It is relatively easy now to see the correspondance with the pseudocode in Fig. 2, and with the Python version (Fig. 6). Also, as mentioned before, the generated code is equivalent to the plain Prolog recursive versions, and the default bytecode grade compilation of Fig. 8 is comparable in performance to the Python code.

4   Some Experimental Results

The proposed extensions are provided as separate Ciao packages **hiordx**, **loops**, **statevars**, and **arrays**, which can be selectively enabled as required. These extensions are implemented as previously described and depend on the `xsyntax` extension and the `xcontrol` internal phases, which together provide coherent support for all the proposed features.

In order to test the convenience, implementation, and performance of these extensions, we have chosen to use a large set of problems from the Euler Project [11]. The choice of these benchmarks is motivated in part by the variety of problems and algorithms involved, which allows illustrating the expressiveness and flexibility of the proposed extensions, and also because encodings of many of these problems are available in several imperative languages, and in particular a good number of them are accessible from the `Picat` web site. As mentioned before, `Picat` is also a logic-based language, different from Prolog, that has loops, state variables, and array index notation in addition to constraints and tabling, and thus we consider it a very good point of reference.

We have encoded the examples in Ciao using our extensions. The resulting code[6] constitutes perhaps the best illustration of the approach. In particular, these programs test the use of the array-like structures, state variables, and loops presented, as well as other Ciao extensions like *clpfd*, *tabling*, *assoc*, or *pmrules*. The coding used typically involves an imperative syntactic style, but often makes use also of Prolog's search, unification, constraint solving, etc., thus illustrating how our approach allows synergistically mixing both styles.

Regarding performance, we have carried out a comparison with `Picat`, which is known to be quite performant, so we also consider it a very good point of reference from this point of view. In this sense our objective is not to perform an in-depth performance comparison, since both the implementation and the problem encodings can still be improved, but rather to have an estimation of whether the approach is competitive.

Table 1 shows the execution times of each program, in seconds, in `Picat` and `Ciao`, grouped in different subtables by the extensions or utilities they use. The symbol '-' means that no output/answer is produced for some reason. The experiments were run on a MacBook Pro, 3,1 GHz Dual-Core Intel Core i5; 16 GB 2133 MHz LPDDR3; macOS: Ventura 13.7.4 (22H420).[7] The results computed in both languages are identical for all cases.

Table 1a presents examples that use only loops, including state variables, without any other extensions. These examples demonstrate that Ciao's implementation of state variables and loops is competitive with `Picat`'s. We observe some performance differences, which may be due to variations in the virtual machine implementations. Table 1b presents examples that use tabling, showing similar performance overall. However, in `Picat`, they execute slightly faster and comparing this with Table 1a, we can infer that the difference is likely to be because of variations in the tabling implementation. Table 1c presents examples that use loops and index notation over lists from the new array extension. The performance is generally similar in both languages, with some exceptions such as

---

[6] See: https://gitlab.software.imdea.org/ciao-lang/ciaoimp-benchmarks.

[7] In order to save space we have left out of the table the problems for which the execution times were too low to be significant.

Table 1. Experimental results on Euler Project problems in Picat and Ciao.

File	Picat	Ciao	Picat/Ciao
p004	0.750	0.102	7.288
p007	0.299	0.172	1.731
p012	11.250	6.975	1.612
p016	0.001	0.000	6.134
p020	0.001	0.000	13.157
p022	0.021	0.021	0.957
p025	3.392	2.117	1.601
p029	2.353	2.288	1.028
p030	1.114	2.220	0.501
p034	0.403	0.289	1.392
p036	1.250	0.841	1.485
p045	0.043	0.030	1.388
p046	0.041	0.027	1.517
p048	0.826	0.017	47.906
p056	0.781	0.210	3.704

(a) Examples that just use loops.

File	Picat	Ciao	Picat/Ciao
p021	0.173	0.137	1.257
p027	1.823	4.482	0.406
p037	3.029	4.278	0.707
p041	0.012	0.014	0.834
p053	0.041	0.036	1.112
p055	0.073	0.070	1.029

(b) Examples that use loops and tabling.

File	Picat	Ciao	Picat/Ciao
p017	0.011	0.016	0.665
p019	0.051	0.050	1.016
p024	1.150	8.596	0.133
p026	0.074	1.946	0.038
p040	0.197	0.161	1.218
p042	0.025	0.030	0.829
p060	142.493	91.048	1.565
p076	0.003	0.057	0.052
p077	0.013	0.204	0.063

(c) Examples that use loops and index notation in lists.

File	Picat	Ciao	Picat/Ciao
p010_log	-	9.778	
p010_mut	0.909	0.933	0.973
p047_log	-	10.553	
p047_mut	0.804	1.184	0.678
p050_log	0.282	1.909	0.147

(d) Examples that use loops and index notation in arrays.

File	Picat	Ciao	Picat/Ciao
Loops and assoc			
p032	2.398	2.005	1.195
p044	1.465	2.458	0.595
p062	0.032	0.168	0.190
Loops and pmrule			
p052	0.418	0.538	0.775
p049	0.138	0.113	1.218

(e) Examples that use loops and other extensions.

p024, p026, p076, and p077. These are likely to be due to the fact that replacing an element in a list is destructive in `Picat` but not in Ciao. Table 1d presents examples that use loops and index notation over arrays from the new array extension. Specifically, they are implemented in Ciao using both logarithmic and mutable arrays, indicated by file name suffix. Performance in mutable arrays is similar to `Picat`'s, which makes sense since `Picat`'s array implementation is also mutable. Table 1e presents other examples that use loops. The examples using single-side unification rules (denoted as *pmrule*) show performance comparable with `Picat`. The other examples use *maps*, for which we have used simply the traditional `library(assoc)` module, and the performance difference is likely due to the faster destructive map updates in `Picat`.

In general, these results suggest that our implementation approach achieves the objective of supporting a customizable and rich set of imperative constructs within Prolog with competitive performance.

5   Conclusion

We have proposed a number of imperative-style constructs that build on and extend the `FSyntax` and `Hiord` syntactic extensions to Prolog. The proposed extensions have been designed so that they combine well with the basic functional notation and the higher-order facilities as well as with other extensions, such as constraints, tabling, etc. In addition, our approach is based on a set of primitives and a simplified, higher-level expansion mechanism that together have allowed us to easily add features such as array notation, state variables, loops, etc. We have also made on the way instrumental extensions to the previous work on `Hiord` and `FSyntax`. We have implemented and evaluated the proposed mechanisms by defining a set of imperative features and exercising their usefulness by translating idiomatically, in imperative style, but also using simultaneously Prolog's characteristics, a large collection of small but interesting programs from the Euler Project. Apart from their intrinsic interest, the choice of these benchmarks was also motivated by the fact that encodings of many of these problems are available in a number of imperative languages, and in particular in `Picat`, which, as we have argued, is a very good point of reference. We have also studied the performance of the translated programs. While some imperative-style constructs were previously available in some form or another in some Prolog systems, and more comprehensively in non-Prolog systems like `Picat`, we argue that our Prolog-based proposal is comprehensive, coherent, and extensible, as well as offering competitive performance.

References

1. Apt, K.R., Brunekreef, J., Partington, V., Schaerf, A.: Alma-O: an imperative language that supports declarative programming. ACM Trans. Program. Lang. Syst. **20**(5), 1014–1066 (1998). https://doi.org/10.1145/293677.293679
2. Cabeza, D., Hermenegildo, M.: A New Module System for Prolog. In: Lloyd, J., et al. (eds.) CL 2000. LNCS (LNAI), vol. 1861, pp. 131–148. Springer, Heidelberg (2000). https://doi.org/10.1007/3-540-44957-4_9
3. Cabeza, D., Hermenegildo, M., Lipton, J.: Hiord: a type-free higher-order logic programming language with predicate abstraction. In: Maher, M.J. (ed.) ASIAN 2004. LNCS, vol. 3321, pp. 93–108. Springer, Heidelberg (2004). https://doi.org/10.1007/978-3-540-30502-6_7
4. Carlsson, M., Mildner, P.: SICStus Prolog - the First 25 Years. Theory Pract. Logic Program. **12**(1–2), 35–66 (2012). https://doi.org/10.1017/S1471068411000482
5. Casas, A., Cabeza, D., Hermenegildo, M.: A syntactic approach to combining functional notation, lazy evaluation and higher-order in LP systems. In: The 8th International Symposium on Functional and Logic Programming (FLOPS 2006), Fuji Susono (Japan), pp. 142–162 (April 2006)
6. Fages, F.: A constraint-based mathematical modeling library in prolog with answer constraint semantics (2024), https://arxiv.org/abs/2402.17286
7. Garcia-Contreras, I., Morales, J.F., Hermenegildo, M.V.: Incremental analysis of logic programs with assertions and open predicates. In: Gabbrielli, M. (ed.) LOPSTR 2019. LNCS, vol. 12042, pp. 36–56. Springer, Cham (2020). https://doi.org/10.1007/978-3-030-45260-5_3

8. Hanus, M.: Curry: An integrated functional logic language (vers. 0.9.0) (2013). http://www.curry-language.org language Report
9. Henderson, F., et al.: The Mercury Language Reference Manual. State Variables. The University of Melbourne (2014). https://mercurylang.org/information/doc-release/mercury_ref/State-variables.html
10. Hermenegildo, M.V., et al.: An overview of ciao and its design philosophy. Theory Pract. Logic Programm. **12**(1–2), 219–252 (2012). https://doi.org/10.1017/S1471068411000457
11. Hughes, C.: Project euler (2025). https://projecteuler.net
12. McGrail, R.: Monads and Control in Logic Programming. Ph.D. thesis, Wesleyan University (1999)
13. Nethercote, N., Stuckey, P.J., Becket, R., Brand, S., Duck, G.J., Tack, G.: MiniZinc: towards a Standard CP modelling language. In: Bessière, C. (ed.) CP 2007. LNCS, vol. 4741, pp. 529–543. Springer, Heidelberg (2007). https://doi.org/10.1007/978-3-540-74970-7_38
14. O'Neill, M.: The genuine sieve of eratosthenes. J. Funct. Program. **19**, 95–106 (2009). https://doi.org/10.1017/S0956796808007004
15. Roy, P.V.: A useful extension to prolog's definite clause grammar notation. ACM SIGPLAN Notices **24**(11), 132–134 (1989)
16. Santos Costa, V., Rocha, R., Damas, L.: The YAP prolog system. Theory Pract. Logic Program. **12**(1–2), 5–34 (2012). https://doi.org/10.1017/S1471068411000512
17. Schimpf, J.: Logical loops. In: Stuckey, P.J. (ed.) ICLP 2002. LNCS, vol. 2401, pp. 224–238. Springer, Heidelberg (2002). https://doi.org/10.1007/3-540-45619-8_16
18. Stuckey, P.J., Marriott, K., Tack, G.: MiniZinc Documentation. https://docs.minizinc.dev/en/stable/index.html
19. Swift, T., Warren, D.S.: XSB: extending prolog with tabled logic programming. Theory Pract. Logic Program. **12**(1–2), 157–187 (2012). https://doi.org/10.1017/S1471068411000500
20. Wielemaker, J., Schrijvers, T., Triska, M., Lager, T.: SWI-Prolog. Theory Pract. Logic Program. **12**(1–2), 67–96 (2012). https://doi.org/10.1017/S1471068411000494
21. Zhou, N.F.: Picat: a scalable logic-based language and system. In: 2nd Symposium on Languages, Applications and Technologies. Open Access Series in Informatics (OASIcs), vol. 29, pp. 5–6. Schloss Dagstuhl–Leibniz-Zentrum für Informatik (2013). https://doi.org/10.4230/OASIcs.SLATE.2013.5, https://drops.dagstuhl.de/entities/document/10.4230/OASIcs.SLATE.2013.5
22. Zhou, N.F., Fruhman, J.: Picat Guide (2025) https://picat-lang.org/download/picat_guide.pdf

Higher-Order Pattern Unification Modulo Similarity Relations

Besik Dundua[1,2(✉)] [iD] and Temur Kutsia[3] [iD]

[1] VIAM, Tbilisi State University, Tbilisi, Georgia
bdundua@gmail.com
[2] Kutaisi International University, Kutaisi, Georgia
[3] RISC, Johannes Kepler University, Linz, Austria
kutsia@risc.jku.at

Abstract. The combination of higher-order theories and fuzzy logic can be useful in decision-making tasks that involve reasoning across abstract functions and predicates, where exact matches are often rare or unnecessary. Developing efficient reasoning and computational techniques for such a combined formalism presents a significant challenge. In this paper, we adopt a more straightforward approach aiming at integrating two well-established and computationally well-behaved components: higher-order patterns on one side and fuzzy equivalences expressed through similarity relations based on minimum T-norm on the other. We propose a unification algorithm for higher-order patterns modulo these similarity relations and prove its termination, soundness, and completeness. This unification problem, like its crisp counterpart, is unitary. The algorithm computes a most general unifier with the highest degree of approximation when the given terms are unifiable.

Keywords: Unification · Higher-order patterns · Fuzzy similarity relations

1 Introduction

Approximate reasoning involves making decisions or performing inferences based on vague or imprecise information, which is often modeled using fuzzy logic. Fuzzy similarity (and proximity) relations are key tools in this type of reasoning, allowing for working with uncertain or imprecise data. Fuzzy similarity refers to the degree to which two elements or objects are alike, using a value in the range of 0 to 1, where 0 represents no similarity and 1 represents complete similarity. These relations can be used to determine how similar a new situation is to past experiences or data. This is particularly useful in scenarios where precise comparisons are impossible or where "similar enough" is acceptable. (See, e.g., [9, 14, 19, 21, 24, 29, 31, 32] in the context of using similarity relations in automated approximate reasoning.)

3. Escobar and L. Titolo (Eds.): LOPSTR 2025, LNCS 16117, pp. 75–93, 2026.
https://doi.org/10.1007/978-3-032-04848-6_5

Fuzzy similarity and proximity relations have been incorporated into knowledge representation and inference processes in the area of logic programming [8,10,12,13,16,18,32], making it possible to reason or compute with vague concepts having imprecise boundaries. It helps to deal with the ambiguity inherent in real-world data, where exact matches are rare, and allows systems to make reasonable inferences even with imprecise or incomplete information. In order for this approach to work, one needs a fundamental computational mechanism such as unification to make an "approximate inference step". Motivated by this application, first-order unification with fuzzy relations has been investigated both from theoretical and practical points of view, see, e.g., [1,6,9,11,15,17,19,20,23,29,30,32–34]. In [7], this technique was studied in a more general setting where the quantitative approximate information is specified using quantales, having the fuzzy quantale as a special case.

The cited works focus on fuzzy reasoning and computation within a first-order framework. However, decision-making often requires higher-order reasoning across abstract layers of functions and predicates, where exact matches are rare or even unnecessary. For instance, when two functions are not identical but exhibit a high degree of similarity in behavior or output, fuzzy similarity relations would enable the system to recognize this resemblance and apply approximate reasoning for inference or prediction. This can be especially useful in fields such as natural language processing, knowledge representation, and complex decision-making systems, where human-like reasoning and the handling of uncertainty are essential. This idea is a primary motivation for our work.

It is important to note that the existing higher-order fuzzy logics (e.g., [22,28]) are highly expressive formalisms, but because of this expressive power, developing efficient reasoning and computational techniques for them is a significant challenge. We adopt a more straightforward approach, concentrating on the integration of established and computationally well-behaved fragments: higher-order patterns on one hand, and fuzzy equivalences expressed through minimum-T-norm-based similarity relations on the other. The first step in supporting reasoning for this integration is the development of fundamental computational techniques, such as unification, which is the subject of this paper.

Our Contribution. We define the notion of similarity for simply-typed lambda terms and study the unification problem for higher-order patterns à la Miller [25]. In this framework, the equality relation modulo $\alpha\beta\eta$-equivalence is replaced by fuzzy similarity modulo $\alpha\beta\eta$ with the minimum T-norm (Gödel T-norm). We develop a rule-based unification algorithm for such problems and prove its termination, soundness, and completeness. The unification problem, like its crisp counterpart, is unitary, that is, any unifiable problem has a *single* (modulo $\alpha\beta\eta$-equivalence) *most general unifier* (mgu) with respect to fuzzy similarity using minimum T-norm. The algorithm returns such an mgu for the given terms, along with an associated approximation degree, which indicates how similar the instances of the terms are under the unifier. Importantly, the computed unifier has the maximal possible approximation degree. This degree must meet or exceed a user-defined threshold (also known as a cut value). When the threshold is set to the maximal value 1, the algorithm computes standard (i.e., crisp) unifiers. In this case, it can be viewed as a rule-based version of the standard higher-order pattern unification algorithm.

Our presentation differs from traditional accounts of higher-order pattern unification and fuzzy unification by introducing a dedicated subalgorithm for variable elimination. This design has two main benefits. First, it simplifies the termination proof. Second, it enhances modularity, making it easier to integrate alternative T-norms: only the subalgorithm requires modification in such cases.

Organization. Section 2 introduces the basic notions and establishes fundamental properties. The core of the paper is Sect. 3, where we define the algorithm and prove its termination, soundness, and completeness. In Sect. 4, we discuss two topics: (a) the crisp counterpart of our algorithm and its relation to existing higher-order pattern unification algorithms; and (b) possible extensions using T-norms other than the minimum (Gödel) T-norm employed in this work. Section 5 concludes the paper. The missing proofs can be found in the technical report [5].

2   Preliminaries

Term Language. Given a set of basic types, whose elements are denoted by δ, *simple types* are constructed using the grammar $\tau ::= \delta \mid \tau \to \tau$, where τ is associative to the right. The alphabet of our language consists of the set $\mathcal{V}$ of variables and $\mathcal{F}$ of constants. They are disjoint and countably infinite and their elements have assigned types. It is assumed that for each basic type, there is at least one function symbol (types are not empty). Variables are typically denoted by $F, G, H, X, Y, Z, x, y, z, \ldots$ and constants by $f, g, a, b, c, \ldots$. The set of *terms* over $\mathcal{F}$ and $\mathcal{V}$, denoted by $\mathcal{T}(\mathcal{F}, \mathcal{V})$, is defined by the grammar

$$t ::= x \mid c \mid \lambda x.t \mid (t_1\, t_2),$$

where $\lambda x.t$ is called an *abstraction* and $(t_1\, t_2)$ is called an *application*. We denote terms by t, s, r.

The following standard abbreviations are used: $(t_1\, t_2\, t_3 \cdots t_n)$, $n \geq 3$, for $(\cdots ((t_1\, t_2)\, t_3) \cdots t_n)$, and $\lambda x_1, \ldots, x_n.t$, $n \geq 2$, for $\lambda x_1.(\lambda x_2.(\ldots (\lambda x_n.t)))$.

A term t is said to *have the type* τ if either

- t is a constant or a variable of type τ,
- $t = \lambda x.s$, the variable x has type ρ, the term s has type ϕ, and $\tau = \rho \to \phi$,
- $t = (s\, r)$, where the term s has type $\rho \to \tau$ and the term r has type ρ for some ρ.

The standard concepts of the simply-typed λ-calculus, such as bound and free occurrences of variables, position in a term, α-conversion, β-reduction, and η-long β-normal form, are defined in the usual way, see, e.g., [2,4]. The set of positions of a term t is denoted by $Pos(t)$. The η-long β-normal form of a term t is denoted by $t \uparrow^{\eta}_{\beta}$. For any t, the term $t \uparrow^{\eta}_{\beta}$ has the form $\lambda x_1, \ldots x_n.(h\, t_1 \cdots t_m)$, where $n, m \geq 0$, the symbol h (called the *head* of the term) is either a constant or a variable, and each t_i (for $i = 1, \ldots, m$) follows the same structural form. Moreover, the term $(h\, t_1 \cdots t_m)$ has a basic type. We follow the standard convention of writing terms in η-long β-normal form as $\lambda x_1, \ldots, x_n.h(t_1, \ldots, t_m)$. When we write an equality between two λ-terms, we mean that they are equivalent modulo α-, β-, and η-equivalence. The size of a term t, denoted $size(t)$, is defined recursively as $size(x) = size(f) = 1$, $size((t_1\, t_2)) = size(t_1) + size(t_2)$, and $size(\lambda x.t) = 1 + size(t)$.

The sets of free and bound variables of a term t are denoted by $\mathtt{fv}(t)$ and $\mathtt{bv}(t)$, respectively. As a convention and for the sake of clarity, in what follows, we distinguish bound and free variables syntactically. In particular, we use lowercase letters x, y, z for bound variables and capital letters X, Y, Z, F, G, H for free variables. A term is called *rigid* if its head symbol is a constant or a bound variable, and it is called *flexible*, if its head symbol is a free variable.

Definition 1 (Higher-order patterns). *A higher-order pattern is a term where, when written in η-long β-normal form, all free variable occurrences are applied to lists of pairwise distinct (η-long forms of) bound variables.*

A *substitution* σ is a mapping from variables to terms such that for each variable x of type τ, the term $\sigma(x)$ is of type τ, and all but finitely many variables are mapped to themselves (modulo $\alpha\beta\eta$). Greek letters $\sigma, \vartheta, \varphi, \tau, \varepsilon$ are used for substitutions, where ε denotes the identity substitution. Each substitution σ is represented as a finite set of pairs $\{x_1 \mapsto \sigma(x_1), \ldots, x_n \mapsto \sigma(x_n)\}$ where the x's are variables for which $\sigma(x_i) \neq x_i$. The sets $Dom(\sigma) = \{x_1, \ldots, x_n\}$ and $Ran(\sigma) = \{\sigma(x_1), \ldots, \sigma(x_n)\}$ are called the *domain* and the *range* of σ, respectively. The set $\mathtt{fv}(\sigma)$ is defined as $\mathtt{fv}(\sigma) = Dom(\sigma) \cup \mathtt{fv}(Ran(\sigma))$ where $\mathtt{fv}(Ran(\sigma)) = \cup_{i=1}^{n}\mathtt{fv}(\sigma(x_i))$

The *application* of a substitution σ to t replaces each *free* occurrence of a variable x in t with $\sigma(x)$. It is defined inductively:

$$x\sigma = \sigma(x), \qquad\qquad\qquad \text{if } x \in Dom(\sigma).$$
$$x\sigma = x, \qquad\qquad\qquad\quad \text{if } x \notin Dom(\sigma).$$
$$f\sigma = f.$$
$$(\lambda x.t)\sigma = \lambda x.t\sigma, \qquad\qquad \text{if } x \notin \mathtt{fv}(\sigma).$$
$$(\lambda x.t)\sigma = \lambda y.t\{x \mapsto y\}\sigma, \qquad \text{if } x \in \mathtt{fv}(\sigma) \text{ and } y \text{ is fresh.}$$
$$(t\, s)\sigma = (t\sigma\, s\sigma).$$

Fuzzy Relations. We define basic notions about fuzzy relations following [32]. A binary *fuzzy relation* on a set S is a mapping from $S \times S$ to the real interval $[0, 1]$. If $\mathcal{R}$ is a fuzzy relation on S and μ is a number $0 < \mu \leq 1$ (called *cut value*), then the μ-*cut* of $\mathcal{R}$ on S, denoted $\mathcal{R}_\mu$, is an ordinary (crisp) relation on S defined as $\mathcal{R}_\mu := \{(s_1, s_2) \mid \mathcal{R}(s_1, s_2) \geq \mu\}$.

A *T-norm* $\wedge$ is an associative, commutative, non-decreasing binary operation on $[0, 1]$ with 1 as the unit element. Some of the most prominent T-norms are

- Gödel (or minimum) T-norm: $s_1 \wedge s_2 = \min(s_1, s_2)$,

- Product T-norm: $s_1 \wedge s_2 = s_1 * s_2$,
- Łukasiewicz T-norm: $s_1 \wedge s_2 = \max(0, s_1 + s_2 - 1)$.

Definition 2 (Similarity relation). *A fuzzy relation $\mathcal{R}$ on a set S is called a proximity relation, if it is reflexive ($\mathcal{R}(s,s) = 1$ for all $s \in S$) and symmetric ($\mathcal{R}(s_1, s_2) = \mathcal{R}(s_2, s_1)$ for all $s_1, s_2 \in S$). A proximity relation is called a similarity relation if it is $\wedge$-transitive: $\mathcal{R}(s_1, s_2) \geq \mathcal{R}(s_1, s) \wedge \mathcal{R}(s, s_2)$ for any $s_1, s_2, s \in S$.*

In the role of S, we take the set of terms of our language. First, we assume a fuzzy relation $\mathcal{R}_A$ to be defined on the alphabet $\mathcal{F} \cup \mathcal{V}$ in such a way that

- $\mathcal{R}_A(x, y) = 0$ for all $x, y \in \mathcal{V}$ with $x \neq y$,
- $\mathcal{R}_A(f, g) = 0$ for all $f, g \in \mathcal{F}$ such that f and g have different types.
- $\mathcal{R}_A(x, f) = \mathcal{R}_A(f, x) = 0$ for all $x \in \mathcal{V}$ and $f \in \mathcal{F}$.

Definition 3 (Fuzzy relation on terms). *Given a fuzzy relation $\mathcal{R}_A$ on the alphabet $\mathcal{F} \cup \mathcal{V}$, we define a fuzzy relation $\mathcal{R}$ on the set of terms $T(\mathcal{F}, \mathcal{V})$ using the T-norm $\wedge$.*

1. If t and s are in η-long β-normal form, then $\mathcal{R}(t, s)$ is defined as follows:

$$\mathcal{R}(a, b) = \mathcal{R}_A(a, b), \quad \text{where } a, b \in \mathcal{F} \cup \mathcal{V},$$
$$\mathcal{R}((t_1\, s_1), (t_2\, s_2)) = \mathcal{R}(t_1, t_2) \wedge \mathcal{R}(s_1, s_2),$$
$$\mathcal{R}(\lambda x.t, \lambda y.s) = \mathcal{R}(t\{x \mapsto z\}, s\{y \mapsto z\}),$$
where x, y, and z have the same type and z is a fresh variable,
$$\mathcal{R}(t, s) = 0 \ \text{otherwise.}$$

2. Otherwise, $\mathcal{R}(t, s) = \mathcal{R}(t \uparrow_\beta^\eta, s \uparrow_\beta^\eta).$

It is easy to see that if $\mathcal{R}_A$ is a proximity relation on the alphabet, then $\mathcal{R}$ is a proximity relation on terms for any T-norm. This definition also implies that if $\mathcal{R}(t, s) > 0$, then

- t and s have the same type,
- $Pos(t \uparrow_\beta^\eta) = Pos(s \uparrow_\beta^\eta)$,
- for each $p \in Pos(t \uparrow_\beta^\eta)$, symbols occurring at position p in $t \uparrow_\beta^\eta$ and $s \uparrow_\beta^\eta$ have the same type,
- a variable (resp. a constant) occurs at position p in $t \uparrow_\beta^\eta$ iff a variable (resp. a constant) occurs at position p in $s \uparrow_\beta^\eta$,
- a free variable X occurs at position p in $t \uparrow_\beta^\eta$ iff the same variable X occurs at position p in $s \uparrow_\beta^\eta$.

Note that if the T-norm is not idempotent, one can find a substitution σ such that $\mathcal{R}(t, s) > 0$ does not imply $\mathcal{R}(t, s) = \mathcal{R}(t\sigma, s\sigma)$. For instance, for the product T-norm, $\mathcal{R}(a, b) = 0.5$, and $\sigma = \{X \mapsto \lambda x.f(x, x)\}$ we have

$$\mathcal{R}(X(a), X(b)) = 0.5,$$
$$\mathcal{R}(X(a)\sigma, X(b)\sigma) = \mathcal{R}(f(a, a), f(b, b)) = 0.5 * 0.5 = 0.25.$$

However, this problem does not arise when the T-norm is idempotent, or when terms are higher-order patterns:

Proposition 1. *Let $\mathcal{R}$ be a similarity relation on terms using the T-norm $\wedge$, t and s be terms, and σ be a substitution. Then $\mathcal{R}(t, s) > 0$ implies $\mathcal{R}(t, s) = \mathcal{R}(t\sigma, s\sigma)$ if (a) $\wedge$ is idempotent, or (b) t and s are higher-order patterns.*

Proof. Assume without loss of generality that t and s are in η-long β-normal form. They have the same structure, since $\mathcal{R}(t, s) > 0$. We proceed by structural induction.

t and s are variables. Then $t = s$, $t\sigma = s\sigma$, and $\mathcal{R}(t\sigma, s\sigma) = \mathcal{R}(t, s) = 1$.

t and s are constants. Then $t\sigma = t$, $s\sigma = s$, and $\mathcal{R}(t\sigma, s\sigma) = \mathcal{R}(t, s)$.

$t = \lambda x_1, \ldots, x_n.h_1(t'_1, \ldots, t'_m)$ and $s = \lambda x_1, \ldots, x_n.h_2(s'_1, \ldots, s'_m)$, where h_1 and h_2 are either both variables or both constants. Then $\mathcal{R}(t, s) = \mathcal{R}_A(h_1, h_2) \wedge \mathcal{R}(t'_1, s'_1) \wedge \cdots \wedge \mathcal{R}(t'_m, s'_m)$. By the induction hypothesis, $\mathcal{R}(t'_i, s'_i) = \mathcal{R}(t'_i\sigma, s'_i\sigma)$ for all $1 \leq i \leq m$.

- If h_1 and h_2 are constants or bound variables, then $h_1\sigma = h_1$, $h_2\sigma = h_2$ and $\mathcal{R}(t\sigma, s\sigma) = \mathcal{R}(t, s)$.
- If h_1 and h_2 are free variables, then they should be the same (since $\mathcal{R}(t, s) > 0$), say X. We consider two cases:
  - t and s are patterns. Then $t'_i = s'_i \in \{x_1, \ldots, x_n\}$. Therefore, $t = s$ and $\mathcal{R}(t\sigma, s\sigma) = \mathcal{R}(t, s) = 1$.
  - t and s are not patterns. If $X \notin Dom(\sigma)$, then the reasoning is like for bound variables above. If $X \in Dom(\sigma)$, then let $X\sigma = \lambda y_1, \ldots, y_m.r$. Then

$$t\sigma = \lambda x_1, \ldots, x_n.r\{y_1 \mapsto t'_1\} \cdots \{y_m \mapsto t'_m\},$$
$$s\sigma = \lambda x_1, \ldots, x_n.r\{y_1 \mapsto s'_1\} \cdots \{y_m \mapsto s'_m\}.$$

If r is linear (i.e., no y_i occurs in it more than once), then $\mathcal{R}(t\sigma, s\sigma) = \mathcal{R}(t'_1, s'_1) \wedge \cdots \wedge \mathcal{R}(t'_m, s'_m) = \mathcal{R}(t, s)$. Now let $\wedge$ be idempotent and assume without loss of generality that y_1 appears in r twice. Then $\mathcal{R}(t\sigma, s\sigma) = \mathcal{R}(t'_1, s'_1) \wedge \mathcal{R}(t'_1, s'_1) \wedge \cdots \wedge \mathcal{R}(t'_m, s'_m) =$ (by idempotence of $\wedge$) $= \mathcal{R}(t'_1, s'_1) \wedge \cdots \wedge \mathcal{R}(t'_m, s'_m) = \mathcal{R}(t, s)$. □

Theorem 1. *If $\mathcal{R}_A$ is a similarity relation on the alphabet, then $\mathcal{R}$ is a similarity relation on terms for any T-norm.*

Proof. We only need to show that for arbitrary terms t, s, r in η-long β-normal form and a T-norm $\wedge$, the $\wedge$-transitivity property holds: $\mathcal{R}(t, r) \geq \mathcal{R}(t, s) \wedge \mathcal{R}(s, r)$. Assume without loss of generality that $\mathcal{R}(t, s) \wedge \mathcal{R}(s, r) > 0$. Then by the monotonicity of T-norms we have $\mathcal{R}(t, s) > 0$ and $\mathcal{R}(s, r) > 0$, which implies that t, s, and r have the same structure. We proceed by induction on this structure.

- When $\{t, s, r\} \in \mathcal{F} \cup \mathcal{V}$, the property follows from the assumption that $\mathcal{R}_A$ is a similarity.
- Let $t = (t_1 t_2)$, $s = (s_1 s_2)$, and $r = (r_1 r_2)$. By definition of $\mathcal{R}$, we have $\mathcal{R}(t, r) = \mathcal{R}(t_1, r_1) \wedge \mathcal{R}(t_2, r_2)$, $\mathcal{R}(t, s) = \mathcal{R}(t_1, s_1) \wedge \mathcal{R}(t_2, s_2)$, and $\mathcal{R}(s, r) = \mathcal{R}(s_1, r_1) \wedge \mathcal{R}(s_2, r_2)$. By the induction hypothesis, we know $\mathcal{R}(t_i, r_i) \geq \mathcal{R}(t_i, s_i) \wedge \mathcal{R}(s_i, r_i)$, $i = 1, 2$. Then, by monotonicity of T-norms, we get $\mathcal{R}(t_1, r_1) \wedge \mathcal{R}(t_2, r_2) \geq \mathcal{R}(t_1, s_1) \wedge \mathcal{R}(s_1, r_1) \wedge \mathcal{R}(t_2, s_2) \wedge \mathcal{R}(s_2, r_2)$, from which, by associativity and commutativity of $\wedge$ and the definition of $\mathcal{R}$, we get $\mathcal{R}((t_1 t_2), (r_1 r_2)) \geq \mathcal{R}((t_1 t_2), (s_1 s_2)) \wedge \mathcal{R}((s_1 s_2), (r_1 r_2))$ for any T-norm $\wedge$.
- Let $t = \lambda x.t'$, $s = \lambda y.s'$, and $r = \lambda z.r'$, where x, y, z have the same type. By definition of $\mathcal{R}$, without loss of generality, we can choose a fresh variable u of the same type such that $\mathcal{R}(\lambda x.t', \lambda z.r') = \mathcal{R}(t'\{x \mapsto u\}, r'\{z \mapsto u\})$, $\mathcal{R}(\lambda x.t', \lambda y.s') = \mathcal{R}(t'\{x \mapsto u\}, s'\{y \mapsto u\})$, and $\mathcal{R}(\lambda y.s', \lambda z.r') = \mathcal{R}(s'\{y \mapsto u\}, r'\{z \mapsto u\})$. By the induction hypothesis, we have $\mathcal{R}(t'\{x \mapsto u\}, r'\{z \mapsto u\}) \geq \mathcal{R}(t'\{x \mapsto u\}, s'\{y \mapsto u\}) \wedge \mathcal{R}(s'\{y \mapsto u\}, r'\{z \mapsto u\})$ for any T-norm, which implies $\mathcal{R}(\lambda x.t', \lambda z.r') \geq \mathcal{R}(\lambda x.t', \lambda y.s') \wedge \mathcal{R}(\lambda y.s', \lambda z.r')$ for any T-norm. $\square$

Given a similarity relation $\mathcal{R}$, cut value μ, and two terms t, s, we write $t \simeq_{\mathcal{R}, \mu} s$ if $\mathcal{R}(t, s) \geq \mu$. The number $\mathcal{R}(t, s)$ is called the $\mathcal{R}$-*similarity degree* of t and s.

We say σ is $(\mathcal{R}, \mu)$-*more general* than ϑ with variable restriction V, written $\sigma \preceq_{\mathcal{R}, \mu}^{V} \vartheta$, if there exists a substitution τ such that $x\sigma\tau \simeq_{\mathcal{R}, \mu} x\vartheta$ for all $x \in V$.

Definition 4 (Unification problem, unifier, unification degree, mgu).
An $(\mathcal{R}, \mu)$-unification equation between terms t and s is written as $t \simeq_{\mathcal{R}, \mu}^{?} s$, where $\mathcal{R}$ is a similarity relation and μ is a cut value. An $(\mathcal{R}, \mu)$-unification problem is a finite set of $(\mathcal{R}, \mu)$-unification equations. A substitution σ is a unifier (or a solution) of an $(\mathcal{R}, \mu)$-unification problem $\{t_1 \simeq_{\mathcal{R}, \mu}^{?} s_1, \ldots, t_1 \simeq_{\mathcal{R}, \mu}^{?} s_1\}$ with unification degree $\mathfrak{d}$ if $\mathcal{R}(t_1\sigma, s_1\sigma) \wedge \cdots \wedge \mathcal{R}(t_n\sigma, s_n\sigma) = \mathfrak{d} \geq \mu$.

Given an $(\mathcal{R}, \mu)$-unification problem P, we say that its $(\mathcal{R}, \mu)$-unifier σ is a most general $(\mathcal{R}, \mu)$-unifier of P if for any $(\mathcal{R}, \mu)$-unifier ϑ of P we have $\sigma \preceq_{\mathcal{R}, \mu}^{\mathtt{fv}(P)} \vartheta$.

We consider a special case of this problem: all terms that appear in the unification problems and unifiers should be higher-order patterns. In the rest of the paper, we make the following assumptions (those related to terms follow [27]):

- min: T-norm $\wedge$ is the minimum T-norm,
- α: α-equivalent terms are identified,
- β: terms are β-normalized by default,
- η: terms are in η-expanded form except for the arguments of free variables, which are in η-normal form, i.e., bound variables.

Example 1. Higher-order pattern $(\mathcal{R}, \mu)$-unification problems may have most general unifiers that are or are not degree-maximal, and may have degree-maximal unifiers that are or are not most general. We illustrate it with an $(\mathcal{R}, \mu)$-unification problem between

$$t = \lambda x.\lambda y.f(F(x), F(y)) \text{ and}$$
$$s = \lambda x.\lambda y.g(a(G(y, x)), b(G(x, y))),$$

where $\mathcal{R}$ is defined as $\mathcal{R}(f, g) = 0.8$, $\mathcal{R}(a, b) = 0.6$, $\mathcal{R}(b, c) = \mathcal{R}(a, c) = 0.5$, and the cut value is $\mu = 0.4$. Consider the following $(\mathcal{R}, \mu)$-unifiers of t and s together with their unification degrees:

$$\sigma_1 = \{F \mapsto \lambda x.a(H(x)), G \mapsto \lambda y.\lambda x.H(x)\}, \qquad \eth_1 = 0.6.$$
$$\sigma_2 = \{F \mapsto \lambda x.b(H(x)), G \mapsto \lambda y.\lambda x.H(x)\}, \qquad \eth_2 = 0.6.$$
$$\sigma_3 = \{F \mapsto \lambda x.c(H(x)), G \mapsto \lambda y.\lambda x.H(x)\}, \qquad \eth_3 = 0.5.$$
$$\sigma_4 = \{F \mapsto \lambda x.a(a(x)), G \mapsto \lambda y.\lambda x.a(x)\}, \qquad \eth_4 = 0.6.$$
$$\sigma_5 = \{F \mapsto \lambda x.c(a(x)), G \mapsto \lambda y.\lambda x.a(x)\}, \qquad \eth_5 = 0.5.$$

From these unifiers, σ_1, σ_2 and σ_3 are most general ones on $V = \{F, G\}$. (They are equivalent to each other modulo similarity.) Hence, we have two most general unifiers σ_1, σ_2 with the maximum degree, and one with a lower degree. The unifier σ_4 is strictly less general on V than the first three, yet its unification degree is maximal. As for σ_5, it is neither most general nor degree-maximal unifier.

Our goal is to design an algorithm that computes a degree-maximal most general unifier. Hence, for this problem, computing either σ_1 or σ_2 would be the desired outcome.

3 Similarity-Based Unification of Higher-Order Patterns

In this section, we formulate a similarity-based unification algorithm in a rule-based manner. The rules operate on triples P; σ; $\eth$, referred to as unification *configurations*, where P is a similarity-based unification problem, σ is the substitution computed so far, and $\eth$ is the approximation degree, also computed so far. The similarity relation $\mathcal{R}$ and the cut value μ are implicit parameters, and it is assumed that $\eth \geq \mu$ in configurations.

The rules are given below. The symbol $\uplus$ stands for disjoint union. The rule LF calls an auxiliary function VarElim (which is also defined below) with the sides of the selected equation as arguments.

Abs: **Abstraction**

$$\{\lambda x.t \simeq^?_{\mathcal{R},\mu} \lambda x.s\} \uplus P;\ \sigma;\mathfrak{d} \rightsquigarrow \{t \simeq^?_{\mathcal{R},\mu} s\} \cup P;\ \sigma;\mathfrak{d}.$$

Dec: **Decomposition**

$$\{f(t_1,\ldots,t_n) \simeq^?_{\mathcal{R},\mu} g(s_1,\ldots,s_n)\} \uplus P;\ \sigma;\mathfrak{d} \rightsquigarrow$$
$$\{t_1 \simeq^?_{\mathcal{R},\mu} s_1,\ldots,t_n \simeq^?_{\mathcal{R},\mu} s_n\} \cup P;\ \sigma;\mathfrak{d} \wedge \mathcal{R}(f,g),$$
where $n \geq 0$ and $(\mathfrak{d} \wedge \mathcal{R}(f,g)) \geq \mu$.

SV: **Same variables**

$$\{F(x_1,\ldots,x_n) \simeq^?_{\mathcal{R},\mu} F(y_1,\ldots,y_n)\} \uplus P;\ \sigma;\ \mathfrak{d} \rightsquigarrow P\vartheta;\ \sigma\vartheta;\ \mathfrak{d},$$
where $n \geq 0$ and

- $\{z_1,\ldots,z_m\} = \{x_i \mid x_i = y_i, 1 \leq i \leq n\}$, $m \geq 0$ (i.e., each z is a variable that appears in the same position in both the sequences $x_1,\ldots,x_n$ and $y_1,\ldots,y_n$),
- $\vartheta = \{F \mapsto \lambda x_1,\ldots,x_n.H(z_1,\ldots,z_m)\}$ for a fresh variable H of the appropriate type.

Ori: **Orient**

$$\{a(s_1,\ldots,s_m) \simeq^?_{\mathcal{R},\mu} F(x_1,\ldots,x_n)\} \uplus P;\ \sigma;\mathfrak{d} \rightsquigarrow$$
$$\{F(x_1,\ldots,x_n) \simeq^?_{\mathcal{R},\mu} a(s_1,\ldots,s_m)\} \cup P;\ \sigma;\mathfrak{d},$$
where $n, m \geq 0$, F is a free variable and a is a constant or $a \in \{x_1,\ldots,x_n\}$.

LF: **Left-flex**

$$\{F(x_1,\ldots,x_n) \simeq^?_{\mathcal{R},\mu} a(s_1,\ldots,s_m)\} \uplus P;\ \sigma;\ \mathfrak{d} \rightsquigarrow P\vartheta;\ \sigma\vartheta;\ \mathfrak{d}$$
where $n, m \geq 0$ and

- $F \notin \mathtt{fv}(a(s_1,\ldots,s_m))$,
- a is a constant, free variable, or $a \in \{x_1,\ldots,x_n\}$,
- $\mathsf{VarElim}(F(x_1,\ldots,x_n), a(s_1,\ldots,s_m)) = \varphi$,
- $\vartheta = \varphi|_V$, where $V = \{F\} \cup \mathtt{fv}(a(s_1,\ldots,s_m))$.

Fail: **Failure**

$$\{t \simeq^?_{\mathcal{R},\mu} s\} \uplus P;\ \sigma;\ \mathfrak{d} \rightsquigarrow \bot,$$
if no other rule applies to the selected equation $t \simeq^?_{\mathcal{R},\mu} s$.

For our minimum T-norm, it would suffice to have $\mathcal{R}(f,g) \geq \mu$ instead of $(\mathfrak{d} \wedge \mathcal{R}(f,g)) \geq \mu$ in the condition of the Dec rule. However, we decided to keep this more general requirement since it can be used with any T-norm. See also Sect. 4 for related discussion.

Analyzing the rules, it is not hard to see that when the failure rule applies, we have one of the following three cases:

- t and s have different types,
- $t = f(t_1,\ldots,t_n)$, $s = g(s_1,\ldots,s_n)$, and $(\mathfrak{d} \wedge \mathcal{R}(f,g)) < \mu$, or
- $t = F(x_1,\ldots,x_n)$, $s = a(s_1,\ldots,s_m)$, and $F \in \mathtt{fv}(a(s_1,\ldots,s_m))$.

In each of these cases, $t \simeq^?_{\mathcal{R},\mu} s$ is unsolvable, which justifies the name of the rule.

In the LF rule, if a is a free variable, then $s_1, \ldots, s_m$ are distinct bound variables (since we work only with higher-order patterns). By this rule, in order to unify a flexible term t and a term s, the auxiliary function $\mathsf{VarElim}(t, s)$ is called, which creates an initial configuration $\{t \simeq^? s\}; \varepsilon$ and applies the VE1 and VE2 rules below as long as possible. If the process stops with the configuration $\emptyset; \varphi$, we say that φ is the answer computed by $\mathsf{VarElim}$ for t and s and write $\mathsf{VarElim}(t, s) = \varphi$. Note that φ might contain bindings for variables introduced in the process of $\mathsf{VarElim}$, which appear neither in t nor in s. Therefore, in ϑ, we keep only those bindings from φ that are relevant to t and s. Note also that $\mathsf{VarElim}$ is independent of $\mathcal{R}$ and does not involve the degree computation.

VE1: **Variable elimination 1**

$$\{F(x_1, \ldots, x_n) \simeq^? a(s_1, \ldots, s_m)\} \uplus P; \sigma \rightsquigarrow$$
$$\{H_1(x_1, \ldots, x_n) \simeq^? s_1, \ldots, H_m(x_1, \ldots, x_n) \simeq^? s_m\} \cup P; \sigma\vartheta,$$
where $n, m \geq 0$ and

- a is a constant or $a \in \{x_1, \ldots, x_n\}$,
- $\vartheta = \{F \mapsto \lambda x_1, \ldots, x_n.a(H_1(x_1, \ldots, x_n), \ldots, H_m(x_1, \ldots, x_n))\}$ where the variables $H_1, \ldots, H_m$ are fresh and have appropriate types.
- (Note that if s_i for $1 \leq i \leq m$, is of function type, the term $H_i(x_1, \ldots, x_n)$ must be η-expanded in both the new configuration and the substitution.)

VE2: **Variable elimination 2**

$$\{F(x_1, \ldots, x_n) \simeq^? G(y_1, \ldots, y_m)\} \uplus P; \sigma \rightsquigarrow P\vartheta; \sigma\vartheta,$$
where $n, m \geq 0$, and

- $\{x_1, \ldots, x_n\} \cap \{y_1, \ldots, y_m\} = \{z_1, \ldots, z_k\}$,
- $\vartheta = \{F \mapsto \lambda x_1, \ldots, x_n.H(z_1, \ldots, z_k), G \mapsto \lambda y_1, \ldots, y_m.H(z_1, \ldots, z_k)\}$ with H being a fresh variable of the appropriate type.

Note that when $\mathsf{VarElim}$ is invoked, it is always called with terms t and s where t has the form $F(x_1, \ldots, x_n)$ such that the variable F does not occur in s. Applying VE1 or VE2 to the initial configuration $\{F(x_1, \ldots, x_n) \simeq^? s\}; \varepsilon$ creates a new configuration in which F does not appear anymore, and if the variables introduced instead of it appear on the left-hand sides, then they are unique again. Hence, the configurations $P; \sigma$ to which VE1 and VE2 apply satisfy the following invariant:

- If an equation of the form $F(x_1, \ldots, x_n) \simeq^? s$ appears in P, then F is unique.

Consequently, in VE1, it does not make sense to apply the generated substitution to the remaining unification problem. That is why we have P and not $P\vartheta$ on the right-hand side of VE1. On the other hand, we need $P\vartheta$ in VE2, because P might contain G.

Given a similarity relation $\mathcal{R}$, the cut value μ, and two terms t and s, to find an $(\mathcal{R}, \mu)$-unifier of t and s, the algorithm HOPS creates the initial configuration $\{t \simeq^?_{\mathcal{R},\mu} s\}; \varepsilon; 1$ and applies the rules above as long as possible. It means that HOPS can be defined as the following strategy where nf stands for normal form:

$$\text{HOPS} := \text{nf}(\text{Step}). \qquad \text{Step} := \text{choice}(\text{Abs}, \text{Dec}, \text{SV}, \text{Ori}, \text{LF}, \text{Fail}).$$

It is easy to see that for each selected equation, only one rule applies. Hence, Step is deterministic in the sense that it transforms a given configuration C in only one way. We refer to the result of transformation as $\text{Step}(C)$.

Example 2. We illustrate the algorithm to solve an $(\mathcal{R}, \mu)$-unification problem from Example 1. We create the initial configuration

$$\{\lambda x.\lambda y.f(F(x), F(y)) \simeq^?_{\mathcal{R},0.4} \lambda x.\lambda y.g(a(G(y, x)), b(G(x, y)))\}; \varepsilon; 1$$

and apply the transformation rules as follows:

$$\{\lambda x.\lambda y.f(F(x), F(y)) \simeq^?_{\mathcal{R},0.4} \lambda x.\lambda y.g(a(G(y, x)), b(G(x, y)))\}; \varepsilon; 1 \rightsquigarrow_{\text{Abs}}$$
$$\{\lambda y.f(F(x), F(y)) \simeq^?_{\mathcal{R},0.4} \lambda y.g(a(G(y, x)), b(G(x, y)))\}; \varepsilon; 1 \rightsquigarrow_{\text{Abs}}$$
$$\{f(F(x), F(y)) \simeq^?_{\mathcal{R},0.4} y(a(G(y, x)), b(G(x, y)))\}; \varepsilon; 1 \rightsquigarrow_{\text{Dec}}$$
$$\{F(x) \simeq^?_{\mathcal{R},0.4} a(G(y, x)), F(y) \simeq^?_{\mathcal{R},0.4} b(G(x, y))\}; \varepsilon; 0.8 \rightsquigarrow_{\text{LF}}$$

Application of LF requires steps of the VarElim :

$$\{F(x) \simeq^? a(G(y, x))\}; \varepsilon \rightsquigarrow_{\text{VE1}}$$
$$\{H_1(x) \simeq^? G(y, x)\}; \{F \mapsto \lambda x.a(H_1(x))\} \rightsquigarrow_{\text{VE2}}$$
$$\emptyset; \{F \mapsto \lambda x.a(H_2(x)), G \mapsto \lambda y\lambda x.H_2(x), H_1 \mapsto \lambda x.H_2(x)\}$$

VarElim returns $\{F \mapsto \lambda x.a(H_2(x)), G \mapsto \lambda y\lambda x.H_2(x)\}$ and we continue:

$$\{a(H_2(y)) \simeq^?_{\mathcal{R},0.4} b(H_2(y))\};$$
$$\{F \mapsto \lambda x.a(H_2(x)), G \mapsto \lambda y\lambda x.H_2(x)\}; 0.8 \rightsquigarrow_{\text{Dec}}$$
$$\{H_2(y) \simeq^?_{\mathcal{R},0.4} H_2(y)\}; \{F \mapsto \lambda x.a(H_2(x)), G \mapsto \lambda y\lambda x.H_2(x)\}; 0.6 \rightsquigarrow_{\text{SV}}$$
$$\emptyset; \{F \mapsto \lambda x.a(H(x)), G \mapsto \lambda y\lambda x.H(x), H_2 \mapsto \lambda x.H(x)\}; 0.6$$

Hence, we obtained the substitution $\{F \mapsto \lambda x.a(H(x)), G \mapsto \lambda y\lambda x.H(x), H_2 \mapsto \lambda x.H(x)\}$ and the degree 0.6. It is easy to check that the substitution is indeed a unifier of the given terms with degree 0.6. Note also that not all the bindings from the substitution are relevant: we can restrict it only to the free variables of the given terms, getting $\{F \mapsto \lambda x.a(H(x)), G \mapsto \lambda y\lambda x.H(x)\}$, which corresponds to σ_1 from Example 1. If we applied the LF rule to the second equation $F(y) \simeq^?_{\mathcal{R},0.4} b(G(x, y))$ instead of the first one, we would get the unifier σ_2 from Example 1.

If we increase the cut value to, say, 0.7, the problem does not have a solution and the algorithm reaches a configuration to which the failure rule applies:

$$\{a(H_2(y)) \simeq^?_{\mathcal{R},0.7} b(H_2(y))\}; \{F \mapsto \lambda x.a(H_2(x)), G \mapsto \lambda y\lambda x.H_2(x)\}; 0.8 \rightsquigarrow_{\text{Fail}} \perp.$$

When $\mu = 1$, the problem is a crisp (i.e., standard) higher-order pattern unification problem, which obviously is not solvable due to the mismatch between f and g. The algorithm detects it, stopping with failure after the application of the abstraction steps.

Theorem 2 (Termination of HOPS). HOPS *terminates for any input either with* $\emptyset; \sigma; \eth$ *or with* $\bot$.

Proof. We first establish that $\mathsf{VarElim}(t, s)$ always terminates. This procedure starts by constructing the initial configuration $\{t \simeq^?_{\mathcal{R},\mu} s\}; \varepsilon$ and then repeatedly applies the **VE1** and **VE2** rules. To each configuration $P; \sigma$ we associate a complexity measure as the multiset of the sizes of equations in P, denoted by $ms(P) := \{\!\{size(t) + size(s) \mid t \simeq^?_{\mathcal{R},\mu} s \in P\}\!\}$. To order the measures, we use the multiset extension of the standard ordering on natural numbers (Dershowitz-Manna ordering [3]). Both **VE1** and **VE2** rules strictly decrease this measure, ensuring that the reduction process cannot continue indefinitely. Consequently, $\mathsf{VarElim}(t, s)$ must terminate.

Now we show termination of HOPS. For this, we define a complexity measure $cm(C)$ for a configuration $C = (P; \sigma; \eth)$, and show that $cm(C) > cm(\mathsf{Step}(C))$ holds. The measure is the triple $cm(C) = \langle N_1, N_2, N_3 \rangle$ defined as follows:

- N_1 is the number of distinct variables in P,
- $N_2 := ms(P)$,
- N_3 is the number of equations in P with a rigid left-hand side and a flexible right-hand side (rigid-flex equations).

We treat $\bot$ as a special configuration and define its measure as $cm(\bot) = \langle 0, \emptyset, 0 \rangle$. Measures are compared lexicographically. For N_2, we use the Dershowitz-Manna ordering. The table below shows which rule reduces which component of the measure. Hence, each rule strictly reduces $cm(C)$. Since the

Rule	N_1	N_2	N_3
LF	$>$		
Abs, Dec, SV, Fail	$\geq$	$>$	
Ori	$\geq$	$\geq$	$>$

ordering is well-founded, it implies the termination of the algorithm. It is obvious that there are only two alternatives for the final configuration: either the first component is empty, or it is $\bot$. It finishes the proof. $\square$

When HOPS stops with $\emptyset; \sigma; \eth$, we say that HOPS *succeeds* with the *computed answer* $(\sigma, \eth)$ (or *computes* $(\sigma, \eth)$). If it stops with $\bot$, we say that HOPS *fails*. For a similarity relation $\mathcal{R}$, a cut value μ, and two terms t and s, if HOPS computes $(\sigma, \eth)$, we write $\mathrm{HOPS}(t, s, \mathcal{R}, \mu) = (\sigma, \eth)$.

Lemma 1. *Let $\mathcal{R}$ be a similarity relation, μ a cut value and $P; \sigma; \mathfrak{d}$ a configuration. If $\mathsf{Step}(P; \sigma; \mathfrak{d}) = (P'; \sigma\vartheta; \mathfrak{d} \wedge \mathfrak{d}')$ and τ is an $(\mathcal{R}, \mu)$-unifier of P' with degree $\mathfrak{d}''$, then $\vartheta\tau$ is an $(\mathcal{R}, \mu)$-unifier of P with degree $\mathfrak{d}' \wedge \mathfrak{d}''$.*

Proof. See [5]. □

Theorem 3 (Soundness of Hops). *Given a similarity relation $\mathcal{R}$, a cut value μ, and two terms t and s, if $\mathrm{Hops}(t, s, \mathcal{R}, \mu) = (\sigma, \mathfrak{d})$, then $\mathfrak{d} \geq \mu$ and $\mathcal{R}(t\sigma, s\sigma) = \mathfrak{d}$, i.e., σ is an $(\mathcal{R}, \mu)$-unifier of t and s with degree $\mathfrak{d}$.*

Proof. From $\mathrm{Hops}(t, s, \mathcal{R}, \mu) = (\sigma, \mathfrak{d})$ we have the derivation

$$P_0; \sigma_0; \mathfrak{d}_0 \rightsquigarrow P_1; \sigma_0\vartheta_1; \mathfrak{d}_0 \wedge \mathfrak{d}_1 \rightsquigarrow^* P_n; \sigma_0\vartheta_1 \cdots \vartheta_n; \mathfrak{d}_0 \wedge \mathfrak{d}_1 \wedge \cdots \wedge \mathfrak{d}_n,$$

where

$$P_0 = \{t \simeq^?_{\mathcal{R}, \mu} s\}, \quad \sigma_0 = \varepsilon, \quad \mathfrak{d}_0 = 1,$$
$$P_n = \emptyset, \quad \sigma = \sigma_0\vartheta_1 \cdots \vartheta_n = \vartheta_1 \cdots \vartheta_n,$$
$$\mathfrak{d} = \mathfrak{d}_0 \wedge \mathfrak{d}_1 \wedge \cdots \wedge \mathfrak{d}_n = \mathfrak{d}_1 \wedge \cdots \wedge \mathfrak{d}_n.$$

Therefore, we get the desired result using induction on the length of the derivation with Lemma 1. □

Lemma 2. *Let $\mathcal{R}$ be a similarity relation, μ a cut value and $P_0; \sigma_0; \mathfrak{d}_0$ a configuration. Assume τ is an $(\mathcal{R}, \mu)$-unifier of P_0 with degree $\mathfrak{d}_\tau \geq \mu$ and $\sigma_0 \preceq^{Dom(\tau)}_{\mathcal{R}, \mu} \tau$. Then we can make a step $\mathsf{Step}(P_0; \sigma_0; \mathfrak{d}_0) = (P_1; \sigma_1; \mathfrak{d}_1)$ such that*

- *$\mathfrak{d}_1 = \mathfrak{d}_0 \wedge \mathfrak{d}'_1$ for some $\mathfrak{d}'_1$,*
- *there exists a substitution φ_1 such that*
  - *$Dom(\varphi_1) = \mathtt{fv}(P_1) \setminus \mathtt{fv}(P_0)$ (the set of new free variables in P_1),*
  - *$\mathtt{fv}(Ran(\varphi_1)) \cap Dom(\tau) = \emptyset$,*
  - *$\varphi_1\tau$ is an $(\mathcal{R}, \mu)$-unifier of P_1 with degree $\mathfrak{d}_{\varphi_1\tau} \geq \mu$ such that $\mathfrak{d}_\tau \leq \mathfrak{d}'_1 \wedge \mathfrak{d}_{\varphi_1\tau}$, and*
  - *$\sigma_1 \simeq^{Dom(\varphi_1\tau)}_{\mathcal{R}, \mu} \varphi_1\tau$.*

Proof. See [5]. □

Theorem 4 (Completeness of Hops). *Given a similarity relation $\mathcal{R}$, a cut value μ, and two terms t and s, if there exists an $(\mathcal{R}, \mu)$-unifier τ of t and s with degree $\mathfrak{d}_\tau \geq \mu$, then $\mathrm{Hops}(t, s, \mathcal{R}, \mu)$ computes an answer $(\sigma, \mathfrak{d})$ such that $\sigma \simeq^{Dom(\tau)}_{\mathcal{R}, \mu} \tau$ and $\mathfrak{d} \geq \mathfrak{d}_\tau$.*

Proof. First note that for any configuration $P; \sigma; \mathfrak{d}$, if P is $(\mathcal{R}, \mu)$-unifiable then $\mathsf{Step}(P; \sigma; \mathfrak{d}) \neq \bot$. This is based on the observation that Step gives $\bot$ in only three cases: if P contains an equation between terms of different types, or an equation $f(t_1, \ldots, t_n) \simeq^?_{\mathcal{R}, \mu} g(s_1, \ldots, s_n)$ with $\mathfrak{d} \wedge \mathcal{R}(f, g) < \mu$, or an equation $F(t_1, \ldots, t_n) \simeq^?_{\mathcal{R}, \mu} a(s_1, \ldots, s_n)$ with $F \in \mathtt{fv}(a(s_1, \ldots, s_n))$. But in none of these cases is P $(\mathcal{R}, \mu)$-unifiable.

Hence, for the initial configuration $P_0; \sigma_0; \mathfrak{d}_0 = \{t \simeq^?_{\mathcal{R}, \mu} s\}; \varepsilon; 1$ we have that τ is an $(\mathcal{R}, \mu)$-unifier of P_0 with degree $\mathfrak{d}_\tau \geq \mu$ and $\sigma_0 \simeq^{Dom(\tau)}_{\mathcal{R}, \mu} \tau$. By Lemma 2, we can make $\mathsf{Step}(P_0; \sigma_0; \mathfrak{d}_0) = (P_1; \sigma_1; \mathfrak{d}_1)$ such that

- $\mathfrak{d}_1 = \mathfrak{d}_0 \wedge \mathfrak{d}_1'$ for some $\mathfrak{d}_1'$,
- there exists a substitution φ_1 such that
  - $Dom(\varphi_1) = \mathtt{fv}(P_1) \setminus \mathtt{fv}(P_0)$ (the set of new free variables in P_1),
  - $\mathtt{fv}(Ran(\varphi_1)) \cap Dom(\tau) = \emptyset$,
  - $\varphi_1\tau$ is an $(\mathcal{R}, \mu)$-unifier of P_1 with degree $\mathfrak{d}_\tau' \geq \mu$ such that $\mathfrak{d}_\tau \leq \mathfrak{d}_1' \wedge \mathfrak{d}_\tau'$, and
  - $\sigma_1 \precsim_{\mathcal{R},\mu}^{Dom(\varphi_1\tau)} \varphi_1\tau$.

The obtained configuration $P_1;\sigma_1;\mathfrak{d}_1$ and $\varphi_1\tau$ satisfy the conditions of Lemma 2. Hence, we can iterate applications of Step (finitely many times, due to Theorem 2), obtaining the maximal chain of configurations $P_1;\sigma_1;\mathfrak{d}_1 \rightsquigarrow \cdots \rightsquigarrow P_n;\sigma_n;\mathfrak{d}_n$. Then

- $P_n = \emptyset$, otherwise it would contradict the fact that it has a solution;
- $\sigma_n \precsim_{\mathcal{R},\mu}^{Dom(\varphi_1\cdots\varphi_n\tau)} \varphi_1\cdots\varphi_n\tau$;
- $\mathfrak{d}_n = \mathfrak{d}_0 \wedge \mathfrak{d}_1' \wedge \cdots \wedge \mathfrak{d}_n'$, where $\mathfrak{d}_0 = 1$ and for all $1 \leq i \leq n$, $\mathfrak{d}_i'$ is such that $\mathfrak{d}_i = \mathfrak{d}_{i-1} \wedge \mathfrak{d}_i'$.

Hence, we obtained $\mathrm{Hops}(t, s, \mathcal{R}, \mu) = (\sigma_n, \mathfrak{d}_n)$, where $\sigma_n \precsim_{\mathcal{R},\mu}^{Dom(\varphi_1\cdots\varphi_n\tau)} \varphi_1\cdots\varphi_n\tau$, and there exists $\mathfrak{d}_\tau'$ such that $\mathfrak{d}_\tau \leq \mathfrak{d}_1' \wedge \cdots \wedge \mathfrak{d}_n' \wedge \mathfrak{d}_\tau' = \mathfrak{d}_n \wedge \mathfrak{d}_\tau' \leq \mathfrak{d}_n$. Since $Dom(\varphi_1\cdots\varphi_n) \cap Dom(\tau) = \emptyset$ and $\mathtt{fv}(Ran(\varphi_1\cdots\varphi_n)) \cap Dom(\tau) = \emptyset$, the composition $\varphi_1\cdots\varphi_n\tau$ can be also represented as the disjoint union of the set representations of these substitutions: $(\varphi_1\cdots\varphi_n) \uplus \tau$. Therefore, from $\sigma_n \precsim_{\mathcal{R},\mu}^{Dom(\varphi_1\cdots\varphi_n\tau)} \varphi_1\cdots\varphi_n\tau$ we get $\sigma_n \precsim_{\mathcal{R},\mu}^{Dom(\tau)} \tau$. We can take σ_n and $\mathfrak{d}_n$ in the role of σ and $\mathfrak{d}$, respectively, which finishes the proof. $\qquad\square$

4   Discussion

From Fuzzy to Crisp. When $\mu = 1$, we are essentially in the crisp case, and our algorithm can be seen as a rule-based variant of the higher-order pattern unification algorithm [25,27]. It is closer to Nipkow's version [27] as our use of VarElim introduces a form of configuration transformation strategy. On the other hand, our approach is more flexible in selecting which equations to transform, since our rules operate on sets rather than lists. In [27], it was noted that using sets instead of lists would lead to divergence, but with our rules and control, it does not happen. We imitate Nipkow's requirement to work at the head of the list, but only when the left-hand side of the selected equation is a flexible term. Below is an example demonstrating how our algorithm handles problematic equations $\{F =^? c(G), G =^? c(F)\}$ from [27]:

$$\{F \simeq_{\mathcal{R},1}^? c(G),\ G \simeq_{\mathcal{R},1}^? c(F)\}; \varepsilon; 1 \rightsquigarrow_{\mathsf{LF}}$$

Calling VarElim :

$$\{F \simeq^? c(G)\}; \varepsilon \rightsquigarrow_{\mathsf{VE1}}$$

$$\{H \simeq^? G\}; \{F \mapsto c(H)\} \rightsquigarrow_{\mathsf{VE2}}$$

$$\emptyset; \{F \mapsto c(G),\ H \mapsto G\}$$

$$\{G \simeq^?_{\mathcal{R},1} c(c(G))\}; \{F \mapsto c(G)\}; 1 \rightsquigarrow_{\mathsf{Fail}}$$
$$\bot.$$

Hence, HOPS fails, as expected.

It should also be mentioned that our rules allow a rather simple termination measure that facilitates the direct termination proof (instead of translating the problem into first-order unification).

T-Norms. Note that using the minimum T-norm (in fact, its idempotence property) is important for the completeness of the algorithm as well as for computing unifiers with the maximum approximation degree. (This is not specific to the higher-order case: it holds even in the first-order case.) The condition $(\partial \wedge \mathcal{R}(f,g)) > \mu$ in the decomposition rule (which is the rule actually computing degrees) is general and applies to any T-norm. For nonidempotent T-norms, we should treat unification problems as multisets. However, even under this modification, the algorithm would be incomplete. To illustrate this, consider a simple similarity relation $\mathcal{R}(a,b) = 0.5$ and the product T-norm defined as $s_1 \wedge s_2 = s_1 * s_2$. Let $t = f(X,X,X)$, $s = f(a,b,b)$, and the cut value $\mu = 0.3$. Then the unification problem $t \simeq^?_{\mathcal{R},\mu} s$ has a unifier $\{X \mapsto b\}$, because $\mathcal{R}(f(b,b,b), f(a,b,b)) = 0.5 > 0.3$. However, the (modified) algorithm fails to compute it:

$$\{\!\{f(X,X,X) \simeq^?_{\mathcal{R},0.3} f(a,b,b)\}\!\}; \varepsilon; 1 \rightsquigarrow_{\mathsf{Dec}}$$
$$\{\!\{X \simeq^?_{\mathcal{R},0.3} a, X \simeq^?_{\mathcal{R},0.3} b, X \simeq^?_{\mathcal{R},0.3} b\}\!\}; \varepsilon; 1 \rightsquigarrow_{\mathsf{LF}}$$
$$\{\!\{a \simeq^?_{\mathcal{R},0.3} b, a \simeq^?_{\mathcal{R},0.3} b\}\!\}; \{X \mapsto a\}; 1 \rightsquigarrow_{\mathsf{Dec}}$$
$$\{\!\{a \simeq^?_{\mathcal{R},0.3} b\}\!\}; \{X \mapsto a\}; 0.5 \rightsquigarrow_{\mathsf{Fail}}$$
$$\bot$$

The computation stops with failure because the decomposition attempt of a and b would involve the check $0.5 * \mathcal{R}(a,b) \geq 0.3$, which fails since $0.5 * \mathcal{R}(a,b) = 0.5 * 0.5 = 0.25 < 0.3$.

For a lower cut value, e.g., $\mu = 0.1$, the algorithm would compute a solution $\{X \mapsto a\}$ with degree 0.25, failing to discover that there exists another unifier, $\{X \mapsto b\}$, with a better degree 0.3.

However, if we consider only linear unification problems (i.e., those where no free variable occurs more than once), the modified algorithm is complete and computes a unifier with the highest degree even for nonidempotent T-norms.

It is possible to regain completeness for nonidempotent T-norms for the general case by modifying the subprocedure VarElim: In the VE1 rule, allow the variable F to be replaced not only by the term

$$\lambda x_1, \ldots, x_n.a(H_1(x_1, \ldots, x_n), \ldots, H_m(x_1, \ldots, x_n)),$$

but by any term (non-deterministically)

$$\lambda x_1, \ldots, x_n.b(H_1(x_1, \ldots, x_n), \ldots, H_m(x_1, \ldots, x_n))$$

where b is similar to a (provided that it still keeps the degree computed so far above the cut value). The computed degree should be also changed accordingly. Such a modification would lead to multiple (finitely many) most general unifiers, out of which one would need to keep only those that have the highest unification degrees. A detailed discussion of this algorithm goes beyond the scope of this paper, though.

5   Conclusion

We studied unification of higher-order patterns modulo fuzzy similarity relations, using the minimum T-norm. This problem, like its classical (crisp) counterpart, is unitary. We developed a rule-based unification algorithm and proved its termination, soundness, and completeness. The computed most general unifier has the best approximation degree. Our work extends, on one hand, the well-known higher-order pattern unification [25,27] to accommodate fuzzy similarity relations. On the other hand, it generalizes the weak unification algorithm [32] from first-order terms to simply-typed lambda terms.

There are some interesting directions for future work, which involve both practical applications and further theoretical developments:

- Incorporating the unification algorithm developed in this paper into a higher-order fuzzy logic programming formalism combining the powers of languages like Lambda-Prolog [26] and FASILL [13]. It can serve as a foundation of a flexible higher-order knowledge-based system.
- Relaxing similarity relations to adapt to more diverse scenarios. One possibility is, e.g., lifting the transitivity requirement and considering proximity relations. This can lead to the generalization of block-based [15] or class-based [20,30] approximate unification algorithms to the higher-order setting. Another option is defining approximation based on (Lawverean) quantales like in quantitative algebras and generalizing the results from [7] to a higher-order case.

Acknowledgments. This work was supported by the Austrian Science Fund (FWF) project P 35530, and NATO Science for Peace and Security (SPS) Programme G6133.

Disclosure of Interests. The authors have no competing interests to declare that are relevant to the content of this article.

References

1. Aït-Kaci, H., Pasi, G.: Fuzzy lattice operations on first-order terms over signatures with similar constructors: a constraint-based approach. Fuzzy Sets Syst. **391**, 1–46 (2020). https://doi.org/10.1016/J.FSS.2019.03.019
2. Barendregt, H., Manzonetto, G.: A Lambda Calculus Satellite. College Publications (2022)

3. Dershowitz, N., Manna, Z.: Proving termination with multiset orderings. Commun. ACM **22**(8), 465–476 (1979). https://doi.org/10.1145/359138.359142
4. Dowek, G.: Higher-order unification and matching. In: Robinson, J.A., Voronkov, A. (eds.) Handbook of Automated Reasoning (in 2 volumes), pp. 1009–1062. Elsevier and MIT Press (2001). https://doi.org/10.1016/B978-044450813-3/50018-7
5. Dundua, B., Kutsia, T.: Higher-order pattern unification modulo similarity relations. CoRR arxiv:2507.13208 (2025). https://doi.org/10.48550/ARXIV.2507.13208
6. Dundua, B., Kutsia, T., Marin, M., Pau, C.: Constraint solving over multiple similarity relations. In: Ariola, Z.M. (ed.) 5th International Conference on Formal Structures for Computation and Deduction, FSCD 2020, Paris, France (Virtual Conference), 29 June–6 July 2020. LIPIcs, vol. 167, pp. 30:1–30:19. Schloss Dagstuhl - Leibniz-Zentrum für Informatik (2020). https://doi.org/10.4230/LIPICS.FSCD.2020.30
7. Ehling, G., Kutsia, T.: Solving quantitative equations. In: Benzmüller, C., Heule, M.J.H., Schmidt, R.A. (eds.) Automated Reasoning - 12th International Joint Conference, IJCAR 2024, Nancy, France, 3–6 July 2024, Proceedings, Part II. Lecture Notes in Computer Science, vol. 14740, pp. 381–400. Springer, Heidelberg (2024). https://doi.org/10.1007/978-3-031-63501-4_20
8. Fontana, F.A., Formato, F.: Likelog: a logic programming language for flexible data retrieval. In: Bryant, B.R., Lamont, G.B., Haddad, H., Carroll, J.H. (eds.) Proceedings of the 1999 ACM Symposium on Applied Computing, SAC'99, San Antonio, Texas, USA, 28 February–2 March 1999, pp. 260–267. ACM (1999). https://doi.org/10.1145/298151.298348
9. Fontana, F.A., Formato, F.: A similarity-based resolution rule. Int. J. Intell. Syst. **17**(9), 853–872 (2002). https://doi.org/10.1002/int.10067
10. Formato, F., Gerla, G., Sessa, M.I.: Extension of logic programming by similarity. In: Meo, M.C., Vilares Ferro, M. (eds.) 1999 Joint Conference on Declarative Programming, AGP'99, L'Aquila, Italy, 6–9 September 1999, pp. 397–410 (1999)
11. Formato, F., Gerla, G., Sessa, M.I.: Similarity-based unification. Fund. Inf. **41**(4), 393–414 (2000). https://doi.org/10.3233/FI-2000-41402
12. Guerrero, J.A., Moreno, G., Riaza, J.A., Sanchez, J.: Smart design of similarity relations for fuzzy logic programming environments. In: IEEE Symposium Series on Computational Intelligence, SSCI 2018, Bangalore, India, 18–21 November 2018, pp. 220–227. IEEE (2018). https://doi.org/10.1109/SSCI.2018.8628871
13. Julián Iranzo, P., Moreno, G., Riaza, J.A.: The fuzzy logic programming language FASILL: design and implementation. Int. J. Approx. Reason. **125**, 139–168 (2020). https://doi.org/10.1016/J.IJAR.2020.06.002
14. Julián Iranzo, P., Moreno, G., Riaza, J.A.: Some properties of substitutions in the framework of similarity relations. Fuzzy Sets Syst. **465**, 108510 (2023). https://doi.org/10.1016/J.FSS.2023.03.013
15. Julián-Iranzo, P., Rubio-Manzano, C.: Proximity-based unification theory. Fuzzy Sets Syst. **262**, 21–43 (2015). https://doi.org/10.1016/j.fss.2014.07.006
16. Julián Iranzo, P., Rubio-Manzano, C.: A sound and complete semantics for a similarity-based logic programming language. Fuzzy Sets Syst. **317**, 1–26 (2017). https://doi.org/10.1016/j.fss.2016.12.016
17. Julián Iranzo, P., Sáenz-Pérez, F.: An efficient proximity-based unification algorithm. In: 2018 IEEE International Conference on Fuzzy Systems, FUZZ-IEEE 2018, Rio de Janeiro, Brazil, 8–13 July 2018, pp. 1–8. IEEE (2018). https://doi.org/10.1109/FUZZ-IEEE.2018.8491593

18. Julián Iranzo, P., Sáenz-Pérez, F.: Bousi~Prolog: design and implementation of a proximity-based fuzzy logic programming language. Expert Syst. Appl. **213**(Part), 118858 (2023). https://doi.org/10.1016/J.ESWA.2022.118858
19. Krajči, S., Lencses, R., Medina, J., Ojeda-Aciego, M., Vojtáš, P.: A similarity-based unification model for flexible querying. In: Carbonell, J.G., Siekmann, J., Andreasen, T., Christiansen, H., Motro, A., Legind Larsen, H. (eds.) FQAS 2002. LNCS (LNAI), vol. 2522, pp. 263–273. Springer, Heidelberg (2002). https://doi.org/10.1007/3-540-36109-X_21
20. Kutsia, T., Pau, C.: Solving proximity constraints. In: Gabbrielli, M. (ed.) LOPSTR 2019. LNCS, vol. 12042, pp. 107–122. Springer, Cham (2020). https://doi.org/10.1007/978-3-030-45260-5_7
21. Loia, V., Senatore, S., Sessa, M.I.: Similarity-based SLD resolution and its role for web knowledge discovery. Fuzzy Sets Syst. **144**(1), 151–171 (2004). https://doi.org/10.1016/J.FSS.2003.10.018
22. Maruyama, Y.: Higher-order fuzzy logics and their categorical semantics: Higher-order linear completeness and Baaz translation via substructural tripos theory. In: 30th IEEE International Conference on Fuzzy Systems, FUZZ-IEEE 2021, Luxembourg, 11–14 July 2021, pp. 1–6. IEEE (2021). https://doi.org/10.1109/FUZZ45933.2021.9494453
23. Medina, J., Ojeda-Aciego, M., Vojtás, P.: Similarity-based unification: a multi-adjoint approach. Fuzzy Sets Syst. **146**(1), 43–62 (2004). https://doi.org/10.1016/j.fss.2003.11.005
24. Milanese, G.C., Pasi, G.: Similarity-based reasoning with order-sorted feature logic. IEEE Trans. Fuzzy Syst. **32**(5), 2797–2810 (2024). https://doi.org/10.1109/TFUZZ.2024.3362897
25. Miller, D.: A logic programming language with lambda-abstraction, function variables, and simple unification. J. Log. Comput. **1**(4), 497–536 (1991). https://doi.org/10.1093/LOGCOM/1.4.497
26. Miller, D., Nadathur, G.: Programming with Higher-Order Logic. Cambridge University Press, Cambridge (2012). https://doi.org/10.1017/CBO9781139021326
27. Nipkow, T.: Functional unification of higher-order patterns. In: Proceedings of the Eighth Annual Symposium on Logic in Computer Science (LICS '93), Montreal, Canada, 19–23 June 1993, pp. 64–74. IEEE Computer Society (1993). https://doi.org/10.1109/LICS.1993.287599
28. Novák, V.: Elements of model theory in higher-order fuzzy logic. Fuzzy Sets Syst. **205**, 101–115 (2012). https://doi.org/10.1016/J.FSS.2012.03.006
29. Pau, C.: Symbolic Techniques for Approximate Reasoning. Ph.D. thesis, Research Institute for Symbolic Computation, Johannes Kepler University Linz, Austria (2022)
30. Pau, C., Kutsia, T.: Proximity-based unification and matching for fully fuzzy signatures. In: 30th IEEE International Conference on Fuzzy Systems, FUZZ-IEEE 2021, Luxembourg, 11–14 July 2021, pp. 1–6. IEEE (2021). https://doi.org/10.1109/FUZZ45933.2021.9494438
31. Sandri, S.A., Mendonça, J., Martins-Bedé, F.T., Guimarães, R., Carvalho, O.S.: Weighted fuzzy similarity relations in case-based reasoning: a case study in classification. In: FUZZ-IEEE 2012, IEEE International Conference on Fuzzy Systems, Brisbane, Australia, 10–15 June 2012, Proceedings, pp. 1–7. IEEE (2012). https://doi.org/10.1109/FUZZ-IEEE.2012.6251149
32. Sessa, M.I.: Approximate reasoning by similarity-based SLD resolution. Theor. Comput. Sci. **275**(1–2), 389–426 (2002). https://doi.org/10.1016/S0304-3975(01)00188-8

33. Virtanen, H.: Vague domains, S-unification, logic programming. Electr. Notes Theor. Comput. Sci. **66**(5), 86–103 (2002). https://doi.org/10.1016/S1571-0661(04)80516-4

34. Vojtás, P.: Declarative and procedural semantics of fuzzy similarity based unification. Kybernetika **36**(6), 707–720 (2000). http://www.kybernetika.cz/content/2000/6/707

A Completion Procedure for Equational Rewriting Systems with Binders

Maribel Fernández[1] , Daniele Nantes-Sobrinho[2] ,
and Daniella Santaguida[2]([✉])

[1] Department of Informatics, King's College London, London, UK
`maribel.fernandez@kcl.ac.uk`
[2] Department of Mathematics, University of Brasília, Brasília, Brazil
`dnantes@unb.br, daniella@mat.unb.br`

Abstract. Completion of first-order rewriting has been extensively studied; however, challenges remain in languages that include binders – addressing them is crucial to enable theorem proving applications. In practice, the α-equivalence generated by the binders has to be combined with an $\mathcal{E}$-equivalence generated by equational axioms. The extension of first-order rewriting to work modulo both α-equivalence and equational axioms $\mathcal{E}$ is not straightforward: particular care is needed when dealing with freshness constraints and renamings, since these can interact with $\mathcal{E}$. In this paper, we define equational nominal rewrite systems (ENRSs) and present a critical pair theorem and a generalised notion of closedness. In addition, we design a completion procedure for closed ENRSs, based on a generalisation of the recursive path ordering, using a novel notion of irrelevance of freshness contexts.

Keywords: Nominal rewriting · Equational Theories · Completion

1 Introduction

Term rewriting provides efficient techniques to work with equations [2,22]. Rewriting can help decide equality of terms within an equational theory $\mathcal{E}$, provided the set of equational axioms can be oriented to create a confluent and terminating, i.e., convergent, set of rules. Completion procedures [16] can be used to try to transform a rewrite system into an equivalent convergent one; however, some axioms cannot be oriented to define a convergent system (e.g., commutativity) [3,19]. In this case, *equational rewriting* (rewriting modulo $\mathcal{E}$) can help.

Some equational theories are generated by identities containing binding operators such as the (η) identity for the λ-calculus, the $\forall$-scope in/ex-trusion or the $\forall$-commute in first-order logic:

$$
\begin{aligned}
(\eta) \quad & \lambda a.Ma \approx M, \text{ if } a \notin fv(M) \\
(\forall\text{-scope}) \quad & \forall a.(\varphi \wedge \psi) \approx \varphi \wedge (\forall a.\psi), \text{ if } a \notin fv(\varphi) \\
(\forall\text{-com}) \quad & \forall a.\forall b.\varphi \approx \forall b.\forall a.\varphi
\end{aligned}
\tag{1}
$$

This study was financed in part by the Coordenação de Aperfeiçoamento de Pessoal de Nível Superior - Brasil (CAPES) - Finance Code 001.

S. Escobar and L. Titolo (Eds.): LOPSTR 2025, LNCS 16117, pp. 94–112, 2026.
https://doi.org/10.1007/978-3-032-04848-6_6

where $fv(-)$ denotes the set of free variables of $-$. Theories including these identities require reasoning modulo α-equality under freshness constraints. Note that the ($\forall$-scope) also requires reasoning modulo associativity and commutativity of $\wedge$. Some identities are better used when oriented as rewriting rules and others are better left to work modulo their congruence [21] as, for e.g., orienting a commutative identity as a rewriting rule leads to non-termination.

The nominal framework [9] stands out as an effective approach for managing languages with binders, such as the λ-calculus and first-order logic (FOL). In this framework, equality directly corresponds to α-equivalence, denoted as $\approx_\alpha$, and freshness constraints are seamlessly integrated into nominal reasoning rather than being pushed to the meta-language. For example, the expression $a\#X$ (read "a is fresh for X") states that the name a cannot occur free in X. This way, the identities in 1 can be formally specified.

Nominal rewriting modulo $\mathcal{E}$ is challenging, due to the interplay between the theory of α-equivalence and $\mathcal{E}$. Special care is needed when extending well-known properties, such as sufficient conditions for confluence and termination, which are used in completion procedures. The first difficulty arises because there are always infinite classes of terms due to α-renaming. For example, for a binary symbol R we have $\forall[a]R(a,b) \approx_\alpha \forall[c]R(c,b) \approx_\alpha \ldots$ for infinite countable atoms. The second and trickier challenge is that the α-equivalence classes of terms with variables are defined under freshness constraints. For example, the α-equivalence class of $\forall[a]R(a,X)$ contains itself and also $\forall[c]R(c,X)$ under the freshness constraints $a\#X$ and $c\#X$. With more constraints, we may have more elements in the class. This behaviour cannot be mimicked in first- or higher-order approaches as, for e.g. freshness constraints are not handled by their languages.

In this paper, we consider nominal rewriting modulo equational theories (ENRS) and investigate fundamental properties such as confluence and termination (convergence). Our framework extends the classical notion of equational rewriting, as developed by Stickel and Lankford [17,20], to languages with binders. We also present a novel completion procedure designed to transform a given ENRS into an equivalent convergent one. Our focus is on closed ENRSs—systems in which no free atoms appear in rules or equations—as they offer high expressive power and correspond to higher-order rewriting systems [6].

Contributions. We provide definitions of rewriting, critical pairs, confluence and termination, taking into account an equational theory $\mathcal{E}$ for a language with binders. First, we establish conditions for the decidability of $\mathcal{R}\cup\mathcal{E}\cup\alpha$-equivalence (Thm. 1), closure is fundamental for this result, as it avoids investigating all possible renamings of rules. Second, we give a novel formulation of a nominal version of the Critical Pair Theorem modulo $\mathcal{E}$ for closed ENRSs (Thm. 2). Building on this, we design a completion procedure for closed ENRSs in the style of Bachmair and Dershowitz (Fig. 3). This procedure incorporates a simplification step based on a novel notion of irrelevance of contexts (Def. 7) which is defined using the *semantics* of critical pairs. This notion allows us to disregard freshness constraints that are not semantically meaningful within the context of a rule.

2   Preliminaries

We briefly recall some basic definitions. For more details, we refer to [8]. We will use $\equiv$ for syntactic equality, $=$ for definitions and $\approx_\alpha$ for α-equality.

Syntax. Fix countable infinite pairwise disjoint sets of *atoms* $\mathbb{A} = \{a, b, c, \dots\}$ and *variables* $\mathcal{X} = \{X, Y, Z, \dots\}$. Atoms follow the *atom convention*: atoms $a, b, c, \dots$ over $\mathbb{A}$ represent different names. Let Σ be a finite set of term-formers $f : n$, disjoint from $\mathbb{A}$ and $\mathcal{X}$, where n is the arity of f. A *permutation* π is a bijection on $\mathbb{A}$ with finite domain. The identity permutation is denoted id. The composition of π and π' is denoted $\pi \circ \pi'$ and π^{-1} denotes the inverse of π.

Nominal terms are defined by the grammar: $s, t, u ::= a \mid \pi \cdot X \mid [a]t \mid f(t_1, \dots, t_n)$, where a is an *atom*, $\pi \cdot X$ is a variable, $[a]t$ is the *abstraction* of a in the term t, and $f(t_1, \dots, t_n)$, sometimes denoted as $f(\overline{t_n})$, is a *function application* with $f \in \Sigma$ and $f : n$. We abbreviate $id \cdot X$ as X. We write $V(-)$ and $A(-)$ to denote the set of variables and the set of atoms, respectively, of $-$. A term is *ground* if $V(t) = \emptyset$. The set $\mathcal{P}os(t)$ of *positions* of a term t is defined as expected. Non-variable positions are called *ground*. The *subterm* of t at position p is denoted by $t|_p$ and $s[t]_p$ is the term obtained by replacing the subterm of s in position p by t.

The *action* of π on a term t is defined inductively: $\pi \cdot a = \pi(a)$, $\pi \cdot (\pi' \cdot X) = (\pi \circ \pi') \cdot X$, $\pi \cdot [a]t = [\pi \cdot a](\pi \cdot t)$, $\pi \cdot f(t) = f(\pi \cdot t)$. The *meta-action of permutation* π over a term t, denoted as t^π, consists of the term obtained by applying π to the atoms of t. A *substitution* θ is a mapping from a finite set of variables to terms, its action on terms is defined inductively: $a\theta = a$, $(\pi \cdot X)\theta = \pi \cdot (X\theta)$, $([a]t)\theta = [a](t\theta)$, and $f(t)\theta = f(t\theta)$. The identity substitution is denoted Id; composition of substitutions is denoted by simple juxtaposition.

There are two kinds of constraints: (alpha-)equality, written $s \approx_\alpha t$, and freshness, written $a\#t$. *Primitive constraints* have the form $a\#X$ and ∇, Δ denote finite sets of primitive constraints. We write Δ, ∇ to denote the union of both sets, and $a, b\#X$ to denote the set $\{a\#X, b\#X\}$. *Judgements* have the form $\Delta \vdash s \approx_\alpha t$ or $\Delta \vdash a\#t$ and are derived using the rules in Fig. 1. The *difference set* of two permutations $ds(\pi, \pi') := \{n \mid \pi \cdot n \neq \pi' \cdot n\}$. In rule $(\approx_\alpha \text{X})$, the expression $ds(\pi, \pi')\#X$ represents the set of constraints $\{n\#X \mid n \in ds(\pi, \pi')\}$.

A *term in context* $\Delta \vdash t$ expresses that the term t has the freshness constraints Δ. For example, $a\#X \vdash f(X, h(b))$ indicates that a cannot occur free in instances of X, that is, if a occurs inside X, it must be under an abstraction. A problem Pr is a set of constraints and we write $\Delta \vdash Pr$ when for all $P \in Pr$ there is a proof using the rules in Fig. 1, taking elements of the context Δ as assumptions. Given a finite set of freshness constraints Δ, θ and π, $\Delta\theta = \{a\#X\theta \mid a\#X \in \Delta\}$, $\langle \Delta\theta \rangle_{nf}$ denotes the least freshness context such that $\langle \Delta\theta \rangle_{nf} \vdash \Delta\theta$ (if one exists) and $\Delta^\pi = \{\pi(a)\#X \mid a\#X \in \Delta\}$.

Nominal $\alpha, \mathcal{E}$-Equality and Unification. A nominal *identity* $\nabla \vdash l \approx r$ consists of a pair of nominal terms l and r under a (possibly empty) freshness context ∇. For example, we can express $\forall$-scope extrusion using the nominal identity

$$\frac{}{\Delta \vdash a \# b}\ (\#\mathrm{A}) \qquad \frac{(\pi^{-1} \cdot (a) \# X) \in \Delta}{\Delta \vdash a \# \pi \cdot X}\ (\#\mathrm{X}) \qquad \frac{}{\Delta \vdash a \# [a] t}\ (\#\mathrm{ABA})$$

$$\frac{\Delta \vdash a \# [b] t}{\Delta \vdash a \# t}\ (\#\mathrm{ABB}) \qquad \frac{\Delta \vdash a \# t_1 \quad \cdots \quad \Delta \vdash a \# t_n}{\Delta \vdash a \# f(t_1, \cdots, t_n)}\ (\#\mathrm{F})$$

$$\frac{}{\Delta \vdash a \approx_\alpha a}\ (\approx_\alpha \mathrm{A}) \qquad \frac{ds(\pi, \pi') \# X \in \Delta}{\Delta \vdash \pi \cdot X \approx_\alpha \pi' \cdot X}\ (\approx_\alpha \mathrm{X}) \qquad \frac{\Delta \vdash s \approx_\alpha t}{\Delta \vdash [a] s \approx_\alpha [a] t}\ (\approx_\alpha \mathrm{ABA})$$

$$\frac{\Delta \vdash s_1 \approx_\alpha t_1 \ \cdots \Delta \vdash s_n \approx_\alpha t_n}{\Delta \vdash f(s_1, \cdots, s_n) \approx_\alpha f(t_1, \cdots, t_n)}\ (\approx_\alpha \mathrm{F}) \qquad \frac{\Delta \vdash s \approx_\alpha (a\ b) \cdot t \quad \Delta \vdash a \# t}{\Delta \vdash [a] s \approx_\alpha [b] t}\ (\approx_\alpha \mathrm{ABB})$$

Fig. 1. Rules for $\#$ and $\approx_\alpha$.

$\mathcal{E}_\forall = \{a \# X \vdash \forall [a] X \approx X\}$. As a is an object-level variable, its name is irrelevant, therefore, this identity could be written using a different name, say $b, c, \ldots$. We use the meta-action of a permutation to rename atoms in identities: for example, $\mathcal{E}_\forall^{(a\ c)} = \{c \# X \vdash \forall [c] X \approx X\}$. In fact, we implicitly work with the *equivariant closure* of identities: *eq-closure*$(\mathcal{E}) = \{E^{(a\ b)} \mid E \in \mathcal{E}$ for all atoms $a, b \in \mathbb{A}\}$. From now on, $\mathcal{E}$ denotes the equivariant closure of the identities in $\mathcal{E}$.

The *equational theory* generated by $\mathcal{E}$ under Δ, denoted $\Delta \vdash s \approx_{\alpha, \mathcal{E}} t$, is the least transitive reflexive symmetric relation such that for some $(\nabla \vdash l \approx r) \in \mathcal{E}$, position p, substitution θ, and fresh context[1] Γ (so if $a \# X \in \Gamma$ then a is not mentioned in Δ, s, t):

$$\frac{\Delta, \Gamma \vdash \nabla\theta, \qquad \Delta, \Gamma \vdash s|_p \approx_\alpha l\theta, \qquad \Delta, \Gamma \vdash s[r\theta]_p \approx_\alpha t}{\Delta \vdash s \approx_{\alpha, \mathcal{E}} t}\ (Ax_\mathcal{E})$$

By abuse of language we write $\mathcal{E}$ to refer to both the set of identities and its equational theory. From now on, we will write simply $\approx_\mathcal{E}$ instead of $\approx_{\alpha, \mathcal{E}}$. The class of a term t with variables is defined under context, say ∇: $[(\nabla, t)]_{\alpha, \mathcal{E}} = \{t' \mid \nabla \vdash t \approx_{\alpha, \mathcal{E}} t'\}$. The class of a ground term t will be denoted simply as $[t]_{\alpha, \mathcal{E}}$ instead of $[(\emptyset, t)]_{\alpha, \mathcal{E}}$. Below, $\mathcal{E}(g)$ denotes the equational theory of the symbol g. From now on, we will write $\mathcal{C}$ to denote the equational theory for commutativity.

Remark 1 (On the cardinality of $\alpha, \mathcal{E}$-equivalence classes). The $\alpha, \mathcal{E}$-equivalence classes of ground nominal terms with abstracted atoms are always infinite. Terms without abstracted atoms may have a finite class depending on $\mathcal{E}$. The cardinality of the class of a term with variables depends on a given freshness constraint.

Example 1. Consider the empty theory $\mathcal{E} = \emptyset$, we have $[f(a, b)]_\alpha = \{f(a, b)\}$. For the commutative theory $\mathcal{C}(g)$, the class of $g(a, b)$ is $[g(a, b)]_{\alpha, \mathcal{C}} = \{g(a, b), g(b, a)\}$. For $\mathcal{N}(h) = \{h(X, 0) \approx 0\}$, one example is the class of $h(a, 0)$: $[h(a, 0)]_{\alpha, \mathcal{N}} = \{0, h(a, 0), h(a, h(a, 0)), \ldots\}$. Terms with variables are tricky: $[(\emptyset, g([a] X, b)]_{\alpha, \mathcal{C}} =$

---

[1] For more details about the need of this fresh context see [10].

$\{g([a]X, b), g(b, [a]X)\}$. The term $g([c]X, b)$ is not in the class: we cannot prove $\emptyset \vdash g([a]X, b) \approx_{\alpha, \mathcal{C}} g([c]X, b)$ as it requires $a, c \# X$. However, under the given context $\nabla = \{a, c \# X\}$, the class of the term $g([a]X, b)$ is $[(\nabla, g([a]X, b))]_{\alpha, \mathcal{C}} = \{g([a]X, b), g(b, [a]X), g([c]X, b), g(b, [c]X)\}$

An $\mathcal{E}$-unification problem (in-context) $\mathcal{P}$ is a finite set of equations of the form $(\nabla \vdash l) \stackrel{\mathcal{E}}{\underset{?}{\approx}} (\Delta \vdash s)$. The pair (Δ', θ) is an $\mathcal{E}$-solution (or $\mathcal{E}$-unifier) of $\mathcal{P}$ iff (Δ', θ) solves every equation in $\mathcal{P}$ that is, for each $(\nabla \vdash l) \stackrel{\mathcal{E}}{\underset{?}{\approx}} (\Delta \vdash s)$ the following properties hold: (i) $\Delta' \vdash \nabla\theta$ (ii) $\Delta' \vdash \Delta\theta$; and (iii) $\Delta' \vdash l\theta \approx_{\mathcal{E}} s\theta$. If there is no (Δ', θ), then we say that $\mathcal{P}$ is *unsolvable*. $\mathcal{U}_{\mathcal{E}}(\mathcal{P})$ denotes the set of E-unifiers of $\mathcal{P}$. Minimal complete sets of E-unifiers are defined in the standard way. We say $\mathcal{E}$ is *finitary* if there exists an $\mathcal{E}$-unification algorithm that computes a finite minimal complete set of $\mathcal{E}$-unifiers.

An $\mathcal{E}$-*matching problem*, denoted $(\nabla \vdash l) \stackrel{\mathcal{E}}{\underset{?}{\approx}} (\Delta \vdash s)$, is a particular kind of $\mathcal{E}$-unification problem where substitutions apply only to one side (here, left).

Example 2 (A simple $\mathcal{C}$-unification problem). Consider the $\mathcal{C}$-unification problem in-context $(a \# X \vdash f^{\mathcal{C}}(X, b)) \stackrel{\mathcal{C}}{\underset{?}{\approx}} (\emptyset \vdash f^{\mathcal{C}}(Y, [b]Z))$. This problem has only one $\mathcal{C}$-solution, $(\{a \# Z\}, [X \mapsto [b]Z, Y \mapsto b])$ as there is not instance of Z that can unify the abstraction $[b]Z$ with the atom b.

Closed Nominal Rewriting. A nominal rewrite rule $R \equiv \nabla \vdash l \to r$ is a tuple of a freshness context ∇ and terms l, r such that $V(r, \nabla) \subseteq V(l)$. For efficiency, we will work with closed rewrite systems. First, we define the concept of a *freshened variant* of a term or a context: given a term t, we say that t'' is a *freshened variant* of t when t'' has the same structure of t, except that the atoms and unknowns have been replaced by 'fresh' ones. Similarly, ∇'' will denote a freshened variant of ∇, that is, if $a \# X \in \nabla$ then $a'' \# X'' \in \nabla''$ where a'' and X'' are chosen fresh. This notion naturally extends to other syntactic objects such as equality and rewrite judgements.

Example 3. $[a''][b'']X''$ is a freshened variant of $[a][b]X$. Also $a'' \# X''$ is a freshened variant of $a \# X$, and $\emptyset \vdash f([a'']X'') \to [a'']X''$ is a freshened variant of $\emptyset \vdash f([a]X) \to [a]X$. Neither $[a''][a'']X''$ nor $[a''][b'']X$ are freshened variants of $[a][b]X$.

A term-in-context $\nabla \vdash l$ is *closed* if there exists a solution for the matching problem $(\nabla'' \vdash l'') \stackrel{}{\underset{?}{\approx}} (\nabla, A(\nabla'', l'') \# V(\nabla, l) \vdash l)$. A rule $R = (\nabla \vdash l \to r)$ and an identity $E = (\nabla \vdash l \approx r)$ are *closed* when $\nabla \vdash (l, r)$ is closed. Intuitively, in closed terms there are no occurrences of free atoms and closed axioms are identities between closed terms. Closed axioms do not allow abstracted atoms to become free. E.g., the rule $R \equiv \emptyset \vdash [a]f(a, X) \to a$ is not closed because there is no solution to $(\emptyset \vdash [a']f(a', X'), a') \stackrel{}{\underset{?}{\approx}} (a' \# X \vdash [a]f(a, X), a)$.

Let $\mathcal{R}$ be a set of closed rules. The *one-step closed rewrite relation* $\Delta \vdash s \to_{\mathcal{R}} t$ is the least relation such that for some $R = (\nabla \vdash l \to r) \in \mathcal{R}$ and term-in-context $\Delta \vdash s$, there is some R'' a freshened variant of R (so fresh for R, Δ, s, t), position p, and substitution θ, such that the following hold:

$$\frac{\Delta, A(R^\pi)\#V(\Delta, s, t) \vdash (\nabla^\pi\theta, \ s|_p \approx_\alpha l^\pi\theta, \ s[r^\pi\theta]_p \approx_\alpha t)}{\Delta \vdash s \to t}$$

Write $\Delta \vdash s \leftrightarrow_\mathcal{R} t$ and $\Delta \vdash s \to^*_\mathcal{R} t$ to denote the symmetric and the reflexive-transitive closure of $\to_\mathcal{R}$, respectively.

3   Closed Nominal Rewriting Modulo $\mathcal{E}$

In this section, we consider the notion of *closed* nominal rewriting modulo an equational theory $\mathcal{E}$ and consider the theory defined by $\mathcal{R} \cup \{\alpha\} \cup \mathcal{E}$, where $\mathcal{R}$ is a set of closed rewrite rules and $\mathcal{E}$ is a set of closed identities. First, we define the relations $\to_{\mathcal{R}/\mathcal{E}}$ and $\to_{\mathcal{R},\mathcal{E}}$, which operate under freshness constraints, and modulo renaming of abstracted atoms. Second, we extend to the nominal framework standard properties of rewriting such as termination, confluence and Church-Rosser modulo $\mathcal{E}$. Due to the unlimited availability of atom renamings in the equivariant closure of identities, we are always dealing with an infinite set of rewriting rules $\mathcal{R}$ and there are always $\approx_\mathcal{E}$-equivalence classes that are infinite. Thus, first-order approaches do not trivially extend to our setting.

3.1   Nominal Rewriting Relations

A closed *equational nominal rewrite system* (ENRS) is built from a set of closed nominal identities $\mathcal{T}$ that can be partitioned into two components as follows: a set $\mathcal{R}$ of closed rewrite rules of the form $\nabla \vdash l \to r$, and a set $\mathcal{E}$ of (unordered) closed identities. We denote this decomposition as $\mathcal{R} \cup \alpha \cup \mathcal{E}$, or more concisely, $\mathcal{R} \cup \mathcal{E}_\alpha$. Following the standard idea [12,20], we will work with $\alpha, \mathcal{E}$-equivalence classes, and work with individual terms as representatives of their class.

Definition 1 (Closed Nominal $\mathcal{R}/\mathcal{E}$-rewriting). *Let $\mathcal{R} \cup \mathcal{E}_\alpha$ be a closed ENRS. The relation $\to_{\mathcal{R}/\mathcal{E}}$ is induced by the composition $\approx_\mathcal{E} \circ \to_\mathcal{R} \circ \approx_\mathcal{E}$. A nominal term-in-context $\Delta \vdash s$ reduces with $\to_{\mathcal{R}/\mathcal{E}}$, when a term in its $\mathcal{E}$-equivalence class reduces via $\to_\mathcal{R}$ as below:*

$$\Delta \vdash (s \to_{\mathcal{R}/\mathcal{E}} t) \ \text{iff there exist } s', t' \text{ such that } \Delta \vdash (s \approx_\mathcal{E} s' \to_\mathcal{R} t' \approx_\mathcal{E} t).$$

$\mathcal{R}$ is confluent modulo $\mathcal{E}$ (or $\mathcal{E}$-confluent) iff whenever $\Delta \vdash t \to^*_{\mathcal{R}/\mathcal{E}} u$ and $\Delta \vdash t \to^*_{\mathcal{R}/\mathcal{E}} v$ then there are u' and v' such that $\Delta \vdash u \to^*_{\mathcal{R}/\mathcal{E}} u', \Delta \vdash v \to^*_{\mathcal{R}/\mathcal{E}} v'$, and $\Delta \vdash u' \approx_\mathcal{E} v'$, and we say that u and v are $\mathcal{E}$-joinable, denoted $u\downarrow_{\mathcal{R}/\mathcal{E}}v$ (or just $u\downarrow v$). $\mathcal{R}$ is terminating modulo $\mathcal{E}$ (or $\mathcal{E}$-terminating) iff $\mathcal{R}/\mathcal{E}$ is noetherian, i.e., there is no infinite $\to_{\mathcal{R}/\mathcal{E}}$ sequence. $\mathcal{R}$ is called $\mathcal{E}$-convergent if it is $\mathcal{E}$-confluent and $\mathcal{E}$-terminating. A term t is said to be in $\mathcal{R}/\mathcal{E}$-normal form whenever one cannot apply another step of $\to_{\mathcal{R}/\mathcal{E}}$.

We use a computationally simpler approach [5] which considers $\mathcal{E}$-equivalence classes of the instances of left-sides of rewrite rules. Next, we define relation $\to_{\mathcal{R},\mathcal{E}}$ that deals with nominal $\mathcal{E}$-matching instead of inspecting the whole $\alpha, \mathcal{E}$-congruence class of a term.

Definition 2 (Closed Nominal $\mathcal{R}, \mathcal{E}$-rewriting). *The one-step closed $\mathcal{E}$-rewrite relation $\Delta \vdash s \to_{\mathcal{R},\mathcal{E}} t$ is the least relation such that for some $R = (\nabla \vdash l \to r) \in \mathcal{R}$ and term-in-context $\Delta \vdash s$, there is some R'' a freshened variant of R (so fresh for R, Δ, s, t), position p, and substitution θ, the following hold:*

$$\frac{\Delta, A(R'')\#V(\Delta, s, t) \vdash \left(\nabla''\theta,\ s|_p \approx_{\mathcal{E}} l''\theta,\ s[r''\theta]_p \approx_\alpha t\right)}{\Delta \vdash s \to_{\mathcal{R},\mathcal{E}} t}$$

$\mathcal{R}, \mathcal{E}$ *is* confluent modulo $\mathcal{E}$ *iff whenever $\Delta \vdash t \to^*_{\mathcal{R},\mathcal{E}} u$ and $\Delta \vdash t \to^*_{\mathcal{R},\mathcal{E}} v$ then there are u' and v' such that $\Delta \vdash u \to^*_{\mathcal{R},\mathcal{E}} u'$, $\Delta \vdash v \to^*_{\mathcal{R},\mathcal{E}} v'$, and $\Delta \vdash u' \approx_{\mathcal{E}} v'$, and we say that u and v are $\mathcal{E}$-joinable by $\mathcal{R}, \mathcal{E}$, denoted $u\downarrow_{\mathcal{R},\mathcal{E}} v$. $\mathcal{R}, \mathcal{E}$ is* terminating modulo $\mathcal{E}$ *iff $\mathcal{R}, \mathcal{E}$ is noetherian, i.e., there is no infinite $\to_{\mathcal{R},\mathcal{E}}$ sequence. A term t is said to be in $\mathcal{R}, \mathcal{E}$-normal form whenever one cannot apply another step of $\to_{\mathcal{R},\mathcal{E}}$.*

Example 4 (Prenex normal form rules). Consider the signature of first-order logic $\Sigma = \{\forall, \exists, \neg, \wedge, \vee\}$, let $\mathcal{C} = \{\vdash P \vee Q \approx Q \vee P, \vdash P \wedge Q \approx Q \wedge P\}$ be the commutative theory. The prenex normal form rules are specified by the following set $\mathcal{R}$ of closed nominal rewrite rules:

$R_1 : a\#P \vdash\ P \wedge \forall[a]Q \to \forall[a](P \wedge Q)$ $R_4 : a\#P \vdash\ P \vee \exists[a]Q \to \exists[a](P \vee Q)$
$R_2 : a\#P \vdash\ P \vee \forall[a]Q \to \forall[a](P \vee Q)$ $R_5 :\qquad \vdash\ \neg(\exists[a]Q) \to \forall[a]\neg Q$
$R_3 : a\#P \vdash\ P \wedge \exists[a]Q \to \exists[a](P \wedge Q)$ $R_6 :\qquad \vdash\ \neg(\forall[a]Q) \to \exists[a]\neg Q$

The following is a one-step $\mathcal{C}$-rewrite with rule (R_4):

$$\underbrace{a\#P'}_{\Delta} \vdash S' \vee \underbrace{(\exists[a]Q' \vee P')}_{s|_2} \to_{\mathcal{R},\mathcal{C}} S' \vee (\exists[a](P' \vee Q'))$$

Take $\theta = [P \mapsto P', Q \mapsto Q']$ then: (i) $\Delta \vdash a\#P' = \nabla\theta$; (ii) $s|_2 = \exists[a]Q' \vee P' \approx_{\mathcal{C}} (P \vee \exists[a]Q)\theta = l\theta$; and (iii) $s[r\theta]_2 = s[(\exists[a](P \vee Q))\theta]_2 = S' \vee (\exists[a](P' \vee Q')) \approx_\alpha t$.

In first-order rewriting, it is well established that $\mathcal{R}, \mathcal{E}$-reducibility is decidable if $\mathcal{E}$-matching is decidable [7]. Following the work of Jouannaud et al. [13], a sufficient condition for this decidability is the existence of a finite and complete $\mathcal{E}$-unification algorithm. However, nominal $\mathcal{E}$-unification introduces an additional challenge due to the need to handle α-equality under meta-variables. This significantly complicates the process of obtaining finite and complete sets of nominal $\mathcal{E}$-unifiers. For instance, nominal $\mathcal{C}$-unification is not finitary when solutions are represented using freshness constraints and substitutions [1].

3.2   Decidability of $\mathcal{R} \cup \mathcal{E}_\alpha$-Equivalence

Our goal in this paper is to find a way to decide $\mathcal{R} \cup \mathcal{E}_\alpha$-equivalence using the more efficient relation $\to_{\mathcal{R},\mathcal{E}}$. The main result is established in Theorem 1, and relies on the nominal version of the Church-Rosser modulo $\mathcal{E}$ property for $\mathcal{R}/\mathcal{E}$ and $\mathcal{R}, \mathcal{E}$ rewriting. By definition, $\mathcal{R} \subseteq \mathcal{R}, \mathcal{E} \subseteq \mathcal{R}/\mathcal{E}$. From this inclusion, it follows that if $\mathcal{R}/\mathcal{E}$ is noetherian then $\mathcal{R}, \mathcal{E}$ is as well.

Definition 3 (Church-Rosser modulo $\mathcal{E}$). *Let $\mathcal{R} \cup \mathcal{E}_\alpha$ be an ENRS.*

1. $\mathcal{R}$ *is* Church-Rosser modulo $\mathcal{E}$ *iff for all Δ, s, t such that $\Delta \vdash s \leftrightarrow^*_{\mathcal{R} \cup \mathcal{E}} t$ there are terms s', t' such that $\Delta \vdash s \rightarrow^*_{\mathcal{R}/\mathcal{E}} s' \approx_{\mathcal{E}} t' \leftarrow^*_{\mathcal{R}/\mathcal{E}} t$.*
2. $\mathcal{R}$ *is* $\mathcal{R}, \mathcal{E}$-Church-Rosser modulo $\mathcal{E}$ *iff for all Δ, s, t such that $\Delta \vdash s \leftrightarrow^*_{\mathcal{R} \cup \mathcal{E}} t$ there are terms s', t' such that $\Delta \vdash s \rightarrow^*_{\mathcal{R}, \mathcal{E}} s' \approx_{\mathcal{E}} t' \leftarrow^*_{\mathcal{R}, \mathcal{E}} t$.*

The next result establishes a relation between the two forms of Church-Rosser modulo $\mathcal{E}$:

Lemma 1. *If $\mathcal{R}$ is $\mathcal{R}, \mathcal{E}$-Church-Rosser modulo $\mathcal{E}$ then $\mathcal{R}$ is also Church-Rosser modulo $\mathcal{E}$.*

Now we can state the main result of this section:

Theorem 1. *Let $\mathcal{R}$ be a finite and closed rewrite system and $\mathcal{E}$ a closed equational theory. If all of the following hold:*

1. $\mathcal{R}, \mathcal{E}$ *is decidable;*
2. $\mathcal{R}$ *is $\mathcal{E}$-terminating;*
3. $\mathcal{R}$ *is Church-Rosser modulo $\mathcal{E}$,*

then $\mathcal{R} \cup \mathcal{E}_\alpha$-equivalence is decidable, by normalising with $\mathcal{R}, \mathcal{E}$.

In the rest of the paper, we present novel techniques to ensure items 1 to 3. The first item relies on theories for which $\mathcal{E}$-matching is decidable. Well-founded orderings can provide the second item. The third item requires more work: we will show sufficient conditions to guarantee that $\mathcal{R}$ is $\mathcal{R}, \mathcal{E}$-*Church-Rosser modulo* $\mathcal{E}$, which implies $\mathcal{R}$ to be Church-Rosser modulo $\mathcal{E}$ by checking $\mathcal{E}$-joinability with $\mathcal{R}, \mathcal{E}$ of our $\mathcal{E}$-critical pairs (cf. Sect. 4).

4   Confluence Modulo $\mathcal{E}$

In this section, we introduce new definitions of critical pairs modulo $\mathcal{E}$ in the nominal setting. These definitions are aimed at proving a nominal version of the Critical Pair Theorem modulo $\mathcal{E}$ for closed ENRSs (Theorem 2). This theorem provides necessary and sufficient conditions for an ENRS $\mathcal{R}$ to be $\mathcal{R}, \mathcal{E}$-Church-Rosser modulo $\mathcal{E}$—a property that is essential for ensuring the decidability of equality modulo $\mathcal{R} \cup \mathcal{E}_\alpha$, as established in Theorem 1.

4.1   Nominal Critical Pairs Modulo $\mathcal{E}$

To compute overlaps between nominal terms and identify critical pairs between nominal rewrite rules modulo a closed equational theory $\mathcal{E}$, we require that $\mathcal{E}$ admits a nominal unification algorithm capable of producing a finite and complete set of $\mathcal{E}$-unifiers.

Fig. 2. $\mathcal{E}$-overlapping and $\mathcal{E}$-critical pair.

Definition 4 ($\mathcal{E}$-overlaps). *A term-in-context $(\Delta_1 \vdash s)$, at a ground position $p \in \mathcal{P}os(s)$, $\mathcal{E}$-overlaps a non-variable[2] term-in-context $(\Delta_2 \vdash t)$ if there exists an $\mathcal{E}$-unifier for $(\Delta_1 \vdash s|_p) \mathbin{?\!\overset{\mathcal{E}}{\approx}_?} (\Delta_2 \vdash t)$. If $\mathcal{E} = \emptyset$ we simply call it an overlap. If there exists a complete set of $\mathcal{E}$-unifiers we obtain a complete set $\mathfrak{S}$ of $\mathcal{E}$-overlaps (see Fig. 2, left).*

Example 5 (Cont. Example 4). The term-in-context $(a_1\#P_1 \vdash P_1 \wedge \forall[a_1]Q_1)$, at root-position, $\mathcal{C}$-overlaps $(a_3\#P_3 \vdash P_3 \wedge \exists[a_3]Q_3)$ with a complete set of $\mathcal{C}$-unifiers $\mathfrak{S} \neq \emptyset$. In fact, the $\mathcal{C}$-unification problem

$$(a_1\#P_1 \vdash P_1 \wedge \forall[a_1]Q_1) \mathbin{?\!\overset{\mathcal{C}}{\approx}_?} (a_3\#P_3 \vdash P_3 \wedge \exists[a_3]Q_3)$$

has a $\mathcal{C}$-unifier $(\Gamma_{\mathcal{CP}_1}, \theta) = (\{a_1\#Q_3, a_3\#Q_1\}, [P_1 \mapsto \exists[a_3]Q_3, P_3 \mapsto \forall[a_1]Q_1])$.

The nominal version of $\mathcal{E}$-critical pairs are pairs of terms-in-context as rules may contain freshness conditions on meta-variables.

Definition 5 ($\mathcal{E}$-critical pairs). *Let $R_1 = \nabla_1 \vdash l_1 \to r_1$ and $R_2 = \nabla_2 \vdash l_2 \to r_2$ be freshened versions of closed rules such that $V(R_1) \cap V(R_2) = \emptyset$. Suppose that $\nabla_1 \vdash l_1$, at a ground position $p \in \mathcal{P}os(l_1)$, $\mathcal{E}$-overlaps $\nabla_2 \vdash l_2$ with a complete set $\mathfrak{S}$ of $\mathcal{E}$-overlappings. The set*

$$\mathsf{CP}_{\mathcal{E}}(R_1, R_2, p) = \{\Gamma \vdash \langle r_1\theta, l_1\theta[r_2\theta]_p\rangle \mid \text{for all } (\Gamma, \theta) \in \mathfrak{S}\} \quad (\text{see Fig. 2, right})$$

is called a complete set of $\mathcal{E}$-critical pairs *of the rule R_1 at position p on the rule R_2. For $\mathcal{E} = \emptyset$, we have simply a* critical pair, *as the set $\mathsf{CP}_{\mathcal{E}}(R_1, R_2, p)$ is unitary.*

A critical pair $\Gamma \vdash \langle u_1, u_2 \rangle$ is *trivial* iff u_1 and u_2 are identical up to renaming of variables, otherwise they are *non-trivial*. An overlap is *proper* if it is not trivial.

Example 6 (Cont. Example 5). Consider the rules

$$R_1 : a_1\#P_1 \vdash P_1 \wedge \forall[a_1]Q_1 \to \forall[a_1](P_1 \wedge Q_1)$$
$$R_3 : a_3\#P_3 \vdash P_3 \wedge \exists[a_3]Q_3 \to \exists[a_3](P_3 \wedge Q_3).$$

The $\mathcal{C}$-critical pair is $\Gamma_{\mathcal{CP}_1} \vdash \langle \forall[a_1](\exists[a_3]Q_3 \wedge Q_1), \exists[a_3](\forall[a_1]Q_1 \wedge Q_3)\rangle$. Similarly, R_2 and R_4 yield the $\mathcal{C}$-critical pair $\Gamma_{\mathcal{CP}_2} \vdash \langle \forall[a_2](\exists[a_4]Q_4 \vee Q_2), \exists[a_4](\forall[a_2]Q_2 \vee Q_4)\rangle$, where $\Gamma_{\mathcal{CP}_2} = \{a_2\#Q_4, a_4\#Q_2\}$.

---

[2] t is not a variable.

Lemma 2 (Technical result). *Let $\mathcal{R}$ be a closed ENRS. The following hold:*

1. *If $\Delta \vdash t$ is closed and $\Delta \vdash t \approx_{\mathcal{E}} t'$ then $\Delta \vdash t'$ is closed.*
2. *If $\Delta \vdash (s,t)$ is a critical pair from a closed ENRS, then $\Delta \vdash (s,t)$ is closed.*
3. *If $\Delta \vdash s$ is closed and $\Delta \vdash s \rightarrow_{\mathcal{R},\mathcal{E}} t$ then $\Delta \vdash (s,t)$ is closed.*
4. *If $\Delta \vdash (s,t)$ is closed and $\Delta \vdash t \rightarrow_{\mathcal{R},\mathcal{E}} u$ then $\Delta \vdash (s,u)$ is closed.*

Observe that $\nabla_1 \vdash l_1 \rightarrow r_1$ and $\nabla_2 \vdash l_2 \rightarrow r_2$ do not play a symmetrical role in the definition of critical pairs.

Definition 6. *There are three types of $\mathcal{E}$-critical pairs: between two rules, between a rule and an oriented identity, and between an oriented identity and a rule. Formally,*

1. $\mathsf{CP}_{\mathcal{E}}(\mathcal{R},\mathcal{R})$ *is the set of non-trivial $\mathcal{E}$-critical pairs between any $\nabla_1 \vdash l_1 \rightarrow r_1$ and $\nabla_2 \vdash l_2 \rightarrow r_2$ in $\mathcal{R}$;*
2. $\mathsf{CP}_{\mathcal{E}}(\mathcal{R},\mathcal{E})$ *is the set of non-trivial $\mathcal{E}$-critical pairs between any $\nabla_1 \vdash l_1 \rightarrow r_1$ in $\mathcal{R}$ and any $\nabla_2 \vdash l_2 \rightarrow r_2$ or $\nabla_2 \vdash r_2 \rightarrow l_2$ such that $\nabla_2 \vdash l_2 \approx r_2$ in $\mathcal{E}$;*
3. $\mathsf{CP}_{\mathcal{E}}(\mathcal{E},\mathcal{R})$ *is the set of non-trivial $\mathcal{E}$-critical pairs between any $\nabla_1 \vdash l_1 \rightarrow r_1$ or $\nabla_1 \vdash r_1 \rightarrow l_1$ such that $\nabla_1 \vdash l_1 \approx r_1$ in $\mathcal{E}$ and any $\nabla_2 \vdash l_2 \rightarrow r_2$ in $\mathcal{R}$.*

Example 7. From the computation in Example 6, we have:

$$\mathsf{CP}_{\mathcal{C}}(\mathcal{R},\mathcal{R}) = \{\Gamma_{\mathcal{CP}_1} \vdash \langle \forall[a_1](\exists[a_3]Q_3 \wedge Q_1), \exists[a_3](\forall[a_1]Q_1 \wedge Q_3)\rangle,$$
$$\Gamma_{\mathcal{CP}_2} \vdash \langle \forall[a_2](\exists[a_4]Q_4 \vee Q_2), \exists[a_4](\forall[a_2]Q_2 \vee Q_4)\rangle\}$$

In addition, $(a_1\#P_1 \vdash P_1 \wedge \forall[a_1]Q_1)$, at root-position, $\mathcal{C}$-overlaps $(\emptyset \vdash P \wedge Q)$ with a complete set of $\mathcal{C}$-unifiers $\mathfrak{S}' \neq \emptyset$. Similarly, R_2, R_3 and R_4 with $\mathcal{C}$ yield the $\mathcal{C}$-critical pair set:

$$\mathsf{CP}_{\mathcal{C}}(\mathcal{R},\mathcal{C}) = \{a_1\#P_1 \vdash \langle \forall[a_1](P_1 \wedge Q_1), \forall[a_1]Q_1 \wedge P_1\rangle$$
$$a_2\#P_2 \vdash \langle \forall[a_2](P_2 \vee Q_2), \forall[a_2]Q_2 \vee P_2\rangle$$
$$a_3\#P_3 \vdash \langle \exists[a_3](P_3 \wedge Q_3), \exists[a_3]Q_3 \wedge P_3\rangle$$
$$a_4\#P_4 \vdash \langle \exists[a_4](P_4 \vee Q_4), \exists[a_4]Q_4 \vee P_4\rangle\}$$

In this example, $\mathsf{CP}_{\mathcal{C}}(\mathcal{C},\mathcal{R}) = \mathsf{CP}_{\mathcal{C}}(\mathcal{R},\mathcal{C})$. In general, this is not always the case.

4.2 Critical Pair Theorem Modulo $\mathcal{E}$ for Closed Rewriting

The next result guarantees the existence of an $\mathcal{E}$-critical pair whenever we have a *peak*, that is, whenever there are two terms u and v such that $\Delta \vdash s \rightarrow_{\mathcal{R},\mathcal{E}} u$ and $\Delta \vdash s \rightarrow_{\mathcal{R}} v$, or a *cliff*, that is whenever there are two terms u and v such that $\Delta \vdash s \rightarrow_{\mathcal{R},\mathcal{E}} u$ and $\Delta \vdash s \leftrightarrow_{\mathcal{E}} v$. We write $\Delta \vdash s \rightarrow_{\mathcal{R},\mathcal{E}}^{[p,\sigma,R]} t$ to be explicit about the position p, substitution σ and the rule R used in a rewriting step.

Lemma 3 (Critical Pair Lemma). *Let $\mathcal{R} \cup \mathcal{E}_\alpha$ be a closed ENRS. Assume we have $\Delta \vdash t \rightarrow_{\mathcal{R}}^{[\epsilon,\theta,R_1]} t_1$ (or $\Delta \vdash t \approx_{\mathcal{E}}^{[\epsilon,\theta,R_1]} t_1$) and $\Delta \vdash t \rightarrow_{\mathcal{R},\mathcal{E}}^{[p,\theta,R_2]} t_2$, with rule $R_1 = \nabla_1 \vdash l_1 \rightarrow r_1$ (or equation $R_1 = \nabla_1 \vdash l_1 \approx r_1$) and rule $R_2 = \nabla_2 \vdash l_2 \rightarrow r_2$ freshened variants of rules and with p a ground position of l_1 ($p \neq \epsilon$ if $R_1 \in \mathcal{E}$). Then there exists a critical pair $\Delta \vdash \langle u_1, u_2 \rangle$ in a complete set of $\mathcal{E}$-critical pairs of the rule R_1 at position p on the rule R_2 and a substitution σ such that $\Delta \vdash t_i \approx_{\mathcal{E}} u_i\sigma$ and $\Delta \vdash \nabla_i\theta$ for $i = 1, 2$.*

As observed earlier, $\mathcal{E}$-congruence classes of nominal terms are almost always infinite due to α-renaming (see Example 1). This complicates the study of the decidability of the reducibility of terms by $\mathcal{R}/\mathcal{E}$ as one would need to investigate the whole class of a term before applying a rule. Thus, we are interested in a characterisation of theories for which $\mathcal{E}$-congruence classes of terms can be fully generated by from a finite set of representatives.

Example 8. Consider the signature $\Sigma = \{\forall, f, >\}$, where f and $>$ are binary symbols. Consider $\mathcal{E}_{\forall_C} = \{\emptyset \vdash \forall[a]\forall[b]X \approx \forall[b]\forall[a]X\}$. The $\alpha, \mathcal{E}_{\forall_C}$-equivalence class of the term $s = \forall[a]\forall[b](f(a,b) > 0)$ includes

$$[s]_{\alpha, \mathcal{E}_{\forall_C}} = \left\{ \begin{array}{l} \forall[a]\forall[b](f(a,b) > 0), \forall[b]\forall[a](f(a,b) > 0), \\ \forall[c]\forall[b](f(c,b) > 0), \forall[b]\forall[c](f(c,b) > 0), \\ \forall[c]\forall[d](f(c,d) > 0), \forall[d]\forall[c](f(d,c) > 0), \ldots \end{array} \right\}.$$

Observe that both α-renaming of bound variables and the commutativity of quantifiers (via $\mathcal{E}_{\forall_C}$) contribute to generating new representatives of the same equivalence class. However, all the representatives are atom-renamings of the first two. Thus, the whole class can be generated from the first two representatives $\{\forall[a]\forall[b](f(a,b) > 0), \forall[b]\forall[a](f(a,b) > 0)\}$. We will call this class *finitely generated up to* α, as we could have chosen the representatives in the second line as the *generators* of the class.

Now we can give a version of the Critical Pair Theorem modulo $\mathcal{E}$ for closed rewriting. It requires the additional hypothesis of a theory $\mathcal{E}$ having congruence classes that are finitely generated up to α, as its proof requires investigating the whole $\mathcal{E}$-congruence class of terms. As in [14, Theorem 16], the additional $\mathcal{R}, \mathcal{E}$-step given in items 2. and 3. is needed due to $\mathcal{E}$-termination.

Theorem 2 (Critical Pair Theorem modulo $\mathcal{E}$). *Let $\mathcal{R} \cup \mathcal{E}_\alpha$ be a closed ENRS such that $\mathcal{R}$ is $\mathcal{E}$-terminating, $\mathcal{E}$ is finitary and $\mathcal{E}$-congruence classes are finitely generated up to α. Then $\mathcal{R}$ is $\mathcal{R}, \mathcal{E}$-Church-Rosser modulo $\mathcal{E}$ iff*

1. *all pairs in $\mathsf{CP}_\mathcal{E}(\mathcal{R}, \mathcal{R})$ are $\mathcal{E}$-joinable by $\mathcal{R}, \mathcal{E}$;*
2. *for each pair $\langle u_1, u_2 \rangle$ in $\mathsf{CP}_\mathcal{E}(\mathcal{R}, \mathcal{E})$, there exists u_2' such that $u_2 \rightarrow_{\mathcal{R}, \mathcal{E}} u_2'$ and the pair $\langle u_1, u_2' \rangle$ is $\mathcal{E}$-joinable by $\mathcal{R}, \mathcal{E}$.*
3. *for each pair $\langle u_1, u_2 \rangle$ in $\mathsf{CP}_\mathcal{E}(\mathcal{E}, \mathcal{R})$, there exists u_1' such that $u_1 \rightarrow_{\mathcal{R}, \mathcal{E}} u_1'$ and the pair $\langle u_1', u_2 \rangle$ is $\mathcal{E}$-joinable by $\mathcal{R}, \mathcal{E}$.*

We already know that $\mathcal{C}$ is not finitary [1] if we use freshness contexts and substitutions to represent solutions, and that is due to fixed-point equations. However, if we consider left-linear rules and knowing that the intersection between variables of each rule is empty, then we do not have fixed-point equations anymore. Thus, the rules have a *finite* complete set of $\mathcal{C}$-critical pairs, that is $\mathsf{CP}_\mathcal{C}(\mathcal{R}, \mathcal{R}) \cup \mathsf{CP}_\mathcal{C}(\mathcal{R}, \mathcal{C}) \cup \mathsf{CP}_\mathcal{C}(\mathcal{C}, \mathcal{R})$ is finite.

4.3   On the Semantics of Critical Pairs

Closedness is not a sufficient condition to guarantee that all the freshness constraints are relevant for a rule. First, we give semantics for pairs $\nabla \vdash (l, r)$ by considering ground instances of (l, r) that satisfy ∇ and also consider renamings of the atoms occurring in ∇, l and r, by considering meta-level permutation of atoms. Second, we verify that some freshness constraints are irrelevant for the semantics of pairs. Next, leveraging from the function application rule (with $(\_, \_)$ as a binary operator) we write $(s, t) \approx_\mathcal{E} (s', t')$ instead of $s \approx_\mathcal{E} s' \wedge t \approx_\mathcal{E} t'$.

Definition 7. *The* semantics *of a* pair-in-context *$\nabla \vdash (l, r)$, represented by $[\![(\nabla, l, r)]\!]$, is the set of (equivalence classes of) ground instances of (l, r) that satisfy ∇, i.e.,*

$$[\![(\nabla, l, r)]\!] := \{[(l', r')]_{\approx_\mathcal{E}} \mid \exists \sigma, \pi. \, l', r' \, ground \colon (l', r') \approx_\mathcal{E} (l^\pi \sigma, r^\pi \sigma) \wedge \nabla^\pi \sigma \, hold\}$$

where $[(l', r')]_{\approx_\mathcal{E}}$ denotes the equivalence class of l', r' modulo $\approx_\mathcal{E}$.

For example, $[\![(a \# X, \forall[a]X, X)]\!] = \{[(\forall[a]b, b)]_{\approx_\mathcal{E}}, [(\forall[b]a, a)]_{\approx_\mathcal{E}}, \ldots\}$. More interestingly, for f a unary function symbol and 0 a constant symbol in a signature, we have $[\![(a \# X, f(X), 0)]\!] = \{[(f(b), 0)]_{\approx_\mathcal{E}}, [(f(c), 0)]_{\approx_\mathcal{E}}, [(f(a), 0)]_{\approx_\mathcal{E}}, \ldots\}$; also, note that $[(f(a), 0)]_{\approx_\mathcal{E}}$ is in the class, because if we take $\sigma = [X \mapsto b]$ and $\pi = (a\ b)(a\ c)$ then $(f(a), 0) \approx_\mathcal{E} (f(X)^\pi \sigma, 0^\pi \sigma) = (f(b)^\pi, 0)$, and $(a \# X)^\pi \sigma = (\pi(a) \# X)\sigma = c \# b$ holds. We can verify $[\![(\emptyset, (f(X), 0))]\!] = [\![(a \# X, (f(X), 0))]\!]$. Note that the constraint $a \# X$ is *irrelevant* for the semantics of the pair $(f(X), 0)$.

The semantics of pairs gives semantics to rewrite rules $\nabla \vdash l \rightarrow r$ as expected.

Definition 8. *Let $R : \nabla \vdash l \rightarrow r$ and consider the pairs-in-context $\nabla \vdash (l, r)$ and $\nabla' \vdash (l, r)$ such that $\nabla' \subseteq \nabla$. Let $\Delta = \nabla \backslash \nabla'$. We call Δ irrelevant for $l \rightarrow r$ iff the semantics of $\nabla \vdash (l, r)$ coincides with the semantics of $\nabla' \vdash (l, r)$, i.e., $[\![(\nabla, l, r)]\!] = [\![(\nabla', l, r)]\!]$. If the equality does not hold, then Δ is called* relevant.

Note that the closed rule $R = a \# X \vdash f(X) \rightarrow 0$ has an irrelevant freshness constraint. Thus, R has the same semantics as the rule $R' = \emptyset \vdash f(X) \rightarrow 0$.

We can find whether a freshness constraint is irrelevant by solving an $\mathcal{E}$-matching problem as follows.

Theorem 3. *Given the closed pairs in context $\nabla \vdash (l, r)$ and $\nabla' \vdash (l, r)$ with $\nabla' \subset \nabla$. We can check whether they have the same semantics by solving the following matching problem:*

$$(\nabla'' \vdash (l'', r'')) \overset{\mathcal{E}}{?\approx} (\nabla', A(\nabla'', l'', r'') \# V(\nabla', l, r) \vdash (l, r))$$

Thus, to check whether $\{a \# X\}$ is irrelevant for $R = a \# X \vdash f(X) \rightarrow 0$ we solve the $\mathcal{E}$-matching problem $(a'' \# X'' \vdash (f(X''), 0)) \overset{\mathcal{E}}{?\approx} (\emptyset, \{a'' \# X\} \vdash (f(X), 0))$. It has a solution: $\theta = [X'' \rightarrow X]$. Next, we return to our running example.

Example 9. Let $\Gamma_{\mathcal{CP}_1} \vdash \langle \underbrace{\forall[a_1](\exists[a_3]Q_3 \wedge Q_1)}_{l}, \underbrace{\exists[a_3](\forall[a_1]Q_1 \wedge Q_3)}_{r} \rangle$ be the crit-

ical pair from Example 6, where $\Gamma_{\mathcal{CP}_1} = \{a_1\#Q_3, a_3\#Q_1\}$. The $\mathcal{C}$-matching
problem: $(a_1^u\#Q_3^u, a_3^u\#Q_1^u \vdash (l^u, r^u)) \overset{\mathcal{C}}{?\approx} (a_1^u\#Q_1, Q_3, a_3\#Q_1, Q_3 \vdash (l, r))$ does not
have a solution. By Theorem 3, the context $\Gamma_{\mathcal{CP}_1}$ is *relevant* for $l \to r$.

5   Completion Procedure for ENRS

In this section, we present a procedure for completion modulo $\mathcal{E}$ (a finite set
of permutative equations) for closed nominal rules $\mathcal{R}$, to build an $\mathcal{E}$-convergent
rewrite system $\mathcal{R} \cup \mathcal{E}_\alpha$. The completion procedure uses a well-founded ordering. In
the case of closed ENRSs, critical pairs are also closed (Lemma 2). Therefore, we
can create a completion method in the style of Knuth and Bendix for equational
nominal systems.

5.1   The Inference System

The completion procedure for closed ENRSs is specified as an inference system $\mathcal{I}$
that operates on triples $(\mathcal{P}, \mathcal{N}, \mathcal{R})$ consisting of a set $\mathcal{P}$ of equations, and a set of
closed nominal rewriting rules that we split into a set $\mathcal{N}$ of *non-protected* and a
set $\mathcal{R}$ of *protected* rules. The protected rules are immune to certain simplification
rules of $\mathcal{I}$. The $\mathcal{E}$-completion procedure checks the $\mathcal{R}, \mathcal{E}$-Church-Rosser modulo
$\mathcal{E}$ property of an ENRS made up from a constant set of equations $\mathcal{E}$ and an
$\mathcal{E}$-terminating set $\mathcal{R}$ of rules.

The Completion Procedure. The input to $\mathcal{I}$ is $(\mathcal{P}, \mathcal{N}, \mathcal{R})$ with $\mathcal{P}$ and $\mathcal{N}$ empty
and $\mathcal{R}$ itself, whose rules must be protected, and a (well-founded) reduction
ordering $>$ between terms. The transformation rules are presented in Fig. 3. We
write $(\mathcal{P}, \mathcal{N}, \mathcal{R}) \vdash_{\mathcal{I}} (\mathcal{P}', \mathcal{N}', \mathcal{R}')$ to indicate that $(\mathcal{P}, \mathcal{N}, \mathcal{R})$ can be transformed
to $(\mathcal{P}', \mathcal{N}', \mathcal{R}')$ by applying one of the inference rules in Fig. 3. A possibly infi-
nite sequence of the form $(\mathcal{P}_0, \mathcal{N}_0, \mathcal{R}_0) \vdash_{\mathcal{I}} (\mathcal{P}_1, \mathcal{N}_1, \mathcal{R}_1) \vdash_{\mathcal{I}} (\mathcal{P}_2, \mathcal{N}_2, \mathcal{R}_2) \vdash_{\mathcal{I}} \cdots$
is called a *run* of the procedure. We will extend every finite run of the form
$(\mathcal{P}_0, \mathcal{N}_0, \mathcal{R}_0) \vdash_{\mathcal{I}} \cdots \vdash_{\mathcal{I}} (\mathcal{P}_n, \mathcal{N}_n, \mathcal{R}_n)$ to an infinite one by setting, for all $i \geq 1$,
$(\mathcal{P}_{n+i}, \mathcal{N}_{n+i}, \mathcal{R}_{n+i}) := (\mathcal{P}_n, \mathcal{N}_n, \mathcal{R}_n)$.

Definition 9. *The set* $\mathcal{P}_\omega$ *of persistent identities and the set* $\mathcal{R}_\omega$ *of persistent
rules of a run are defined as* $\mathcal{P}_\omega := \bigcup_{i \geq 0} \bigcap_{j \geq i} \mathcal{P}_j$ *and* $\mathcal{R}_\omega := \bigcup_{i \geq 0} \bigcap_{j \geq i} \mathcal{R}_j$. *For a finite
run,* $\mathcal{P}_\omega := \mathcal{P}_n$ *and* $\mathcal{R}_\omega := \mathcal{R}_n$. *For an infinite run,* $\mathcal{P}_\omega$ *and* $\mathcal{R}_\omega$ *are identities
and rules that are never removed in later inference steps. We define* $\mathcal{R}^\infty = \bigcup_{i \geq 0} \mathcal{R}_i$
and $\mathcal{P}^\infty = \bigcup_{i \geq 0} \mathcal{P}_i$.

We call a run *non-failing* if it terminates successfully or if it does not termi-
nate, hence we have $\mathcal{P}_\omega = \emptyset$ and $\mathcal{R}_\omega = \mathcal{R}^\infty$. A completion procedure is *correct*
if and only if every non-failing run succeeds, i.e., $\mathcal{P}_\omega = \emptyset$ and $\mathcal{R}_\omega$ is convergent
and equivalent to $\mathcal{R}_0$ ($\mathcal{R}_\omega$ is canonical modulo $\mathcal{E}$).

1. $(\mathcal{P}, \mathcal{N}, \mathcal{R})$	$\Rightarrow (\mathcal{P} \cup \{\Delta' \vdash s = t\}, \mathcal{N}, \mathcal{R})$	if $\Delta \vdash (s, t)$ is a non-joinable CP of $\mathcal{R}$ and $\Delta \backslash \Delta'$ is irrelevant for $s \to t$ for some $\Delta' \subseteq \Delta$
2. $(\mathcal{P} \cup \{\Delta \vdash s = t\}, \mathcal{N}, \mathcal{R})$	$\Rightarrow (\mathcal{P}, \mathcal{N} \cup \{\Delta \vdash s \to t\}, \mathcal{R})$	if $\Delta \vdash s > t$
3. $(\mathcal{P} \cup \{\Delta \vdash s = t\}, \mathcal{N}, \mathcal{R})$	$\Rightarrow (\mathcal{P}, \mathcal{N} \cup \{\Delta \vdash t \to s\}, \mathcal{R})$	if $\Delta \vdash t > s$
4. $(\mathcal{P} \cup \{\Delta \vdash s = t\}, \mathcal{N}, \mathcal{R})$	$\Rightarrow (\mathcal{P}, \mathcal{N}, \mathcal{R})$	if $\Delta \vdash s \approx_\mathcal{E} t$
5. $(\mathcal{P} \cup \{\Delta \vdash s = t\}, \mathcal{N}, \mathcal{R})$	$\Rightarrow (\mathcal{P} \cup \{\Delta \vdash s' = t\}, \mathcal{N}, \mathcal{R})$	if $\Delta \vdash s \to^c_{\mathcal{R}/\mathcal{E}} s'$
6. $(\mathcal{P} \cup \{\Delta \vdash s = t\}, \mathcal{N}, \mathcal{R})$	$\Rightarrow (\mathcal{P} \cup \{\Delta \vdash s = t'\}, \mathcal{N}, \mathcal{R})$	if $\Delta \vdash t \to^c_{\mathcal{R}/\mathcal{E}} t'$
7. $(\mathcal{P}, \mathcal{N} \cup \{\Delta \vdash s \to t\}, \mathcal{R})$	$\Rightarrow (\mathcal{P}, \mathcal{N} \cup \{\Delta \vdash s \to t'\}, \mathcal{R})$	if $\Delta \vdash t \to^c_{\mathcal{R}/\mathcal{E}} t'$
8. $(\mathcal{P}, \mathcal{N}, \mathcal{R} \cup \{\Delta \vdash s \to t\})$	$\Rightarrow (\mathcal{P}, \mathcal{N}, \mathcal{R} \cup \{\Delta \vdash s \to t'\})$	if $\Delta \vdash t \to^c_{\mathcal{R}/\mathcal{E}} t'$
9. $(\mathcal{P}, \mathcal{N} \cup \{\Delta \vdash s \to t\}, \mathcal{R})$	$\Rightarrow (\mathcal{P} \cup \{\Delta \vdash s' = t\}, \mathcal{N}, \mathcal{R})$	if $\Delta \vdash s \to_{\mathcal{R}, \mathcal{E}} s'$ using $\nabla \vdash l \to r \in \mathcal{R}$ and l does not reduce with $\Delta \vdash s \to t$
10. $(\mathcal{P}, \mathcal{N}, \mathcal{R})$	$\Rightarrow (\mathcal{P}, \mathcal{N}, \mathcal{R} \cup \{\Delta \vdash s \to t\})$	if $s = t \in EXT_\mathcal{E}(\mathcal{R})$
11. $(\mathcal{P}, \mathcal{N} \cup \{\Delta \vdash s \to t\}, \mathcal{R})$	$\Rightarrow (\mathcal{P}, \mathcal{N}, \mathcal{R} \cup \{\Delta \vdash s \to t\})$	

Fig. 3. Transformation Rules of the Completion procedure for ENRS.

5.2   Correctness of the $\mathcal{E}$-Completion Procedure

Now we need to find sufficient conditions for the correctness of the $\mathcal{E}$-completion procedure, which will use *proof orderings*. First, a *proof* $\mathbb{P}$ of an identity $\Delta \vdash s \approx t$ in $\mathcal{R}^\infty \cup \mathcal{E}^\infty$ is a finite sequence $(s_0, \ldots, s_n)$ of length $n + 1 > 0$ such that $s_0 = s$ and $s_n = t$, and for all i, $1 \le i \le n$: (i) $s_{i-1} \leftrightarrow_{\mathcal{E}^\infty} s_i$, or (ii) $s_{i-1} \to_{\mathcal{R}^\infty} s_i$, or (iii) $s_i \to_{\mathcal{R}^\infty} s_{i-1}$. We call a triple (Δ, s_{i-1}, s_i) a *proof step* for $i = 1, \ldots, n$.

By a peak $\Delta \vdash s \leftarrow_\mathcal{R} u \to_{\mathcal{R}, \mathcal{E}} t$ (resp. a cliff $\Delta \vdash s \leftrightarrow_\mathcal{E} u \to_{\mathcal{R}, \mathcal{E}} t$) we intend a proof in which the first proof step is not strictly below any other step. The set of such peaks (and cliffs) and their inverses is denoted $\mathbb{N}_\mathcal{I}$. We call a proof a *normal-form proof* when none of its subproofs are in $\mathbb{N}_\mathcal{I}$: A peak $\Delta \vdash s \leftarrow_\mathcal{R} u \to_{\mathcal{R}, \mathcal{E}} t$ represents a proof $\Delta \vdash s \leftarrow_\mathcal{R} u \leftrightarrow_\mathcal{E} u_1 \leftrightarrow_{\mathcal{R}, \mathcal{E}} \cdots \leftrightarrow_\mathcal{E} u_n \leftrightarrow_{\mathcal{R}, \mathcal{E}} t$, where the proof steps apply at positions $p, q_1, \ldots, q_n$ and q in this order such that p is not strictly below q, and q_i is below q. We use the same notion for cliffs.

We start by giving a Noetherian relation $\Rightarrow_\mathcal{I}$ on proofs such that for every run $(\mathcal{P}_0, \mathcal{N}_0, \mathcal{R}_0) \vdash_\mathcal{I} (\mathcal{P}_1, \mathcal{N}_1, \mathcal{R}_1) \vdash_\mathcal{I} \cdots$ and proof $\mathbb{P}_i$ in $\mathcal{R}_i \cup \mathcal{P}_i \cup \mathcal{E}$ there is a sequence of proofs $\mathbb{P}_i \Rightarrow_\mathcal{I} \mathbb{P}_{i+1} \Rightarrow_\mathcal{I} \cdots$, where $\mathbb{P}_j$, for all $j \ge i$, is a proof in $\mathcal{R}_j \cup \mathcal{P}_j \cup \mathcal{E}$ and $\mathbb{P}_n = \mathbb{P}_{n+1} = \cdots$ for some $n \ge i$. Note that $\mathbb{P}_n$ has to be a proof in $\mathcal{R}^\infty \cup \mathcal{P}^\infty \cup \mathcal{E}$. Hence, to prove that $\mathcal{R}_\mathcal{E}^\infty$ is Church-Rosser modulo $\mathcal{E}$, it suffices to show that for each proof $\mathbb{P}_i$ in $\mathcal{R}_i \cup \mathcal{P}_i \cup \mathcal{E}$ there is a sequence of proof transformations such that $\mathbb{P}_n$ is a normal-form proof with respect to $\mathbb{N}_\mathcal{I}$. Next, items 1. to 11. refer to labels of the rules in Fig 3.

The rules 2., 3. (for orientation), 4. (for deletion), and 11. (for protection) are reflected by proof transformation rules

$$\Delta \vdash s \leftrightarrow_{\mathcal{P}} t \;\Rightarrow\; \Delta \vdash s \to_{\mathcal{N}} t \;\text{ if } \Delta \vdash s > t$$
$$\Delta \vdash s \leftrightarrow_{\mathcal{P}} t \;\Rightarrow\; \Delta \vdash t \to_{\mathcal{N}} s \;\text{ if } \Delta \vdash t > s$$
$$\Delta \vdash s \leftrightarrow_{\mathcal{P}} t \;\Rightarrow\; \Delta \vdash s \leftrightarrow_{\mathcal{E}}^{*} t$$
$$\Delta \vdash s \to_{\mathcal{N}} t \;\Rightarrow\; \Delta \vdash s \to_{\mathcal{R}} t$$

where $\mathcal{P}$ is a finite set of nominal equations and $\mathcal{N}$ and $\mathcal{R}$ are finite nominal rewrite systems contained in $>$. Inference rules 5., 6. (for simplification), 7., 8. (for composition) and 9. (for collapse) are mirrored by proof transformation rules

$$\Delta \vdash s \leftrightarrow_{\mathcal{P}} t \;\Rightarrow\; \Delta \vdash s \to_{\mathcal{R}/\mathcal{E}} s' \leftrightarrow_{\mathcal{P}} t$$
$$\Delta \vdash s \leftrightarrow_{\mathcal{P}} t \;\Rightarrow\; \Delta \vdash t \to_{\mathcal{R}/\mathcal{E}} t' \leftrightarrow_{\mathcal{P}} s$$
$$\Delta \vdash s \to_{\mathcal{N}} t \;\Rightarrow\; \Delta \vdash s \to_{\mathcal{N}} t' \leftarrow_{\mathcal{R}/\mathcal{E}} t$$
$$\Delta \vdash s \to_{\mathcal{R}} t \;\Rightarrow\; \Delta \vdash s \to_{\mathcal{R}} t' \leftarrow_{\mathcal{R}/\mathcal{E}} t$$
$$\Delta \vdash s \to_{\mathcal{N}} t \;\Rightarrow\; \Delta \vdash s \to_{\mathcal{R},\mathcal{E}} s' \leftrightarrow_{\mathcal{P}} t$$

where $s \to_{\mathcal{N}} t$ and $s \to_{\mathcal{R}} t$ are by application of rule $s \to t$, and the rewrite step in $s \to_{\mathcal{R},\mathcal{E}} s'$ is by rule $l \to r$ where l does not reduce with $s \to t$.

The rule 1., for deduction, eliminates peaks, as expressed by the rule

$$\Delta \vdash s \leftarrow_{\mathcal{N} \cup \mathcal{R}} u \to_{\mathcal{R},\mathcal{E}} t \;\Rightarrow\; \Delta' \vdash s \leftrightarrow_{\mathcal{E}}^{*} s' \leftrightarrow_{\mathcal{P}} t' \leftrightarrow_{\mathcal{E}}^{*} t$$

where $\to_{\mathcal{N} \cup \mathcal{R}}$ is the application of $\to_{\mathcal{N}}$ or $\to_{\mathcal{R}}$, $\to_{\mathcal{R},\mathcal{E}}$ is the $\mathcal{R}, \mathcal{E}$-rewriting step and Δ' is such that $\Delta \setminus \Delta'$ is irrelevant for $s \to t$.

The rule 10., for extension, eliminates cliffs that are proper overlaps, and is reflected by the rule

$$\Delta \vdash s \to_{\mathcal{N} \cup \mathcal{R}, \{u \approx v\}} t \;\Rightarrow\; \Delta \vdash s \to_{\mathcal{R}, \{w[u]_p \approx w[v]_p\}} t$$

The next result establishes that proofs are preserved by transformation rules.

Lemma 4. *If* $(\mathcal{P}, \mathcal{N}, \mathcal{R}) \vdash_{\mathcal{I}} (\mathcal{P}', \mathcal{N}', \mathcal{R}')$ *and* $\mathbb{P}$ *is a proof in* $\mathcal{R} \cup \mathcal{P} \cup \mathcal{E}$, *then there exists a proof* $\mathbb{P}'$ *in* $\mathcal{R}' \cup \mathcal{P}' \cup \mathcal{E}$, *such that* $\mathbb{P} \Rightarrow_{\mathcal{I}}^{*} \mathbb{P}'$.

Theorem 4 (Termination). *The proof relation* $\Rightarrow_{\mathcal{I}}^{+}$ *induced by the rewrite system* $\mathcal{R}$ *is noetherian, that is, it terminates.*

We will need a notion of extended rules, as follows:

Definition 10. *Let* $R = \Delta \vdash s \to t$ *be a rule and* $E = \Delta \vdash u \approx v$ *be an equation such that some proper non-variable subterm* $u|_p$ *is* $\mathcal{E}$-*unifiable with* s. *Then,* $\Delta \vdash u[s]_p \to u[t]_p$ *is called an* extended rule *of* R *with respect to* E. *By* $EXT_{\mathcal{E}}(\mathcal{R})$ *we denote the set of all extended rules of* $\mathcal{R}$ *with respect to* $\mathcal{E}$.

A run of a completion procedure is called *fair with respect to extensions* if $\mathsf{CP}_{\mathcal{E}}(\mathcal{R}^{\infty}) \subseteq \bigcup_{i \geq 0} \mathcal{P}_i$ and $EXT_{\mathcal{E}}(\mathcal{R}^{\infty}) \subseteq \bigcup_{i \geq 0} \mathcal{R}_i$. A completion procedure is *fair with respect to extensions* iff every non-failing run is fair w.r.t. extensions.

Theorem 5 (Correctness). *The fair completion procedure is correct. Let $\mathcal{E}$ be a set of equations for which minimal, complete sets of unifiers exist. If an $\mathcal{E}$-completion procedure is fair with respect to extensions and does not fail for given input, then $\mathcal{R}_{\mathcal{E}}^{\infty}$ is canonical modulo $\mathcal{E}$.*

Example 10. Suppose we want to apply the completion procedure in the closed prenex normal form rules (cf. Ex. 4) to check if the system is $\mathcal{C}$-confluent. From Ex. 6 we know that the following are critical pairs of $\mathcal{R}$:

$$\Gamma_{\mathcal{CP}_1} \vdash \langle \forall [a_1](\exists [a_3]Q_3 \wedge Q_1), \exists [a_3](\forall [a_1]Q_1 \wedge Q_3) \rangle$$
$$\Gamma_{\mathcal{CP}_2} \vdash \langle \forall [a_2](\exists [a_4]Q_4 \vee Q_2), \exists [a_4](\forall [a_2]Q_2 \vee Q_4) \rangle$$

Non-joinability can be checked using the rules for $\mathcal{I}$:

$$(\emptyset, \mathcal{R}) \Longrightarrow^{1,5,6,3} (\emptyset, \mathcal{R} \cup R_7) \Longrightarrow^{1,5,6,3} (\emptyset, \mathcal{R} \cup R_7 \cup R_8)$$

where $R_7 = \{\Gamma_{\mathcal{CP}_1} \vdash \exists [a_3](\forall [a_1](Q_3 \wedge Q_1)) \rightarrow \forall [a_1](\exists [a_3](Q_3 \wedge Q_1))\}$ and $R_8 = \{\Gamma_{\mathcal{CP}_2} \vdash \exists [a_4](\forall [a_2](Q_4 \vee Q_2)) \rightarrow \forall [a_2](\exists [a_4](Q_4 \vee Q_2))\}$.

With these two new rules the system becomes $\mathcal{C}$-confluent.

6   Conclusion and Related Work

We have provided several results for equational nominal rewriting systems. In particular, the Nominal Critical Pair Lemma modulo $\mathcal{E}$ helps analysing critical pairs in this setting. We also introduced a novel concept of semantics of critical pairs, enabling the refinement of freshness constraints and improving the efficiency of the completion procedure. Finally, we provided a procedure for constructing $\mathcal{E}$-confluent closed ENRSs, advancing the practical applicability of these theoretical results. The next step is to apply these results to extend a rewrite-based programming language, such as Maude, to deal with binders and equational axioms.

Related Work. Formalisations in Isabelle/HOL have been made for confluence of first-order left-linear systems [15], for pattern completeness that can be used to verify ground confluence proofs by rewriting induction [23] and for confluence of term rewrite systems using parallel critical pairs [11]. The last one also analyses particular cases modulo a set of confluent rewrite rules.

Huet's alternative approach to completion for first-order rewriting modulo an equational theory $\mathcal{E}$ uses a simpler rewrite relation and avoids $\mathcal{E}$-unification by restricting to left-linear systems. This approach has been recently applied to $\mathcal{AC}$ theories [19]. In this paper, we generalise to the nominal setting the general approach [3,14,16] for equational rewriting (relations $\mathcal{R}, \mathcal{E}$ and $\mathcal{R}/\mathcal{E}$) and use $\mathcal{E}$-unification to compute critical pairs.

A recent work investigating the confluence of conditional term rewriting systems modulo an equational theory, where the conditions are atomic formulas of the form $P(t_1, \ldots, t_n)$ for a predicate symbol P and first-order terms $t_1, \ldots, t_n$, can be found in [18]. Nominal rewriting can be seen as a form of conditional rewriting in which the conditions are freshness predicates of the form $a \# X$, where $a \in \mathbb{A}$ are nominal atoms that act as object-level variables, and $X \in \mathcal{X}$ are meta-variables. Additionally, ENRS involves binding constructs. Both features—freshness conditions and binding—are not directly expressible in first-order conditional rewriting. A detailed comparison between [18] and this paper is left for future work. Another application of completion procedures is proofs by induction [4], which we will explore in future work.

Acknowledgements. We thank the anonymous reviewers and Salvador Lucas for their valuable suggestions and comments, which have contributed to improving this paper.

References

1. Ayala-Rincón, M., de Carvalho Segundo, W., Fernández, M., Silva, G.F., Nantes-Sobrinho, D.: Formalising nominal C-unification generalised with protected variables. Math. Struct. Comput. Sci. **31**(3), 286–311 (2021). https://doi.org/10.1017/S0960129521000050

2. Baader, F., Nipkow, T.: Term Rewriting and All That. Cambridge University Press, Cambridge (1998)

3. Bachmair, L., Dershowitz, N.: Completion for rewriting modulo a congruence. Theor. Comput. Sci. **67**(2&3), 173–201 (1989). https://doi.org/10.1016/0304-3975(89)90003-0

4. Comon, H.: Inductionless induction. In: Robinson, J.A., Voronkov, A. (eds.) Handbook of Automated Reasoning (in 2 volumes), pp. 913–962. Elsevier and MIT Press (2001). https://doi.org/10.1016/B978-044450813-3/50016-3

5. Dershowitz, N., Plaisted, D.A.: Rewriting. In: Robinson, J.A., Voronkov, A. (eds.) Handbook of Automated Reasoning (in 2 volumes), pp. 535–610. Elsevier and MIT Press (2001). https://doi.org/10.1016/B978-044450813-3/50011-4

6. Domínguez, J., Fernández, M.: From nominal to higher-order rewriting and back again. Log. Methods Comput. Sci. **11**(4) (2015). https://doi.org/10.2168/LMCS-11(4:9)2015

7. Escobar, S., Meseguer, J., Sasse, R.: Variant narrowing and equational unification. In: Rosu, G. (ed.) Proceedings of the Seventh International Workshop on Rewriting Logic and its Applications, WRLA 2008. Electronic Notes in Theoretical Computer Science, vol. 238, pp. 103–119. Elsevier (2008). https://doi.org/10.1016/j.entcs.2009.05.015

8. Fernández, M., Gabbay, M.: Nominal rewriting. Inf. Comput. **205**(6), 917–965 (2007). https://doi.org/10.1016/j.ic.2006.12.002

9. Gabbay, M., Pitts, A.M.: A new approach to abstract syntax with variable binding. Formal Aspects Comput. **13**(3-5), 341–363 (2002). https://doi.org/10.1007/s001650200016

10. Gabbay, M.J., Mathijssen, A.: Nominal (universal) algebra: equational logic with names and binding. J. Logic Comput. **19**(6), 1455–1508 (2009). https://doi.org/10.1093/logcom/exp033

11. Hirokawa, N., Kim, D., Shintani, K., Thiemann, R.: Certification of confluence- and commutation-proofs via parallel critical pairs. In: Proceedings of the 13th ACM SIGPLAN International Conference on Certified Programs and Proofs, CPP 2024, pp. 147–161. Association for Computing Machinery, New York (2024). https://doi.org/10.1145/3636501.3636949

12. Jouannaud, J.-P.: Confluent and coherent equational term rewriting systems application to proofs in abstract data types. In: Ausiello, G., Protasi, M. (eds.) CAAP 1983. LNCS, vol. 159, pp. 269–283. Springer, Heidelberg (1983). https://doi.org/10.1007/3-540-12727-5_16

13. Jouannaud, J.-P., Kirchner, C., Kirchner, H.: Incremental construction of unification algorithms in equational theories. In: Diaz, J. (ed.) ICALP 1983. LNCS, vol. 154, pp. 361–373. Springer, Heidelberg (1983). https://doi.org/10.1007/BFb0036921

14. Jouannaud, J., Kirchner, H.: Completion of a set of rules modulo a set of equations. SIAM J. Comput. **15**(4), 1155–1194 (1986). https://doi.org/10.1137/0215084

15. Kirk, C., Middeldorp, A.: Formalizing simultaneous critical pairs for confluence of left-linear rewrite systems. In: Proceedings of the 14th ACM SIGPLAN International Conference on Certified Programs and Proofs, CPP '25, pp. 156–170. Association for Computing Machinery (2025). https://doi.org/10.1145/3703595.3705881

16. Knuth, D.E., Bendix, P.B.: Simple word problems in universal algebras. In: Leech, J. (ed.) Computational Problems in Abstract Algebra, pp. 263–297. Pergamon (1970). https://doi.org/10.1016/B978-0-08-012975-4.50028-X

17. Lankford, D.S.: Canonical inference. Report ATP-32, Departments of Mathematics and Computer Sciences, University of Texas at Austin (1975)

18. Lucas, S.: Confluence of conditional rewriting modulo. In: Murano, A., Silva, A. (eds.) 32nd EACSL Annual Conference on Computer Science Logic (CSL 2024). Leibniz International Proceedings in Informatics (LIPIcs), vol. 288, pp. 37:1–37:21. Schloss Dagstuhl – Leibniz-Zentrum für Informatik, Dagstuhl (2024). https://doi.org/10.4230/LIPIcs.CSL.2024.37

19. Niederhauser, J., Hirokawa, N., Middeldorp, A.: Left-linear completion with AC axioms. Log. Methods Comput. Sci. **21**(2) (2025). https://doi.org/10.46298/LMCS-21(2:10)2025

20. Peterson, G.E., Stickel, M.E.: Complete sets of reductions for some equational theories. J. ACM **28**(2), 233–264 (1981). https://doi.org/10.1145/322248.322251

21. Robinson, J.A., Voronkov, A. (eds.): Handbook of Automated Reasoning (in 2 volumes). Elsevier and MIT Press (2001)

22. Terese: Term rewriting systems, Cambridge tracts in theoretical computer science, vol. 55. Cambridge University Press (2003)
23. Thiemann, R., Yamada, A.: A verified algorithm for deciding pattern completeness. In: Rehof, J. (ed.) 9th Internatioanl Conference on Formal Structures for Computation and Deduction (FSCD 2024). Leibniz International Proceedings in Informatics (LIPIcs), vol. 299, pp. 27:1–27:17. Schloss Dagstuhl – Leibniz-Zentrum für Informatik, Dagstuhl (2024). https://doi.org/10.4230/LIPIcs.FSCD.2024.27

Automated Certification of Logic Program Groundness Analysis

Thierry Marianne$^{(\boxtimes)}$ (ID), Fred Mesnard (ID), and Etienne Payet (ID)

LIM, University of Reunion, Saint-Denis, France
{thierry.marianne,frederic.mesnard,etienne.payet}@univ-reunion.fr

Abstract. In this paper, we are interested in the combination of abstract interpretation and interactive theorem proving, which stand at the opposite ends of the program verification automation spectrum. Our idea is to take advantage of the respective strengths of these two techniques. As a first case study, we focus on groundness analysis of logic programs. Using the proof assistant LPTP (*Logic Program Theorem Prover*), we automate the formal certification of groundness invariants generated by abstract interpretation. We present an experimental evaluation of our approach by applying it to a set of logic programs. Our experiments are twofold. On the one hand, to certify groundness invariants we use automated theorem provers drawing on the theoretical framework of LPTP. On the other hand, we generate and certify natural deduction proofs of groundness invariants with the proof checker of LPTP.

Keywords: Abstract interpretation · Certification · Groundness analysis

1 Introduction

Abstract interpretation [8] is a tool of choice for the static analysis of programming languages. In practice, abstract interpreters are complex programs and potentially contain defects, which raises the question of the validity of the computed information [5]. This article describes two possible answers in the context of groundness analysis of logic programs. Our goal is to automatically certify groundness properties inferred by bottom-up abstract interpretation. We rely on the theoretical framework of LPTP (*Logic Program Theorem Prover*) [17] and its implementation. On the one hand, we use automated demonstration to prove our target conjectures expressed in the specification language of LPTP axiomatized in first order logic. On the other hand, we first construct derivations of the groundness properties by running an implemented completeness theorem for propositional natural deduction, as natural deduction is the proof format of LPTP. Then we certify these derivations by using the proof checker integrated in LPTP.

© The Author(s), under exclusive license to Springer Nature Switzerland AG 2026
S. Escobar and L. Titolo (Eds.): LOPSTR 2025, LNCS 16117, pp. 113–122, 2026.
https://doi.org/10.1007/978-3-032-04848-6_7

This article is organized as follow. In Sect. 2, we introduce some preliminary notions. Section 3 highlights analysis techniques based on abstract interpretation applied to logic programs to infer inter-arguments relations as boolean relations. In Sect. 4, we leverage automated theorem proving to generate proofs of groundness properties expressed in FOF (*First Order Form*), a well-known logic language from TPTP (*Thousands of Problems for Theorem Provers*) [18] for expressing first-order logic axioms and conjectures. Section 5 describes how we formulate groundness properties in LPTP syntax directly from the invariants inferred by abstract interpretation. We present an algorithm to construct a derivation in natural deduction for these properties in the theoretical framework of LPTP. To do so, we explicit elements based on the proof by induction of a propositional formula. Finally, in Sect. 6, we present an experimental evaluation of the two approaches on several logic programs.

2 Preliminaries

We refer to [1,13] for the basics of logic programming including SLD resolution for the operational semantics. We only consider *positive logic programs* and our reference semantics is the s-semantics [3], a non-ground semantics of logic programs. Let P be a positive logic program. Elements of the least fixpoint of the immediate consequences operator T_P are approximated by abstract compilation, for instance using a boolean bottom-up implementation of T_P.

We will prove that these elements belong to the non-ground representation of the least term model M_P of P with LPTP. According to [3], as $M_P = lfp(T_P)$, these proofs certify that these elements belong to the least fixpoint of T_P for the s-semantics.

3 Groundness Analysis

Abstract interpretation [8] is a formal method applied to approximate program semantics by collecting information about data flow for concrete domains, which can be unbounded when the program is executed. The result of this static analysis is an abstraction of the program behaviour [7]. Abstract interpretation was extended to the analysis of logic programs [4,9].

In the context of cTI (*constraint-based Termination Inference*) [15], an abstract interpretation technique named *abstract compilation* provides approximations of the analysed program. These approximations are expressed as inter-arguments relations in the form of boolean relations. We use them to formulate groundness properties. Indeed, dependencies between variables groundness can be represented by boolean constraints [2]. For instance, a relation such as "if the variable Y is instantiated to a ground term, then the variable X is ground" can be denoted by the boolean constraint $y \Rightarrow x$. The boolean variable y (resp. x) represents the instantiation state (ground or possibly not ground) of the variable Y (resp. X).

Let us consider the logic program P defining the predicate append/3:

```
append([], Xs, Xs).
append([X|Xs], Ys, [X|Zs]) :-
    append(Xs, Ys, Zs).
```

The analysis of P by abstract interpretation provides the inter-argument dependency relation $(x \wedge y) \Leftrightarrow z$. This formula expresses the fact that if the call append(x, y, z) succeeds, then, after its proof (via SLD-resolution or bottom-up computation) the third argument z is ground if and only if the first argument x and the second argument y are ground.

4 Automatic Proofs by Automated Theorem Proving

In the mid-90s, Robert F. Stärk showed that for any logic programs P, if $gr(t)$ is provable, ($gr/1$ is a predefined predicate of IND(P), the theoretical framework of LPTP), then t is ground [17]. So $gr(t)$ actually expresses the groundness of a term t. IND(P) consists of first-order logic axioms associated to P. This theory includes Clark's completion [6] and induction along the definition of the predicates. This guarantee allows us to formulate groundness properties about P in the specification language of LPTP, whose semantics is the first-order calculus of classical logic [17].

We follow the methodology introduced in [14] to prove groundness properties inferred by abstract interpretation. The requirements for proving a property are the corresponding logic program P (*append* in our running example) and the invariant to be certified. We compile P into the FOF version of IND(P). Moreover, the groundness property to prove and its induction axiom are compiled as a FOF conjecture. Both this conjecture and IND(P) are stored in a single file. For instance, for our running example, the conjecture is

```
fof('lemma-append3', conjecture,
    ! [Xx1,Xx2,Xx3] : ( append_succeeds(Xx1,Xx2,Xx3)
    => ( ( ( ( ( gr(Xx3) & gr(Xx2) ) & gr(Xx1) ) |
    ( ( ~ ( gr(Xx3) ) & gr(Xx2) ) & ~ ( gr(Xx1) ) ) ) |
    ( ( ~ ( gr(Xx3) ) & ~ ( gr(Xx2) ) ) & gr(Xx1) ) ) |
    ( ( ~ ( gr(Xx3) ) & ~ ( gr(Xx2) ) ) & ~ ( gr(Xx1) ) ) ) )
).
```

Then we apply both *Vampire* [12] and *E Theorem Prover* [16] to the FOF file to try to prove the conjecture within a time limit. So we get either a positive answer or a "don't know" answer. We also have a trace of the positive answer. This trace is not expressed as a LPTP derivation but in a FOF format. The results of our experiments on several logic programs are reported in Sect. 6.

5   Automatic Generation of LPTP Proofs

We consider a groundness property formula provided by cTI for a pure logic program P. In [14], we showed $IND(P)$ (see [17]) allows us the generate an induction axiom for a directly recursive predicate and a formula to prove. For example, let us prove Lemma *append3_gr* below that is inferred by abstract interpretation, where the expression $\mathbf{S}\,\text{append}(x_1, x_2, x_3)$ expresses success of the goal $\text{append}(x_1, x_2, x_3)$ and the unary predicate gr of LPTP expresses groundness of its argument.

Lemma $[append3\_gr]$ $\forall x_1, x_2, x_3 \,(\mathbf{S}\,\text{append}(x_1, x_2, x_3) \rightarrow$
$(gr(x_3) \wedge gr(x_2) \wedge gr(x_1)) \vee (\neg gr(x_3) \wedge gr(x_2) \wedge \neg gr(x_1)) \vee$
$(\neg gr(x_3) \wedge \neg gr(x_2) \wedge gr(x_1)) \vee (\neg gr(x_3) \wedge \neg gr(x_2) \wedge \neg gr(x_1)))$.

Axiom II of $IND(P)$, whose application is hard-coded in LPTP, allows one to introduce equivalences involving gr applied to compound terms:

Axiom II of IND(P) for gr [17]
  4. $gr(c)$ [if c is a constant]
  5. $gr(x_1) \wedge \ldots \wedge gr(x_m) \leftrightarrow gr(f(x_1, \ldots, x_m))$ [f is m-ary]

The automatic translation by LPTP of the code of $\text{append}/3$ into an inductive definition results in the formula:

$$\forall x, y, z \Big(\mathbf{S}\,\text{append}(x, y, z) \leftrightarrow (x = [\,] \wedge z = y) \vee$$

$$\exists v_0, xs, zs(x = [v_0 | xs] \wedge z = [v_0 | zs] \wedge \mathbf{S}\,\text{append}(xs, y, zs)) \Big)$$

The general form of the groundness property to prove is an implication whose conclusion is in clausal disjunctive normal form. It is derived from the groundness formula inferred by cTI:

$$\forall x_1, \ldots, x_n \,\mathbf{S}\,R(x_1, \ldots, x_n) \rightarrow \bigvee \bigwedge gr\_ngr(x_j)$$

where R is a n-ary user-defined predicate and $gr\_ngr(x_j)$ denotes either $gr(x_j)$ or $\neg gr(x_j)$.

We implement an algorithm inspired by the proof of the next proposition, which is used in [11] to show the completeness of natural deduction for propositional logic.

Proposition 1 (Prop. 1.38 of [11]). *Let ϕ be a formula such that $p_1, \ldots, p_n$ are its only propositional atoms. Let l be any line number in ϕ's truth table. For all $1 \leq i \leq n$, let $\hat{p}_i$ be p_i if the entry in line l of p_i is True, otherwise $\hat{p}_i$ is $\neg p_i$. Then we have*

  1. $\hat{p}_1, \ldots, \hat{p}_n \vdash \phi$ *is provable if the entry for ϕ in line l is True.*
  2. $\hat{p}_1, \ldots, \hat{p}_n \vdash \neg\phi$ *is provable if the entry for ϕ in line l is False.*

This result is proved by structural induction on ϕ. Taking our inspiration from it, we replace the propositional variables in the groundness formula to prove by calls to gr. As LPTP is implemented in Prolog, we reuse its syntax, its declarative operator **S** for predicate success and its tactics to mechanize the generation of a complete proof term.

First of all, we enumerate the variables of the target groundness formula ϕ. The idea is to generate a proof matching the lines of the truth table of ϕ. We note that the number of lines of the table is 2^n, where n is the number of variables. We implemented the procedure prove_with_premises, given in pseudo-code below. It returns a derivation (Deriv) from a groundness property (Phi), some premises (Premises) and a truth value (TruthValue). It considers all possible relations (groundness gr, negation ~, conjunction &, disjunction \/ and implication =>) and contains recursive calls on the sub-formulas of Phi (see Form, Phi1 and Phi2 below). The procedure assemble_derivation transforms the groundness sub-formulas by application of Axiom II of IND(P) before assembling the groundness formula derivation in LPTP syntax from the sole Premises passed as argument for the formula truth value (TruthValue) to be shown.

```
prove_with_premises(Phi, TruthValue, Premises)
  switch Phi
    case gr(Form) :
      Deriv := assemble_derivation(gr(Form), TruthValue, Premises)
    case ~ Form :
      Deriv := prove_with_premises(Form, ~ TruthValue, Premises)
    case Phi1 & Phi2 :
      D1 := prove_with_premises(Phi1, TruthValue, Premises)
      D2 := prove_with_premises(Phi2, TruthValue, Premises)
      Deriv := concat(D1, D2)
    case Phi1 \/ Phi2 :
      D1 := prove_with_premises(
        Phi1, TruthValue, concat(~ Phi2, Premises)
      )
      D2 := prove_with_premises(
        Phi2, TruthValue, concat(~ Phi1, Premises)
      )
      Deriv := concat(D1, D2)
    case Phi1 => Phi2 :
      Deriv := prove_with_premises(
        Phi2, TruthValue, concat(Phi1, Premises)
      )
  return Deriv
```

We apply the disjunction elimination rule in a systematic way from the 2^n cases we get. This can be translated directly in LPTP by the recursive application of the *cases* tactic for disjunctions expressing that a variable is ground or free. The target groundness formula ϕ is reduced by syntactic decomposition to produce a derivation. Hence, the sequents we get depend solely on the premises originating from the successive application of the law of excluded middle for each variable. As a result, we cover all 2^n groundness cases for all variables at stake by grouping these sequents altogether.

Back to our running example, the induction axiom schema for append/3 and the groundness formula provided by abstract interpretation allow us to generate a proof of Lemma *append3_gr* with two gaps (**GAP**), one in the base case and one in the induction step. We apply the algorithm described above to fill these gaps. In both cases, we aim at proving a tautology (for all possible variables groundness) in disjunctive normal form. Beginning with the base case (between the two horizontal lines below), we observe that $gr([])$ is true by application of Axiom II.4 of IND(P). Moreover, we find the unique variable x_4, so two cases must be considered depending on its groundness. The algorithm previously described provides the following excerpt after filling the gap in the base case.

Lemma [*append3_gr*] $\forall x_1, x_2, x_3$ (**S** append$(x_1, x_2, x_3) \rightarrow$
$(gr(x_3) \wedge gr(x_2) \wedge gr(x_1)) \vee (\neg gr(x_3) \wedge gr(x_2) \wedge \neg gr(x_1)) \vee$
$(\neg gr(x_3) \wedge \neg gr(x_2) \wedge gr(x_1)) \vee (\neg gr(x_3) \wedge \neg gr(x_2) \wedge \neg gr(x_1)))$.

Proof.

Induction$_0$: $\forall x_1, x_2, x_3$ (**S** append$(x_1, x_2, x_3) \rightarrow$
$(gr(x_3) \wedge gr(x_2) \wedge gr(x_1)) \vee (\neg gr(x_3) \wedge gr(x_2) \wedge \neg gr(x_1)) \vee$
$(\neg gr(x_3) \wedge \neg gr(x_2) \wedge gr(x_1)) \vee (\neg gr(x_3) \wedge \neg gr(x_2) \wedge \neg gr(x_1)))$.

Hypothesis$_1$: none.
   Case$_2$: $gr(x_4)$. $gr(x_4) \wedge gr(x_4)$. $gr(x_4) \wedge gr(x_4) \wedge gr([])$.
    $(gr(x_4) \wedge gr(x_4) \wedge gr([])) \vee (\neg gr(x_4) \wedge gr(x_4) \wedge \neg gr([]))$.
    $(gr(x_4) \wedge gr(x_4) \wedge gr([])) \vee (\neg gr(x_4) \wedge gr(x_4) \wedge \neg gr([])) \vee$
    $(\neg gr(x_4) \wedge \neg gr(x_4) \wedge gr([]))$.
    $(gr(x_4) \wedge gr(x_4) \wedge gr([])) \vee (\neg gr(x_4) \wedge gr(x_4) \wedge \neg gr([])) \vee$
    $(\neg gr(x_4) \wedge \neg gr(x_4) \wedge gr([])) \vee (\neg gr(x_4) \wedge \neg gr(x_4) \wedge \neg gr([]))$.
   Case$_2$: $\neg gr(x_4)$. $\neg gr(x_4) \wedge \neg gr(x_4)$.
    $\neg gr(x_4) \wedge \neg gr(x_4) \wedge gr([])$. $(gr(x_4) \wedge gr(x_4) \wedge gr([])) \vee$
    $(\neg gr(x_4) \wedge gr(x_4) \wedge \neg gr([])) \vee (\neg gr(x_4) \wedge \neg gr(x_4) \wedge gr([]))$.
    $(gr(x_4) \wedge gr(x_4) \wedge gr([])) \vee (\neg gr(x_4) \wedge gr(x_4) \wedge \neg gr([])) \vee$
    $(\neg gr(x_4) \wedge \neg gr(x_4) \wedge gr([])) \vee (\neg gr(x_4) \wedge \neg gr(x_4) \wedge \neg gr([]))$.
   Hence$_2$, in all cases: $(gr(x_4) \wedge gr(x_4) \wedge gr([])) \vee (\neg gr(x_4) \wedge gr(x_4) \wedge \neg gr([])) \vee$
   $(\neg gr(x_4) \wedge \neg gr(x_4) \wedge gr([])) \vee (\neg gr(x_4) \wedge \neg gr(x_4) \wedge \neg gr([]))$.
   Conclusion$_1$: $(gr(x_4) \wedge gr(x_4) \wedge gr([])) \vee (\neg gr(x_4) \wedge gr(x_4) \wedge \neg gr([])) \vee$
   $(\neg gr(x_4) \wedge \neg gr(x_4) \wedge gr([])) \vee (\neg gr(x_4) \wedge \neg gr(x_4) \wedge \neg gr([]))$.

Hypothesis$_1$: $\forall x_5, x_6, x_7, x_8$ $(gr(x_8) \wedge gr(x_7) \wedge gr(x_6) \vee$
   $\neg gr(x_8) \wedge gr(x_7) \wedge \neg gr(x_6) \vee \neg gr(x_8) \wedge \neg gr(x_7) \wedge gr(x_6) \vee$
   $\neg gr(x_8) \wedge \neg gr(x_7) \wedge \neg gr(x_6)$ and **S** append$(x_6, x_7, x_8))$. $\bot$ by **GAP**.

Conclusion$_1$: $(gr([x_5|x_8]) \wedge gr(x_7) \wedge gr([x_5|x_6])) \vee$
$(\neg gr([x_5|x_8]) \wedge gr(x_7) \wedge \neg gr([x_5|x_6])) \vee (\neg gr([x_5|x_8]) \wedge \neg gr(x_7) \wedge gr([x_5|x_6])) \vee$
$(\neg gr([x_5|x_8]) \wedge \neg gr(x_7) \wedge \neg gr([x_5|x_6]))$. $\square$

We apply the same technique to the induction step after enumerating its variables (x_5, x_6, x_7, x_8). The complete derivations are publicly available online[1]. Finally, we check the generated proof term with LPTP to certify the derivations that we have built.

6   Experimentation

We experimented our methodology using programs from the LPTP library, to which other programs were added, see Table 1, sorted in ascending order of number of lines of code in LPTP format (column LOC).

Table 1. Experimental results

Prog.	Prop.	Vars	Inf. (ms)	V/E (ms)	FOF LOC	Deriv. (ms)	Cert. (ms)	LOC
member.pl	1	3	3	3	66	6	7	269
for.pl	2	4	4	8	243	8	6	273
addmul.pl	2	6	4	18	1412	9	16	911
ackermann.pl	1	3	4	17	1972	8	16	949
fib.pl	2	5	5	19	1768	10	14	970
nat.pl	4	8	6	166	2383	11	16	975
int.pl	6	11	10	55	6386	16	19	1049
split.pl	1	3	9	10	974	14	28	1123
suffix.pl	4	10	12	17	554	18	22	1203
list.pl	5	12	19	2456	6760	26	67	2873
derivDLS.pl	1	3	20	12306	4705	263	146	3931
reverse.pl	4	10	20	493	3451	43	93	3958
average1.pl	3	7	7	22	752	17	116	8846
permutation.pl	7	19	22	215	2864	36	216	9335
transitiveclosure.pl	6	18	43	105	10220	541	654	14213
sort.pl	9	22	72	12755	867612	319	12187	71067

We used SWI-Prolog version 9.2.2 and an Apple MacBook Pro M2 running macOS Sonoma 14.6.1. For each program (column Prog.), we measured the number of groundness properties inferred by cTI (column Prop.), the total number of variables that these properties contain (column Vars) and the time it takes

---

[1] github.com/atp-lptp/automated-certification-of-logic-program-groundness-analysis.

for cTI to compute them (column Inf.). Using the methodology described in Sect. 4 (without proof reconstruction in LPTP format), we successfully certified all these properties automatically using *Vampire* (version 4.9) and *E Theorem Prover* (version 3.1), with a time limit of 1 min. The shortest certification time performed by either *Vampire* or *E Theorem Prover* has been reported in column V/E. The number of lines of the proofs in FOF format is provided in column FOF LOC. We also applied the technique presented in Sect. 5. We measured the time required to construct the groundness properties proof (column Deriv.) and the time to certify their derivations with LPTP (column Cert.).

We didn't find any wrong invariant from this limited experiment. Such a case would result in a timeout in the V/E column and a failure to construct the LPTP derivation for the wrong invariant.

We observe that the number of lines in the FOF format proofs (column FOF LOC) ranges from comparable to up to an order of magnitude greater than the number of lines of code in LPTP format (column LOC). Moreover, the space complexity to generate the derivation cases is exponential in the number of variables occurring in each groundness property. This complexity is one of the main limitations of our implementation. It originates from the choice of Huth and Ryan's algorithm to construct a tautology in natural deduction.

7   Conclusion

Proof assistants like Isabelle with *Sledgehammer* use tools like *cvc5*[2] without abstract interpretation. Using such tools participates in saving time when proving facts by suggesting lemmas and tactics. In order to keep the possibility for users to check entire proofs, a proof reconstruction mechanism based on certificates has been introduced [10].

This article illustrated this idea in the context of logic programming. We combine the advantage of invariants algorithmic generation by abstract interpretation and formal verification offered by an interactive proof assistant. We have considered two techniques to certify groundness properties. First, we leveraged automated theorem provers without guaranteed termination and no proof in LPTP format. Second, we have used the proof checker integrated within LPTP by automatically constructing proofs for each groundness property by applying Huth and Ryan's algorithm, which always terminates, with a complexity exponential in the number of propositional variables.

More in-depth work is needed to better compare these two techniques. We would like to take into account negation by failure as well. We aim at reducing computing time complexity exposed above. Other inter-arguments relations types, matching other abstract domains and proof procedures, belong to paths yet to be explored to show the genericity of our approach.

Acknowledgments. We are thankful to Manuel Hermenegildo, Pedro Lopez and José Morales for all the discussions we had on this topic. We also thank the anonymous reviewers for their insightful and constructive criticisms.

---

[2] https://cvc5.github.io/blog/2024/03/15/isabelle-reconstruction.html.

Disclosure of Interests. The authors have no competing interests to declare that are relevant to the content of this article.

References

1. Apt, K.R.: Logic programming. In: van Leeuwen, J. (ed.) Handbook of Theoretical Computer Science, Volume B: Formal Models and Semantics, pp. 493–574. Elsevier and MIT Press (1990)
2. Armstrong, T., Marriott, K., Schachte, P., Søndergaard, H.: Two classes of boolean functions for dependency analysis. Sci. Comput. Program. **31**(1), 3–45 (1998). https://doi.org/10.1016/S0167-6423(96)00039-1
3. Bossi, A., Gabbrielli, M., Levi, G., Martelli, M.: The s-semantics approach: theory and applications. J. Log. Program. **19**(20), 149–197 (1994). https://doi.org/10.1016/0743-1066(94)90026-4
4. Bruynooghe, M.: A framework for the abstract interpretation of logic programs. Department of Computer Science, K.U.Leuven, Leuven, Belgium (1987-10-01). https://doi.org/10.1016/0743-1066(91)80001-T
5. Casso, I., Morales, J.F., López-García, P., Hermenegildo, M.V.: Testing Your (Static Analysis) Truths. In: Fernández, M. (ed.) Logic-Based Program Synthesis and Transformation, pp. 271–292. Springer International Publishing, Cham (2021). https://doi.org/10.1007/978-3-030-68446-4_14
6. Clark, K.L.: Negation as failure. In: Gallaire, H., Minker, J. (eds.) Logic and Data Bases, Symposium on Logic and Data Bases, Centre d'études et de recherches de Toulouse, France, pp. 293–322. Advances in Data Base Theory, Plemum Press, New York (1977). https://doi.org/10.1007/978-1-4684-3384-5_11
7. Cousot, P., Cousot, R.: Abstract interpretation frameworks. J. Log. Comput. **2**(4), 511–547 (1992). https://doi.org/10.1093/logcom/2.4.511
8. Cousot, P., Cousot, R.: Abstract interpretation: a unified lattice model for static analysis of programs by construction or approximation of fixpoints. In: Proceedings of the 4th ACM SIGACT-SIGPLAN Symposium on Principles of Programming Languages, pp. 238–252 (1977). https://doi.org/10.1145/512950.512973
9. Cousot, P., Cousot, R.: Abstract interpretation and application to logic programs. J. Log. Program. **13**(2&3), 103–179 (1992). https://doi.org/10.1016/0743-1066(92)90030-7
10. Fleury, M., Schurr, H.J.: Reconstructing veriT Proofs in Isabelle/HOL. Electr. Proc. Theoret. Comput. Sci. **301**, 36–50 (2019). https://doi.org/10.4204/EPTCS.301.6
11. Huth, M., Ryan, M.: Logic in Computer Science: Modelling and Reasoning about Systems. Logic in Computer Science: Modelling and Reasoning about Systems, Cambridge University Press (2000)
12. Kovács, L., Voronkov, A.: First-order theorem proving and vampire. In: Sharygina, N., Veith, H. (eds.) CAV 2013. LNCS, vol. 8044, pp. 1–35. Springer (2013). https://doi.org/10.1007/978-3-642-39799-8_1
13. Lloyd, J.W.: Foundations of Logic Programming, 2nd Edition. Springer (1987)
14. Mesnard, F., Marianne, T., Payet, E.: Automated theorem proving for Prolog verification. In: Bjørner, N., Heule, M., Voronkov, A. (eds.) LPAR 2024 Complementary Volume. Kalpa Publications in Computing, vol. 18, pp. 137–151. EasyChair (2024). https://doi.org/10.29007/c25r

15. Mesnard, F., Neumerkel, Ulrich et Payet, E.: cTI : un outil pour l'inférence de conditions optimales de terminaison pour Prolog. In: 10eme Journées francophones de programmation logique et programmation par contraintes (JFPLC 2001), pp. 271–286. Association Française pour la Programmation en Logique et la programmation par Contraintes (AFPLC), Hermes Science Publications, Paris, France (Apr 2001)
16. Schulz, S., Cruanes, S., Vukmirović, P.: Faster, higher, stronger: E 2.3. In: Fontaine, P. (ed.) CADE 2019. LNCS (LNAI), vol. 11716, pp. 495–507. Springer, Cham (2019). https://doi.org/10.1007/978-3-030-29436-6_29
17. Stärk, R.F.: The theoretical foundations of LPTP (a logic program theorem prover). J. Logic Program. **36**(3), 241–269 (1998). https://doi.org/10.1016/S0743-1066(97)10013-9
18. Sutcliffe, G.: The logic languages of the TPTP world. Logic J. IGPL **31**(6), 1153–1169 (2023). https://doi.org/10.1093/jigpal/jzac068

CurryInfo: Managing Analysis and Verification Information about Curry Packages

Michael Hanus$^{(\boxtimes)}$

Institut für Informatik, Kiel University, Kiel, Germany
mh@informatik.uni-kiel.de

Abstract. CurryInfo is a tool to manage information about program entities defined in modules of Curry packages. CurryInfo is designed as a generic and extensible system so that the kind of information ranges from syntactic (e.g., comments, types, source code) to semantic aspects (e.g., determinism, termination, total definition, non-failing). CurryInfo collects such information and provides various methods to access them. For instance, one can show this information in a REPL or IDE to help the programmer to select or use operations in an appropriate manner. Another application is to include this information in other tools to analyze or verify programs. Since CurryInfo manages a cache containing information about all Curry packages, this can speed up such tools on larger applications.

1 Introduction

Larger software system are usually not developed from scratch but by re-using many existing pieces of software—typically organized in packages. Although such packages provide an API describing its use, the knowledge of the API information does often not suffice for its correct use. For instance, in a strongly typed programming language, the API is a collection of signatures of operations exported by the package so that the type-correct use of these operations can be checked by the compiler. However, the knowledge about the signature is sometimes not sufficient. For instance, in imperative languages, operations might have side effects which are not explicitly mentioned in their interfaces. Although side effects cannot occur in declarative languages, there are other aspects relevant to the programmer, like determinism or termination behavior, or conditions for the non-failing execution of an operation. Since declarative languages are a good basis to infer or approximate such semantic aspects, one can show them to the programmer instead of manually browsing through the source code.

This is one of the motivations to develop the system described in this paper. As the name indicates, CurryInfo is a system to support the development and analysis of programs written in the multi-paradigm declarative language Curry[1] which amalgamates features of functional and logic programming. Due to this combination, operations have various semantic properties which are not immediately visible from their definition. For instance,

---

[1] https://www.curry-lang.org.

© The Author(s), under exclusive license to Springer Nature Switzerland AG 2026
S. Escobar and L. Titolo (Eds.): LOPSTR 2025, LNCS 16117, pp. 123–134, 2026.
https://doi.org/10.1007/978-3-032-04848-6_8

- Operations might be non-deterministic [9], i.e., might yield more than one value for a given argument: although this is an important concept of contemporary functional logic languages (see [3,9] for more details about the advantages of non-deterministic operations), such operations must be used with care in top-level computations involving I/O, since non-deterministic computations need to be encapsulated inside deterministic I/O operations.
- Operations might be non-terminating: in lazy functional languages, computing with non-terminating operations is a feature supporting modularity [20] but they must be used with care. Hence, it is useful to see the termination status of operations during program development.
- Operations might fail on some arguments: when partially defined operations are used, one should either check before the call the admissibility of the arguments or check after the call whether it has failed (e.g., by encapsulated search or exception handlers). Thus, it is important to know whether an operation is totally defined or has a specific non-fail condition [13].

In the language Mercury [23], some of these properties, like non-determinism and possible failures, are part of the source programs and used to generate efficient target code. As a consequence, explicitly defined properties restrict the set of admissible Mercury programs whereas we are interested to keep the flexibility of Curry but approximate semantic properties at compile time [15,16,18]. Since such approximations require non-trivial program analyses based on fixpoint computations, their computation needs some time for larger applications with dozens or hundreds of modules. To avoid a time-consuming computation in an interactive programming environment (e.g., REPL or IDE), CurryInfo provides an infrastructure to compute and collect such information when packages are uploaded, stores this information in a central cache, and provides methods to deliver this information in various formats so that it can be used by different tools. This has the following advantages:

- The use of CurryInfo during program development (e.g., in a REPL or IDE) supports the programmer to consider non-trivial semantic properties of operations when they are applied.
- The use of CurryInfo in other analysis or verification tools can speed up their computations since they can fetch information about imported packages from CurryInfo instead of locally (re)computing it.

After a short introduction to Curry and existing analysis and verification tools in Sect. 2, we survey the information managed by CurryInfo in Sect. 3 and show the basic usage of CurryInfo in Sect. 4. Section 5 describes the structure and implementation of CurryInfo and the methods provided to extend CurryInfo in a modular manner. Section 6 contains our conclusions with a short evaluation.

2   Analysis and Verification of Curry Programs

The declarative language Curry [19] amalgamates features from functional programming (demand-driven evaluation, strong typing, higher-order functions) and logic programming (computing with partial information, unification, constraints), see [3,10] for surveys. The syntax of Curry is close to Haskell [22]. In addition to Haskell, Curry applies rules with overlapping left-hand sides in a (don't know) non-deterministic manner (where Haskell always selects the first matching rule) and allows *free (logic) variables* in conditions and right-hand sides of defining rules. For instance, the following operation inserts an element at an unspecified position into a list:

```
insert :: a  → [a]  → [a]
insert x []    = [x]
insert x (y:ys) = x : y : ys
insert x (y:ys) = y : insert x ys
```

Note that both of the last two rules can be applied when the second argument of `insert` is a non-empty list. Thus, the expression `insert 0 [1,2]` non-deterministically evaluates to any of the values `[0,1,2]`, `[1,0,2]`, or `[1,2,0]`. `insert` can be used to define permutations of lists in a simple manner:

```
perm :: [a]  → [a]
perm []    = []
perm (x:xs) = insert x (perm xs)
```

Note that `perm` is defined by non-overlapping rules, but `perm [1,2,3,4]` non-deterministically evaluates to any of the 24 permutations of the input list. This demonstrates that the (non-)determinism status of `perm` is not directly visible from its signature or definition.

In order to help the programmer to recognize semantic properties of operations which might depend on the behavior of directly or indirectly used operations, there exist various tools to approximate such properties. For instance, the generic analysis system CASS [18] provides an infrastructure for fixpoint computations which is incremental w.r.t. a given modular structure of programs to enable the analysis of larger applications. CASS is based on the idea of abstract interpretation [7] so that abstract domains and the corresponding abstract operations can be defined and plugged into the infrastructure of CASS. Currently, CASS supports more than 30 different analyses[2] on Curry programs to approximate properties like determinism, totally definedness, termination, demanded arguments, groundness, etc. It has been used in various applications, e.g., to transform Boolean equalities into unification to reduce search spaces [5], to detect non-deterministic operations relevant to top-level computations [4], or to optimize programs [6].

Another recent tool targets the safe execution of Curry programs by verifying the absence of failures at compile time [16]. For this purpose, non-fail conditions [13], which approximate arguments that ensure the fail-free execution of operations, are automatically inferred. For instance, consider the operations

```
last :: [a]  → a              fac :: Int  → Int
last [x]     = x              fac n | n == 0 = 1
last (_:x:xs) = last (x:xs)         | n > 0  = n * fac (n-1)
```

---

[2] See https://cpm.curry-lang.org/webapps/cass/main.cgi?DOC_Analyses for more details.

The tool described in [16] infers that, if the argument of `last` is a non-empty list, it does not fail. This is done by an inference with a domain of abstract types and using properties approximated by CASS. Furthermore, the non-fail condition "`n==0 || n>0`" is inferred for `fac` by combining this approach with solving arithmetic constraints [15], for which an SMT solver [8] is used. If `last` or `fac` are used in other operations, either the non-fail conditions are satisfied in these uses or they imply new non-fail conditions of operations using them. Altogether, the inference and verification of non-fail conditions can be time-consuming on larger applications.

Since Curry is a universal programming language intended to implement larger applications, it has many additional features not described here, like monadic I/O [24] for declarative input/output, set functions [2] to encapsulate non-deterministic search, or functional patterns [1] to specify complex transformations in a high-level manner. Curry programs are structured in modules[3] and modules can be organized in packages The Curry package manager[4] provides access to currently more than 140 packages with several hundred modules.[5] Since non-trivial applications written in Curry are based on dozens of packages (e.g., the Curry package manager is written in Curry and uses 40 packages and more than 130 modules), it is relevant to have information about imported program entities during the development of such applications. This is one of the main motivations for the development of CurryInfo.

3   Information Managed by CurryInfo

CurryInfo is intended to provide an overview of entities defined in Curry packages. This section surveys the entities and the information managed by CurryInfo.

A *package* contains the implementation of some functionality in a particular application domain. Since the implementation and functionality evolves over time, packages come in different *versions* with unique identifiers. The semantic versioning standard[6] is a recommendation to associate meaningful identifiers to different versions of a package. The Curry package manager supports checking these recommendations [12].

A package contains, apart from management information, documentation, or test suites, a set of *modules*. Each module defines *operations* to implement the required functionality. Since Curry is strongly typed with a Haskell-like type system, a module might also contain definitions of *types* (data types or type synonyms) and *classes* (type classes [25] or type constructor classes [21]).

To reflect this structure, CurryInfo manages various information about packages, versions, modules, operations, types, and classes, which are also called *entities* in CurryInfo. For each entity, one can ask CurryInfo for different pieces of

---

[3] The module system is almost identical to Haskell's module system.

[4] https://curry-lang.org/tools/cpm.

[5] https://cpm.curry-lang.org/.

[6] http://www.semver.org/.

information which are called *requests* of CurryInfo. Some of the requests for the different entities are:[7]

- *package requests*: the name and the identifiers of the versions of a package
  version requests: the version identifier, documentation, modules, and package dependencies of this version
- *module requests*: name, documentation, source code, lists of exported operations, types, and classes
- *operation requests*: name, documentation, definition, signature, fixity, and various semantic properties, like determinism, demanded arguments, solution completeness, termination, totally definedness, result values, non-fail conditions
- *type requests*: name, documentation, definition, and list of constructors
- *class requests*: name, documentation, definition, and list of methods

Since CurryInfo is designed to be extensible, new requests can easily be added provided that a tool is available to compute them (see Sect. 5).

4   Usage

Before we show details of the implementation of CurryInfo, we survey various use cases of CurryInfo in this section.

Basically, the executable of CurryInfo can be invoked with options to specify an entity and the requests to be shown for this entity. For instance, requests about the operation `length` defined in the module `Prelude` of package `base` with version `3.3.0` can be shown as follows:

```
curry-info --package=base --version=3.3.0 --module=Prelude
  --operation=length documentation deterministic totally-defined
  terminating demand failfree
```

Requests are computed on-demand or taken from a cache (see Sect. 5) if they have already been computed.

Since this raw access to requests is cumbersome, there is also the tiny wrapper tool `cpm-query`[8] so that one can compute the same information as above by the command

```
cpm-query Prelude length
```

`cpm-query` searches for a package version containing `length` in module `Prelude` according to the current load path. Moreover, the default requests shown for a given kind of entity can be specified in a configuration file. Thus, `cpm-query` provides a simple method to access analysis and verification information by other tools, as shown next.

Curry systems come with an interactive REPL (Read-Eval-Print-Loop) which has commands to load modules or to evaluate expressions. The recent

---

[7] The page https://cpm.curry-lang.org/curry-info/run.cgi?--requests shows the actual list of all requests supported by CurryInfo.

[8] https://cpm.curry-lang.org/pkgs/cpm-query.html.

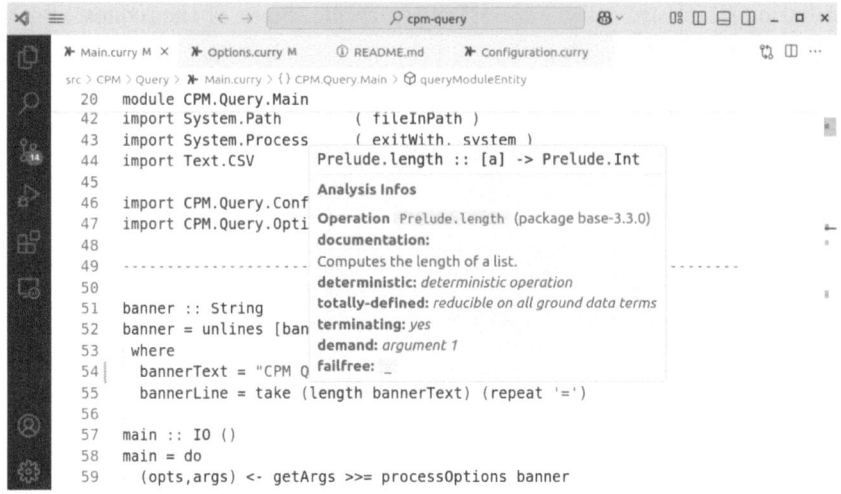

Fig. 1. Showing analysis information of `length` by CurryInfo in Visual Studio Code.

release of PAKCS [17] has a command ":`info`" which invokes `cpm-query` to show requests of operations, types, or classes. For instance, the command

> `:info length`

returns the same information as the call to `cpm-query` shown above provided that the `Prelude` operation `length` is in the scope of the REPL expression (otherwise, one has to qualify the operation with its module name).

The most convenient use of CurryInfo is via the Curry Language Server[9] since it supports an extension to invoke any command when hovering over particular program entities, like operations, types, or classes, in a program editor supporting the language server protocol. If this extension is configured to invoke `cpm-query`,[10] hovering over an occurrence of `length` in the editor pops up a window with analysis and verification information provided by CurryInfo. Figure 1 shows a screenshot when hovering over `length` using this extension in Visual Studio Code.

A further use of CurryInfo is to speed up the computation of other analysis or verification tools. For instance, in global program analyses, such as mentioned in Sect. 2, CASS analyzes all imported modules before analyzing the current module [18]. This means that all imported packages are analyzed before the main modules of an application can be analyzed which might be time-consuming for larger applications. A concrete implementation of this usage is evaluated in Appendix A.

---

[9] https://github.com/fwcd/curry-language-server.

[10] See https://github.com/curry-packages/cpm-query/blob/main/README.md.

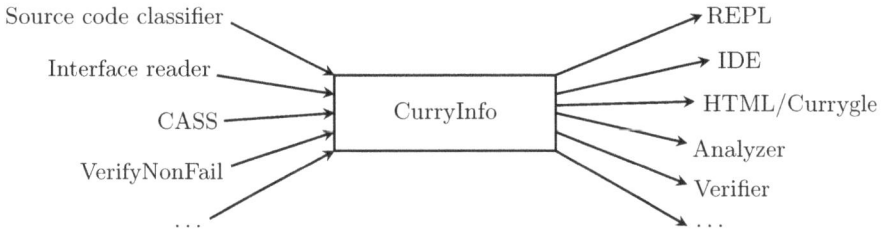

Fig. 2. Structure of the CurryInfo system.

5   System Structure and Implementation

CurryInfo provides a generic infrastructure to collect information about Curry packages from different sources and delivers the collected information in various forms, as shown in Fig. 2. Currently, the following tools contribute information:

– Information about documentation comments and definitions of operations, types, and classes in the source text is extracted by a specific source code classifier[11] which performs a lexical and syntactical analysis of Curry programs to group the source text.
– The front end of Curry implementations generates interface files to organize the independent compilation of modules. These interface files are processed by a specific interface reader[12] in order to extract the signature and fixity information of operations defined in modules.
– Analysis and verification information is obtained from external tools, like [15,16,18]. Since these tools can deliver their results also in a standard JSON format, it is easier to parse these results instead of integrating these complex tools in CurryInfo.

In order to get requests from CurryInfo for various purposes, CurryInfo can deliver results in different output formats, like human-readable text, optional with markdown syntax, JSON, or as Curry data terms. Moreover, CurryInfo can be invoked in different modes:

– *command mode* (as shown in Sect. 4): parameters are passed as options and the results are printed on the output stream.
– *server mode*: communication with CurryInfo is done via a socket connection and a specified protocol so that CurryInfo is kept active until the communication is closed.
– *web service mode*: this is similar to the command mode but parameters are passed by the environment variable `QUERY_STRING` so that the executable `curry-info` can be used as a CGI script on a web server. The default installation of this web service is at https://cpm.curry-lang.org/curry-info/. When a new package version is uploaded, this web service will be informed so that it

---

[11] https://cpm.curry-lang.org/pkgs/curry-source.html.
[12] https://cpm.curry-lang.org/pkgs/curry-interface.html.

automatically starts to compute all requests for this package and stores this information in its cache.

In its default mode, `cpm-query` contacts this web service to request information. Thus, when using `cpm-query` in a REPL or IDE, as discussed in Sect. 4, it is not necessary to have a local installation of CurryInfo.

CurryInfo also stores all information in human-readable HTML format in static web pages. The Curry API search engine Curr(y)gle[13] delivers references to the information stored in the CurryInfo web pages so that Curry users have immediate access to analysis and verification information of operations defined in published packages.

Since the actual computation of requests can be costly in the case of complex analysis or verification tasks, CurryInfo caches already computed results for program entities. For this purpose, CurryInfo associates a file to each entity which contains a JSON object with request names as keys.[14] For requests dealing with source texts (documentation comments, definitions), only references to the original source files are stored in the JSON objects to limit their sizes.

As already mentioned, CurryInfo is designed to be extensible, i.e., new requests can easily be added to the implementation of CurryInfo. For this purpose, CurryInfo has a configuration module where the requests for the different entities are defined by calls to the generic operation

```
registerRequest :: ConvertJSON b => String  →  String
    →  Generator a b  →  Printer b  →  RegisteredRequest a
```

Here, `a` is the type of entities (package, module, operation,...) and `b` is the type of values of the request. Since these values are stored in the cache in JSON format, the class constraint "`ConvertJSON b`" requires conversion operations to and from JSON. The first argument is an identifier of the request and the second argument a short description (to be shown in the help menu). The third argument is an operation which generates, for an entity of type `a`, the requested value of type `b`. The fourth argument prints a value of the request as a string (according to output format options). Hence, in order to add a new kind of request to CurryInfo, one has to implement a generator for this request, e.g., by using an external analysis tool, and a pretty printer for request values, and add them to the implementation of CurryInfo[15] by using `registerRequest`.

6   Conclusions

We presented CurryInfo, an infrastructure to collect information about entities defined in Curry packages and to distribute them to different applications. CurryInfo is generic in the kind of information so that it can cover syntactic as well

---

[13] https://cpm.curry-lang.org/currygle/.

[14] In principle, one can also use a data base for all entities. Since there is a direct mapping from entities to files, the use of JSON files was advantageous for debugging during the development of CurryInfo.

[15] Available at https://github.com/curry-language/curry-info-system.

as semantic properties of program entities, like information inferred by program analysis or verification systems. Providing information about semantic aspects is quite relevant since computing them is time consuming for larger packages. Therefore, CurryInfo caches this information so that it is immediately available when required by a REPL or IDE.

To get an impression of the usability of CurryInfo in an IDE, we measured the time[16] to execute `cpm-query` to compute the results as shown in Fig. 1. The elapsed time of this execution is 0.3 s when using the remote CurryInfo web service (which runs on a different server outside the local network), which is an acceptable time in an IDE. This time reduces to 0.1 s when a local installation of CurryInfo is used (for this purpose, the CurryInfo web server allows to download its cache so that it can be locally installed). Although this difference seems relevant, it is hardly recognizable when hovering in an IDE. On the other hand, the on-demand analysis of the same information without CurryInfo requires more than a minute. This clearly demonstrates the advantage of CurryInfo and its information caching. The use of CurryInfo to speed up other analysis tools is discussed and evaluated in Appendix A.

For future work it is interesting to evaluate whether the use of a database for the cache might provide an efficiency improvement, to add further requests that could be helpful to the programmer, like verified contracts [14], or to use CurryInfo in other analysis or verification systems.

A   Using CurryInfo in Analysis Tools

As mentioned in Sect. 4, the information managed by CurryInfo can be useful to speed up the computation of other analysis or verification tools. To evaluate this potential usage, we modified the Curry analysis system CASS [18] by adding an option to force CASS to query CurryInfo for required analysis information: if CurryInfo has this information available, it will be copied from CurryInfo instead of computing it locally by CASS. One can also choose to contact the CurryInfo web service or a local installation of CurryInfo.

The subsequent table shows the timings of these different usages (on the same machine as described in Sect. 6). We compared the elapsed times (in seconds) of two implementations of CASS: one compiled with PAKCS [17] (which compiles to Prolog and uses SICStus-Prolog 4.9.0 as back end) and one compiled with KiCS2 [6] (which compiles to Haskell and uses GHC 9.4.5 as back end). For each Curry application shown in the first column, we show the timings for the analysis without CurryInfo (*no CI*), with the CurryInfo web service (*web*), and a local installation of CurryInfo (*local*). Moreover, the "Modules" column shows the total number of modules of the application (*all*), the number of modules from imported packages (*imp*) where the results can be copied from CurryInfo, and the number of local modules (*loc*) which must always be analyzed by CASS. The applications used in these tests are the CurryInfo system, CASS [18], the

---

[16]   We used a Linux machine running Ubuntu 22.04 with an Intel Core i7-1165G7 (2.80GHz) processor with eight cores. The tools were executed with KiCS2 [6].

inference and verification system for non-fail conditions [15,16], the property-based testing tool CurryCheck [11], the Curry Package Manager CPM [12], and cpm-manage, a tool to generate the web pages of the CPM repository. For all these applications, we analyzed the determinism behavior of the operations in the main module.

	Modules			CASS (PAKCS)			CASS (KiCS2)		
	all	imp	loc	no CI	web	local	no CI	web	local
CurryInfo	83	58	25	6:48.81	3:14.27	3:01.10	19.85	23.01	11.79
CASS	89	74	15	7:47.93	3:17.15	4:47.05	17.70	23.77	9.43
VerifyNonFail	122	103	19	14:52.85	8:07.68	4:42.85	29.98	34.80	15.16
CurryCheck	122	111	11	9:57.19	4:51.37	3:41.69	25.33	34.57	13.25
CPM	134	105	29	8:36.62	6:42.24	4:56.29	32.45	37.67	17.25
cpm-manage	64	59	5	6:01.36	3:41.91	2:27.37	14.03	19.51	8.09

As one can see, the speed-up obtained by copying analysis information from CurryInfo depends on the implementation of CASS, the network connection or time to copy and parse the analysis results, and the complexity of the analysis process. For instance, KiCS2 is quite efficient for purely functional programs. Hence, the network connection to the CurryInfo web service causes a substantial delay so that the use of the local installation of CurryInfo is much faster.[17]

One can expect that for more complex systems, like the inference and verification of non-fail conditions, where also external SMT-solvers are used [15], the efficiency improvements are higher than for the CASS analyses tested above.

References

1. Antoy, S., Hanus, M.: Declarative programming with function patterns. In: Hill, P.M. (ed.) LOPSTR 2005. LNCS, vol. 3901, pp. 6–22. Springer, Heidelberg (2006). https://doi.org/10.1007/11680093_2
2. Antoy, S., Hanus, M.: Set functions for functional logic programming. In: Proceedings of the 11th ACM SIGPLAN International Conference on Principles and Practice of Declarative Programming (PPDP'09), pp. 73–82. ACM Press (2009)
3. Antoy, S., Hanus, M.: Functional logic programming. Commun. ACM **53**(4), 74–85 (2010)
4. Antoy, S., Hanus, M.: Eliminating irrelevant non-determinism in functional logic programs. In: Lierler, Y., Taha, W. (eds.) PADL 2017. LNCS, vol. 10137, pp. 1–18. Springer, Cham (2017). https://doi.org/10.1007/978-3-319-51676-9_1
5. Antoy, S., Hanus, M.: Transforming boolean equalities into constraints. Formal Aspects Comput. **29**(3), 475–494 (2017)

---

[17] Due to this reason, the CurryInfo web service provides a copy of its cache which can easily be downloaded and locally installed.

6. Braßel, B., Hanus, M., Peemöller, B., Reck, F.: KiCS2: a new compiler from curry to haskell. In: Kuchen, H. (ed.) WFLP 2011. LNCS, vol. 6816, pp. 1–18. Springer, Heidelberg (2011). https://doi.org/10.1007/978-3-642-22531-4_1

7. Cousot, P., Cousot, R.: Abstract interpretation: a unified lattice model for static analysis of programs by construction of approximation of fixpoints. In: Proc. of the 4th ACM Symposium on Principles of Programming Languages, pp. 238–252 (1977)

8. de Moura, L., Bjørner, N.: Z3: an efficient SMT solver. In: Ramakrishnan, C.R., Rehof, J. (eds.) TACAS 2008. LNCS, vol. 4963, pp. 337–340. Springer, Heidelberg (2008). https://doi.org/10.1007/978-3-540-78800-3_24

9. González-Moreno, J.C., Hortalá-González, M.T., López-Fraguas, F.J., Rodríguez-Artalejo, M.: An approach to declarative programming based on a rewriting logic. J. Log. Program. **40**, 47–87 (1999)

10. Hanus, M.: Functional logic programming: from theory to Curry. In: Voronkov, A., Weidenbach, C. (eds.) Programming Logics. LNCS, vol. 7797, pp. 123–168. Springer, Heidelberg (2013). https://doi.org/10.1007/978-3-642-37651-1_6

11. Hanus, M.: CurryCheck: checking properties of curry programs. In: Hermenegildo, M.V., Lopez-Garcia, P. (eds.) LOPSTR 2016. LNCS, vol. 10184, pp. 222–239. Springer, Cham (2017). https://doi.org/10.1007/978-3-319-63139-4_13

12. Hanus, M.: Semantic versioning checking in a declarative package manager. In: Technical Communications of the 33rd International Conference on Logic Programming (ICLP 2017), OpenAccess Series in Informatics (OASIcs), pp. 6:1–6:16. Schloss Dagstuhl - Leibniz-Zentrum fuer Informatik (2017)

13. Hanus, M.: Verifying fail-free declarative programs. In: Proceedings of the 20th International Symposium on Principles and Practice of Declarative Programming (PPDP 2018), pp. 12:1–12:13. ACM Press (2018)

14. Hanus, M.: Combining static and dynamic contract checking for Curry. Fund. Inform. **173**(4), 285–314 (2020)

15. Hanus, M.: Hybrid verification of declarative programs with arithmetic non-fail conditions. In: Kiselyov, O. (eds.) Programming Languages and Systems. APLAS 2024. LNCS, vol 15194. Springer, Singapore (2025). https://doi.org/10.1007/978-981-97-8943-6_6

16. Hanus, M.: Inferring Non-failure Conditions for Declarative Programs. In: Gibbons, J., Miller, D. (eds) Functional and Logic Programming. FLOPS 2024. LNCS, vol. 14659. Springer, Singapore (2024). https://doi.org/10.1007/978-981-97-2300-3_10

17. Hanus, M., et al.: PAKCS: The Portland Aachen Kiel Curry System (2025). https://www.curry-lang.org/pakcs/

18. Hanus, M., Skrlac, F.: A modular and generic analysis server system for functional logic programs. In: Proc. of the ACM SIGPLAN 2014 Workshop on Partial Evaluation and Program Manipulation (PEPM 2014), pp. 181–188. ACM Press (2014)

19. Hanus, M., (ed.). Curry: An integrated functional logic language (vers. 0.9.0) (2016). http://www.curry-lang.org

20. Hughes, J.: Why functional programming matters. Comput. J. **32**(2), 98–107 (1989)

21. Jones, M.P.: A system of constructor classes: overloading and implicit higher-order polymorphism. J. Funct. Program. **5**(1), 1–35 (1995)

22. Peyton Jones, S. (ed.) Haskell 98 Language and Libraries—The Revised Report. Cambridge University Press (2003)

23. Somogyi, Z., Henderson, F., Conway, T.: The execution algorithm of Mercury, an efficient purely declarative logic programming language. J. Log. Program. **29**(1–3), 17–64 (1996)
24. Wadler, P.: How to declare an imperative. ACM Comput. Surv. **29**(3), 240–263 (1997)
25. Wadler, P., Blott, S.: How to make ad-hoc polymorphism less ad hoc. In: Proc. of the 16th ACM Symposium on Principles of Programming Languages (POPL 1989), pp. 60–76 (1989)

Program Synthesis for Geometric Modeling

Romain Pascual[1]($^{(\boxtimes)}$) (ID), Pascale Le Gall[1] (ID), Hakim Belhaouari[2] (ID),
and Agnès Arnould[2] (ID)

[1] MICS, CentraleSupélec, Université Paris-Saclay, Gif-sur-Yvette, France
{romain.pascual,pascale.legall}@centralesupelec.fr
[2] Université de Poitiers, Univ. Limoges, CNRS, XLIM, Poitiers, France
{hakim.belhaouari,agnes.arnould}@univ-poitiers.fr

Abstract. Implementing geometric modeling operations in a programming language can be inherently challenging despite their seemingly simple input-to-output descriptions. We propose a program synthesis method to generate executable code from representative examples. We focus on geometric computations in topology-based modeling, where nD objects are decomposed into cells with added geometric information. This domain uses combinatorial structures represented as graphs, with operations formalized as graph transformation rules and geometric modifications given by code-like annotations on the rule's graph nodes.

Keywords: Programming-by-example · Domain-specific language · Topology-based geometric modeling · Constraint-solving

1 Introduction

Program synthesis, often described as "the holy grail of Computer Science" [23], aims to automatically generate executable programs from high-level specifications, alleviating the burden of manual coding. Inductive synthesis, in particular, infers programs from input-to-output examples [4,50], such as the FlashFill feature in Microsoft Excel [21]. In this work, we investigate program synthesis in a specific application domain, geometric modeling, which provides methods and algorithms to represent and manipulate geometric shapes. Geometric modeling operations are typically implemented in a low-level programming language like C or C++, with advanced performance optimizations, making them difficult to adapt. While APIs exist to define custom operations [9,20,49], they often exceed domain experts' skills. Therefore, a means to create custom operations remains a longstanding aspiration, one that a program synthesis approach could fulfill. Rather than synthesizing low-level code, we propose to synthesize modeling operations in a Domain-Specific Language (DSL) based on graph transformations [14,25] at the core ot the Jerboa platform [3] to benefit from the high-level representation of operations and associated formal verification mechanisms [2,42].

Related Work. Prior work has explored program synthesis for generating geometric objects with desired properties, e.g., from patterns [7], program traces [8,26], ruler-compass constructions [22], geometric constraints [37], or an underlying

© The Author(s), under exclusive license to Springer Nature Switzerland AG 2026
S. Escobar and L. Titolo (Eds.): LOPSTR 2025, LNCS 16117, pp. 135–153, 2026.
https://doi.org/10.1007/978-3-032-04848-6_9

L-sytems [24,45,52]. While not advertised as program synthesis, inverse procedural modeling aims to retrieve the procedure that generated an object to build similar-looking objects from variations of the procedure [15,27,51]. Other works have applied program synthesis techniques to CAD using Constructive Solid Geometry (CSG) [30,47]. In particular, [13] proposes to synthesize CSG trees from surface meshes using the SKETCH system [48]. These methods are similar in spirit to ours but distinct in goal: they aim to generate objects, whereas we are interested in synthesizing transformations of geometric objects. Closer to our goal, in [34] the authors generate geometric expressions from examples with a neural network learning the parameters of a subdivision scheme. While interesting, this approach diverges from our goal as we aim to compute the target geometry while supporting arbitrary topological changes.

Contributions. We propose an automatic generation of geometric expressions over arbitrary topological modifications from an input-to-output example, tailoring established synthesis methods to geometric modeling. Building on Jerboa's DSL and prior work on inferring topological transformations [41], we complete the synthesis of modeling operations by retrieving the missing geometric expressions. Inspired by component- and sketch-based synthesis [22,28,48], we treat the synthesis task as completing a sketch skeleton describing an affine combination of components, called *values of interest*, grounded in topological abstractions. The resulting constraints, derived from the input-to-output example provided by the user, are solved via a solver. We present JerboaStudio, a tool integrated into the Jerboa platform, to empirically validate our method.

Paper Organization. Section 2 clarifies our goal using a running example, the flat extrusion, while Sect. 3 revisits generalized maps for object representation and Jerboa's DSL. We outline our synthesis method in Sect. 4, with practical implementation details discussed in Sect. 5. Section 6 evaluates our framework with a benchmark on subdivision schemes. Section 7 provides some concluding remarks.

2   Motivation and Running Example

To illustrate our motivation, consider a 2D flat extrusion. The user provides two objects (Fig. 1a): an initial pentagonal face and a modified version with a shrunk copy, sharing the same barycenter and connected vertex-to-vertex with the original. Our goal is to synthesize a program that computes the new vertex positions. Using the annotations in Fig. 1b, we aim to compute the *output* positions $o_1, \ldots, o_5$ (in orange) from the *input* positions $i_1, \ldots, i_5$ (in blue). Since the added face is a homothety, each o_k for $k \in 1..5$ can be expressed as a linear combination $o_k = p \cdot i_k + (1 - p) \cdot C$ where i_k is the corresponding input vertex, $C = \frac{1}{5} \sum_{k=1}^{5} i_k$ is the barycenter of the original face, and p is the homothety ratio. Since all o_k share the same expression, the synthesis task reduces to inferring the correct value of p and producing a program that computes this expression. Importantly, the expression must generalize beyond pentagons to

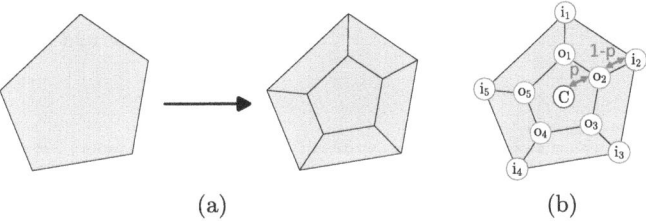

Fig. 1. Synthesis of a geometric computation: (a) a geometric modeling operation, (b) explanation about the geometric computations.

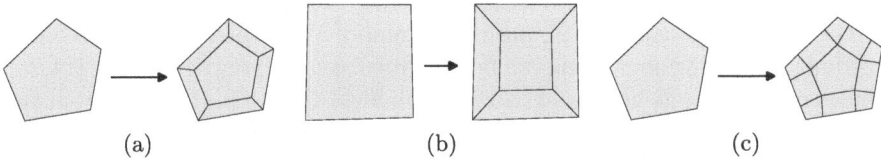

Fig. 2. Variations on the modeling operation of Fig. 1a: (a) different geometry,(b) different initial topology,(c) different topological modification.

support reuse across contexts. For example, a quad as inputs (see Fig. 2b) yields the same equation for each o_k with now $k \in 1..4$. We abstract the computation into the symbolic expression $O = p \cdot I + (1 - p) \cdot C$, where I and O are meta-variables for the input and output families. From this symbolic form, we can recover the concrete expressions with the input-to-output example of Fig. 1a.

The objects of Fig. 1a are meshes, described by an internal arrangement of cells (vertices, edges, faces) – the *topology* – enriched with data attached to the cells (positions to vertices, curvatures to edges, and colors to faces) – the *geometry*. The operation in Fig. 2a uses the same topological modification as the flat extrusion of Fig. 1a but with different positions: the geometric computation only differs in the value of p. Figure 2b results from the same operation but applied to a quad. If we synthesize the operation from the pentagonal example in Fig. 1a and apply it to this quad, we should recover the correct output. Put differently, both input-to-output examples should synthesize the same operation. Finally, Fig. 2c shows a different modeling operation, the ternary subdivision [32], which performs a different topological modification.

3   A DSL for Topology-Based Geometric Modeling

Geometric modeling requires an internal representation of shapes. For our synthesis framework, the representation must be precise enough to express fine-grained edits but regular enough to support automated reasoning. We adopt *generalized maps* (Gmaps) [11,33], which offer a combinatorial structure to describe how cells (vertices, edges, faces, etc.) are connected. Gmaps are well-suited for our synthesis framework because (1) they support arbitrary-dimensional meshes (e.g., surfaces, volumes); (2) they can be interpreted as graphs with regular

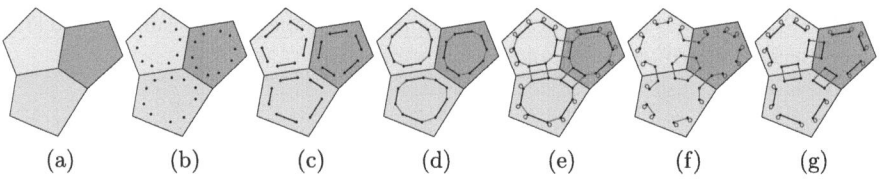

```
1    // Position for n0
2    return n0.position;
```

(a)   (b)

```
1    // Position for n4
2    return Point3::midpt(Point3::middle(<0,1>_position(n0)),n0.position);
```

(c)

Fig. 3. Flat extrusion: (a) rule scheme, (b) expression for $n0$, (c) expression for $n4$.

patterns, enabling rule-based rewriting; (3) they separate the *topology* (connectivity) from the *geometry* (e.g., positions, colors). With the encoding of Gmaps as graphs, modeling operations can be described as graph rewriting rules [14,25]. These consist of a left-hand side (LHS) graph identifying a pattern to match and a right-hand side (RHS) graph for the modified pattern. In Jerboa, rules are generalized to rule schemes as illustrated in Fig. 3a, where the rule structure defines topological edits and node annotations (e.g., `position`) provides the computational expressions to update the geometry. These expressions, given in Figs. 3b and 3c are the target of our synthesis framework detailed in Sect. 4. The remainder of this section introduces the formal background required to interpret such rules.

3.1   Embedded Generalized Maps

Generalized maps can be formalized as a specific subclass of graphs with constraints that ensure the topological correctness of the structure.

Definition 1 (Generalized map (see [42]). *Given* $n \in \mathbb{N}$ *, a generalized map of dimension* n*, n-Gmap or simply Gmap, is an undirected graph* $G = (N, A)$ *with arcs labeled by a dimension* d *in* $0..n$ *(then called a d-arc) satisfying:*

Incidence constraint: *each node has exactly one incident arc per dimension,*
Cycle constraint: *every path labelled* $ijij$ *(with* $i + 2 \leq j$*) forms a cycle.*

(a)   (b)   (c)   (d)   (e)   (f)   (g)

Fig. 4. Gmap construction: (a) 2D object, (b) darts (•) for each valid vertex-edge-face triplet, (c) 0-arcs (•—•) link darts in the same face and edge but not the same vertex, (d) 1-arcs (•—•) link edges, (e) 2-arcs (•—•) link faces. Cells: (f) $\langle 1, 2 \rangle$-orbit (vertices), (g) $\langle 0, 2 \rangle$-orbit (edges), (d) $\langle 0, 1 \rangle$-orbit (faces).

The incidence constraint enables unambiguous path descriptions as sequences of dimensions. To distinguish between nodes in Gmaps and in our DSL rules, we refer to the nodes in N as *darts*, following [11]. The semantics of a dart is given by a tuple of incident cells, and a *d*-arc connects darts differing only at dimension d. In a 2-Gmap, darts represent vertex-edge-face triplets, and 0-arcs connect darts in different vertices of the same edge and face. Figure 4 illustrates the progressive construction of a Gmap: darts are created (Fig. 4b), then connected via arcs (Figs. 4c to 4e), forming the object's topology. Darts on the boundary of a cell are self-linked along the corresponding dimension (see 2-loops in Fig. 4e). Cells, such as vertices, edges, or faces, correspond to subgraphs called orbits.

Definition 2 (Orbit (see [42]). *Let G be an n-Gmap, v a dart of G and $o \subseteq 0..n$ a subset of dimensions. The* orbit $G\langle o \rangle (v)$ *is the maximal subgraph induced by the dimensions in o and containing v.*

The orbit $G\langle o \rangle (v)$ is of type $\langle o \rangle$ or is an $\langle o \rangle$-orbit.

The $\langle o \rangle$-orbits are the connected components after ignoring arcs labeled outside $\langle o \rangle$. Since 0-arcs split vertices but preserve edges and faces, $\langle 1, 2 \rangle$-orbits contain all darts belonging to a vertex and encode the vertices (Fig. 4f). Similarly, faces correspond to $\langle 0, 1 \rangle$-orbits (Fig. 4d) and edges to $\langle 0, 2 \rangle$-orbits (Fig. 4g).

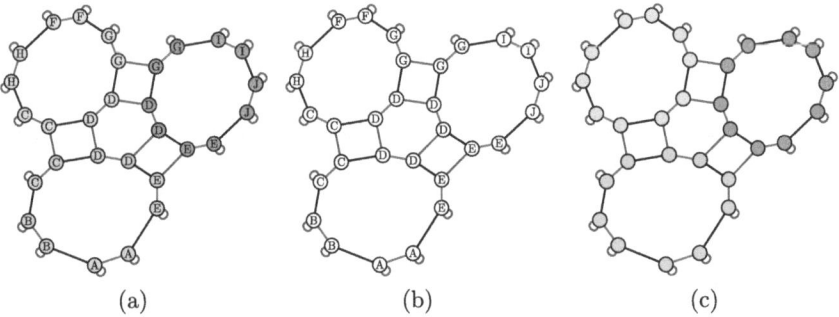

(a)   (b)   (c)

Fig. 5. Embeddings: (a) embedded Gmap, (b) `position` : $\langle 1, 2 \rangle \to$ `Point3`, (c) `color` : $\langle 0, 1 \rangle \to$ `Color3`.

Geometry and attributes, such as vertex positions or face colors, are attached via embedding functions associating orbits to data types [2], similar to graph attribution [14,25]. For example, vertex positions are encoded by `position` : $\langle 1, 2 \rangle \to$ `Point3` and face colors by `color` : $\langle 0, 1 \rangle \to$ `Color3`.

Definition 3 (Embedded generalized map (see [2])). *Let $\pi : \langle o_\pi \rangle \to \tau_\pi$ be an embedding symbol π together with an orbit type $\langle o_\pi \rangle$ and a data type τ_π. A Gmap embedded on π is a pair (G, π_G) where $G = (N, A)$ is a Gmap and π_G is a function $N \to \tau_\pi$ satisfying:*

Embedding constraint *all darts of an $\langle o_\pi \rangle$-orbit share the same value of type τ_π.*

Embedded Gmaps can be extended to support multiple embedding symbols. Figure 5 shows the position and color embeddings of the Gmap from Fig. 4.

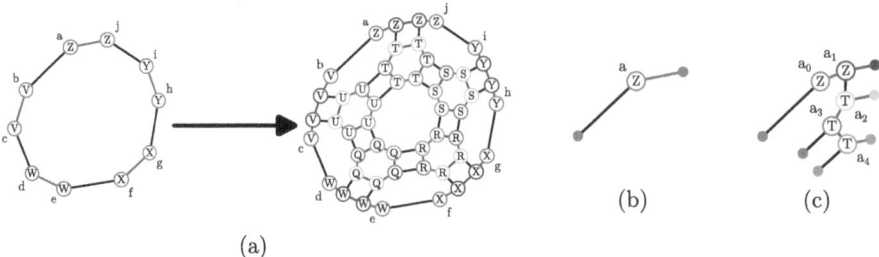

Fig. 6. Instantiation of the flat extrusion based on the rule scheme of Fig. 3a: (a) instantiated rule, (b) zoom on the LHS and (c) RHS instantiations, a_0 in (c) coincides with a in (b) sharing the same position Z.

3.2   Modeling Operations as Graph Transformations

In Jerboa [3], rules are extended to rule schemes parameterized by orbit types to abstract topological changes [42]: nodes become placeholders for orbits, labeled by their orbit type. Replacing a node with an orbit is called *instantiation*. A distinguished LHS node, the *hook*, anchors the matching. Other nodes encode transformations via relabeling functions derived from the hook's orbit type and theirs. Figure 3a shows the rule scheme for the flat extrusion from Fig. 1. The hook $n0$ (double line) of type $\langle 0, 1 \rangle$ is modified to $\langle 0, \_ \rangle$, encoding the function $\langle 0, 1 \rangle \mapsto \langle 0, \_ \rangle$, i.e., $\{0 \mapsto 0, 1 \mapsto \_\}$. The symbol $\_$ denotes the removal of the initial dimension. Node $n4$ with type $\langle 0, 1 \rangle$ encodes the identity function, creating the homothetic copy of the initial face.

Instantiating this rule on a pentagon (Fig. 6a) replaces the hook $n0$ with the $\langle 0, 1 \rangle$-orbit containing the darts $a, \ldots, j$. Five copies are created for each RHS node (color-coded to match the nodes in Fig. 3a), relabeled accordingly. Finally, the copies are connected following the arcs of the rule scheme: an arc between two nodes results in an arc between each pair of twin darts in the two copies. Figures 6b and 6c zoom on dart a. Subscripts indicate the node index from Fig. 3a. The transformations builds a 1012-path between a_0 and a_4, while arcs connecting same-color darts originate from the node orbit types. This high-level explanation elucidates the abstraction used within our synthesis framework. For further details on the instantiation, we refer the reader to the set-based explanation in [39].

In Fig. 3a, RHS nodes $n0$ and $n4$ carry geometric expressions as indicated by the annotation `position`. For $n0$, the expression (Fig. 3b) preserves the initial positions. For $n4$, the expression (Fig. 3c) computes:

$$\texttt{midpt}(\texttt{middle}(\langle 0, 1 \rangle\_ \texttt{position}(n0)), \texttt{position}(n0)). \tag{1}$$

where `position` gives the position, `midpt` the midpoint between two positions, `middle` the barycenter of a collection of positions, and $\langle 0, 1 \rangle\_$ `position` a collection of positions in an orbit $\langle 0, 1 \rangle$. This collection is retrieved by a dedicated operator in Jerboa's DSL, leveraging the high regularity of Gmaps to gather embedding values within an orbit. During instantiation, $n0$ is substituted by the darts associated with $n0$ before modification. For dart a, we derive $\mathtt{midpt}(\mathtt{middle}(\langle 0, 1 \rangle \_ \mathtt{position}(a)), \mathtt{position}(a))$. Substituting $n0$ by a makes the expression computable as it solely relies on dart identifiers. First, $\mathtt{middle}(\langle 0, 1 \rangle \_ \mathtt{position}(a))$ computes the barycenter $C = \frac{1}{5} \sum_{k=1}^{5} i_k$ from Fig. 1b. All darts $a, \ldots, j$ compute the same value. Then, $\mathtt{midpt}(\ldots, \mathtt{position}(a))$ computes the midpoint between the barycenter and the position of a, as in the expression $p.I + (1 - p).C$ of Sect. 2 with $p = \frac{1}{2}$.

Geometric expressions for rules over embedded Gmaps can be formalized with algebraic data types [2]. An embedded Gmap enriches a Gmap with an algebra over a signature combining node variables (from LHS nodes), standard operations (e.g., $\mathtt{middle}$ for the data type $\mathtt{Point3}$), and topological operators such as collect operators $\pi_{\langle o \rangle}$, (e.g., $\langle 0, 1 \rangle \_ \mathtt{position}$ in Eq. (1)), retrieving τ_π-values within an orbit $\langle o \rangle$. These last operators allow concise expressions for geometric computations, justifying the expression $O = p \cdot I + (1 - p) \cdot C$ in Sect. 2. Jerboa allows the user to declare and implement new functions (in Java) to be used in an imperative language for geometric expressions, part of Jerboa's DSL. The expressions are replaced with the implemented functions when the rule is translated into an efficient program via code generation. In this work, we will use a fragment of the native expressions available in Jerboa (see Sect. 4.2).

4   Synthesizing Geometric Expressions

Section 3 explained that Jerboa's DSL edits the topology via graph rewriting rules and the geometry via node-based expressions, enabling the separate synthesis of each kind of change. In [41], we introduced the *topological folding algorithm* extracting topological changes by folding an input-to-output example into a rule scheme, leaving only the geometric expressions to be synthesized. Embeddings, parameterized by orbit types, anchor geometric expressions in the topological structure, providing convenient access to *values of interest*. We propose to synthesize linear combinations of such values of interest.

Program synthesis faces two core challenges: the intractability of the program space and the interpretation of the user intent [23]. Designing a program synthesis method involves choosing how to represent the user intent, define the program space, and analyze it to find a candidate program. These choices are interdependent; for example, a grammar-encoded search space favors enumeration-based analysis [1]. We now elucidate our choices and rationale, while focusing on the synthesis of positions.

4.1   User Intent

We adopt a programming-by-example approach to synthesize geometric expressions of modeling operations, using the same user-provided input-to-output example and leveraging intermediate results from the topological folding algorithm [41]. The user provides (1) an input instance, (2) an output instance, (3) a mapping of preserved parts. This process is comparable to the substring analysis in FlashFill [21] but becomes exponentially harder with graphs (see [38, Sec. 7.2] for details). The algorithm also records the set of darts in the input-to-output example associated with each node of the rule scheme. We aim to automatically insert geometric expressions to ensure that instantiating the rule scheme yields the input-to-output example.

The first step is to identify the RHS nodes requiring a geometric expression. Jerboa enforces the embedding constraint by propagating the computed embedding values on partially matched orbits [2,3]. For instance, if part of a vertex is translated, propagation ensures that all darts within the $\langle 1, 2 \rangle$-orbit share the same position after modification. Only one position expression is needed (and thus has to be synthesized) per $\langle 1, 2 \rangle$-orbit in the rule scheme. For the rule scheme of Fig. 3a, the RHS contains two $\langle 1, 2 \rangle$-orbits, one with $n0$ and $n1$, and the other with $n2$, $n3$, and $n4$. The first orbit contains a preserved node ($n0$) associated with the darts $(a, b, \ldots, j)$ that have the same positions $(A, B, \ldots, E)$ in both input and output. We could add the expression `return n0.position`. No expression is needed in practice since the initial values can be propagated. For the second orbit, we must choose one of the nodes $n2$, $n3$, or $n4$ as a candidate for a geometric expression. In the sequel, we will consider the synthesis of a position expression for $n4$. Having identified the programs to be synthesized from the user-provided example, we now delimit the set of candidate expressions before validating them against all darts associated with the node.

4.2 Search Space

In the programming-by-example paradygm, program specifications are partial mappings corresponding to the input-to-output example(s). To mitigate overfitting when synthesizing programs, we constrain the search space to a subset of Jerboa's geometric expressions used as components in a sketching approach. Specifically, we focus on orbit-dependent built-in functions.

Component-Based Synthesis. Component-based synthesis generates programs from domain-specific primitives called *components* [17,22,28]. Because of the abstraction layer induced by rule schemes, we seek functions that do not depend on a specific instantiation, which we call *points of interest* (POI). Such functions should be independent of the (size of the) input orbit and remain invariant to changes in the dart chosen for computation. Orbit-based barycenters of positions satisfy these conditions, with a generic expression given by:

$$\texttt{middle}(\langle o \rangle \_ \texttt{position}(x)), \qquad (2)$$

generalizing $\texttt{middle}(\langle 0, 1 \rangle \_ \texttt{position}(x))$ (Sect. 3.2). Orbit types $\langle o \rangle$ induce an equivalence relation $\equiv_{\langle o \rangle} \subseteq N \times N$ between darts in the same $\langle o \rangle$-orbit, which extends to embeddings $\pi : \langle o_\pi \rangle \to \tau_\pi$ such that $\equiv_{\langle o_\pi \rangle}$-equivalent darts share the same τ_π-value [2, Def. 7]. For instance, $\texttt{position} : \langle 1, 2 \rangle \to \texttt{Point3}$ partitions a 2-Gmap into vertices where all darts have the same `Point3`-value. This reduces the orbit-based barycenters of positions to four: vertices, edges, faces, and connected components, written $\texttt{poi}_{\langle o \rangle}$. The expressions are given in Fig. 7a and illustrated in Fig. 7b. Geometric expressions on RHS nodes refer to values of LHS

Point of interest	Name	Expression
vertex	$p_v = \text{poi}_{\langle 1,2 \rangle}$	$\texttt{middle}(\langle 1,2 \rangle\_\texttt{position}(d))$
edge	$p_e = \text{poi}_{\langle 0,2 \rangle}$	$\texttt{middle}(\langle 0,2 \rangle\_\texttt{position}(d))$
face	$p_f = \text{poi}_{\langle 0,1 \rangle}$	$\texttt{middle}(\langle 0,1 \rangle\_\texttt{position}(d))$
component	$p_c = \text{poi}_{\langle 0,1,2 \rangle}$	$\texttt{middle}(\langle 0,1,2 \rangle\_\texttt{position}(d))$

(a)

(b)

Fig. 7. Points of interest: (a) geometric expressions, (b) examples of computations.

nodes, similar to contract programming practices. Thus, the components are the POI $\text{poi}_{\langle o \rangle}$ from one LHS node per $\langle o \rangle$-orbit ($n0$ for the flat extrusion). The choice of orbit-based barycenters as components meets the standard way in geometric modeling of using barycentric [10] and generalized barycentric coordinates [18] to interpolate or deform geometric objects from known positions [29]. Limiting POIs to orbit-based barycenters aligns well with the program-by-example setting and offers a minimal yet expressive set of components compatible with rule schemes: they abstract local geometry while remaining invariant under dart permutations.

Sketching. POIs provide elementary built-in functions for synthesis. We complement them with a control structure akin to a sketch with holes for the numerical values to be retrieved, delimiting a search space of valid candidates. Here, we seek to retrieve affine combinations of POIs, similar to the approach of [48]. For a node n_R, the synthesized code defines a symbolic equation of the form:

$$\texttt{position}(n_R) = t + \sum_{\langle o \rangle \in 0..2/\sim_{\langle 1,2 \rangle}} \sum_{n_L \in N_L/\equiv_{\langle o \rangle}} w_{\text{poi}_{\langle o \rangle}(n_L)} \cdot \text{poi}_{\langle o \rangle}(n_L) \qquad (3)$$

where $0..2/\sim_{\langle 1,2 \rangle}$ is the quotient of dimensions by the equivalent relation induced by $\langle 1,2 \rangle$ (the rows of Fig. 7a), and $N_L/\equiv_{\langle o \rangle}$ the quotient of LHS nodes by the $\langle o \rangle$-induced relation. The weights $w_{\text{poi}_{\langle o \rangle}(n_L)}$ and the translation t are the values to be synthesized, encoded by the keyword $\texttt{??}$ in the sketch skeleton of Fig. 8. The sketch is the same for all RHS nodes. For $n4$ in the flat extrusion, it exactly matches Fig. 8 with $\texttt{#node#}$ replaced by $\texttt{n0}$, specializing Eq. (3) into:

$$\texttt{position}(n4) = t + \underbrace{w_v \cdot p_v(n0)}_{\text{vertex}} + \underbrace{w_e \cdot p_e(n0)}_{\text{edge}} + \underbrace{w_f \cdot p_f(n0)}_{\text{face}} + \underbrace{w_c \cdot p_c(n0)}_{\text{component}}. \qquad (4)$$

4.3   Resolution via a Solver

During instantiation, geometric expressions are evaluated by substituting the node with each associated dart. Mimicking this process, we treat the sketch as a parametric equation with unknown weights (keyword $\texttt{??}$) and generate one

```
1   // translation
2   Point3 res = new Point3 ( ?? , ?? , ?? );
3
4   // per #node# in <1,2>-orbit of the left hand side
5   Point3 pV_#node# = Point3 :: middle (<1,2>_position ( #node# ));
6   pV_#node#.scaleVect ( ?? );
7   res.addVect (pV_#node#);
8
9   // per #node# in <0,2>-orbit of the left hand side
10  Point3 pE_#node# = Point3 :: middle (<0,2>_position ( #node# ));
11  pE_#node#.scaleVect ( ?? );
12  res.addVect (pE_#node#);
13
14  // per #node# in <0,1>-orbit of the left hand side
15  Point3 pF_#node# = Point3 :: middle (<0,1>_position ( #node# ));
16  pF_#node#.scaleVect ( ?? );
17  res.addVect (pF_#node#);
18
19  // per #node# in <0,1,2>-orbit of the left hand side
20  Point3 pC_#node# = Point3 :: middle (<0,1,2>_position ( #node# ));
21  pC_#node#.scaleVect ( ?? );
22  res.addVect (pC_#node#);
23
24  return res;
```

Fig. 8. Sketch skeleton for a geometric expression, where ?? encodes the values to be synthesized. Line 2 is a placeholder for the translation t. For each POI, the sketch operates in three steps: (1) the expressions `middle(<o>_position(#node#))` (lines, 5 10, 15, and 20) compute the POIs $\text{poi}_{\langle o \rangle}(n_L)$, where `#node#` is replaced by one n_L (per equivalence class in $N_L/\equiv_{\langle o \rangle}$); (2) these `Point3` values are multiplied by weights $w_{\text{poi}_{\langle o \rangle}(n_L)}$ via `scaleVect` (lines, 6 11, 16, and 21); (3) each POI's contribution is added to the global computation via `addVect`.

constraint per associated dart. This transformation is valid because (1) the components (the POIs) only depend on input nodes, and (2) the output value is known from the user-provided example. We instantiate Eq. (3) by substituting n_R and n_L with darts from the input-output example. For the flat extrusion, substituting $n0$ with a (Fig. 6b) and $n4$ with a_4 (Fig. 6c) in Eq. (4) yields a constraint involving w_v, w_e, w_f, w_c, and t. The 10 darts from the pentagon of Fig. 6a yield 10 vector constraints, which we decompose into 30 scalar constraints (one per coordinate axis) over 4 weights and 3 translation components.

The constrained problem is a system of linear equations over real-valued variables and delegated to a solver. We experimented with Google OR-Tools with GLOP and Z3 with quantifier-free floating-point arithmetic. Z3 is a Satisfiability Modulo Theories (SMT) solver allowing soft constraints and prioritization, while GLOP is a simple-to-integrate linear programming solver. The results of Sect. 6 were obtained with OR-Tools as a backend. To break ties between valid solutions, we bias the solver toward simpler orbits – vertices, edges, faces, and finally, connected components – with cells preferred over the translation to avoid overfitting, similar to ranking or optimization methods [23]. For the flat extrusion, the solution is $w_v = 0.5$, $w_e = 0.0$, $w_f = 0.5$, $w_c = 0.0$, $t_x = 0.0$, $t_y = 0.0$, and $t_z = 0.0$. As postprocessing, we discard POIs with weight below an (adjustable) threshold of 10^{-3}, removing edge and connected component POIs in Fig. 9.

```
1   // no translation
2   Point3 res = new Point3 (0.0 ,0.0 ,0.0) ;
3
4   // vertex
5   Point3 p0 = Point3 :: middle (<1,2> _ position (n0));
6   p0 . scaleVect (0.5) ;
7   res . addVect (p0) ;
8
9   // face
10  Point3 p2 = Point3 :: middle (<0,1> _ position (n0));
11  p2 . scaleVect (0.5) ;
12  res . addVect (p2) ;
13
14  return res ;
```

Fig. 9. Synthesized geometric expression for $n4$.

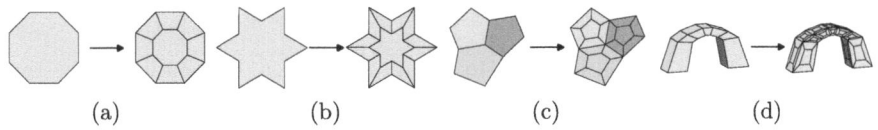

(a)   (b)   (c)   (d)

Fig. 10. Applications of the synthesized flat extrusion to other faces:(a) to an octo-gon,(b) to a snowflake. Applications of the synthesized operation generalized to sur-faces: (c) to the geometric object of Fig. 4,(d) to an arche.

For the variations in Fig. 2, we obtain the same expression for Fig. 2a with the modified weights $w_v = 0.67$ and $w_f = 0.33$, while the additional vertices of Fig. 2c have $w_v = 0.5$ and $w_e = 0.5$. Our approach follows [16], splitting the synthesis task into *sketch generation* from components and *sketch completion* using constraint-solving, jointly encoding component structure, syntactic sketch restrictions, and user intent into a unified problem which guarantees syntactic and semantic correctness.

4.4   Application of the Synthesized Operation

As discussed in Sect. 2, our goal is to synthesize geometric expressions for model-ing operations that generalize across shapes. Having synthesized the expressions for the flat extrusion (Fig. 1), we can apply it to other faces, such as the quad in Fig. 2b, producing the expected result. As shown in Fig. 10a and 10b, the synthesized operation can edit various shapes. We can also run the topological folding algorithm on the same example with the orbit type $\langle 0, 1, 2 \rangle$ to obtain a rule scheme similar to Fig. 3a with $n0$ carrying $\langle 0, 1, 2 \rangle$, and RHS nodes adjusted accordingly. The synthesized geometric expression remains unchanged, general-izing the flat extrusion to surfaces (Figs. 10c and 10d).

5   Implementation and Practical Details

5.1   Generalization to Vector Spaces and 3D Objects

Our synthesis method is independent of the embedding type and extends beyond positions. We enrich Jerboa's standard signature with a type **VectorialEbd** and

Table 1. Example of vectorial embeddings on a 2-Gmap.

Embedding	Data Type	Orbit Type	Array length	Clamp
position	Point3	$\langle 1, 2 \rangle$	3	No
color	Color3	$\langle 0, 1 \rangle$	3	Yes
transparency	Transparency	$\langle 0, 1 \rangle$	1	Yes
normal	Vector3	$\langle 0, 1 \rangle$	3	No

(a)   (b)   (c)   (d)   (e)

Fig. 11. Layering of subsoil horizons. Input (a) and output (b) data for synthesizing position and color expressions for the layering operation, with an application of the synthesized operation to a scene: (c) initial surfaces, (d) result of the layering operation, and (e) volume explosion hiding the initial surfaces to reveal inner volumes.

functions `scaleVect`, `addVect`, and `middle`. `VectorialEbd` serves as a generic interface, enabling generalization from barycentric *points* to *values* of interest. Subtypes of `VectorialEbd` are arrays of fixed length. Table 1 summarizes standard data types and associated embeddings for which our synthesis mechanism works. To deal with `Color3` and `Transparency` having bounded values, the result of the computation is clamped via the call to a function `clampVect` right before the return statement of line 24 in Fig. 8. Our approach generalizes to volumetric models (3-Gmaps). We demonstrate this on a layering operation used in geological modeling [43], where interpolated soil horizons are synthesized between two input surfaces (Fig. 11). The 3D operation involves both position and color embeddings, resp. defined on $\langle 1, 2, 3 \rangle$- and $\langle 0, 1 \rangle$-orbits. The system synthesized 25 expressions – 6 for positions, 19 for colors – via barycentric interpolation. Complete synthesis took under 55ms, which is negligible compared to the time needed to choose (or build) a representative input-to-output example or implement the operation.

5.2   JerboaStudio

Jerboa includes (1) an editor for designing operations, (2) a kernel for generating efficient code from rules, and (3) a generic Gmap viewer for applying operations. The editor allows specialists to create software that domain experts can use through the viewer. We integrated these components in a tool called JerboaStudio, available online[1] and illustrated in Fig. 12. In Fig. 12a, the user provides input and output shapes and hints for the input-to-output mapping. Figure 12b displays the rule and a synthesized embedding expression. JerboaStudio offers a

---

[1] Last consulted on July 16th, 2025 : https://gitlab.com/jerboateam/jerboa-studio.

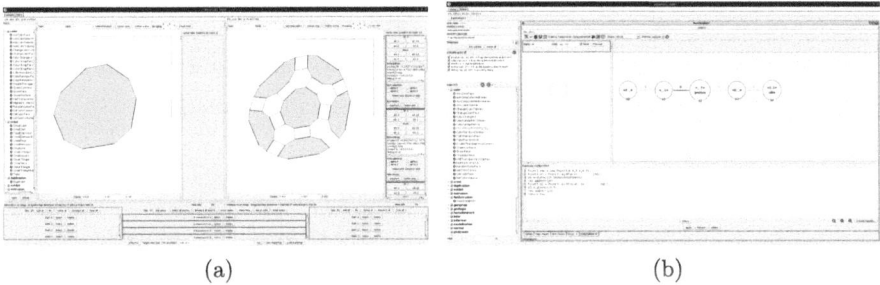

(a)   (b)

Fig. 12. JerboaStudio: (a) viewer with a pentagonal face as input (left), the extruded face as output(right), and the input-to-output mapping (bottom); and (b) editor with the retrieved rule scheme and a synthesized geometric expression (bottom).

solution for the automatic construction of modeling operations combining program synthesis for geometric expressions and the topological folding algorithm from [41].

5.3 Limits

Syntax-guided synthesis [1] may fail when the target expression lies outside the syntactic search space. Our search space consists of linear combinations of orbit barycenters, which can lead to overfitting or no solution being found, as in the example of the von Koch curve (Fig. 13). From a square (Fig. 13a), we construct the first iteration (Fig. 13b) and synthesize an operation. Applying it once provides the expected result, but reapplying it again yields an invalid second iteration (Fig. 13c): one expression (computed from edge midpoints) is correct; the other, involving a derivation angle from the original edge, is not. Our method computes the latter using the face's barycenter and translates the vertex in the wrong direction. A skilled user could edit the synthesized expression to fix it and obtain the desired second iteration (Fig. 13d). Figures 14a and 14b show the input and output, with preservation links identified by the darts (a to h). The synthesized expressions (Fig. 14c) for $n3$ combine edge ($poi_{\langle 0 \rangle}$) and face ($poi_{\langle 0,1 \rangle}$)

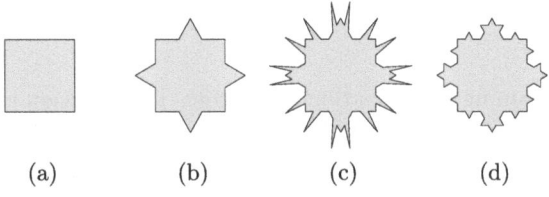

(a)   (b)   (c)   (d)

Fig. 13. Synthesis of the von Koch curve: (a) a square, (b) the first iteration of the operation, (c) invalid second iteration obtained by applying the synthesized operation, (d) valid second iteration built after fixing the geometric expression.

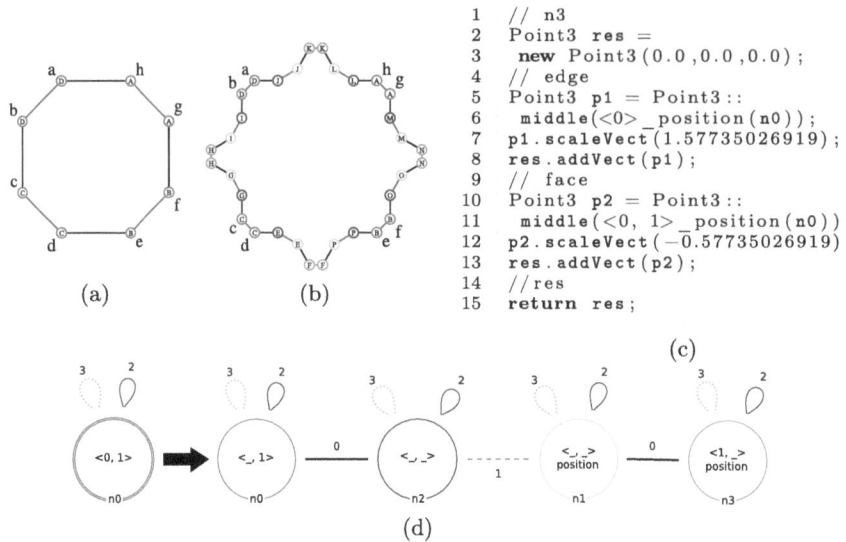

```
1   // n3
2   Point3 res =
3     new Point3(0.0,0.0,0.0);
4   // edge
5   Point3 p1 = Point3::
6     middle(<0>_position(n0));
7   p1.scaleVect(1.57735026919);
8   res.addVect(p1);
9   // face
10  Point3 p2 = Point3::
11    middle(<0, 1>_position(n0));
12  p2.scaleVect(-0.57735026919);
13  res.addVect(p2);
14  //res
15  return res;
```

(a)   (b)   (c)

(d)

Fig. 14. Synthesizing the von Koch curve: (a) input and (b) output as a part of an embedded Gmap, (d) rule scheme deduced from the topological folding algorithm (node colors encode the retrieved associations), (c) synthesized position expression for $n3$.

```
1   Point3 src; Point3 tgt; Vector3 fNormal;
2   if (n0.orient){
3     src = n0.position;
4     tgt = n0@0.position;
5     fNormal = Vector3::newellMethod(n0);
6   } else{
7     src = n0@0.position;
8     tgt = n0.position;
9     fNormal = Vector3::newellMethod(n0@0);
10  }
11  Vector3 eVect = new Vector3(src,tgt);
12  Vector3 eNormal = eVect.cross(fNormal).normalize();
13  eNormal.scale(Point3::sqrt3 / 6 * eVect.norm());
14  eNormal.add(Point3::midpt(n0.position, n0@0.position));
15  return eNormal;
```

Fig. 15. Explanation for the synthesized expression of Fig. 14c: fixing the expression for $n3$, requires expression outside the current search space as the new vertices are combinations of the face and edge barycenters.

barycenters, explaining the deviation in Fig. 13c. This solution is found based on the regularity of the input square but would not be with subsequent iterations for which no expression exists within our syntactic space. The corrected version (Fig. 15) uses Jerboa features outside the original syntactic space.

Table 2. Benchmark Summary

Operation	# Expr	# Synth (%)	# Correct (%)	SolT (ms)	SynT (ms)
Surface Subdivisions					
Catmull-Clark [6]	3	3 (100%)	1 (33%)	1.2	10
Doo-Sabin [12]	1	1 (100%)	0 (0%)	0.4	11
Powell-Sabin [44]	2	2 (100%)	2 (100%)	0.9	11
Blender's Subdivide [19]	2	2 (100%)	2 (100%)	0.9	9
Sierpinski Carpet [35]	2	2 (100%)	2 (100%)	1.0	13
$\sqrt{3}$ [31]	2	2 (100%)	1 (50%)	0.9	11
Volume Subdivisions					
Menger [36]	3	3 (100%)	3 (100%)	1.4	26
$(2, 2, 2)$-Menger [46]	9	9 (100%)	9 (100%)	2.9	64
Surface to Volume Refinements					
Mesh to Tet	1	1 (100%)	1 (100%)	0.5	12
Mesh to Hex	3	3 (100%)	3 (100%)	1.2	16

6 Evaluation

We synthesized geometric expressions for subdivision schemes to validate our approach. These are standard operations used in modeling to refine shapes by applying changes to entire connected components. Table 2 reports results for 6 surface subdivisions, 2 volume subdivisions, and 2 surface-to-volume refinements. Each rule has a single LHS node. We use the same cube (48 darts) as a shared input instance for all operations leading to sketches with 8 unknowns solved on 48 equations. The experiments were conducted with Java 11, and OR-Tools 9.6.2534, on an Intel® Core™ Ultra 7, @4.80 GHz with 32 GB RAM. For each operation, we report the number of expressions to synthesize (# Expr), synthesized (# Synth), semantically correct after manual inspection (# Correct), solver time in ms (SolT), and complete synthesis time in ms (SynT). The artifacts for reproducing the benchmark are available as supplementary material [40] hosted on Zenodo. The solver handled each sketch in 0.3–0.5 ms. Full integration (from example to editor-ready operation) takes 0.5–2 s, making the pipeline responsive enough for interactive use. We correctly synthesized 24 out of 28 expressions, completing 7 of 10 operations, with failures due to expressions lying outside the search space. The method generalizes well to typical modeling tasks, while more expressive sketches (either in the control structure or components used) would be needed to address the remaining cases.

7 Conclusion

We presented a new method for automatically generating efficient code for geometric modeling operations with arbitrary topological changes. We use a rule-based DSL combined with an algebraically rooted language for geometric computations. Our component-based strategy uses a sketch as a control structure to define a search space of affine combinations over values of interest, completed by a solver from generated constraints. Future work includes interactive synthesis, where users can refine results through (counter)examples, posing challenges for user interaction, especially with 3D objects. Another promising direction is adapting Metasketches [5], which partitions the search space into ordered sets of sketches and guides the search with a gradient function.

Disclosure of Interests. The authors have no competing interests to declare that are relevant to the content of this article.

References

1. Alur, R., et al.: Syntax-guided synthesis. In: 2013 Formal Methods in Computer-Aided Design, pp. 1–8 (October 2013). https://doi.org/10.1109/FMCAD.2013.6679385
2. Arnould, A., Belhaouari, H., Bellet, T., Le Gall, P., Pascual, R.: Preserving consistency in geometric modeling with graph transformations. Math. Struct. Comput. Sci. **32**(3), 300–347 (2022). https://doi.org/10.1017/S0960129522000226
3. Belhaouari, H., Arnould, A., Le Gall, P., Bellet, T.: Jerboa: a graph transformation library for topology-based geometric modeling. In: Giese, H., König, B. (eds.) ICGT 2014. LNCS, vol. 8571, pp. 269–284. Springer, Cham (2014). https://doi.org/10.1007/978-3-319-09108-2_18
4. Biermann, A.W.: The inference of regular LISP programs from examples. IEEE Trans. Syst. Man Cybern. **8**(8), 585–600 (1978). https://doi.org/10.1109/TSMC.1978.4310035
5. Bornholt, J., Torlak, E., Grossman, D., Ceze, L.: Optimizing synthesis with metasketches. In: Proceedings of the 43rd Annual ACM SIGPLAN-SIGACT Symposium on Principles of Programming Languages, pp. 775–788 (January 2016). https://doi.org/10.1145/2837614.2837666
6. Catmull, E., Clark, J.: Recursively generated B-spline surfaces on arbitrary topological meshes. Comput. Aided Des. **10**(6), 350–355 (1978). https://doi.org/10.1016/0010-4485(78)90110-0
7. Cheema, S., Buchanan, S., Gulwani, S., LaViola, J.J.: A practical framework for constructing structured drawings. In: Proceedings of the 19th International Conference on Intelligent User Interfaces, pp. 311–316 (February 2014). https://doi.org/10.1145/2557500.2557522
8. Chugh, R., Hempel, B., Spradlin, M., Albers, J.: Programmatic and direct manipulation, together at last. ACM SIGPLAN Notices **51**(6), 341–354 (2016). https://doi.org/10.1145/2980983.2908103
9. Conlan, C.: The Blender Python API. Apress, Berkeley, CA (2017). https://doi.org/10.1007/978-1-4842-2802-9
10. Coxeter, H.S.M.: Introduction to Geometry. John Wiley, Hoboken (1969)
11. Damiand, G., Lienhardt, P.: Combinatorial Maps: Efficient Data Structures for Computer Graphics and Image Processing. CRC Press, Boca Raton (September 2014)

12. Doo, D., Sabin, M.A.: Behaviour of recursive division surfaces near extraordinary points. Comput. Aided Des. **10**(6), 356–360 (1978). https://doi.org/10.1016/0010-4485(78)90111-2

13. Du, T., et al.: InverseCSG: automatic conversion of 3D models to CSG trees. ACM Trans. Graph. **37**(6), 213:1–213:16 (2018). https://doi.org/10.1145/3272127.3275006

14. Ehrig, H., Ehrig, K., Prange, U., Taentzer, G.: Fundamentals of Algebraic Graph Transformation. MTCSAES, Springer, Heidelberg (2006). https://doi.org/10.1007/3-540-31188-2

15. Emilien, A., Vimont, U., Cani, M.P., Poulin, P., Benes, B.: WorldBrush: interactive example-based synthesis of procedural virtual worlds. ACM Trans. Graph. **34**(4), 106:1–106:11 (2015). https://doi.org/10.1145/2766975

16. Feng, Y., Martins, R., Wang, Y., Dillig, I., Reps, T.W.: Component-based synthesis for complex APIs. In: Proceedings of the 44th ACM SIGPLAN Symposium on Principles of Programming Languages, pp. 599–612 (January 2017). https://doi.org/10.1145/3009837.3009851

17. Feser, J.K., Chaudhuri, S., Dillig, I.: Synthesizing data structure transformations from input-output examples. ACM SIGPLAN Notices **50**(6), 229–239 (2015). https://doi.org/10.1145/2813885.2737977

18. Floater, M.S.: Generalized barycentric coordinates and applications. Acta Numer **24**, 161–214 (2015). https://doi.org/10.1017/S0962492914000129

19. Foundation, B.: Blender. https://www.blender.org/

20. Gould, D.: Complete Maya Programming: An Extensive Guide to MEL and C++ API, 1 edn. Elsevier, Amsterdam (2003). https://doi.org/10.1016/B978-1-55860-835-1.X5000-9

21. Gulwani, S.: Automating string processing in spreadsheets using input-output examples. ACM SIGPLAN Notices **46**(1), 317–330 (2011). https://doi.org/10.1145/1925844.1926423

22. Gulwani, S., Korthikanti, V.A., Tiwari, A.: Synthesizing geometry constructions. ACM SIGPLAN Notices **46**(6), 50–61 (2011). https://doi.org/10.1145/1993316.1993505

23. Gulwani, S., Polozov, O., Singh, R.: Program synthesis. Found. Trends® Program. Lang. **4**(1-2), 1–119 (2017). https://doi.org/10.1561/2500000010

24. Guo, J., et al.: Inverse procedural modeling of branching structures by inferring L-systems. ACM Trans. Graph. **39**(5), 155:1–155:13 (2020). https://doi.org/10.1145/3394105

25. Heckel, R., Taentzer, G.: Graph Transformation for Software Engineers: With Applications to Model-Based Development and Domain-Specific Language Engineering. Springer, Cham (2020). https://doi.org/10.1007/978-3-030-43916-3

26. Hempel, B., Chugh, R.: Semi-automated SVG programming via direct manipulation. In: Proceedings of the 29th Annual Symposium on User Interface Software and Technology, pp. 379–390 (October 2016). https://doi.org/10.1145/2984511.2984575

27. Hu, Y., Dorsey, J., Rushmeier, H.: A novel framework for inverse procedural texture modeling. ACM Trans. Graph. **38**(6), 186:1–186:14 (2019). https://doi.org/10.1145/3355089.3356516

28. Jha, S., Gulwani, S., Seshia, S.A., Tiwari, A.: Oracle-guided component-based program synthesis. In: Proceedings of the 32nd ACM/IEEE International Conference on Software Engineering, vol. 1, pp. 215–224 (May 2010). https://doi.org/10.1145/1806799.1806833

29. Ju, T., Schaefer, S., Warren, J.: Mean value coordinates for closed triangular meshes. ACM Trans. Graph. **24**(3), 561–566 (2005). https://doi.org/10.1145/1073204.1073229

30. Kania, K., Zięba, M., Kajdanowicz, T.: UCSG-NET- unsupervised discovering of constructive solid geometry Tree. In: Proceedings of the 34th International Conference on Neural Information Processing Systems, pp. 8776–8786 (December 2020)

31. Kobbelt, L.: sqrt(3)-subdivision. In: Proceedings of the 27th Annual Conference on Computer Graphics and Interactive Techniques, pp. 103–112 (July 2000). https://doi.org/10.1145/344779.344835

32. Lieng, H., Kosinka, J., Shen, J., Dodgson, N.A.: A colour interpolation scheme for topologically unrestricted gradient meshes. Comput. Graph. Forum **36**(6), 112–121 (2017). https://doi.org/10.1111/cgf.12862

33. Lienhardt, P.: Topological models for boundary representation: a comparison with n-dimensional generalized maps. Comput. Aided Des. **23**(11), 59–82 (1991). https://doi.org/10.1016/0010-4485(91)90100-B

34. Liu, H.T.D., Kim, V.G., Chaudhuri, S., Aigerman, N., Jacobson, A.: Neural subdivision. ACM Trans. Graph. **39**(4), 124:124:1–124:124:16 (2020). https://doi.org/10.1145/3386569.3392418

35. Mandelbrot, B.B.: Fractals : Form, Chance, and Dimension. Freeman, Dallas (1977)

36. Menger, K.: Dimensionstheorie. B.G. Teubner, Berlin (1928)

37. Merrell, P., Manocha, D.: Constraint-based model synthesis. In: 2009 SIAM/ACM Joint Conference on Geometric and Physical Modeling, pp. 101–111 (2009). https://doi.org/10.1145/1629255.1629269

38. Pascual, R.: Inference of graph transformation rules for the design of geometric modeling operations. PhD Thesis, Université Paris-Saclay (November 2022). https://www.theses.fr/2022UPAST146

39. Pascual, R.: Instantiation of Jerboa Rule Schemes, a Set-based Explanation (November 2024). https://doi.org/10.48550/arXiv.2411.15986

40. Pascual, R., Belhaouari, H.: Program Synthesis for Geometric Modeling - Benchmark Artifacts (2025). https://doi.org/10.5281/zenodo.15982906

41. Pascual, R., Belhaouari, H., Arnould, A., Le Gall, P.: Inferring topological operations on generalized maps: application to subdivision schemes. Graph. Vis. Comput. **6**, 200049 (2022). https://doi.org/10.1016/j.gvc.2022.200049

42. Pascual, R., Le Gall, P., Arnould, A., Belhaouari, H.: Topological consistency preservation with graph transformation schemes. Sci. Comput. Program. **214**, 102728 (2022). https://doi.org/10.1016/j.scico.2021.102728

43. Perrin, M., Rainaud, J.F.: Shared Earth Modeling: Knowledge Driven Solutions for Building and Managing Subsurface 3D Geological Models. Editions TECHNIP (2013)

44. Powell, M.J.D., Sabin, M.A.: Piecewise quadratic approximations on triangles. ACM Trans. Math. Softw. **3**(4), 316–325 (1977). https://doi.org/10.1145/355759.355761

45. Prusinkiewicz, P., Samavati, F., Smith, C., Karwowski, R.: L-system description of subdivision curves. Int. J. Shape Model. **09**(01), 41–59 (2003). https://doi.org/10.1142/S0218654303000048

46. Richaume, L., Andres, E., Largeteau-Skapin, G., Zrour, R.: Unfolding level 1 Menger Polycubes of arbitrary size with help of outer faces. In: Couprie, M., Cousty, J., Kenmochi, Y., Mustafa, N. (eds.) DGCI 2019. LNCS, vol. 11414, pp. 457–468. Springer, Cham (2019). https://doi.org/10.1007/978-3-030-14085-4_36

47. Sharma, G., Goyal, R., Liu, D., Kalogerakis, E., Maji, S.: CSGNet: neural shape parser for constructive solid geometry. In: Proceedings of the IEEE Conference on Computer Vision and Pattern Recognition (CVPR), pp. 5515–5523 (2018). https://doi.org/10.48550/arXiv.1712.08290

48. Solar-Lezama, A.: Program sketching. Int. J. Softw. Tools Technol. Transf. 475–495 (2012). https://doi.org/10.1007/s10009-012-0249-7

49. Squillacote, A.H., Ahrens, J., Law, C., Geveci, B., Moreland, K., King, B.: The ParaView guide. Kitware (2007)

50. Summers, P.D.: A methodology for LISP program construction from examples. J. ACM **24**(1), 161–175 (1977). https://doi.org/10.1145/321992.322002

51. Wu, F., Yan, D.M., Dong, W., Zhang, X., Wonka, P.: Inverse procedural modeling of facade layouts. ACM Trans. Graph. **33**(4), 121:1–121:10 (2014). https://doi.org/10.1145/2601097.2601162

52. Šťava, O., Beneš, B., Měch, R., Aliaga, D.G., Krištof, P.: Inverse procedural modeling by automatic generation of L-systems. Comput. Graph. Forum **29**(2), 665–674 (2010). https://doi.org/10.1111/j.1467-8659.2009.01636.x

Recurrent Pairs Revisited

Etienne Payet[(✉)] [iD]

LIM - Université de la Réunion, Réunion, France
etienne.payet@univ-reunion.fr
http://lim.univ-reunion.fr/staff/epayet/

Abstract. In this short paper, we consider non-looping non-termination in term rewriting and logic programming. We describe a strict generalisation of the recurrent pair approach that we introduced previously. We also present an experimental evaluation of our contribution that we implemented in our tool NTI.

Keywords: Non-Termination · Non-Looping · Term Rewriting · Logic Programming

1 Introduction

This paper is concerned with non-termination in term rewriting and logic programming, where one rewrites terms or sequences of terms according to the operational semantics described, *e.g.*, in [1,2]. Rewriting is formalised by binary relations $\Rightarrow_r$ indexed by rules r from a given program and non-termination as the existence of an infinite rewrite sequence $t_0 \Rightarrow_{r_1} t_1 \Rightarrow_{r_2} \cdots$. The vast majority of the papers related to this topic provide necessary or sufficient conditions for the existence of *loops*, *i.e.*, finite rewrite sequences $t_0 \Rightarrow_{r_1} \cdots \Rightarrow_{r_n} t_n$ where t_n satisfies a condition C which entails the possibility of starting again, *i.e.*, $t_n \Rightarrow_{r_1} \cdots \Rightarrow_{r_n} t_{2n}$ where t_{2n} also satisfies C, and so on.

In this paper, we rather consider *non-looping* non-termination, *i.e.*, infinite rewrite sequences that do not embed any loop. Our contribution is a strict extension of an approach introduced previously [8,9] for detecting non-termination of the form $t_0 \left(\Rightarrow_{w_1}^* \circ \Rightarrow_{w_2} \right) t_1 \left(\Rightarrow_{w_1}^* \circ \Rightarrow_{w_2} \right) \cdots$, where w_1 and w_2 are finite sequences of rules. We illustrate it by the following example.

Example 1. Consider the term rewrite system or binary logic program consisting of the following rules (*i.e.*, pairs of terms):

$$r_1 = (u_1, v_1) = \bigl(\mathsf{f}(x, \mathsf{s}^3(y)), \mathsf{f}(\mathsf{s}^2(x), \mathsf{s}(y)) \bigr)$$
$$r_2 = (u_2, v_2) = \bigl(\mathsf{f}(x, \mathsf{s}^3(0)), \mathsf{f}(0, \mathsf{s}^7(x)) \bigr)$$

Here, x and y are variables and f, s and 0 are function symbols of arity 2, 1 and 0 respectively. Moreover, by s^n we mean n successive applications of s. Let $\Delta = 2$. We observe that there is a move of s's between the arguments of f. From u_1 to

S. Escobar and L. Titolo (Eds.): LOPSTR 2025, LNCS 16117, pp. 154–164, 2026.
https://doi.org/10.1007/978-3-032-04848-6_10

v_1, Δ occurrences of s are added at the root position of the first argument of f while Δ occurrences are removed from the root position of the second one. On the other hand, suppose that in r_2 the term bound to x has the form $s^m(\cdots)$. Then, in v_2, the number of occurrences of s at the root position of the second argument of f is $7 + m = \Delta \times 2 + m + 3$; so, if $m = \Delta \times n$ for some $n \in \mathbb{N}$, then we have $7 + m = \Delta \times (n + 2) + 3$. Therefore, for all naturals n, we have the infinite rewrite sequence:

$$f\left(0, s^{\Delta \times n+3}(0)\right) \overset{n}{\underset{r_1}{\Rightarrow}} f\left(s^{\Delta \times n}(0), s^3(0)\right) \underset{r_2}{\Rightarrow} f\left(0, s^{\Delta \times (n+2)+3}(0)\right)$$
$$\overset{n+2}{\underset{r_1}{\Rightarrow}} f\left(s^{\Delta \times (n+2)}(0), s^3(0)\right) \underset{r_2}{\Rightarrow} f\left(0, s^{\Delta \times (n+4)+3}(0)\right)$$
$$\overset{n+4}{\underset{r_1}{\Rightarrow}} \cdots$$

It has the form $t_0 \left(\Rightarrow^*_{r_1} \circ \Rightarrow_{r_2}\right) t_1 \left(\Rightarrow^*_{r_1} \circ \Rightarrow_{r_2}\right) \cdots$ and does not embed a loop, because the number of applications of r_1 gradually increases. The approach of this paper detects its existence (see Definition 3 and Corollary 1), contrary to that of [8,9] which only considers the case $\Delta = 1$ (Definition 3 considers any $\Delta \in \mathbb{N}$).

The paper is organised as follows. Section 2 provides some basic definitions and notations, Sect. 3 describes an extension of the *recurrent pair* approach introduced in [8,9], Sect. 4 presents an experimental evaluation, Sect. 5 briefly introduces related work and Sect. 6 concludes with future work.

2   Preliminaries

We let $\mathbb{N}$ denote the set of natural numbers. Let A be a set. Then, $\overline{A}$ is the set of finite sequences of elements of A, which includes the empty sequence, denoted as e. We use the delimiters $\langle$ and $\rangle$ for writing elements of $\overline{A}$ and juxtaposition to denote the concatenation operation, *e.g.*, $\langle a_0, a_1 \rangle \langle a_2, a_3 \rangle = \langle a_0, a_1, a_2, a_3 \rangle$. We generally denote elements of $\overline{A}$ using lowercase letters with an overline, *e.g.*, $\overline{a}$.

2.1   Binary Relations

A binary relation ϕ on a set A is a subset of $A^2 = A \times A$. For all $\varphi \subseteq A^2$, we let $\phi \circ \varphi$ denote the *composition* of ϕ and φ:

$$\phi \circ \varphi = \left\{ (a, a') \in A^2 \mid \exists a_1 \in A : (a, a_1) \in \phi \wedge (a_1, a') \in \varphi \right\}$$

We let ϕ^0 be the identity relation and, for any $n \in \mathbb{N}$, $\phi^{n+1} = \phi^n \circ \phi$. Moreover, $\phi^+ = \bigcup \{\phi^n \mid n > 0\}$ (resp. $\phi^* = \phi^0 \cup \phi^+$) denotes the transitive (resp. reflexive and transitive) *closure* of ϕ. A ϕ-*chain*, or simply *chain* if ϕ is clear from the context, is a (possibly infinite) sequence of elements of A such that $(a, a') \in \phi$ for any two consecutive elements a, a' (hence, the empty sequence and the singletons are chains). For binary relations that have the form of an arrow, *e.g.*, $\Rightarrow$, we may write chains $a_0, a_1, \ldots$ as $a_0 \Rightarrow a_1 \Rightarrow \cdots$.

2.2   Terms and Substitutions

We use the same definitions and notations as [2] for terms. A *signature* is a set of *function symbols*, each element of which has an *arity* in $\mathbb{N}$. The 0-ary elements of a signature are called *constant symbols*. We denote function symbols by letters or digits in the *sans serif* font, *e.g.*, f, 0...

Let Σ be a signature and X be a set of *variables* disjoint from Σ. For $m \in \mathbb{N}$, we let $\Sigma^{(m)}$ denote the set of all m-ary elements of Σ. The set $T(\Sigma, X)$ of Σ-*terms over* X is defined as: $X \subseteq T(\Sigma, X)$ and, for all $m \in \mathbb{N}$, all $f \in \Sigma^{(m)}$ and all $s_1, \ldots, s_m \in T(\Sigma, X)$, $f(s_1, \ldots, s_m) \in T(\Sigma, X)$. For all $s \in T(\Sigma, X)$, we let $Var(s)$ denote the set of variables occurring in s. We use the superscript notation to denote several successive applications of a unary function symbol, *e.g.*, $s^3(0)$ is a shortcut for $s(s(s(0)))$ and $s^0(0) = 0$.

A $T(\Sigma, X)$-*substitution* (or simply *substitution* if the set of terms is irrelevant or clear from the context) is a function θ from X to $T(\Sigma, X)$ such that $\theta(x) \neq x$ for only finitely many variables x. The *domain* of θ is $Dom(\theta) = \{x \in X \mid \theta(x) \neq x\}$. We usually write θ as $\{x_1 \mapsto \theta(x_1), \ldots, x_n \mapsto \theta(x_m)\}$ where $\{x_1, \ldots, x_m\} = Dom(\theta)$ (hence, the identity substitution is written as $\emptyset$). A *(variable) renaming* is a substitution that is a bijection on X. We let $S(\Sigma, X)$ denote the set of all $T(\Sigma, X)$-substitutions.

The application of $\theta \in S(\Sigma, X)$ to $s \in T(\Sigma, X)$ is denoted as $s\theta$ and is defined as: $s\theta = \theta(s)$ if $s \in X$ and $s\theta = f(s_1\theta, \ldots, s_m\theta)$ if $s = f(s_1, \ldots, s_m)$. Application of θ is extended to finite sequences of terms, *i.e.*, $\langle s_1, \ldots, s_m \rangle \theta = \langle s_1\theta, \ldots, s_m\theta \rangle$.

The *composition* of $\sigma, \theta \in S(\Sigma, X)$ is the $T(\Sigma, X)$-substitution denoted as $\sigma\theta$ and defined as: for all $x \in X$, $\sigma\theta(x) = (\sigma(x))\theta$. This is an associative operation, *i.e.*, for all $s \in T(\Sigma, X)$, $(s\sigma)\theta = s(\sigma\theta)$. We say that σ is *more general* than θ if $\theta = \sigma\eta$ for some $\eta \in S(\Sigma, X)$.

Let $s, t \in T(\Sigma, X)$. We say that s *unifies* with t (or that s and t unify) if $s\sigma = t\sigma$ for some $\sigma \in S(\Sigma, X)$. Then, σ is called a *unifier* of s and t. Moreover, σ is called a *most general unifier* (mgu) of s and t if it is a unifier of s and t that is more general than all unifiers of s and t. We let $mgu(s, t)$ denote the set of mgu's of s and t.

2.3   The Signature Used in the Paper

We regard the symbol e denoting the empty sequence as a special constant symbol. To simplify the statements of this paper, from now on we fix a signature Σ and a set $H = \{\Box_n \mid n \in \mathbb{N} \setminus \{0\}\}$ of constant symbols (called *holes*) such that Σ, $\{e\}$ and H are disjoint from each other. We also fix an infinite countable set X of variables disjoint from $\Sigma \cup \{e\} \cup H$. A *term* is an element of $T(\Sigma, X)$. Let n be a positive integer. An n-*context* is an element of $T(\Sigma \cup H, X)$ that contains occurrences of $\Box_1, \ldots, \Box_n$ but no occurrence of another hole. For all n-contexts c and all $s_1, \ldots, s_n \in T(\Sigma \cup H, X)$, we let $c(s_1, \cdots, s_n)$ denote the element of $T(\Sigma \cup H, X)$ obtained from c by replacing all the occurrences of $\Box_i$ by s_i, for all $1 \leq i \leq n$. We use the superscript notation for denoting several successive embeddings of a 1-context c into itself: $c^0 = \Box_1$ and, for all $n \in \mathbb{N}$, $c^{n+1} = c(c^n)$.

Terms are generally denoted by s, t, u, v, variables by x, y and contexts by c, possibly with subscripts and primes.

2.4 Term Rewriting and Logic Programming

We refer to [2] for the basics of term rewriting and to [1] for those of logic programming. For the sake of harmonisation, we consider the following notion of rule that encompasses term rewriting and logic programming rules (in term rewriting, usually the right-hand side of a rule is a term).

Definition 1. *A* program *is a subset of* $T(\Sigma, X) \times \overline{T(\Sigma, X)}$, *every element of which is called a* rule. *A rule* $(u, \overline{v})$ *is* binary *if* $\overline{v}$ *is empty or is a singleton. We let* $\Re$ *denote the set of binary rules. For the sake of readability, we omit the delimiters* $\langle$ *and* $\rangle$ *in the right-hand side of a binary rule, which amounts to considering that* $\Re \subseteq T(\Sigma, X) \times (T(\Sigma, X) \cup \{e\})$.

Given a rule $(u, \overline{v})$, we let $[(u, \overline{v})] = \{(u\gamma, \overline{v}\gamma) \mid \gamma \text{ is a renaming}\}$ denote its *equivalence class modulo renaming*. Moreover, for all sets of rules U and sequences of terms S, we write $\overline{r} \ll_S U$ to denote that $\overline{r}$ is a sequence of elements of U variable disjoint from S and from each other.

The rules of a program allow one to rewrite terms and finite sequences of terms. This is formalised by the following binary relations.

Definition 2. *For all programs* P *and all* $\Rightarrow \in \{\rightarrow, \rightsquigarrow, \hookrightarrow\}$, *we let* $\Rightarrow_P = \bigcup \{\Rightarrow_r \mid r \in P\}$ *where, for all* $r \in P$,

$$\underset{r}{\rightarrow} = \left\{ (s, c(v\theta)) \in T(\Sigma, X)^2 \;\middle|\; \begin{array}{l} r = (u, \langle v \rangle), \; s = c(u\theta), \; \theta \in S(\Sigma, X) \\ c \text{ is a 1-context with exactly one } \square_1 \end{array} \right\}$$

$$\underset{r}{\rightsquigarrow} = \left\{ (\langle s \rangle\, \overline{s}, (\overline{v}\,\overline{s})\theta) \in \overline{T(\Sigma, X)}^2 \;\middle|\; \langle (u, \overline{v}) \rangle \ll_{\langle s \rangle \overline{s}} [r], \; \theta \in mgu(u, s) \right\}$$

$$\underset{r}{\hookrightarrow} = \left\{ (u\theta, v\theta) \in \Re \;\middle|\; r = (u, v) \in \Re, \; Var(v) \subseteq Var(u), \; \theta \in S(\Sigma, X) \right\}$$

For instance, in Example 1, we have $Var(v_1) \subseteq Var(u_1)$. So, for $\theta = \{x \mapsto 0, y \mapsto s(x)\}$, we have $u_1\theta \rightarrow_{r_1} v_1\theta$ where $u_1\theta = f(0, s^4(x))$ and $v_1\theta = f(s^2(0), s^2(x))$. We also have $u_1\theta = c(u_1\theta)$ and $v_1\theta = c(v_1\theta)$ for the 1-context $c = \square_1$. Hence, we have $u_1\theta \rightarrow_{r_1} v_1\theta$. On the other hand, let $u_1' = f(x', s^3(y))$ and $v_1' = f(s^2(x'), s(y))$. Then, we have $\langle (u_1', v_1') \rangle \ll_{\langle u_1\theta \rangle} [r_1]$ and $\theta' \in mgu(u_1', u_1\theta)$ where $\theta' = \{x' \mapsto 0, y \mapsto s(x)\}$. So, we have $\langle u_1\theta \rangle \rightsquigarrow_{r_1} \langle v_1'\theta' \rangle$ where $v_1'\theta' = v_1\theta$ (in this example, the sequence $\overline{s}$ of the definition of $\rightsquigarrow$ is empty).

The binary relation $\rightarrow_P$ (resp. $\rightsquigarrow_P$) corresponds to the operational semantics of term rewriting (resp. logic programming with the leftmost selection rule). In the proofs of Sect. 3, we need the *closure under substitutions* property (Lemma 1 below). Contrary to $\rightarrow_P$, the relation $\rightsquigarrow_P$ does not satisfy it. This is why we introduce $\hookrightarrow_P$: it satisfies this property and is a restriction of $\rightsquigarrow_P$ to binary rules (*i.e.*, for all $r \in P$, $s \hookrightarrow_r t$ implies $\langle s \rangle \rightsquigarrow_r \overline{t}$ where $\overline{t} = e$ if $t = e$ and $\overline{t} = \langle t \rangle$ otherwise, see Lemma 2.15 of [9]). We also note that $\hookrightarrow_P$ is a restriction of $\rightarrow_P$ (*i.e.*, $\hookrightarrow_r \subseteq \rightarrow_r$ for all $r \in P$) where one rewrites terms at the root position only.

Lemma 1. *Let P be a program and $\Rightarrow \in \{\rightarrow, \hookrightarrow\}$. Then, $\Rightarrow_P$ is* closed under substitutions, *i.e., $s \Rightarrow_P t$ implies $s\theta \Rightarrow_P t\theta$ for all terms s, t and substitutions θ.*

In the rest of this paper, given a program P, we only consider the relations $\rightarrow_P$ and $\hookrightarrow_P$. In logic programming with the leftmost selection rule, one may consider the *binary unfolding* [3] of P, denoted as $binunf(P)$, which is a set of binary rules obtained from P that enjoys the following property:

Theorem 1 ([3]). *Let P be a program and $\bar{s}$ be a sequence of terms. Then, there is an infinite $\leadsto_P$-chain that starts from $\bar{s}$ if and only if there is an infinite $\leadsto_{binunf(P)}$-chain that starts from $\bar{s}$.*

Hence, the existence of an infinite $\hookrightarrow_{binunf(P)}$-chain that starts from a term s implies that of an infinite $\leadsto_{binunf(P)}$-chain that starts from $\langle s \rangle$, which itself implies that of an infinite $\leadsto_P$-chain that starts from $\langle s \rangle$.

3   Extending Recurrent Pairs

Let P be a program and $\Rightarrow \in \{\rightarrow, \hookrightarrow\}$. In this section, we describe a technique for detecting infinite $\Rightarrow_P$-chains using a strict extension of recurrent pairs [8,9]. For all $w \in \overline{P}$, we let $\Rightarrow_w$ be the identity relation if w is empty and $\Rightarrow_w = (\Rightarrow_{r_1} \circ \cdots \circ \Rightarrow_{r_n})$ if $w = \langle r_1, \ldots, r_n \rangle$ with $n \geq 1$. So, any finite non-empty $\Rightarrow_P$-chain has the form $s \Rightarrow_w t$ for some $s, t \in T(\Sigma, X)$ and some $w \in \overline{P}$. Moreover, for all $m, n \in \mathbb{N}$, we let $[n]_m$ be the set of integers greater than n that are *congruent to n modulo m*, i.e., $[n]_m = \{n + k \times m \mid k \in \mathbb{N}\}$.

Definition 3. *Let P be a program and $\Rightarrow \in \{\rightarrow, \hookrightarrow\}$. A* recurrent pair *for $\Rightarrow_P$ is a pair $(u_1 \Rightarrow_{w_1} v_1, u_2 \Rightarrow_{w_2} v_2)$ of finite non-empty $\Rightarrow_P$-chains such that*

- $u_1 = c_1(x, c_2^{m_1}(y))$ *and* $v_1 = c_1(c_2^{n_1}(x), c_2^{n_2}(y))$,
- $u_2 = c_1(x, c_2^{m_2}(s))$ *and* $v_2 = c_1(c_2^{n_3}(t), c_2^{n_4}(x))$ *with* $t \in \{s, x\}$,
- c_1 *is a 2-context,* c_2 *is a 1-context,* $x, y \in X$, $s \in T(\Sigma, X)$,
- $x \neq y$ *and* $\{x, y\} \cap Var(c_1, c_2, s) = \emptyset$,
- $\{m_1, m_2, n_1, n_2, n_3, n_4\} \subseteq \mathbb{N}$,
- $n_2 \leq m_1$, $n_2 \leq m_2$ *and* $\{n_1, n_3, n_4 - m_2\} \subseteq [0]_\Delta$ *where* $\Delta = (m_1 - n_2)$.

This definition is a strict generalisation of that provided in [9], which itself is a strict generalisation of that of [8] (we always have $(m_1, n_2, m_2) = (1, 0, 0)$ in [8] and $(m_1, n_2) = (1, 0)$ in [9]). Intuitively, $u_1 \Rightarrow_{w_1} v_1$ and $u_2 \Rightarrow_{w_2} v_2$ are "mutually recursive" $\Rightarrow_P$-chains where occurrences of context c_2 are moved between $\square_1$ and $\square_2$ in c_1 (see Lemma 2 and Lemma 4 below). In some very special situations, the existence of a recurrent pair implies that of a loop, e.g., if $n_3 = 0$ and $m_2 = n_4$ then we have $c_1(s, c_2^{m_2}(s)) \Rightarrow_{w_2} c_1(s, c_2^{m_2}(s)) \Rightarrow_{w_2} \cdots$. But this is not always the case: in this section, we prove that the existence of a recurrent pair implies that of an infinite $(\Rightarrow_{w_1}^* \circ \Rightarrow_{w_2})$-chain (see Corollary 1).

Example 2. In Example 1, let $\Rightarrow \in \{\rightarrow, \hookrightarrow\}$ and $P = \{r_1, r_2\}$. We have $u_1 \Rightarrow_{r_1} v_1$ and $u_2 \Rightarrow_{r_2} v_2$. Moreover, the pair $(u_1 \Rightarrow_{r_1} v_1, u_2 \Rightarrow_{r_2} v_2)$ is recurrent for $\Rightarrow_P$ with $c_1 = \mathsf{f}(\square_1, \square_2)$, $c_2 = \mathsf{s}(\square_1)$, $s = t = 0$, $m_1 = m_2 = 3$, $(n_1, n_2, n_3, n_4) = (2, 1, 0, 7)$ and $\Delta = (m_1 - n_2) = 2$.

Example 3. Let $\Rightarrow \in \{\rightarrow, \hookrightarrow\}$ and P be the program consisting of the rules

$$r_1 = (u_1, v_1) = \big(\mathsf{f}(x, \mathsf{s}^2(y)), \mathsf{f}(x, \mathsf{s}(y))\big)$$
$$r_2 = (u_2, v_2) = (\mathsf{f}(x, \mathsf{s}(0)), \mathsf{f}(\mathsf{s}(x), \mathsf{s}(x)))$$

We have $u_1 \Rightarrow_{r_1} v_1$ and $u_2 \Rightarrow_{r_2} v_2$. Moreover, the pair $(u_1 \Rightarrow_{r_1} v_1, u_2 \Rightarrow_{r_2} v_2)$ is recurrent for $\Rightarrow_P$ with $c_1 = \mathsf{f}(\square_1, \square_2)$, $c_2 = \mathsf{s}(\square_1)$, $s = 0$, $t = x$, $(m_1, m_2) = (2, 1)$, $(n_1, n_2, n_3, n_4) = (0, 1, 1, 1)$ and $\Delta = (m_1 - n_2) = 1$.

Example 4. Let $\Rightarrow \in \{\rightarrow, \hookrightarrow\}$ and P be the program consisting of the rules

$$r_1 = (u_1, v_1) = \big(\mathsf{f}(x, \mathsf{s}^7(y)), \mathsf{f}(\mathsf{s}^3(x), \mathsf{s}^4(y))\big)$$
$$r_2 = (u_2, v_2) = \big(\mathsf{f}(x, \mathsf{s}^6(0)), \mathsf{f}(x, \mathsf{s}^{11}(x))\big)$$

We have $u_1 \Rightarrow_{r_1} v_1$ and $u_2 \Rightarrow_{r_2} v_2$. Moreover, the pair $(u_1 \Rightarrow_{r_1} v_1, u_2 \Rightarrow_{r_2} v_2)$ is recurrent for $\Rightarrow_P$ with $c_1 = \mathsf{f}(\square_1, \square_2)$, $c_2 = \mathsf{s}(\square_1)$, $s = \mathsf{s}(0)$, $t = x$, $(m_1, m_2) = (7, 5)$, $(n_1, n_2, n_3, n_4) = (3, 4, 0, 11)$ and $\Delta = (m_1 - n_2) = 3$. Note that if we choose $s = 0$ instead then we get $m_2 = 6$ and we have $(n_4 - m_2) \notin [0]_\Delta$.

The next statements are parametric in a program P, in $\Rightarrow \in \{\rightarrow, \hookrightarrow\}$ and in a recurrent pair for $\Rightarrow_P$, with the notations of Definition 3 as well as this new one, introduced for the sake of readability:

Definition 4. *For all $m, n \in \mathbb{N}$, $c_1(m, n)$ denotes the term $c_1(c_2^m(s), c_2^n(s))$.*

First, we introduce a couple of technical lemmas stating properties of the relations $\Rightarrow_{w_1}$ and $\Rightarrow_{w_2}$. Their proofs are based on the fact that $\rightarrow$ and $\hookrightarrow$ are closed under substitutions (see Lemma 1).

Lemma 2. *For all $m, n \in \mathbb{N}$ with $m_1 \leq n$, we have*

$$c_1(m, n) \underset{w_1}{\Rightarrow} c_1(m + n_1, n - \Delta)$$

Proof. Let $m, n \in \mathbb{N}$ with $m_1 \leq n$. Then, $c_1(m, n) = c_1(c_2^m(s), c_2^n(s)) = u_1\theta$ where $\theta = \{x \mapsto c_2^m(s), y \mapsto c_2^{n-m_1}(s)\}$. So, as $u_1 \Rightarrow_{w_1} v_1$, by Lemma 1 we have $c_1(m, n) \Rightarrow_{w_1} v_1\theta$ where $v_1\theta = c_1\big(c_2^{m+n_1}(s), c_2^{n_2+n-m_1}(s)\big) = c_1(m + n_1, n_2 + n - m_1)$, where $n_2 + n - m_1 = n - \Delta$. $\square$

By iterating the application of Lemma 2, one gets the following result.

Lemma 3. *For all $m \in \mathbb{N}$ and $n \in [m_2]_\Delta$, there exists $k \in \mathbb{N}$ such that*

$$c_1(m, n) \underset{w_1}{\overset{k}{\Rightarrow}} c_1(m + k \times n_1, m_2)$$

Proof. Let $m \in \mathbb{N}$ and $n \in [m_2]_\Delta$. Then, we have $n = m_2 + k\Delta$ for some $k \in \mathbb{N}$.

- Suppose that $m_1 \leq m_2$. Then, we have $m_1 \leq m_2 \leq n$. Therefore, one can apply Lemma 2 k times to get $c_1(m, n) \Rightarrow_{w_1}^{k} c_1(m + k \times n_1, n - k\Delta)$, with $(n - k\Delta) = m_2$.
- Suppose that $m_2 < m_1$.
  - If $k = 0$ then $n = m_2$ and $c_1(m, n) \Rightarrow_{w_1}^{k} c_1(m + k \times n_1, m_2)$.
  - Otherwise, $m_2 + \Delta = m_2 + (m_1 - n_2) = m_1 + (m_2 - n_2)$, i.e., $m_2 + \Delta - m_1 = m_2 - n_2$. But, as $n_2 \leq m_2$, we have $0 \leq (m_2 - n_2)$. So, $0 \leq (m_2 + \Delta - m_1)$, i.e., $m_1 \leq (m_2 + \Delta)$. Consequently, we have $m_2 < m_1 \leq (m_2 + \Delta) \leq n$. So, one can apply Lemma 2 k times to get $c_1(m, n) \Rightarrow_{w_1}^{k} c_1(m + k \times n_1, n - k\Delta)$, with $(n - k\Delta) = m_2$.   □

Lemma 4. *For all $m \in \mathbb{N}$, we have $c_1(m, m_2) \Rightarrow_{w_2} c_1(n_3 + m', n_4 + m)$ where $m' = 0$ if $t = s$ and $m' = m$ if $t = x$.*

Proof. Let $m \in \mathbb{N}$. We have $c_1(m, m_2) = c_1(c_2^m(s), c_2^{m_2}(s)) = u_2\{x \mapsto c_2^m(s)\}$. So, as $u_2 \Rightarrow_{w_2} v_2$, by Lemma 1 we have $c_1(m, m_2) \Rightarrow_{w_2} v_2\{x \mapsto c_2^m(s)\}$.

- If $t = s$ then $v_2\{x \mapsto c_2^m(s)\} = c_1(c_2^{n_3}(s), c_2^{n_4 + m}(s)) = c_1(n_3, n_4 + m)$.
- If $t = x$ then $v_2\{x \mapsto c_2^m(s)\} = c_1(c_2^{n_3 + m}(s), c_2^{n_4 + m}(s)) = c_1(n_3 + m, n_4 + m)$.   □

By combining Lemma 3 and Lemma 4, one gets the next proposition.

Proposition 1. *For all $m \in [0]_\Delta$ and $n \in [m_2]_\Delta$, there exist $m' \in [0]_\Delta$ and $n' \in [m_2]_\Delta$ such that $c_1(m, n) (\Rightarrow_{w_1}^{*} \circ \Rightarrow_{w_2}) c_1(m', n')$.*

Proof. Let $m \in [0]_\Delta$ and $n \in [m_2]_\Delta$. By Lemma 3, there exists $k \in \mathbb{N}$ such that $c_1(m, n) \Rightarrow_{w_1}^{k} c_1(l, m_2)$ and $l = m + k \times n_1$. By Lemma 4, $c_1(l, m_2) \Rightarrow_{w_2} c_1(n_3 + l', n_4 + l)$ where $l' = 0$ if $t = s$ and $l' = l$ if $t = x$. Therefore, for $m' = n_3 + l'$ and $n' = n_4 + l$, we have $c_1(m, n) (\Rightarrow_{w_1}^{k} \circ \Rightarrow_{w_2}) c_1(m', n')$. We note that $m' \in [0]_\Delta$ because $\{m, n_1, n_3\} \subseteq [0]_\Delta$. Moreover, $(n_4 - m_2) \in [0]_\Delta$ implies that $n_4 \in [m_2]_\Delta$; hence, as $l \in [0]_\Delta$ (because $\{m, n_1\} \subseteq [0]_\Delta$), we have $(n_4 + l) \in [m_2]_\Delta$, i.e., $n' \in [m_2]_\Delta$.   □

The main result of this paper is a straightforward consequence of Proposition 1:

Corollary 1. *Let P be a program, $\Rightarrow \in \{\rightarrow, \hookrightarrow\}$ and $(u_1 \Rightarrow_{w_1} v_1, u_2 \Rightarrow_{w_2} v_2)$ be a recurrent pair for $\Rightarrow_P$, with the notations of Definition 3. Then, for all $m \in [0]_\Delta$ and $n \in [m_2]_\Delta$, the term $c_1(m, n)$ starts an infinite $(\Rightarrow_{w_1}^{*} \circ \Rightarrow_{w_2})$-chain.*

This result implies the existence of infinite chains in the above examples. Each of these chains does not embed any loop because the number of applications of r_1 gradually increases.

Example 5. In Example 1–2, we have the following infinite $(\Rightarrow_{r_1}^* \circ \Rightarrow_{r_2})$-chain:

$$\overbrace{f(0, s^3(0))}^{c_1(0,m_2)} \; (\overset{0}{\underset{r_1}{\Rightarrow}} \circ \underset{r_2}{\Rightarrow}) \; f(0, s^7(0)) \overset{2}{\underset{r_1}{\Rightarrow}} f(s^4(0), s^3(0)) \underset{r_2}{\Rightarrow} f(0, s^{11}(0)) \overset{4}{\underset{r_1}{\Rightarrow}} \cdots$$

It corresponds to the case $n = 0$ in Example 1.

Example 6. In Example 3, we have the following infinite $(\overset{*}{\underset{r_1}{\Rightarrow}} \circ \underset{r_2}{\Rightarrow})$-chain:

$$\overbrace{f(0, s(0))}^{c_1(0,m_2)} \; (\overset{0}{\underset{r_1}{\Rightarrow}} \circ \underset{r_2}{\Rightarrow}) \; f(s(0), s(0)) \; (\overset{0}{\underset{r_1}{\Rightarrow}} \circ \underset{r_2}{\Rightarrow}) \; f(s^2(0), s^2(0))$$

$$\overset{1}{\underset{r_1}{\Rightarrow}} f(s^2(0), s(0)) \underset{r_2}{\Rightarrow} f(s^3(0), s^3(0)) \overset{2}{\underset{r_1}{\Rightarrow}} \cdots$$

Example 7. In Example 4, we have the following infinite $(\Rightarrow_{r_1}^* \circ \Rightarrow_{r_2})$-chain:

$$\overbrace{f(s(0), s^6(0))}^{c_1(0,m_2)} \; (\overset{0}{\underset{r_1}{\Rightarrow}} \circ \underset{r_2}{\Rightarrow}) \; f(s(0), s^{12}(0)) \overset{2}{\underset{r_1}{\Rightarrow}} f(s^7(0), s^6(0)) \underset{r_2}{\Rightarrow} f(s^7(0), s^{18}(0)) \overset{4}{\underset{r_1}{\Rightarrow}} \cdots$$

4 Experimental Evaluation

We have implemented the approach of Sect. 3 in our tool NTI for term rewrite systems (TRSs) and logic programs (LPs). More precisely, NTI unfolds the program under analysis (using a user-provided time limit to stop this possibly infinite process) and tries to detect pairs of unfolded rules $((u_1, v_1), (u_2, v_2))$ that satisfy Definition 3. Since we started to work on this topic a few years ago, we have added several examples of non-looping non-terminating TRSs and LPs to the TPDB.[1] They are all similar to the programs of Example 1–4. In Table 1, we report the results of the analysers participating in the *International Termination Competition*[2] that are capable of detecting non-looping non-terminating TRSs (NTI'24 refers to the version of NTI that implements the approach of this paper). We point out that AProVE and NTI are the only two tools that participate in the "logic programming" category of the competition and that AProVE is not able to detect non-termination of LPs. We note that NTI'24 is the only tool that succeeds on all benchmarks. Our results can be reproduced using our tool and the benchmarks available online.[3]

5 Related Work

Apart from [8,9], we are aware of only a few papers dealing with non-looping non-termination: [7,12] in the field of string rewriting, [4,5,11,12] in term rewriting and [10] in logic programming. How all these approaches are related to ours is an open question that we leave for future work.

---

[1] Termination Problem Data Base: http://termination-portal.org/wiki/TPDB.
[2] http://termination-portal.org/wiki/Termination_Competition.
[3] https://github.com/etiennepayet/nti.

Table 1. Results of the Termination Competition 2024 on the TRSs and LPs we added to the TPDB (time limit = 300 s, see https://termcomp.github.io/Y2024/). The last column on the right gives the values of Δ for the recurrent pairs found by NTI.

Directory of the TPDB	AProVE [6]	AutoNon [5]	NTI'23 [9]	NTI'24	Δ
TRS_Standard/payet_21	0/3	3/3	3/3	3/3	$\{1\}$
TRS_Standard/Payet_23	0/10	0/10	10/10	10/10	$\{1\}$
TRS_Standard/Payet_24	1/5	0/5	0/5	5/5	$\{1, 2, 3, 5\}$
Logic_Programming/Payet_22	0/5	–	4/5	5/5	$\{1\}$
Logic_Programming/Payet_23	0/9	–	9/9	9/9	$\{1\}$
Logic_Programming/Payet_24	0/4	–	0/4	4/4	$\{2, 3, 5\}$

6   Conclusion

We have presented a natural, strict, generalisation of the recurrent pairs of [8,9] to encompass a broader range of infinite rewrite sequences, specifically those where Δ can be any natural number, rather than being restricted to 1. On the theoretical side, this leads to the definition of a wider class of non-terminating behaviours, compared to [8,9]. On the practical side, this allows the detection of infinite rewrite sequences that were not detectable by previous approaches. We still have to investigate whether these infinite sequences correspond to situations arising in real programs or in programs introduced by other sources than ourselves (in the TPDB, our extension only solves problems that we specifically added to illustrate our contribution, contrary to the approach of [8,9] that solves problems from, *e.g.*, [12]).

Future work will also focus on extending our approach to deal with more general situations, *e.g.*, by considering recurrent tuples with more than two rules to detect infinite rewrite sequences $t_0 \rightarrowtail t_1 \rightarrowtail \cdots$ where $\rightarrowtail$ has the form $(\Rightarrow^*_{w_1} \circ \cdots \circ \Rightarrow^*_{w_{n-1}} \circ \Rightarrow_{w_n})$ for some natural $n \geq 1$, some $\Rightarrow \in \{\rightarrow, \hookrightarrow\}$ and some finite sequences of rules $w_1, \ldots, w_n$.

Example 8. Consider the following variant of Example 1:

$$r_1 = (u_1, v_1) = \big(\mathsf{f}(x, \mathsf{s}^3(y), z), \mathsf{f}(\mathsf{s}^2(x), \mathsf{s}(y), z)\big)$$
$$r_2 = (u_2, v_2) = \big(\mathsf{f}(x, y, \mathsf{s}^3(z)), \mathsf{f}(x, y, \mathsf{s}(z))\big)$$
$$r_3 = (u_3, v_3) = \big(\mathsf{f}(x, \mathsf{s}^3(0), \mathsf{s}^3(0)), \mathsf{f}(0, \mathsf{s}^7(x), \mathsf{s}^7(x))\big)$$

Let $\Delta = 2$ and $\Rightarrow\ \in \{\rightarrow, \hookrightarrow\}$. For all $n \in \mathbb{N}$, we have the infinite rewrite sequence

$$\mathsf{f}\left(0, \mathsf{s}^{\Delta \times n + 3}(0), \mathsf{s}^{\Delta \times n + 3}(0)\right) \left(\overset{n}{\underset{r_1}{\Rightarrow}} \circ \overset{n}{\underset{r_2}{\Rightarrow}}\right) \mathsf{f}\left(\mathsf{s}^{\Delta \times n}(0), \mathsf{s}^3(0), \mathsf{s}^3(0)\right)$$

$$\underset{r_3}{\Rightarrow} \mathsf{f}\left(0, \mathsf{s}^{\Delta \times (n+2)+3}(0), \mathsf{s}^{\Delta \times (n+2)+3}(0)\right)$$

$$\left(\overset{n+2}{\underset{r_1}{\Rightarrow}} \circ \overset{n+2}{\underset{r_2}{\Rightarrow}}\right) \mathsf{f}\left(\mathsf{s}^{\Delta \times (n+2)}(0), \mathsf{s}^3(0), \mathsf{s}^3(0)\right)$$

$$\underset{r_3}{\Rightarrow} \mathsf{f}\left(0, \mathsf{s}^{\Delta \times (n+4)+3}(0), \mathsf{s}^{\Delta \times (n+4)+3}(0)\right)$$

$$\left(\overset{n+4}{\underset{r_1}{\Rightarrow}} \circ \overset{n+4}{\underset{r_2}{\Rightarrow}}\right) \cdots$$

It has the form $t_0 \rightarrowtail t_1 \rightarrowtail \cdots$ where $\rightarrowtail\ = (\Rightarrow^*_{r_1} \circ \Rightarrow^*_{r_2} \circ \Rightarrow_{r_3})$ and it does not embed any loop, because the number of applications of r_1 and r_2 gradually increases. Moreover, it is not a $(\Rightarrow^*_{w_1} \circ \Rightarrow_{w_2})$-chain for some finite sequences of rules w_1 and w_2 (see Corollary 1). We observe that the pair (r_1, r_3) is not recurrent: if it was then, in r_1, the context c_1 would be $\mathsf{f}(\square_1, \square_2, z)$ and, in r_3, it would be $\mathsf{f}(\square_1, \square_2, \mathsf{s}^3(0))$ or $\mathsf{f}(\square_1, \mathsf{s}^3(0), \square_2)$, which is not possible because these contexts are different. For the same reasons, the pair (r_2, r_3) is not recurrent either. Hence, our approach does not apply to this example.

Acknowledgments. The author thanks the anonymous reviewers for their insightful and constructive criticisms.

Disclosure of Interests. The author has no competing interests to declare that are relevant to the content of this article.

References

1. Apt, K.R.: From Logic Programming to Prolog. Prentice Hall International series in computer science, Prentice Hall (1997)
2. Baader, F., Nipkow, T.: Term Rewriting and All That. Cambridge University Press, Cambridge (1998)
3. Codish, M., Taboch, C.: A semantic basis for the termination analysis of logic programs. J. Log. Program. **41**(1), 103–123 (1999). https://doi.org/10.1016/S0743-1066(99)00006-0
4. Emmes, F., Enger, T., Giesl, J.: Proving non-looping non-termination automatically. In: Gramlich, B., Miller, D., Sattler, U. (eds.) IJCAR 2012. LNCS (LNAI), vol. 7364, pp. 225–240. Springer, Heidelberg (2012). https://doi.org/10.1007/978-3-642-31365-3_19
5. Endrullis, J., Zantema, H.: Proving non-termination by finite automata. In: Fernández, M. (ed.) Proceedings of the 26th International Conference on Rewriting Techniques and Applications. Leibniz International Proceedings in Informatics, vol. 36, pp. 160–176. Schloss Dagstuhl–Leibniz-Zentrum fuer Informatik (2015).https://doi.org/10.4230/LIPIcs.RTA.2015.160
6. Giesl, J., et al.: Automated Program Verification Environment (2025). http://aprove.informatik.rwth-aachen.de/

7. Oppelt, M.: Automatische Erkennung von Ableitungsmustern in nichttermnieren-den Wortersetzungssystemen. Diploma Thesis, HTWK Leipzig, Germany (2008)

8. Payet, E.: Binary non-termination in term rewriting and logic programming. In: Yamada, A. (ed.) Proceedings of the 19th International Workshop on Termination (2023). https://doi.org/10.48550/arXiv.2307.11549

9. Payet, E.: Non-termination in term rewriting and logic programming. J. Autom. Reason. **68**(4), 24 (2024). https://doi.org/10.1007/S10817-023-09693-Z

10. Payet, E.: Non-termination of logic programs using patterns. Theory and Practice of Logic Programming. Published online 2025:1-17. https://doi.org/10.1017/S1471068425100100

11. Wang, Y., Sakai, M.: On non-looping term rewriting. In: Geser, A., Søndergaard, H. (eds.) Proceedings of the 8th International Workshop on Termination, pp. 17–21 (2006)

12. Zantema, H., Geser, A.: Non-looping rewriting. Universiteit Utrecht. UU-CS, Department of Computer Science, Utrecht University, Netherlands (1996)

Natural Language to LOGICA: Towards Interactive and Explainable Data Analytics

Ojaswa Garg[1], Shayan Mirjafari[1], Yilin Xia[2], Shawn Bowers[3],
Bertram Ludäscher[2], and Evgeny Skvortsov[1(✉)]

[1] Google LLC, Kirkland, WA, USA
evgenys@google.com
[2] University of Illinois, Urbana-Champaign, IL, USA
{yilinx2,ludaesch}@illinois.edu
[3] Gonzaga University, Spokane, WA, USA
bowers@gonzaga.edu

Abstract. We propose to make data analysis more accessible and verifiable by generating LOGICA programs from natural language queries. LOGICA, a logic programming language that compiles to (embedded) SQL, combines the clarity of declarative logic rules with the scalability of robust SQL engines. We evaluate the translation of natural language to LOGICA using the SPIDER 1.0 SQL benchmark, demonstrating that GEMINI 2.5 achieves accuracy comparable to the leading SQL generators. We also explore a 2-step translation via intermediate LOGICLM configurations, i.e., using OLAP-style *measures*, *dimensions*, and *filters*. These configurations serve as another explainable intermediate layer that domain experts can easily validate, even with limited or no SQL, OLAP or logic programming experience. Our analysis reveals that approximately half of the SPIDER 1.0 queries can be expressed as OLAP queries with our approach. By employing LOGICA as an intermediate layer (rather than generating SQL directly), we create a transparent and verifiable path to database queries from natural language.

Keywords: logic programming · databases · explainable AI

1 Introduction

Natural language interfaces promise users the ability to quickly and easily gain insights from data without directly writing analytical queries, e.g., in SQL [3]. However, the implementation of these interfaces presents significant challenges. For instance, as both human analysts and AI systems work with complex data and queries, explainability becomes essential for verification and trust.

In this paper, we explore the use of LOGICA [8,9], a formal logic-based language that compiles into SQL, as an intermediate specification for translating complex data analyses from natural language into executable queries. LOGICA offers a unique combination of SQL's scalability with the clarity and explainability of logic rules. It provides a representation that can help clarify the intent

S. Escobar and L. Titolo (Eds.): LOPSTR 2025, LNCS 16117, pp. 165–179, 2026.
https://doi.org/10.1007/978-3-032-04848-6_11

behind potentially ambiguous natural language queries. Given these advantages, an important research question emerges: Can LOGICA programs be effectively generated from natural language queries using current AI technologies?

Recent advances in LLMS have demonstrated impressive capabilities in code generation, in particular in the Text-to-SQL domain [1, 2, 4–6, 10]. However, it is not clear whether models that have been primarily trained on SQL also reliably generate LOGICA programs. We show that specialized training is *not* necessary: Modern LLMs demonstrate a surprising ability to generate correct LOGICA rules with only minimal specialized prompting. Our approach uses simple prompts containing (1) a LOGICA tutorial, (2) the database schema(s), (3) sample data to recognize constants, and (4) the natural language questions. The result is a method that yields impressive results while remaining easily reproducible.

Our evaluation uses the SPIDER 1.0 SQL benchmark [11], a diverse and challenging dataset for cross-domain semantic parsing. While this benchmark was designed for SQL evaluation, its structure makes it equally valuable for assessing LOGICA program generation. We measured the accuracy of generated LOGICA programs across a wide range of complex queries and database structures.

In addition to the direct generation of LOGICA rules, we also investigate a 2-step translation via LOGICLM [7] configurations. LOGICLM is an open source natural language data analytics interface that uses LOGICA and LLMs to translate natural language queries into OLAP-style queries via intermediate LOGICLM configurations. These configurations, structured around measures, dimensions, and filters, provide a substantially enhanced layer of explainability that makes data analysis accessible to a broader audience. While this approach requires queries to conform to an OLAP structure, our analysis reveals that approximately half of the queries in the SPIDER 1.0 dataset can be expressed in this format. For these queries, LOGICLM configurations offer an intuitive representation that domain experts can validate even without SQL or logic programming knowledge, enabling those who lack the time or background to learn LOGICA to still meaningfully participate in the data analysis process.

Our initial evaluations of LOGICA program generation indicated lower performance than expected, but closer examination revealed several factors affecting accuracy metrics rather than actual generation quality. These included harmless differences such as returning additional columns (which technically differ from reference answers but satisfy user information needs) and ambiguities in natural language questions that allow for multiple valid interpretations. This experience underscores a "recursive" theme in our work: just as LOGICA provides explainability for queries, we found that the evaluation of LOGICA itself requires explainable metrics to accurately assess its true capabilities. Addressing these evaluation nuances provides a more accurate assessment of model performance for direct LOGICA generation.

Contributions. The results of our evaluation demonstrate that GEMINI 2.5 achieves performance comparable to the leading SQL generators from 2023, suggesting that the logic-based structure of LOGICA aligns well with LLMs' reasoning capabilities. This finding has significant implications for the future of natural language interfaces to databases, indicating that the clarity and explainability benefits of logic programming can be obtained without sacrificing generation accuracy. We hypothesize that such explainability could potentially benefit not only human users but also AI systems when reasoning about data transformations: a promising direction for further investigation.

This paper contributes to the growing body of research on natural language interfaces for data analysis by demonstrating the feasibility of generating LOGICA programs with minimal specialized prompting, evaluating the quality of these generations against an established benchmark, and exploring the potential of intermediate representations to enhance explainability. Through this work, we aim to advance the development of data analysis tools that are not only powerful but also transparent and accessible to a broad range of users.

2   Background

LOGICA Overview. LOGICA is a declarative logic programming language designed for data manipulation that bridges the gap between the intuitive nature of logic programming and the practical demands of modern data science. Unlike traditional SQL, which is based on natural language syntax that can become unwieldy for complex queries, LOGICA leverages the precision and clarity of mathematical logic notation to express data transformations and queries. At its core, LOGICA is based on predicate logic, where programs consist of facts and rules. A rule has the form *head* :- *body*, where the conclusion in the *head* is derived whenever the condition in the *body* is satisfied. LOGICA extends Datalog with several key features that make it particularly suitable for data analysis:

Named Arguments. Traditionally, logic programming languages use positional arguments. LOGICA supports *named arguments* to enhance readability when working with tables with many columns. For example, instead of:

```
Human("Socrates", 250, -470, "Athens");
```

LOGICA allows labels for each term:

```
Human(name: "Socrates", iq: 250, yr: -470, loc: "Athens");
```

When using a predicate, only the necessary arguments are needed:

```
AthenianPhilosopher(philosopher:) :-
    Human(name: philosopher, loc: "Athens", iq: iq), iq>200;
```

Functional Notation. LOGICA also supports *functional predicates* that transform input values to output values, enabling a more natural expression of data transformations. Functions in LOGICA are defined using the = operator rather than the :- operator for standard rules:

```
BookAuthor(title: "Frankenstein", year: 1816) = "Shelley";
```

Functional predicates can also be used with rule bodies, allowing for complex transformations. The following query also leverages LOGICA's support for nested data objects.

```
BookAuthor(title:, year: info.pub_yr) = info.author :-
  Book(title:, info:);
```

Functional notation enables the composition of transformations, similar to how functions work in traditional programming languages:

```
S(x) = x * x;
D(x) = 2 * x;
Result(D(S(x))) :- Input(x);
```

This functional style can make data transformations more intuitive and aligns with how many data scientists conceptualize data operations.

Custom Aggregation. LOGICA provides supports aggregation capabilities that extend standard operations like **Sum** and **Count**. Crucially, it allows users to define custom aggregation functions by combining existing aggregators with mathematical operations. For example, the following defines a custom aggregator for calculating the sum of squares.

```
SumOfSquares(x) = Sum(x * x);
```

Similarly, the following example defines the harmonic mean.

```
HarmonicMean(x) = Sum(1) / Sum(1 / x);
```

Custom aggregators, which can be used like built-in aggregation functions, support specialized analytical tasks and forms the foundation for defining OLAP-style measures in LOGICLM, where measures are essentially custom aggregations over facts. As shown below, LOGICA supports both predicate-level aggregation using the **distinct** keyword and aggregating expressions using curly braces.

```
# Predicate-level aggregation with distinct
Fruit(fruit:, total_weight? += weight) distinct :-
  BoxOfFruit(fruit:, weight:);
# Aggregating expression in a rule
PurchaseSummary(p_id:, total_val:, most_expensive:) :-
  Purchase(p_id:, tickets:),
  total_val = Sum{ticket.price :- ticket in tickets},
  most_expensive = Max{ticket.price :- ticket in tickets};
```

SQL Compilation. LOGICA programs compile to SQL, allowing execution on multiple database engines including SQLite, PostgreSQL, DuckDB, and Google BigQuery. By compiling programs to SQL, LOGICA exploits SQL's widespread infrastructure and computational efficiency. Users can easily switch between target engines using a built-in directive (e.g., **Engine("bigquery")**) allowing the same program to run on different underlying database systems. The SQL compilation process is automated and optimized, generating efficient queries that leverage the underlying database engine's capabilities.

LOGICLM Overview. LOGICLM is an interactive data analysis system that combines Large Language Models (LLMs) and LOGICA to provide natural language access to data exploration and visualization. Unlike systems that directly translate natural language to SQL, where errors in the generated SQL can lead to incorrect results without the user's knowledge, LOGICLM introduces a transparent intermediate layer using OLAP-style configurations expressed through LOGICA.

LogicLM Architecture and Workflow. The core innovation of LOGICLM is its two-step approach to translating natural language queries. In the first step, an LLM interprets the natural language query and generates a structured OLAP configuration specifying which measures, dimensions, and filters to apply. Then in the second step, the configuration is displayed to the user for verification and potential modification before being converted into executable LOGICA code, which is then compiled to SQL and executed against the database. This architecture ensures both the accuracy of query translation and user control over the process, allowing for iterative refinement of analyses through the browser-based interface.

OLAP Components as LOGICA Predicates. LOGICLM leverages LOGICA's expressive capabilities to represent OLAP components as logical predicates. A *measure* can be defined using LOGICA's custom aggregation capabilities to create quantitative metrics. For example, counting orders can be defined as:

```
OrderCount(fact) = Count(fact.order_id);
```

A *dimension* is implemented using functional predicates that map facts to categorical values for analysis. For instance, associating orders with customer districts can be performed as follows.

```
CustomerDistrictName(fact) = district_name :-
    District(d_id: fact.cust_district, name: district_name);
```

A *filter* is expressed using standard predicates that specify conditions for data selection. For example, the following filters orders from specific cities.

```
OrdersToCities(fact, city_names:) :-
    Constraint(CustomerCityName(fact) in city_names);
```

Natural-Language Query Generation and Verification. When a user submits a natural language request, LOGICLM translates it into a JSON-formatted query configuration that specifies: (1) the measure(s) to calculate; (2) the dimension(s) to analyze; (3) the filter(s) to apply, including any parameters; and (4) the type of visualization to use for displaying results. For example, the request "*How many deliveries were done to districts of Springfield*" might be translated (depending on the context) into a configuration specifying `OrderCount` as the measure, `CustomerDistrictName` as the dimension, and `OrdersToCities` with the parameter `["Springfield"]` as the filter. This configuration is displayed to the user (as part of the LOGICLM user interface) allowing them to verify that the system has correctly understood their intent prior to query execution. Users can modify any element of the configuration directly through the interface if needed, providing an important safeguard against potential misinterpretations by the LLM.

Metadata and System Configuration. LOGICLM uses a dedicated LOGICA predicate to define the configuration context and its associated metadata:

```
LogicLM(
  title: "Delivery Statistics",
  fact_tables: ["FoodOrderDataSource"],
  dimensions: ["CustomerDistrictName","CustomerCityName"],
  measures: ["OrderCount", "DeliveryDuration"],
  filters: ["OrdersToCities"],
  suffix_lines: [
    "Try using linechart or barchart.",
    "If unsure use a table chart.",
    "Good luck!"]
);
```

The metadata configuration includes the available measures, dimensions, and filters to use as part of natural language queries, as well as providing system-level settings and additional context for the LLM through the **suffix_lines** parameter.

3   Query Generation

We describe two experimental approaches for leveraging LLMs to generate LOGICA programs from natural language queries. The first approach directly translates a user's natural language query to LOGICA only using prompt engineering. The second approach leverages LOGICLM as an intermediate step in the natural-language to LOGICA translation. Queries and experimental results are developed for the SPIDER 1.0 dataset [11], which is a well-known benchmark for evaluating Text-to-SQL systems. For the purposes of this paper, all experiments are run using Gemini (although other LLMs could also be used).

3.1   Overview of the Spider Dataset

SPIDER 1.0 is a large-scale benchmark for complex, cross-domain text-to-SQL tasks. It provides 8,659 training examples from 146 databases, split between **train_spider.json** (7,000 examples, 140 databases) and **train_others.json** (1,659 examples, 6 databases). We focus on the evaluation sets: **dev.json** (DEV) with 1,034 queries from 20 databases, and **test.json** (TEST) with 2,147 queries from 40 databases, which contain only databases unseen in the training set.

While difficulty levels are not directly annotated in the dataset, they can be automatically assigned using the official evaluation script [11]. Each SQL query is categorized as *easy, medium, hard,* or *extra hard,* based on the resulting SQL constructs (e.g., **WHERE, GROUP BY, JOIN**) and structural factors like aggregation count or nested queries. This classification provides a useful lens for analyzing model performance across varying query complexities.

3.2 Approach 1: Prompting LLMs Directly to Generate LOGICA

The first phase of experiments evaluated the LLM's ability to translate natural language into LOGICA using prompt engineering alone. A user prompt was provided to GEMINI 2.5, instructing it to generate a LOGICA program. The resulting program was then executed on the associated dataset to assess its correctness. A snippet of the prompt used is shown below.

This is the Logica Info: _LOGICA_INFO

This is the input schema: _SCHEMA_

This is the snippet of the data in the tables mentioned in the schema: _DATA_

Example Question: What is the name and nation of the singer who have a song having 'Hey' in its name?

Example LOGICA Program:

```
Report(name:, country:) :-
  singer(name:, country:, song_name: s_name),
  Like(s_name, "%Hey%");
```

Provide a LOGICA Program for Input Schema which answers the _QUESTION_ .

In this prompt, the section labeled _LOGICA_INFO provides the LLM with background knowledge about LOGICA, including documentation and syntax guidelines. The _SCHEMA_ and _DATA_ sections are derived from the SPIDER 1.0 dataset: the former defines the structure of the relevant database tables, while the latter presents snippets of actual table contents (typically only the first few rows) to help the model understand potential values within each column. This information is followed by an example consisting of a natural-language question and its corresponding LOGICA program, which serves to demonstrate the expected output format. The prompt ends with a new question from the SPIDER 1.0 dataset telling the LLM to generate the corresponding LOGICA program.

Based on the `pets_1` database, the following query addresses a question marked as being "extra hard" from SPIDER 1.0. The query asks for the first name and the age of students who have a dog but do not have a cat as a pet. The corresponding LOGICA program was generated using our prompting approach:

```
HasDog(stuid:, fname:, age:) :-
  Student(stuid:, fname:, age:),
  Has_Pet(stuid:, petid:),
  Pets(petid:, pettype: "dog");
HasCat(stuid:) :-
  Student(stuid:),
  Has_Pet(stuid:, petid:),
  Pets(petid:, pettype: "cat");
Report(fname:, age:) distinct :-
  HasDog(stuid:, fname:, age:),
```

```
~HasCat(stuid:);
```

The corresponding SQL query compiled from the LOGICA program is:

```
SELECT T1.fname,T1.age
  FROM student AS T1
  JOIN has_pet AS T2
    ON T1.stuid = T2.stuid
  JOIN pets AS T3
    ON T3.petid = T2.petid
 WHERE T3.pettype = 'dog'
   AND T1.stuid NOT IN
       (SELECT T1.stuid
          FROM student AS T1
          JOIN has_pet AS T2
            ON T1.stuid = T2.stuid
          JOIN pets AS T3
            ON T3.petid = T2.petid
         WHERE T3.pettype = 'cat')
```

This example helps to illustrate the potential value of using LOGICA as an intermediate representation in the translation from natural language to SQL via LLMs. In particular, the LOGICA program uses explicit negation in the body of the **Report** rule, whereas in SQL the negation is much less direct, requiring the use of a subquery. For more complex queries, including those that require basic negation, LOGICA can provide a more interpretable result (while still generating the underlying SQL). The modular and declarative nature of LOGICA (via logic-programming constructs) can also make it easier to identify potential errors and to understand more directly how the LLM is interpreting user questions.

3.3   Approach 2: LOGICLM Configurations

Our second method uses LOGICLM as an intermediate step before generating LOGICA programs. LOGICLM configurations are generated automatically by the LLM, which requires reformulation of the input problem as an OLAP-style query. Below is a snippet of the prompt that is used.

This is the Logica Info: **_LOGICA_INFO**

This is the input schema: **_SCHEMA_**

These are the sets of questions: **_QUESTIONS_**

Example LOGICLM Configurations:

```
BabyNames(fact) :- usa_names.usa_1910_current(..fact);
NumberOfBabies(fact) = Sum(fact.number);
Name(fact) = fact.name;
StateIn(fact, states:) :-
  Constraint(fact.state in states);
```

```
ConsolidatingBabyNames(numberofbabies? Aggr=
NumberOfBabies(fact), name: Name(fact)) distinct :-
  BabyNames(fact),
  StateIn(fact, states: ["WA", "OR", "CA"]);
```

Provide a LOGICLM config for the input schema which answers the questions.

As in our first approach, the prompt begins with embedded LOGICA documentation and syntax guidelines. We then provide the _SCHEMA_ and a set of natural language _QUESTIONS_ from SPIDER 1.0, prompting the system to generate a corresponding LOGICLM configuration. These configurations specify measures, dimensions, and filters as logical predicates, serving as interpretable representations of query intent that can be validated by human experts. The resulting configuration, combined with the original questions, is then used to prompt GEMINI 2.5 to generate the final LOGICA program.

4   Evaluation and Accuracy Refinement

We evaluated the LOGICA-based generation approach on 2,147 queries from the `test.json` file (TEST) of the SPIDER 1.0 dataset. Due to an access issue with the `bike_racing` database (17 queries) and the absence of schema files for `art_1` (114 queries), the effective TEST benchmark was reduced to 2,016 queries. Of these, 12 were excluded due to GEMINI 2.5 producing invalid LOGICA queries, resulting in 2,004 valid queries. We experimented with two prompting strategies: one without and one with embedding 5-row dataset snippets. These yielded execution accuracies of 76% and 78.3%, respectively. For details, see the *Without Dataset Snippet* and *With Dataset Snippet* rows in Table 1.

Evaluating the semantic accuracy of generated database queries is a nuanced task. While benchmarks like SPIDER 1.0 provide a crucial baseline, a strict exact execution output matching metric can be misleading, as it often penalizes valid alternative interpretations or superior answers.

Of the 21.7% of queries that did not yield correct results we found that many fell into three categories that should reasonably be considered correct: (1) mismatches between **None** and 0, (2) overly restrictive golden (target) queries, and (3) over-selection of columns. The first two reflect evaluation false negatives, while the third suggests a need for more precise prompt engineering. To incorporate these findings into our accuracy assessment, we developed a script to automatically identify these cases and annotate them as "Equivalence Type" in the JSON file containing the correct answer.

4.1   Mismatch Between None and Zero

Cases where the SQL generated from the LOGICA Program returned **None** instead of 0 for numerical results, particularly in scenarios involving aggregations like

Table 1. Execution accuracy on the `test.json` set from the SPIDER 1.0 benchmark, broken down by SQL query difficulty. Difficulty levels (easy, medium, hard, extra hard) are computed based on the presence of specific SQL components and structural complexity. Equivalence 1: None Check; Equivalence 2: Limit was Artificially Used; Equivalence 3: Multiple Columns Returned.

	easy	medium	hard	extra	all
count	457	779	441	327	2004
Without Dataset Snippet	81.1%	79.0%	71.9%	63.9%	76.0%
With Dataset Snippet	83.2%	81.6%	73.9%	69.7%	78.3%
Dataset Snippet + Equivalence 1&2	84.0%	83.8%	81.9%	82.3%	83.2%
Dataset Snippet + All Equivalences	89.5%	87.7%	83.0%	83.2%	86.3%

`SUM(1)` on an empty set of rows rather than the standard `COUNT(*)`, highlight a specific compiler behavior. While None and 0 are distinct in SQL, from a functional perspective within certain contexts of the LOGICA Program's execution, they might be considered equivalent, representing the absence of a count or value; you can spot these specific cases where this nuance occurs as they are tagged as *"None Check - Equivalence 1"*.

4.2   Overly Restrictive Golden Queries

Some ground truth (golden) SQL queries in SPIDER 1.0 are overly restrictive, returning only a single row even when multiple correct answers exist in the dataset. This is particularly evident in comparative questions (e.g., *"Which year had the most concerts?"*), where the query uses a `LIMIT 1` clause despite the presence of multiple equally valid rows, that is, the years 2014 and 2015 each contained three concerts. In contrast, the generated LOGICA program returns all correct results, capturing a more complete answer set. These cases are annotated as *"Limit was Artificially Used - Equivalence 2"*.

Difficulty Level: hard
Database Name: concert_singer
Question: Which year has most number of concerts?
Golden Query:

```
SELECT YEAR
  FROM concert
 GROUP BY YEAR
 ORDER BY count(*)
  DESC LIMIT 1;
```

LOGICA **Program:**

```
ConcertsPerYear(yr_val:, num_concerts?+=1) distinct :-
    concert(year: yr_val);
```

```
MaxNumConcerts() =
  Max{n :- ConcertsPerYear(num_concerts: n)};
Report(year:) :-
  ConcertsPerYear(yr_val: year, num_concerts: n),
  n == MaxNumConcerts();
```

Golden Output: [(2015)]
Logica Output: [(2014), (2015)]

After reclassifying these two types of cases as correct, the adjusted accuracy of our direct LOGICA program generation rose to 83.2% on the TEST benchmark. See the *Dataset Snippet + Equivalence 1&2* in the Table 1. Notably, this performance was achieved solely through direct prompting, without any fine-tuning on a Text-to-LOGICA dataset.

4.3   Over-Selection of Columns

Even after accounting for the previous two categories of false negatives, 16.8% of queries in the TEST benchmark still showed discrepancies. A common issue was over-selection, where the generated LOGICA program returned more columns than required by the gold query although all required columns have been correctly included. The cases are annotated as *"Multiple Columns Returned - Equivalence 3"*.

For instance, in response to *"What are the earnings of poker players, ordered descending by value?"*, the golden SQL retrieved **earnings**, whereas the generated LOGICA program included **player_name** and **earnings**, as shown below.

Difficulty Level: easy
Database Name: poker_player
Question: What are the earnings of poker players, ordered descending by value?
Golden Query:

```
SELECT Earnings
  FROM poker_player
  ORDER BY Earnings DESC
```

LOGICA Program:

```
Report(player_name:, earnings:) :-
  poker_player(people_id:, earnings:),
  people(people_id:, name: player_name);
@OrderBy("Report", "earnings desc");
```

Golden Output: [(596462.0,), (476090.0,), ...]
Logica Output: [('Maksim Botin', 596462.0), ('Aleksey Ostapenko', 476090.0), ...]

When treating this category as correct, the adjusted accuracy of our direct LOGICA Program generation method increases to 86.3% on the TEST benchmark (see Table 1).

5   Discussion

5.1   Potential Flaws in SPIDER 1.0

In addition to overly restrictive gold queries, our analysis also revealed potential errors in the SPIDER 1.0 dataset's ground truth SQL. For instance, the query for "Who owns the youngest dog? Give me his or her last name." incorrectly selected the owner of the oldest dog by using the maximum dog age, contradicting the question's intent. In contrast, the generated LOGICA query correctly identified the youngest dog using the date_of_birth field. This example highlighted a potential flaw in the benchmark data itself. These observations underscore the complexities involved in evaluating the quality of generated database queries. It also emphasizes the importance of considering both functional correctness and the logical coherence of the generated code.

Difficulty Level: extra hard
Database Name: dog_kennels
Question: Who owns the youngest dog? Give me his or her last name.
Golden Query:

```
SELECT T1.last_name
  FROM Owners AS T1 JOIN Dogs AS T2
    ON T1.owner_id = T2.owner_id
 WHERE T2.age = (SELECT max(age) FROM Dogs);
```

LOGICA Program:

```
YoungestDogBirthDate() = Max{
  dob :- Dogs(date_of_birth: dob)};
OwnerOfYoungestDog(owner_id:)  :-
  Dogs(owner_id:, date_of_birth: dob),
  dob == YoungestDogBirthDate();
Report(last_name:) distinct  :-
  OwnerOfYoungestDog(owner_id: oid),
  Owners(owner_id: oid, last_name:);
```

Golden Output: [(Feil), (Fisher), (Rippin)]
Logica Output: [(Mertz)]

5.2   Study of "incorrect" Logica Queries

Our analysis of "incorrect" queries revealed they were rarely factually wrong. Instead, the discrepancies stemmed from different interpretations of the natural language prompt. In many cases, the LLM generated a LOGICA program for a more comprehensive or literal interpretation of the question than the benchmark's golden SQL, which often represents only one of several valid interpretations. This can be illustrated with the below example:

Difficulty Level: hard
Database Name: cre_Doc_Template_Mgt
Question: Return the id of the document with the fewest paragraphs.
Golden Query:

```
SELECT document_id
  FROM Paragraphs
 GROUP BY document_id
 ORDER BY count(*) ASC LIMIT 1;
```

LOGICA Program:

```
DocParagraphCount(doc_id:, num_paragraphs:) :-
  Documents(document_id: doc_id),
  Paragraphs(document_id: doc_id),
  num_paragraphs = Count{
      para_id :- Paragraphs(document_id: doc_id,
                            paragraph_id: para_id)
  };
DocParagraphCount(doc_id:, num_paragraphs: 0) :-
  Documents(document_id: doc_id),
  Max{1 :- Paragraphs(document_id: doc_id)} is null;
MinParagraphsValue() =
  Min{count :- DocParagraphCount(num_paragraphs:count)};
Report(document_id:) distinct :-
  DocParagraphCount(doc_id: document_id,
                    num_paragraphs: current_count),
  current_count == MinParagraphsValue();
```

Golden Output: [(3)]
Logica Output: [(0), (1), (76), (82), (801801)]

Our interpretation of this LOGICA code is that it considers documents with zero paragraphs as valid entries. This inclusive approach appears to be the source of the observed difference in results compared to the golden SQL, which implicitly excludes documents lacking paragraphs from consideration within the **Paragraphs** table. The majority of inaccuracies in the Logica program's responses appear to originate from its inability to precisely account for the nuances of the underlying data. For example, when asked "*What country is Jetblue Airways affiliated with?*", the golden SQL solution demonstrates knowledge of the exact string "*JetBlue Airways*" in the dataset. Lacking this specific data visibility, the Logica program tends to query using "*Jetblue Airways*", leading to discrepancies with capitalization or other variations in the actual data entries.

Difficulty Level: easy
Database Name: flight_2
Question: What country is Jetblue Airways affiliated with?
Golden Query:

```
SELECT Country
  FROM AIRLINES
 WHERE Airline = "JetBlue Airways"
```

LOGICA Program:

```
Report(country:)  :-
    airlines(airline: "Jetblue Airways", country:);
```

Golden Output: [('USA')]
Logica Output: []

Accompanying this paper are files detailing the results of our evaluations on the DEV and TEST benchmarks, including both correct and incorrect answers. To gain deeper insights into the discrepancies, we conducted a detailed analysis of 10 randomly selected incorrect queries from the TEST benchmark.

Our analysis of 10 discrepancies between Golden and LOGICA Query outputs revealed distinct root causes. Three instances were due to errors in the Golden Query, five stemmed from an incorrect LOGICA Program, and the remaining two resulted from ambiguity in the original natural language question.

Question Info	Description
QN: 1593 Error: Golden Query	The golden query uses LIMIT 1 but sums all boxes, not just those from the largest-capacity warehouse.
QN: 1434 Error: Golden Query	Compares price to average, rather than twice the average as specified in the question.
QN: 986 Error: Golden Query	Sorts affiliations by descending paper count, while the question implies ascending order.
QN: 706 Error: Logica Program	Logica includes related_document_object_id, which inflates the document count.
QN: 1104 Error: Logica Program	Uses lowercase "jones", causing no match due to case sensitivity.
QN: 980 Error: Ambiguous	The question does not specify whether partial name matching (LIKE) is required.
QN: 1449 Error: Ambiguous	"Average for each good" interpreted differently: SQL uses overall average, Logica uses per-good averages.
QN: 768 Error: Logica Program	Uses "Canada" (capitalized), while database stores "CANADA" (uppercase).
QN: 1039 Error: Logica Program	Groups by Affiliation.name instead of affiliation_id, consolidating results.
QN: 1157 Error: Logica Program	Computes average age using max age per pilot, not averaging all values.

References

1. Jacob Devlin, Ming-Wei Chang, Kenton Lee, and Kristina N. Toutanova. BERT: Pre-training of Deep Bidirectional Transformers for Language Understanding. arXiv, 2018
2. Dawei Gao, Haibin Wang, Yaliang Li, Xiuyu Sun, Yichen Qian, Bolin Ding, and Jingren Zhou. Text-to-SQL Empowered by Large Language Models: A Benchmark Evaluation. *Proc. VLDB Endow.*, 17(5):1132–1145, January 2024
3. Boyan Li, Yuyu Luo, Chengliang Chai, Guoliang Li, and Nan Tang. The Dawn of Natural Language to SQL: Are We Fully Ready? *Proc. VLDB Endow.*, 17(11):3318–3331, 2024
4. Matthew E. Peters, Mark Neumann, Mohit Iyyer, Matt Gardner, Christopher Clark, Kenton Lee, and Luke Zettlemoyer. Deep Contextualized Word Representations. In *Annual Conference of the North American Chapter of the Association for Computational Linguistics*, pages 2227–2237, June 2018
5. Mohammadreza Pourreza and Davood Rafiei. Context Learning of Text-to-SQL with Self-Correction. *arXiv*, 2023
6. Mohammed Saeed, Nicola De Cao, and Paolo Papotti. Querying large language models with SQL. In *International Conference on Extending Database Technology, EDBT*, pages 365–372, 2024
7. Evgeny Skvortsov, Shayan Mirjafari, Ojaswa Garg, Yilin Xia, Shawn Bowers, and Bertram Ludäscher. LogicLM:RobustApplicationofLargeLanguageModelswithLogic ProgrammingforDataAnalytics . In *EDBT*, 2025
8. Evgeny S. Skvortsov, Yilin Xia, Shawn Bowers, and Bertram Ludäscher. The Logica System: Elevating SQL Databases to Declarative Data Science Engines. In *Datalog-2.0)*, volume 3801, pages 69–73, 2024
9. Evgeny S. Skvortsov, Yilin Xia, and Bertram Ludäscher. Logica: Declarative Data Science for Mere Mortals. In *EDBT*, pages 842–845, 2024
10. Ashish Vaswani, Noam Shazeer, Niki Parmar, Jakob Uszkoreit, Llion Jones, Aidan N Gomez, Łukasz Kaiser, and Illia Polosukhin. Attention is All you Need. In *Advances in Neural Information Processing Systems*, volume 30, 2017
11. Tao Yu, Rui Zhang, Kai Yang, Michihiro Yasunaga, Dongxu Wang, Zifan Li, James Ma, Irene Li, Qingning Yao, Shanelle Roman, Zilin Zhang, and Dragomir Radev. Spider: A large-scale human-labeled dataset for complex and cross-domain semantic parsing and Text-to-SQL task. In *EMNLP*, 2018

Characterizing Equivalence of Logically Constrained Terms via Existentially Constrained Terms

Kanta Takahata[1], Jonas Schöpf[2(✉)] [iD], Naoki Nishida[3(✉)] [iD],
and Takahito Aoto[1(✉)] [iD]

[1] Niigata University, Niigata, Japan
aoto@ie.niigata-u.ac.jp
[2] University of Innsbruck, Innsbruck, Austria
jonas.schoepf@uibk.ac.at
[3] Nagoya University, Nagoya, Japan
nishida@i.nagoya-u.ac.jp

Abstract. Logically constrained term rewriting is a rewriting framework that supports built-in data structures such as integers and bit vectors. Recently, constrained terms play a key role in various analyses and applications of logically constrained term rewriting. A fundamental question on constrained terms arising there is how to characterize equivalence between them. However, in the current literature only limited progress has been made on this. In this paper, we provide several sound and complete solutions to tackle this problem. Our key idea is the introduction of a novel concept, namely existentially constrained terms, into which the original form of constrained terms can be embedded. We present several syntactic characterizations of equivalence between existentially constrained terms. In particular, we provide two different kinds of complete characterizations: one is designed to facilitate equivalence checking, while the other is intended for theoretical analysis.

Keywords: Logically Constrained Term Rewrite System ·
Constrained Term · Equivalence · Logical Constraint

1 Introduction

The basic formalism of term rewriting is a purely syntactic computational model; due to its simplicity, it is one of the most extensively studied computational models. One of the main issues of term rewriting and its real-world applications is that the basic formalism lacks painless treatment of built-in data structures, such as integers, bit vectors, etc. Logically constrained term rewriting [7] is a relatively new extension of term rewriting that intends to overcome such weaknesses of the basic formalism, while keeping succinctness for theoretical analysis

This work was partially supported by JSPS KAKENHI Grant Numbers JP24K14817 and JP24K02900, and FWF (Austrian Science Fund) project I 5943-N.

as a computational model. Rewrite rules, that are used to model computations, in logically constrained term rewrite systems (LCTRSs) are equipped with constraints over some arbitrary theory, e.g., linear integer arithmetic. Built-in data structures are represented via the satisfiability of constraints within a respective theory. Recent progress on the LCTRS formalism was for example made in confluence analysis [11,12], (non-)termination analysis [5,9], completion [15], rewriting induction [3,8], algebraic semantics [1], and complexity analysis [16].

Recently, constrained terms play a key role in various analyses and applications of logically constrained term rewriting. Here, a *constrained term* consists of a term and a constraint, which restricts the possibilities in which the term is instantiated. For example, $f(x)$ $[x > 2]$ is a constrained term (in LCTRS notation) which can be intuitively considered as a set of terms $\{f(x) \mid x > 2\}$. Two constrained terms are said to be *equivalent* if they denote the same sets of terms. A fundamental question on constrained terms arising there is how to characterize equivalence between them. However, in the current literature, only limited progress has been made on this.

In this paper, we provide several sound and complete solutions to tackle this problem. Our key idea is the introduction of a novel concept, namely existentially constrained terms, into which the original form of constrained terms can be embedded. The idea of existentially constrained terms is very simple—just distinguish variables that appear solely in the constraint but not in the term itself by using existential quantifiers. Nevertheless, the introduction of existential quantifiers takes us a step further in achieving a *syntactic analysis of the equivalence of constrained terms*.

During the analysis of LCTRSs, rewriting constrained terms, called *constrained rewriting*, is frequently used. It is the key part for many different analysis techniques, e.g., for finding specific joining sequences in confluence analysis or is part of several inference rules in rewriting induction. Unfortunately, it is infeasible for LCTRS tools to fully support constrained rewriting due to the heavy non-determinism mainly caused by the equivalence transformations. To overcome this problem, *most general constrained rewriting* has been proposed and commutation of the constrained rewriting and the equivalence transformation has been shown for left-linear LCTRSs [14]. The characterizations on equivalence of existentially constrained terms in this paper provide the theoretical foundation for this work.

The remainder of the paper is organized as follows. After explaining some basics of logically constrained term rewriting in Sect. 2, we introduce existentially constrained terms and their equivalence in Sect. 3. Then, in Sect. 4, we consider equivalence of existentially constrained terms consisting of renamed variants; we additionally give a counterexample to a partial characterization known in the literature and its correction. In Sect. 5, we introduce *pattern-general* existentially constrained terms and show that any existentially constrained term can be transformed into an equivalent pattern-general one. Based on that, we give a sound and complete characterization of equivalent pattern-general existentially constrained terms. Finally, in Sect. 6 we extend our characterization to the equivalence of existentially constrained terms in general. Due to the page limit, omitted (or detailed) proofs are presented in the full version of this paper [13].

2 Preliminaries

In this section, we briefly recall the basic notions of LCTRSs [1,7,11,12] and fix additional notations used throughout this paper. Familiarity with the basic notions of term rewriting is assumed (e.g. see [2,10]).

An LCTRS is based on a sorted signature, thus our signature consists of a set $\mathcal{S}$ of sorts and a set $\mathcal{F}$ of function symbols, where each $f \in \mathcal{F}$ is attached with its sort declaration as $\mathrm{sort}(f) = \tau_1 \times \cdots \times \tau_n \to \tau_0$; we usually write $f \colon \tau_1 \times \cdots \times \tau_n \to \tau_0$ for simplicity. We assume that these sets can be partitioned into two disjoint sets, i.e., $\mathcal{S} = \mathcal{S}_{\mathsf{th}} \uplus \mathcal{S}_{\mathsf{te}}$ and $\mathcal{F} = \mathcal{F}_{\mathsf{th}} \uplus \mathcal{F}_{\mathsf{te}}$, where each $f \colon \tau_1 \times \cdots \times \tau_n \to \tau_0 \in \mathcal{F}_{\mathsf{th}}$ satisfies $\tau_i \in \mathcal{S}_{\mathsf{th}}$ for all $0 \leqslant i \leqslant n$. Elements of $\mathcal{S}_{\mathsf{th}}$ ($\mathcal{F}_{\mathsf{th}}$) and $\mathcal{S}_{\mathsf{te}}$ ($\mathcal{F}_{\mathsf{te}}$) are called theory sorts (symbols) and term sorts (symbols). Each variable and term is equipped with a sort, where the sort of $f(t_1, \ldots, t_n)$ with $\mathrm{sort}(f) = \tau_1 \times \cdots \times \tau_n \to \tau_0$ is τ_0 and a term t of sort $\tau \in \mathcal{S}$ is denoted by t^τ. The sets of $\mathcal{S}$-sorted variables and terms are denoted by $\mathcal{V}$ and $\mathcal{T}(\mathcal{F}, \mathcal{V})$. For any $T \subseteq \mathcal{T}(\mathcal{F}, \mathcal{V})$, the set T^τ consists of terms in T whose sort is τ. We assume a special sort $\mathsf{Bool} \in \mathcal{S}_{\mathsf{th}}$, and call the terms in $\mathcal{T}(\mathcal{F}_{\mathsf{th}}, \mathcal{V})^{\mathsf{Bool}}$ logical constraints. Note that every variable in a logical constraint has a theory sort. We denote the set of variables appearing in terms $t_1, \ldots, t_n$ by $\mathcal{V}(t_1, \ldots, t_n)$. Sometimes sequences of variables and terms are written as $\vec{x}$ and $\vec{t}$. The set of variables occurring in $\vec{x}$ is denoted by $\{\vec{x}\}$. The set of sequences of elements of a set T by T^*, such that $\vec{x} \in \mathcal{V}^*$.

The set of positions in a term t is denoted by $\mathcal{P}\mathsf{os}(t)$. The symbol and subterm occurring at a position $p \in \mathcal{P}\mathsf{os}(t)$ is denoted by $t(p)$ and $t|_p$, respectively. For $U \subseteq \mathcal{F} \cup \mathcal{V}$, we write $\mathcal{P}\mathsf{os}_U(t) = \{p \in \mathcal{P}\mathsf{os}(t) \mid t(p) \in U\}$ for positions with symbols in U. A term obtained from t by replacing subterms at parallel positions $p_1, \ldots, p_n$ by the terms $t_1, \ldots, t_n$, having the same sort as $t|_{p_1}, \ldots, t|_{p_n}$, is written as $t[t_1, \ldots, t_n]_{p_1, \ldots, p_n}$ or just $t[t_1, \ldots, t_n]$ when no confusions arises. Sometimes we consider an expression obtained by replacing those subterms $t|_{p_1}, \ldots, t|_{p_n}$ in t by holes of the same sorts, which is called a multihole context and denoted by $t[\ ]_{p_1, \ldots, p_n}$.

A sort-preserving function σ from $\mathcal{V}$ to $\mathcal{T}(\mathcal{F}, \mathcal{V})$ is called a substitution, where it is identified with its homomorphic extension $\sigma \colon \mathcal{T}(\mathcal{F}, \mathcal{V}) \to \mathcal{T}(\mathcal{F}, \mathcal{V})$. For a set of terms T, we write $\sigma(T) = \{\sigma(t) \mid t \in T\}$; the domain of σ is denoted by $\mathcal{D}\mathsf{om}(\sigma)$: $\mathcal{D}\mathsf{om}(\sigma) = \{x \in \mathcal{V} \mid \sigma(x) \neq x\}$. A substitution σ is written as $\sigma \colon U \to T$ if $U \supseteq \mathcal{D}\mathsf{om}(\sigma)$ and $\sigma(U) \subseteq T$. For a set $U \subseteq \mathcal{V}$, a substitution $\sigma|_U$ is given by $\sigma|_U(x) = \sigma(x)$ if $x \in U$ and $\sigma|_U(x) = x$ otherwise. For substitutions σ_1, σ_2 such that $\mathcal{D}\mathsf{om}(\sigma_1) \cap \mathcal{D}\mathsf{om}(\sigma_2) = \varnothing$, the substitution $\sigma_1 \cup \sigma_2$ is given by $(\sigma_1 \cup \sigma_2)(x) = \sigma_i(x)$ if $x \in \mathcal{D}\mathsf{om}(\sigma_i)$ and $(\sigma_1 \cup \sigma_2)(x) = x$ otherwise. A substitution $\sigma \colon \{x_1, \ldots, x_n\} \to \{t_1, \ldots, t_n\}$ such that $\sigma(x_i) = t_i$ is denoted by $\{x_1 \mapsto t_1, \ldots, x_n \mapsto t_n\}$; for brevity sometimes we write just $\{\vec{x} \mapsto \vec{t}\}$. A bijective substitution $\sigma \colon \mathcal{V} \to \mathcal{V}$ is called a renaming, and its inverse is denoted by σ^{-1}.

A model over a sorted signature $\langle \mathcal{S}_{th}, \mathcal{F}_{th} \rangle$ consists of the two interpretations $\mathcal{I}$ for sorts and $\mathcal{J}$ for function symbols. $\mathcal{I}$ assigns a non-empty set $\mathcal{I}(\tau)$ to $\tau \in \mathcal{S}_{th}$, and $\mathcal{J}$ assigns a function $\mathcal{J}(f): \mathcal{I}(\tau_1) \times \cdots \times \mathcal{I}(\tau_n) \to \mathcal{I}(\tau_0)$ to $f: \tau_1 \times \cdots \times \tau_n \to \tau_0 \in \mathcal{F}_{th}$. We assume a fixed model $\mathcal{M} = \langle \mathcal{I}, \mathcal{J} \rangle$ over the sorted signature $\langle \mathcal{S}_{th}, \mathcal{F}_{th} \rangle$ such that any element $a \in \mathcal{I}(\tau)$ appears as a constant a^τ in $\mathcal{F}_{th}$. These constants are called *values* and the set of all values is denoted by $\mathcal{V}al$. For a term t, we define $\mathcal{V}al(t) = \{ t(p) \mid p \in \mathcal{P}os_{\mathcal{V}al}(t) \}$ and for a substitution γ, we define $\mathcal{V}\mathcal{D}om(\gamma) = \{ x \in \mathcal{V} \mid \gamma(x) \in \mathcal{V}al \}$. Throughout this paper we assume the standard interpretation for the sort $\mathsf{Bool} \in \mathcal{S}_{th}$, namely $\mathcal{I}(\mathsf{Bool}) = \mathbb{B} = \{ \mathsf{true}, \mathsf{false} \}$, and the existence of necessary standard theory function symbols such as $\neg, \wedge, \Rightarrow, =^\tau$, etc. These are required to express constraints together with their default sorts and interpretations.

A valuation ρ on the model $\mathcal{M} = \langle \mathcal{I}, \mathcal{J} \rangle$ is a mapping that assigns any $x^\tau \in \mathcal{V}$ with $\tau \in \mathcal{S}_{th}$ to $\rho(x) \in \mathcal{I}(\tau)$. The interpretation of a term $t^\tau \in \mathcal{T}(\mathcal{F}_{th}, \mathcal{V})$ with $\tau \in \mathcal{S}_{th}$ in the model $\mathcal{M}$ over the valuation ρ is denoted by $[\![t]\!]_{\mathcal{M},\rho}$. For a valuation ρ over the model $\mathcal{M}$, we write $\vDash_{\mathcal{M},\rho} \varphi$ if $[\![\varphi]\!]_{\mathcal{M},\rho} = \mathsf{true}$, and $\vDash_{\mathcal{M}} \varphi$ if $\vDash_{\mathcal{M},\rho} \varphi$ for all valuations ρ. For $X \subseteq \mathcal{V}$, a substitution γ is said to be X-valued if $\gamma(X) \subseteq \mathcal{V}al$. We write $\gamma \vDash_{\mathcal{M}} \varphi$ (and say γ respects φ) if the substitution γ is $\mathcal{V}ar(\varphi)$-valued and $\vDash_{\mathcal{M}} \varphi\gamma$. If no confusion arises then we drop the subscript $\mathcal{M}$ in these notations.

3 Existentially Constrained Terms

In this section, we introduce our novel notion of existentially constrained terms, and give the definition of their equivalence. We start by giving the definition of existential constraints and then proceed to existentially constrained terms in order to show their specific properties.

Definition 3.1 (Existential Constraints). *An existential constraint is a pair $\langle \vec{x}, \varphi \rangle$ of a sequence of variables $\vec{x}$ and a logical constraint φ, written as $\exists \vec{x}. \; \varphi$, such that $\{ \vec{x} \} \subseteq \mathcal{V}ar(\varphi)$. We define the sets of free and bound variables of $\exists \vec{x}. \; \varphi$ as follows: (1) $\mathcal{F}\mathcal{V}ar(\exists \vec{x}. \; \varphi) = \mathcal{V}ar(\varphi) \backslash \{ \vec{x} \}$, and (2) $\mathcal{B}\mathcal{V}ar(\exists \vec{x}. \; \varphi) = \{ \vec{x} \}$.*

We may abbreviate $\exists \vec{x}. \; \varphi$ to φ if $\vec{x}$ is the empty sequence.

Example 3.2. The following are existential constraints: $\exists x. \; (x \geqslant 3) \wedge (y = x * z)$, $\exists x, y, z. \; (y = x * z)$, $(y = x * z)$, and true. However, $(\exists x. \; y = 4 * z) \wedge (\exists z. \; y = 3 * z)$ is not an existential constraint because it does not adhere to the form $\langle \vec{x}, \varphi \rangle$. This is also not the case for $\exists y. \; x \geqslant 3$, because $\{ y \} \not\subseteq \{ x \} = \mathcal{V}ar(x \geqslant 3)$. We have $\mathcal{F}\mathcal{V}ar(\exists x. \; (x \geqslant 3) \wedge (y = x * z)) = \{ y, z \}$ and $\mathcal{B}\mathcal{V}ar(\exists x. \; (x \geqslant 3) \wedge (y = x * z)) = \{ x \}$.

Remark here that, despite its name and form, $\exists \vec{x}. \; \varphi$ is not defined as a usual existentially quantified formula, so that it is not identified modulo renaming of the bound variables $\vec{x}$, ensuring that $\mathcal{B}\mathcal{V}ar$ is well-defined. In fact, "existential quantification" is only considered when the constraint is interpreted in the model (see Definition 3.4).

Lemma 3.3. *Let s be a term and $\exists \vec{x}.\ \varphi$ an existential constraint. Then, the following statements are equivalent: (1) $\mathcal{F}\mathsf{Var}(\exists \vec{x}.\ \varphi) \subseteq \mathsf{Var}(s)$ and $\mathcal{B}\mathsf{Var}(\exists \vec{x}.\ \varphi) \cap \mathsf{Var}(s) = \varnothing$ (2) $\mathcal{B}\mathsf{Var}(\exists \vec{x}.\ \varphi) = \mathsf{Var}(\varphi) \backslash \mathsf{Var}(s)$ (3) $\mathcal{F}\mathsf{Var}(\exists \vec{x}.\ \varphi) = \mathsf{Var}(\varphi) \cap \mathsf{Var}(s)$*

Proof (Sketch). Show (1) $\implies$ (2), (2) $\iff$ (3), and (3) $\implies$ (1). □

As the name suggests, the existential quantifier in existential constraints is interpreted on the model as in the predicate logic. Since constants in our model $\mathcal{M}$ appear as constants (values) in our signature, we define validity and satisfiability as follows.

Definition 3.4 (Validity and Satisfiablity of Existential Constraints).
Let $\exists \vec{x}.\ \varphi$ be an existential constraint, and ρ a valuation. Then, we write $\vDash_{\mathcal{M},\rho} \exists \vec{x}.\ \varphi$ if there exists $\vec{v} \in \mathcal{V}\mathsf{al}^*$ such that $\vDash_{\mathcal{M},\rho} \varphi\kappa$, where $\kappa = \{\vec{x} \mapsto \vec{v}\}$. An existential constraint $\exists \vec{x}.\ \varphi$ is said to be valid, *written as $\vDash_{\mathcal{M}} \exists \vec{x}.\ \varphi$, if $\vDash_{\mathcal{M},\rho} \exists \vec{x}.\ \varphi$ for any valuation ρ. An existential constraint $\exists \vec{x}.\ \varphi$ is said to be* satisfiable *if $\vDash_{\mathcal{M},\rho} \exists \vec{x}.\ \varphi$ for some valuation ρ. For any substitution σ, we write $\sigma \vDash_{\mathcal{M}} \exists \vec{x}.\ \varphi$ (and say σ respects $\exists \vec{x}.\ \varphi$) if $\sigma(\mathcal{F}\mathsf{Var}(\exists \vec{x}.\ \varphi)) \subseteq \mathcal{V}\mathsf{al}$ and $\vDash_{\mathcal{M}} (\exists \vec{x}.\ \varphi)\sigma$. Here, $(\exists \vec{x}.\ \varphi)\sigma$ denotes the application of a substitution σ: $(\exists \vec{x}.\ \varphi)\sigma := \exists \vec{x}.\ (\varphi\sigma|_{\mathcal{F}\mathsf{Var}(\exists \vec{x}.\ \varphi)})$.*

Example 3.5 (Cont'd from Example 3.2). Let $\mathbb{Z}$ be the standard integer model and ρ be a valuation such that $\rho(y) = 6$ and $\rho(z) = 2$. Then $\vDash_{\mathbb{Z},\rho} \exists x.\ (x \geqslant 3) \wedge (y = x \times z)$, because by taking $\kappa = \{x \mapsto 3\}$ we obtain $\vDash_{\mathbb{Z},\rho} (3 \geqslant 3) \wedge (y = 3 \times z)$. Thus, $\exists x.\ (x \geqslant 3) \wedge (y = x \times z)$ is satisfiable. Note that it is not valid—as witness consider a valuation ρ' with $\rho'(y) = 5$ and $\rho'(z) = 2$. For other examples $\exists x.\ (x \geqslant 3) \wedge (y \leqslant 3) \wedge (x < y)$ is not satisfiable, while $\exists x.\ (x \geqslant 3) \wedge (y \leqslant x)$ is valid. Let $\sigma = \{y \mapsto 3 + 3, z \mapsto 2\}$ be a substitution. Then $\sigma \nvDash_{\mathbb{Z}} \exists x.\ (x \geqslant 3) \wedge (y = x \times z)$, as $\sigma(y) \notin \mathcal{V}\mathsf{al}$. On the other hand, we have $\sigma' \vDash_{\mathbb{Z}} \exists x.\ (x \geqslant 3) \wedge (y = x \times z)$ for a substitution $\sigma' = \{x \mapsto 1, y \mapsto 6, z \mapsto 2\}$ as $\{y, z\} \subseteq \mathcal{V}\mathcal{D}\mathsf{om}(\sigma')$ and the application of σ' gives $(\exists x.\ (x \geqslant 3) \wedge (6 = x \times 2))$.

Now, we use existential constraints to define existentially constrained terms.

Definition 3.6 (Existentially Constrained Term). *An* existentially constrained term *is a triple $\langle X, s, \exists \vec{x}.\ \varphi \rangle$, written as $\Pi X.\ s\ [\exists \vec{x}.\ \varphi]$, of a set X of variables, a term s, and an existentially constraint $\exists \vec{x}.\ \varphi$, such that (1) $\mathcal{F}\mathsf{Var}(\exists \vec{x}.\ \varphi) \subseteq X \subseteq \mathsf{Var}(s)$, and (2) $\mathcal{B}\mathsf{Var}(\exists \vec{x}.\ \varphi) \cap \mathsf{Var}(s) = \varnothing$. Variables in X are called* logical variables *(of $\Pi X.\ s\ [\exists \vec{x}.\ \varphi]$).*

Example 3.7. Let $\mathsf{f}, \mathsf{g} \in \mathcal{F}_{\mathsf{te}}$. From this we construct the three existentially constrained terms $\Pi\{x\}.\ \mathsf{g}(x)\ [\exists y.\ x = 3 \times y]$, $\Pi\{x\}.\ \mathsf{f}(x + 2, \mathsf{g}(y))\ [\exists z.\ x = 2 \times z]$, and $\Pi\varnothing.\ \mathsf{g}(x)\ [\mathsf{true}]$. The last one is abbreviated as $\Pi\varnothing.\ \mathsf{g}(x)$. None of the following expressions are existentially constrained terms: $\Pi\{y\}.\ \mathsf{g}(x)\ [\exists z.\ z \geqslant y]$ (y does not appear in $\mathsf{g}(x)$), $\Pi\{y\}.\ \mathsf{g}(x)\ [\exists x.\ x \geqslant y]$ (the bound variable x appears in $\mathsf{g}(x)$), and $\Pi\{x\}.\ \mathsf{f}(x, y)\ [\exists z.\ z \geqslant y]$ (y is not a member of the set $\{x\}$).

Note that the conditions $(1), (2)$ of existentially constrained terms equals the condition (1) of Lemma 3.3 including the condition on X (i.e., $\mathcal{F}Var(\exists \vec{x}.\ \varphi) \subseteq X \subseteq Var(s)$). Thus, Lemma 3.3 states useful equivalences w.r.t. the variable conditions of existentially constrained terms as follows:

Lemma 3.8. *Let X be a set of variables, s a term, and $\exists \vec{x}.\ \varphi$ an existential constraint. Then, the following statements are equivalent:*

(1) $\Pi X.\ s\ [\exists \vec{x}.\ \varphi]$ is an existentially constrained term,
(2) $\mathcal{F}Var(\exists \vec{x}.\ \varphi) \subseteq X \subseteq Var(s)$ and $\mathcal{B}Var(\exists \vec{x}.\ \varphi) = Var(\varphi) \setminus Var(s)$, and
(3) $\mathcal{F}Var(\exists \vec{x}.\ \varphi) \subseteq X \subseteq Var(s)$ and $\mathcal{F}Var(\exists \vec{x}.\ \varphi) = Var(\varphi) \cap Var(s)$.

We give now the notion of equivalence of constrained terms together with the notion of subsumption.

Definition 3.9 (Subsumption and Equivalence). *An existentially constrained term $\Pi X.\ s\ [\exists \vec{x}.\ \varphi]$ is said to be subsumed by an existentially constrained term $\Pi Y.\ t\ [\exists \vec{y}.\ \psi]$, denoted by $\Pi X.\ s\ [\exists \vec{x}.\ \varphi] \subsetsim \Pi Y.\ t\ [\exists \vec{y}.\ \psi]$, if for all X-valued substitutions σ with $\sigma \vDash_{\mathcal{M}} \exists \vec{x}.\ \varphi$ there exists a Y-valued substitution γ with $\gamma \vDash_{\mathcal{M}} \exists \vec{y}.\ \psi$ such that $s\sigma = t\gamma$. Two existentially constrained terms $\Pi X.\ s\ [\exists \vec{x}.\ \varphi]$ and $\Pi Y.\ t\ [\exists \vec{y}.\ \psi]$ are said to be equivalent, denoted by $\Pi X.\ s\ [\exists \vec{x}.\ \varphi] \sim \Pi Y.\ t\ [\exists \vec{y}.\ \psi]$, if $\Pi X.\ s\ [\exists \vec{x}.\ \varphi] \subsetsim \Pi Y.\ t\ [\exists \vec{y}.\ \psi]$ and $\Pi X.\ s\ [\exists \vec{x}.\ \varphi] \supsetsim \Pi Y.\ t\ [\exists \vec{y}.\ \psi]$.*

Example 3.10. Consider $\mathsf{f} \in \mathcal{F}_{\mathsf{te}}$ for a signature of an LCTRS over the theory of integers. We have $\Pi \varnothing.\ \mathsf{f}(1,1)\ [\mathsf{true}] \sim \Pi\{x,y\}.\ \mathsf{f}(x,y)\ [(x=y) \wedge (x=1)] \sim \Pi\{y\}.\ \mathsf{f}(1,y)\ [y=1] \sim \Pi\{x\}.\ \mathsf{f}(x,x)\ [x=1]$. Moreover, the following subsumptions hold: $\Pi\{x\}.\ \mathsf{f}(x,y)\ [x=1] \subsetsim \Pi\{x\}.\ \mathsf{f}(x,y)\ [x \geqslant 1]$, $\Pi\{x\}.\ \mathsf{f}(x,x) \subsetsim \Pi\{x,y\}.\ \mathsf{f}(x,y)$, and $\Pi\{x,y\}.\ \mathsf{f}(x,y) \subsetsim \Pi\{x\}.\ \mathsf{f}(x,y)$. However, equivalence does not hold for any these.

We define satisfiability of existentially constrained terms.

Definition 3.11 (Satifiability of Existentially Constrained Terms). *An existentially constrained term $\Pi X.\ s\ [\exists \vec{x}.\ \varphi]$ is said to be satisfiable if $\exists \vec{x}.\ \varphi$ is satisfiable.*

Below, we often focus on characterizations of equivalence for *satisfiable* existentially constrained terms. However, since all unsatisfiable existentially constrained terms are equivalent, this is no restriction.

The following lemma on satisfiable existentially constrained terms turns out to be very useful in later proofs.

Lemma 3.12. *Let $\Pi X.\ s\ [\exists \vec{x}.\ \varphi]$ be a satisfiable existentially constrained term. Then, there exists an X-valued substitution γ such that $\gamma \vDash_{\mathcal{M}} \exists \vec{x}.\ \varphi$, $Dom(\gamma) = X$, and $\mathcal{P}os(s) = \mathcal{P}os(s\gamma)$.*

Proof. By assumption, the constraint $\exists \vec{x}.\ \varphi$ is satisfiable. Thus, there exists a valuation ρ such that $\vDash_{\mathcal{M},\rho} \exists \vec{x}.\ \varphi$. Take a substitution $\gamma := \rho|_X$. $\square$

Before concluding this section, we relate the notion of existentially constrained terms to the respective original notion introduced in [7]. A term φ is a logical constraint if $\varphi \in \mathcal{T}(\mathcal{F}_{\mathsf{th}}, \mathcal{V})$ with a boolean sort. A logical constraint φ is respected by a substitution σ, written also as $\sigma \vDash \varphi$, if $\sigma(\mathcal{V}\mathsf{ar}(\varphi)) \subseteq \mathcal{V}\mathsf{al}$ and $\vDash_{\mathcal{M}} \varphi\sigma$. A constrained term is a tuple of a term s and a logical constraint φ written as $s\ [\varphi]$ (which we call *non-existentially constrained terms* below). Two non-existentially constrained terms $s\ [\varphi]$, $t\ [\psi]$ are equivalent, written as $s\ [\varphi] \sim t\ [\psi]$, if for all substitutions σ with $\sigma \vDash_{\mathcal{M}} \varphi$ there exists a substitution γ with $\gamma \vDash_{\mathcal{M}} \psi$ such that $s\sigma = t\gamma$, and vice versa. Note that we abuse $\sim$ for both existentially constrained terms and non-existentially ones. The following correspondence follows immediately by definition.

Lemma 3.13. *Let $s\ [\varphi]$ and $t\ [\psi]$ be non-existentially constrained terms, and $\Pi X.\ s\ [\exists\vec{x}.\ \varphi]$ and $\Pi Y.\ t\ [\exists\vec{y}.\ \psi]$ be existentially constrained terms such that $X = \mathcal{V}\mathsf{ar}(s) \cap \mathcal{V}\mathsf{ar}(\varphi)$, $\{\vec{x}\} = \mathcal{V}\mathsf{ar}(\varphi) \setminus \mathcal{V}\mathsf{ar}(s)$, $Y = \mathcal{V}\mathsf{ar}(t) \cap \mathcal{V}\mathsf{ar}(\psi)$, and $\{\vec{y}\} = \mathcal{V}\mathsf{ar}(\psi) \setminus \mathcal{V}\mathsf{ar}(t)$. Then, $s\ [\varphi]$ and $t\ [\psi]$ are equivalent if and only if so are the existentially constrained terms $\Pi X.\ s\ [\exists\vec{x}.\ \varphi]$ and $\Pi Y.\ t\ [\exists\vec{y}.\ \psi]$.*

It is easy to verify the equivalence of non-existentially constrained terms via equivalence of existentially constrained terms. However, in the next section we will see that it is essential to characterize the equivalence of existential constraints.

4   Equivalence of Variable Renamed Existentially Constrained Terms

We start with a sufficient condition for equivalence of existentially constrained terms consisting of renamed variants.

Lemma 4.1. *Let $\Pi X.\ s\ [\exists\vec{x}.\ \varphi]$, $\Pi Y.\ t\ [\exists\vec{y}.\ \psi]$ be existentially constrained terms. Suppose that there exists a renaming δ such that $s\delta = t$, $\delta(X) = Y$, and $\vDash_{\mathcal{M}} (\exists\vec{x}.\ \varphi)\delta \Leftrightarrow (\exists\vec{y}.\ \psi)$. Then, $\Pi X.\ s\ [\exists\vec{x}.\ \varphi] \sim \Pi Y.\ t\ [\exists\vec{y}.\ \psi]$.*

Proof. As δ is a bijection, we can take the inverse renaming by δ^{-1}. From the condition, we have $t = s\delta^{-1}$, $Y = \delta^{-1}(X)$, and $\vDash_{\mathcal{M}} (\exists\vec{y}.\ \psi)\delta^{-1} \Leftrightarrow (\exists\vec{x}.\ \varphi)$. By symmetricity of the definition of equivalence, it suffices to prove $\Pi X.\ s\ [\exists\vec{x}.\ \varphi] \subsetsim \Pi\{x\delta \mid x \in X\}.\ s\delta\ [(\exists\vec{x}.\ \varphi)\delta]$. Fix an X-valued substitution σ with $\sigma \vDash_{\mathcal{M}} \exists\vec{x}.\ \varphi$. Let us define the substitution $\gamma := \sigma \circ \delta^{-1}$. Then one can show that γ is Y-valued, $\gamma \vDash_{\mathcal{M}} \exists\vec{y}.\ \psi$ and $s\sigma = t\gamma$. $\qquad\square$

Example 4.2. Lemma 4.1 gives that $\Pi\{x\}.\ \mathsf{f}(x,y)\ [x \geqslant 0] \sim \Pi\{y\}.\ \mathsf{f}(y,x)\ [y \geqslant 0]$ using a renaming $\delta = \{x \mapsto y, y \mapsto x\}$. Also $\Pi\{x\}.\ \mathsf{f}(x,y)\ [\exists z.\ x = z + z] \sim \Pi\{x\}.\ \mathsf{f}(x,y)\ [(x \mod 2) = 0]$ holds. However, Lemma 4.1 does not imply any of the equivalences in Example 3.10.

In a special case, our sufficient condition for equivalence can be extended to a necessary and sufficient condition—this is our first characterization.

Theorem 4.3. *Let δ be a renaming. Let $\Pi X.\ s\ [\exists \vec{x}.\ \varphi]$, $\Pi Y.\ t\ [\exists \vec{y}.\ \psi]$ be satisfiable existentially constrained terms such that $s\delta = t$. Then, $\Pi X.\ s\ [\exists \vec{x}.\ \varphi] \sim \Pi Y.\ t\ [\exists \vec{y}.\ \psi]$ if and only if $\delta(X) = Y$ and $\vDash_{\mathcal{M}} (\exists \vec{x}.\ \varphi)\delta \Leftrightarrow (\exists \vec{y}.\ \psi)$.*

Proof. As the *if* direction follows from Lemma 4.1, we concentrate on the *only-if* direction. Assume that $\Pi X.\ s\ [\exists \vec{x}.\ \varphi] \sim \Pi Y.\ s\delta\ [\exists \vec{y}.\ \psi]$. We first show by contradiction that $\delta(X) = Y$. Assume that $\delta(X) \neq Y$, hence $X \neq \delta^{-1}(Y)$. By $Y \subseteq \mathcal{V}\mathrm{ar}(t)$, we have $\delta^{-1}(Y) \subseteq \delta^{-1}(\mathcal{V}\mathrm{ar}(t)) = \mathcal{V}\mathrm{ar}(t\delta^{-1}) = \mathcal{V}\mathrm{ar}(s)$. Thus, combining with $X \subseteq \mathcal{V}\mathrm{ar}(s)$, we have that $X \cup \delta^{-1}(Y) \subseteq \mathcal{V}\mathrm{ar}(s)$. Thus, there exists a variable $z \in \mathcal{V}\mathrm{ar}(s)$ such that $z \notin X$ and $z \in \delta^{-1}(Y)$ or vice versa.

We first consider the case that $z \notin X$ and $z \in \delta^{-1}(Y)$. Let p be a position of z in s, i.e., $s|_p = z$. Since $\Pi X.\ s\ [\exists \vec{x}.\ \varphi]$ is satisfiable, there exists an X-valued substitution σ with $\sigma \vDash_{\mathcal{M}} \exists \vec{x}.\ \varphi$ and $\mathcal{D}\mathrm{om}(\sigma) = X$, by Lemma 3.12. As $z \notin X = \mathcal{D}\mathrm{om}(\sigma)$, it follows that $z\sigma \notin \mathcal{V}\mathrm{al}$. By our assumption, there exist a Y-valued substitution γ with $\gamma \vDash_{\mathcal{M}} \exists \vec{y}.\ \psi$ and $s\sigma = s\delta\gamma$. As γ is Y-valued and $\delta(z) \in Y$, we have $(s\delta\gamma)|_p = s|_p\delta\gamma = \delta(z)\gamma \in \mathcal{V}\mathrm{al}$. This contradicts $(s\sigma)|_p = z\sigma \notin \mathcal{V}\mathrm{al}$ and $s\sigma = s\delta\gamma$. The case that $z \in X$ and $z \notin \delta^{-1}(Y)$ follows similarly.

Next, we show that $\vDash_{\mathcal{M}} (\exists \vec{x}.\ \varphi)\delta \Leftrightarrow (\exists \vec{y}.\ \psi)$. To show that $\vDash_{\mathcal{M}} (\exists \vec{x}.\ \varphi)\delta \Rightarrow (\exists \vec{y}.\ \psi)$, let ρ be a valuation such that $\vDash_{\mathcal{M},\rho} (\exists \vec{x}.\ \varphi)\delta$. Then, $\vDash_{\mathcal{M}} (\exists \vec{x}.\ \varphi)(\rho \circ \delta)$. Take a substitution $\sigma := (\rho \circ \delta)|_X$. Then, clearly, σ is X-valued. From $\mathcal{F}\mathcal{V}\mathrm{ar}(\exists \vec{x}.\ \varphi) \subseteq X$ and $\vDash_{\mathcal{M}} (\exists \vec{x}.\ \varphi)\delta\rho$, it also follows $\sigma \vDash_{\mathcal{M}} \exists \vec{x}.\ \varphi$. Using our assumption, one obtains a Y-valued substitution γ with $\gamma \vDash_{\mathcal{M}} \exists \vec{y}.\ \psi$ and $s\sigma = t\gamma = s\delta\gamma$. Thus, we have that $\sigma|_{\mathcal{V}\mathrm{ar}(s)} = (\gamma \circ \delta)|_{\mathcal{V}\mathrm{ar}(s)}$. Hence, $\sigma(\delta^{-1}(x)) = \gamma(x)$ for all $x \in \delta(\mathcal{V}\mathrm{ar}(s)) = \mathcal{V}\mathrm{ar}(t)$. Then, as $\mathcal{F}\mathcal{V}\mathrm{ar}(\exists \vec{y}.\ \psi) \subseteq \mathcal{V}\mathrm{ar}(t)$, it follows from $\gamma \vDash_{\mathcal{M}} \exists \vec{y}.\ \psi$ that $\vDash_{\mathcal{M}} (\exists \vec{y}.\ \psi)\delta^{-1}\sigma$. By our choice of σ, we have $(\rho \circ \delta)|_X = \sigma|_X$. Thus, $\rho(y) = \sigma(\delta^{-1}(y))$ for all $y \in \delta(X) = Y$. Hence, by $\mathcal{F}\mathcal{V}\mathrm{ar}(\exists \vec{y}.\ \psi) \subseteq Y$, it follows $\vDash_{\mathcal{M}} (\exists \vec{y}.\ \psi)\rho$. Thus, $\vDash_{\mathcal{M},\rho} \exists \vec{y}.\ \psi$. To show $\vDash_{\mathcal{M}} (\exists \vec{y}.\ \psi) \Rightarrow (\exists \vec{x}.\ \varphi)\delta$, we apply the proofs so far to the symmetric proposition with replacing δ by δ^{-1}. $\square$

In [3, Section 2.3], the equivalence of two non-existentially constrained terms $s\ [\varphi]$ and $s\ [\psi]$ is characterized by the validity of $(\exists \vec{x}.\ \varphi) \Leftrightarrow (\exists \vec{y}.\ \psi)$, where $\{\vec{x}\} = \mathcal{V}\mathrm{ar}(\varphi) \setminus \mathcal{V}\mathrm{ar}(s)$ and $\{\vec{y}\} = \mathcal{V}\mathrm{ar}(\psi) \setminus \mathcal{V}\mathrm{ar}(t)$. However, this characterization is not correct: $(x = x) \Leftrightarrow \mathsf{true}$ is valid, but $\mathsf{f}(x)\ [x = x] \not\sim \mathsf{f}(x)\ [\mathsf{true}]$. The characterization is recovered and adapted for existentially constrained terms as follows, using Theorem 4.3:

Corollary 4.4. *Let $\Pi X.\ s\ [\exists \vec{x}.\ \varphi]$, $\Pi Y.\ s\ [\exists \vec{y}.\ \psi]$ be satisfiable existentially constrained terms. Then, $\Pi X.\ s\ [\exists \vec{x}.\ \varphi] \sim \Pi Y.\ s\ [\exists \vec{y}.\ \psi]$ if and only if $X = Y$ and $\mathcal{M} \vDash (\exists \vec{x}.\ \varphi) \Leftrightarrow (\exists \vec{y}.\ \psi)$.*

5   Pattern-General Existentially Constrained Terms and Their Equivalence

In this section, we introduce and focus on a notion for a general form of existentially constrained terms. A term s is said to be *linear w.r.t. a set X of variables* if every variable in X appears in s at most once.

Definition 5.1 (Pattern-General Existentially Constrained Term). *An existentially constrained term* $\Pi X.\ s\ [\exists \vec{x}.\ \varphi]$ *is called* pattern-general *if s is X-linear and* $\mathcal{V}\mathsf{al}(s) = \varnothing$.

At this point of the paper, readers may wonder why this condition is named "pattern-general"—we postpone explaining the reason until Lemma 5.10. We call an existentially constrained term $\Pi X.\ s\ [\exists \vec{x}.\ \varphi]$ *value-free* (cf. [6]) if $\mathcal{V}\mathsf{al}(s) = \varnothing$. We call $\Pi X.\ s\ [\exists \vec{x}.\ \varphi]$ *linear w.r.t. logical variables* (LV-linear, for short) if s is X-linear. Thus, $\Pi X.\ s\ [\exists \vec{x}.\ \varphi]$ is pattern-general if and only if it is value-free and LV-linear.

Example 5.2. The term $\Pi \{x\}.\ \mathsf{f}(x, y)\ [x \geqslant 0]$ is pattern-general, while the terms $\Pi \{x\}.\ \mathsf{f}(x, 1)\ [x \geqslant 0]$ and $\Pi \{x\}.\ \mathsf{f}(x, x)\ [x \geqslant 0]$ are not. Note that $\Pi \{x\}.\ \mathsf{f}(y, \mathsf{f}(y, x))\ [x \geqslant 0]$ is indeed pattern-general.

In the following we define the transformation from an existentially constrained term into an equivalent one which is in addition pattern-general.

Definition 5.3 (PG-transformation). *We define the transformation* PG *on existentially constrained terms as follows:* $\mathrm{PG}(\Pi X.\ s\ [\exists \vec{x}.\ \varphi]) = \Pi Y.\ t\ [\exists \vec{y}.\ \psi]$, *where* $Y = \{w_1, \ldots, w_n\}$, $t = s[w_1, \ldots, w_n]_{p_1, \ldots, p_n}$, $\{\vec{y}\} = \{\vec{x}\} \cup X$, *and* $\psi = (\varphi \wedge \bigwedge_{i=1}^{n} (s|_{p_i} = w_i))$ *with pairwise distinct fresh variables* $w_1, \ldots, w_n$ *and positions* $p_1, \ldots, p_n$ *such that* $\mathcal{P}\mathsf{os}_{X \cup \mathcal{V}\mathsf{al}}(s) = \{p_1, \ldots, p_n\}$.

Example 5.4 (Cont'd from Example 5.2). We obtain $\mathrm{PG}(\Pi \{x\}.\ \mathsf{f}(x, 1)\ [x \geqslant 0]) = \Pi \{w_1, w_2\}.\ \mathsf{f}(w_1, w_2)\ [\exists x.\ (x \geqslant 0) \wedge (x = w_1) \wedge (1 = w_2)]$, as well as $\mathrm{PG}(\Pi \{x\}.\ \mathsf{f}(x, x)\ [x \geqslant 0]) = \Pi \{w_1, w_2\}.\ \mathsf{f}(w_1, w_2)\ [\exists x.\ (x \geqslant 0) \wedge (x = w_1) \wedge (x = w_2)]$.

The following lemma proving well-definedness of the PG-transformation can be shown in a straightforward manner.

Lemma 5.5. *Let* $\Pi X.\ s\ [\exists \vec{x}.\ \varphi]$ *be an existentially constrained term. Then, both of the following statements hold:*

(i) $\mathrm{PG}(\Pi X.\ s\ [\exists \vec{x}.\ \varphi])$ *is a pattern-general existentially constrained term, and*
(ii) if $\Pi X.\ s\ [\exists \vec{x}.\ \varphi]$ *is satisfiable, then so is* $\mathrm{PG}(\Pi X.\ s\ [\exists \vec{x}.\ \varphi])$.

The following theorem states the correctness of the PG-transformation.

Theorem 5.6. *Let* $\Pi X.\ s\ [\exists \vec{x}.\ \varphi]$ *be an existentially constrained term. Then, we have* $\Pi X.\ s\ [\exists \vec{x}.\ \varphi] \sim \mathrm{PG}(\Pi X.\ s\ [\exists \vec{x}.\ \varphi])$.

Proof. Let $\mathcal{P}\mathsf{os}_{X \cup \mathcal{V}\mathsf{al}}(s) = \{p_1, \ldots, p_n\}$ and $\mathrm{PG}(\Pi X.\ s\ [\exists \vec{x}.\ \varphi]) = \Pi Y.\ t\ [\exists \vec{y}.\ \psi]$ where $w_1, \ldots, w_n$ are pairwise distinct fresh variables, $t = s[w_1, \ldots, w_n]_{p_1, \ldots, p_n}$, $Y = \{w_1, \ldots, w_n\}$, $\{\vec{y}\} = \{\vec{x}\} \cup X$, and $\psi = (\varphi \wedge \bigwedge_{i=1}^{n} (s|_{p_i} = w_i))$. ($\subseteq$) Let σ be an X-valued substitution such that $\sigma \vDash_{\mathcal{M}} \exists \vec{x}.\ \varphi$. Take a substitution $\gamma = \sigma \circ \{w_i \mapsto s|_{p_i} \mid 1 \leqslant i \leqslant n\}$. Then, we can show that γ is Y-valued, $\gamma \vDash_{\mathcal{M}} \exists \vec{y}.\ \psi$, and $t\gamma = s\sigma$. ($\supseteq$) Let γ be a Y-valued substitution such that $\gamma \vDash_{\mathcal{M}} \exists \vec{y}.\ \psi$. Then, there exists $\vec{v} \in \mathcal{V}\mathsf{al}^*$ such that $\vDash_{\mathcal{M}} \psi \kappa \gamma$, where $\kappa = \{\vec{y} \mapsto \vec{v}\}$. Take $\sigma = \gamma \circ \kappa|_X$. Then, one can show σ is X-valued, $\sigma \vDash_{\mathcal{M}} \exists \vec{x}.\ \varphi$, $s\sigma = t\gamma$. $\square$

The following two lemmata, whose proofs are straightforward, demonstrate useful correspondences between constrained terms before and after the PG transformation.

Lemma 5.7. *Let* $\Pi X.\ s\ [\exists \vec{x}.\ \varphi]$ *be a satisfiable constrained term. Suppose that* $\mathrm{PG}(\Pi X.\ s\ [\exists \vec{x}.\ \varphi]) = (\Pi Y.\ s[w_1, \ldots, w_n]_{p_1, \ldots, p_n}\ [\exists \vec{y}.\ \psi])$ *and* $\sigma = \{w_i \mapsto s|_{p_i} \mid 1 \leqslant i \leqslant n\}$ *where* $\{p_1, \ldots, p_n\} = \mathcal{P}\mathsf{os}_{X \cup \mathcal{V}\mathsf{al}}(s)$. *Then* $\vDash_{\mathcal{M}} (\exists \vec{x}.\ \varphi) \Leftrightarrow (\exists \vec{y}.\ \psi)\sigma$.

Lemma 5.8. *Let* $\Pi X.\ s\ [\exists \vec{x}.\ \varphi]$ *be a satisfiable constrained term. Suppose that* $\mathrm{PG}(\Pi X.\ s\ [\exists \vec{x}.\ \varphi]) = (\Pi Y.\ s[w_1, \ldots, w_n]_{p_1, \ldots, p_n}\ [\exists \vec{y}.\ \psi])$ *where* $\{p_1, \ldots, p_n\} = \mathcal{P}\mathsf{os}_{X \cup \mathcal{V}\mathsf{al}}(s)$.

(1) *For any* $i, j \in \{1, \ldots, n\}$, $\vDash_{\mathcal{M}} (\exists \vec{x}.\ \varphi) \Rightarrow (s|_{p_i} = s|_{p_j})$ *if and only if* $\vDash_{\mathcal{M}} (\exists \vec{y}.\ \psi) \Rightarrow (w_i = w_j)$.
(2) *For any* $i \in \{1, \ldots, n\}$ *and* $v \in \mathcal{V}\mathsf{al}$, $\vDash_{\mathcal{M}} (\exists \vec{x}.\ \varphi) \Rightarrow (s|_{p_i} = v)$ *if and only if* $\vDash_{\mathcal{M}} (\exists \vec{y}.\ \psi) \Rightarrow (w_i = v)$.

Next, we characterize equivalence of satisfiable pattern-general existentially constrained terms. Before the characterization, we show useful fundamental properties of equivalence.

Lemma 5.9. *Let* $\Pi X.\ s\ [\exists \vec{x}.\ \varphi], \Pi Y.\ t\ [\exists \vec{y}.\ \psi]$ *be satisfiable existentially constrained terms such that* $\Pi X.\ s\ [\exists \vec{x}.\ \varphi] \sim \Pi Y.\ t\ [\exists \vec{y}.\ \psi]$. *Then, all of the following statements hold:* (1) $\mathcal{P}\mathsf{os}(s) = \mathcal{P}\mathsf{os}(t)$, (2) $\mathcal{P}\mathsf{os}_{X \cup \mathcal{V}\mathsf{al}}(s) = \mathcal{P}\mathsf{os}_{Y \cup \mathcal{V}\mathsf{al}}(t)$, (3) $\mathcal{P}\mathsf{os}_{\mathcal{V} \setminus X}(s) = \mathcal{P}\mathsf{os}_{\mathcal{V} \setminus Y}(t)$, (4) $\mathcal{P}\mathsf{os}_{\mathcal{F} \setminus \mathcal{V}\mathsf{al}}(s) = \mathcal{P}\mathsf{os}_{\mathcal{F} \setminus \mathcal{V}\mathsf{al}}(t)$, (5) $s(p) = t(p)$ *for any position* $p \in \mathcal{P}\mathsf{os}_{\mathcal{F} \setminus \mathcal{V}\mathsf{al}}(s)$, (6) *for any position* $p \in \mathcal{P}\mathsf{os}(s)$, *if* $s|_p \in X$ *and* $t|_p \in \mathcal{V}\mathsf{al}$, *then* $\sigma(s|_p) = t|_p$ *for any* X-*valued substitution* σ *such that* $\sigma \vDash_{\mathcal{M}} \exists \vec{x}.\ \varphi$, *and* (7) *there exists a renaming* $\theta \colon \mathcal{V}\mathsf{ar}(s) \setminus X \to \mathcal{V}\mathsf{ar}(t) \setminus Y$ *such that* $\theta(s[\ ]_{p_1, \ldots, p_n}) = t[\ ]_{p_1, \ldots, p_n}$, *where* $\{p_1, \ldots, p_n\} = \mathcal{P}\mathsf{os}_{X \cup \mathcal{V}\mathsf{al}}(s)$ *(* $= \mathcal{P}\mathsf{os}_{Y \cup \mathcal{V}\mathsf{al}}(t)$*).*

Proof. We present the proof of (1); all remaining cases are proven similarly. By Lemma 3.12, we have $\sigma \vDash_{\mathcal{M}} \exists \vec{x}.\ \varphi$ and $\mathcal{P}\mathsf{os}(s) = \mathcal{P}\mathsf{os}(s\sigma)$ for some X-valued substitution σ. By assumption, we obtain a Y-valued substitution γ such that $\gamma \vDash_{\mathcal{M}} \exists \vec{y}.\ \psi$ and $s\sigma = t\gamma$. Thus, we have that $\mathcal{P}\mathsf{os}(t) \subseteq \mathcal{P}\mathsf{os}(t\gamma) = \mathcal{P}\mathsf{os}(s\sigma) = \mathcal{P}\mathsf{os}(s)$. Similarly, $\mathcal{P}\mathsf{os}(s) \subseteq \mathcal{P}\mathsf{os}(t)$. Therefore, we have that $\mathcal{P}\mathsf{os}(s) = \mathcal{P}\mathsf{os}(t)$. $\square$

Before proceeding to the actual characterization, let us revisit why our naming "pattern-general" is quite natural. A term s is called *most general* in a set $S \subseteq \mathcal{T}(\mathcal{F}, \mathcal{V})$ of terms whenever for all $t \in S$ there exists a substitution σ such that $s\sigma = t$. We refer to the full version of this paper [13] for the proof.

Lemma 5.10. *Let* $\Pi X.\ s\ [\exists \vec{x}.\ \varphi]$ *be a satisfiable existentially constrained term. Then,* $\Pi X.\ s\ [\exists \vec{x}.\ \varphi]$ *is pattern-general if and only if* s *is most general in* $\{t \mid \Pi X.\ s\ [\exists \vec{x}.\ \varphi] \sim \Pi Y.\ t\ [\exists \vec{y}.\ \psi]\}$.

Note that $\Pi\{x\}.\ \mathsf{g}(x)\ [\mathsf{false}]$ and $\Pi\{x\}.\ x\ [\mathsf{false}]$ are equivalent and pattern-general by definition. Thus, the lemma does not hold if $\Pi X.\ s\ [\exists \vec{x}.\ \varphi]$ is not satisfiable.

We are now ready to present a characterization of equivalence of satisfiable pattern-general existentially constrained terms.

Theorem 5.11. *Let* $\Pi X.\ s\ [\exists \vec{x}.\ \varphi], \Pi Y.\ t\ [\exists \vec{y}.\ \psi]$ *be satisfiable pattern-general existentially constrained terms. Then,* $\Pi X.\ s\ [\exists \vec{x}.\ \varphi] \sim \Pi Y.\ t\ [\exists \vec{y}.\ \psi]$ *if and only if there exists a renaming* ρ *such that* $s\rho = t$, $\rho(X) = Y$, *and* $\vDash_{\mathcal{M}} (\exists \vec{x}.\ \varphi)\rho \Leftrightarrow (\exists \vec{y}.\ \psi)$.

Proof. The *if* part follows from Lemma 4.1. We show the *only-if* part. By our assumption, no value appears in s or t and hence $\mathcal{P}os_{\mathsf{Val}}(s) = \mathcal{P}os_{\mathsf{Val}}(t) = \varnothing$. Using Lemma 5.9, let $\{p_1, \ldots, p_n\} = \mathcal{P}os_X(s) = \mathcal{P}os_Y(t)$, and $s|_{p_i} = z_i$ and $t|_{p_i} = w_i$ for $1 \leqslant i \leqslant n$. As $\Pi X.\ s\ [\exists \vec{x}.\ \varphi]$ and $\Pi Y.\ t\ [\exists \vec{y}.\ \psi]$ are pattern-general, $z_1, \ldots, z_n$ are pairwise distinct variables, and so are $w_1, \ldots, w_n$. Let $\rho = \theta \cup \{z_i \mapsto w_i \mid 1 \leqslant i \leqslant n\}$. Since θ is a renaming, $\{z_1, \ldots, z_n\} \cap (\mathcal{V}ar(s) \setminus X) = \varnothing$, and $\{w_1, \ldots, w_n\} \cap (\mathcal{V}ar(t) \setminus Y) = \varnothing$, we know ρ is well-defined and renaming. Furthermore, $s\rho = (s[z_1, \ldots, z_n]_{p_1,\ldots,p_n})\rho = s\rho[z_1\rho, \ldots, z_n\rho]_{p_1,\ldots,p_n} = s\theta[w_1, \ldots, w_n]_{p_1,\ldots,p_n} = t[w_1, \ldots, w_n]_{p_1,\ldots,p_n} = t$. The rest of the statements follow from this by Theorem 4.3. $\square$

Example 5.12. Recall the equivalent existentially constrained terms of Example 3.10. By applying the PG-transformation to each them, we obtain the following:

$$\mathrm{PG}(\Pi\varnothing.\ \mathsf{f}(1,1)) = \Pi\{w_1, w_2\}.\ \mathsf{f}(w_1, w_2)\ [(1 = w_1) \wedge (1 = w_2)]$$
$$\mathrm{PG}(\Pi\{x, y\}.\ \mathsf{f}(x, y)\ [(x = y) \wedge (x = 1)])$$
$$= \Pi\{w_1, w_2\}.\ \mathsf{f}(w_1, w_2)\ [(x = y) \wedge (x = 1) \wedge (x = w_1) \wedge (y = w_2)]$$
$$\mathrm{PG}(\Pi\{y\}.\ \mathsf{f}(1, y)\ [y = 1])$$
$$= \Pi\{w_1, w_2\}.\ \mathsf{f}(w_1, w_2)\ [\exists y.\ (y = 1) \wedge (1 = w_1) \wedge (y = w_2)]$$
$$\mathrm{PG}(\Pi\{x\}.\ \mathsf{f}(x, x)\ [x = 1])$$
$$= \Pi\{w_1, w_2\}.\ \mathsf{f}(w_1, w_2)\ [\exists x.\ (x = 1) \wedge (x = w_1) \wedge (x = w_2)]$$

It becomes trivial to see the equivalence of these terms by Theorem 5.11, as all of these constraints are logically equivalent.

Together with Theorem 5.6, we have a sound and complete characterization of equivalence of satisfiable existentially constrained terms.

Corollary 5.13. *Let* $\Pi X.\ s\ [\exists \vec{x}.\ \varphi], \Pi Y.\ t\ [\exists \vec{y}.\ \psi]$ *be satisfiable existentially constrained terms. Then,* $\Pi X.\ s\ [\exists \vec{x}.\ \varphi] \sim \Pi Y.\ t\ [\exists \vec{y}.\ \psi]$ *if and only if there exists a renaming* ρ *such that* $s'\rho = t'$, $\rho(X') = Y'$, *and* $\vDash_{\mathcal{M}} (\exists \vec{x}'.\ \varphi')\rho \Leftrightarrow (\exists \vec{y}'.\ \psi')$, *where* $\mathrm{PG}(\Pi X.\ s\ [\exists \vec{x}.\ \varphi]) = \Pi X'.\ s'\ [\exists \vec{x}'.\ \varphi'])$ *and* $\mathrm{PG}(\Pi Y.\ t\ [\exists \vec{y}.\ \psi]) = \Pi Y'.\ t'\ [\exists \vec{y}'.\ \psi'])$.

Transformations of non-existentially constrained terms into *value-free* ones can be seen in [4, 6]. The PG-transformation in this section is an extension to that of existentially constrained terms into pattern-general ones (i.e., not only value-free but also LV-linear ones).

6   General Characterization of Equivalence

To check the equivalence of existentially constrained terms, it is often convenient to apply the PG transformation and use Theorem 5.11. However, in a theoretical analysis, one frequently needs to handle the equivalence of non-pattern-general terms as well, where the PG transformation is less suitable. Therefore, a general criterion for the equivalence of existentially constrained terms is preferred.

In this section, we generalize Theorem 5.11 to arbitrary existentially constrained terms, i.e., we characterize equivalence of existentially constrained terms which are not assumed to be pattern-general. To this end, we introduce new notions and notations.

Definition 6.1. *Let $\Pi X.\ s\ [\exists \vec{x}.\ \varphi]$ be an existentially constrained term. Then, we define a binary relation $\sim_{\mathcal{P}os_{X \cup \mathcal{V}al}(s)}$ over the positions in $\mathcal{P}os_{X \cup \mathcal{V}al}(s)$ as follows: $p \sim_{\mathcal{P}os_{X \cup \mathcal{V}al}(s)} q$ if and only if $\models_{\mathcal{M}} ((\exists \vec{x}.\ \varphi) \Rightarrow s|_p = s|_q)$.*

We may omit the subscript $\mathcal{P}os_{X \cup \mathcal{V}al}(s)$ of $\sim_{\mathcal{P}os_{X \cup \mathcal{V}al}(s)}$ if it is clear from the context.

Example 6.2. Consider an existentially constrained term $\Pi X.\ s\ [\varphi]$ where $X = \{x, x', y, y'\}$, $s = \mathsf{h}(x, x', 0, y, y, y', 0 \times 10)$ with $\mathsf{h} \in \mathcal{F}_{\mathsf{te}}$, and $\varphi = (x = x') \wedge (x' = 0) \wedge (y = y')$. Then, $\mathcal{P}os_{X \cup \mathcal{V}al}(s) = \{1, 2, 3, 4, 5, 6, 7.1, 7.2\}$ and we have $1 \sim 2 \sim 3 \sim 7.1$ and $4 \sim 5 \sim 6$.

The proof of the following lemma is straightforward.

Lemma 6.3. *Let $\Pi X.\ s\ [\exists \vec{x}.\ \varphi]$ be an existentially constrained term. Then,*

(1) $\sim_{\mathcal{P}os_{X \cup \mathcal{V}al}(s)}$ is an equivalence relation over the positions in $\mathcal{P}os_{X \cup \mathcal{V}al}(s)$, and
(2) for any positions $p, q \in \mathcal{P}os_{X \cup \mathcal{V}al}(s)$, if $s|_p = s|_q$, then $p \sim_{\mathcal{P}os_{X \cup \mathcal{V}al}(s)} q$.

The equivalence class of a position $p \in \mathcal{P}os_{X \cup \mathcal{V}al}(s)$ w.r.t. $\sim_{\mathcal{P}os_{X \cup \mathcal{V}al}(s)}$ is denoted by $[p]_{\sim_{\mathcal{P}os_{X \cup \mathcal{V}al}(s)}}$. If it is clear from the context then we may simply denote it by $[p]_{\sim}$. We further denote the representative of $[p]_{\sim}$ by $\hat{p}$.

Definition 6.4. *Let $\Pi X.\ s\ [\exists \vec{x}.\ \varphi]$ be a satisfiable existentially constrained term. Let $\mathcal{P}os_{\mathcal{V}al!}(s) = \{p \in \mathcal{P}os_{X \cup \mathcal{V}al}(s) \mid$ there exists $v \in \mathcal{V}al$ such that $\models_{\mathcal{M}} ((\exists \vec{x}.\ \varphi) \Rightarrow (s|_p = v))\}$.*

Example 6.5 (Cont'd from Example 6.2). Since $\sim$ is an equivalence relation, we have a quotient set $\mathcal{P}os_{X \cup \mathcal{V}al}(s)/\sim = \{\{1, 2, 3, 7.1\}, \{4, 5, 6\}, \{7.2\}\}$. Let 1 and 4 be representatives of the equivalence classes $\{1, 2, 3, 7.1\}$ and $\{4, 5, 6\}$, respectively. Then, for instance $\hat{3} = 1$ and $\hat{5} = 4$. Furthermore, we have $\mathcal{P}os_{\mathcal{V}al!}(s) = \{1, 2, 3, 7.1, 7.2\}$.

It is easy to see the set $\mathcal{P}os_{\mathcal{V}al!}(s)$ is consistent with $\sim_{\mathcal{P}os_{X \cup \mathcal{V}al}(s)}$ as shown in the following lemma.

Lemma 6.6. *For any satisfiable existentially constrained term $\Pi X.\ s\ [\exists \vec{x}.\ \varphi]$, all of the following statements hold:*

(1) For each position $p \in \mathcal{P}os_{\mathcal{V}al!}(s)$, there exists a unique value $v \in \mathcal{V}al$ such that $\models_{\mathcal{M}} ((\exists \vec{x}.\ \varphi) \Rightarrow (s|_p = v))$,

(2) for any positions $p, q \in \mathcal{P}os_{X \cup \mathcal{V}al}(s)$, if $p \in \mathcal{P}os_{\mathcal{V}al!}(s)$ and $p \sim q$, then $q \in \mathcal{P}os_{\mathcal{V}al!}(s)$, and

(3) for any positions $p, q \in \mathcal{P}os_{X \cup \mathcal{V}al}(s)$ and values $v, v' \in \mathcal{V}al$, if $p \sim q$, $\models_{\mathcal{M}} ((\exists \vec{x}.\ \varphi) \Rightarrow (s|_p = v))$, and $\models_{\mathcal{M}} ((\exists \vec{x}.\ \varphi) \Rightarrow (s|_q = v'))$, then $v = v'$.

As mechanism to instantiate the term part of an existentially constrained term by values under the equivalence, we introduce representative substitutions.

Definition 6.7. *Let $\Pi X.\ s\ [\exists \vec{x}.\ \varphi]$ be a satisfiable existentially constrained term.*

(1) For each $p \in \mathcal{P}os_{\mathcal{V}al!}(s)$, there exists a unique value v such that $\mathcal{M} \models (\exists \vec{x}.\ \varphi) \Rightarrow (s|_p = v)$ by Lemma 6.6. We denote such v by $\mathcal{V}al!(p)$.

(2) We define a representative substitution $\mu_X : X \rightarrow X \cup \mathcal{V}al$ of $\Pi X.\ s\ [\exists \vec{x}.\ \varphi]$ as follows:

$$\mu_X(z) = \begin{cases} \mathcal{V}al!(p) & \text{if } s(p) = z \text{ for some } p \in \mathcal{P}os_{\mathcal{V}al!}(s), \\ s(\hat{p}) & \text{otherwise,} \end{cases}$$

where $\hat{p}$ is the representative of the equivalence class $[p]_\sim$. Here note that if $s(p) = z$ for some $p \in \mathcal{P}os_{\mathcal{V}al!}(s)$, then $q \in \mathcal{P}os_{\mathcal{V}al!}(s)$ for any q such that $s(q) = z$ by Lemma 6.6 (2).

(3) Provided it is clear from the contexts, for simplicity, we shorten $\mu_X(x)$ by $\hat{x}$ and so does $\mu_X(X)$ by $\hat{X}$. We also put $\hat{v} = v$ for $v \in \mathcal{V}al$.

Example 6.8 (Cont'd from Example 6.5). We have $\mathcal{V}al!(p) = 0 \in \mathcal{V}al$ for $p \in \{1, 2, 3, 7.1\}$, and $\mathcal{V}al!(7.2) = 10 \in \mathcal{V}al$. Since $X = \{x, x', y, y'\}$, the representative substitution is $\mu_X = \{x \mapsto 0, x' \mapsto 0, y \mapsto y, y' \mapsto y\}$ and $\hat{X} = \{1, y\}$.

Example 6.9 (Cont'd from Example 6.8). Let $\Pi Y.\ t\ [\psi]$ be another existentially constrained term such that $Y = \{x, x', y, z\}$, $t = \mathsf{h}(z, z, z, x, x', x, z \times y)$, and $\psi = ((x \leqslant x') \wedge (x' \leqslant x) \wedge (z = 0) \wedge (y = (z + 2) \times 5))$. Then, we have $\Pi X.\ s\ [\varphi] \sim \Pi Y.\ t\ [\psi]$. Let us see how this equivalence can be observed using our notions. We have $\mathcal{P}os_{X \cup \mathcal{V}al}(s) = \{1, 2, 3, 4, 5, 6, 7.1, 7.2\} = \mathcal{P}os_{X \cup \mathcal{V}al}(t)$, $\sim_{\mathcal{P}os_{X \cup \mathcal{V}al}(s)} = \sim_{\mathcal{P}os_{Y \cup \mathcal{V}al}(t)}$, and $\mathcal{P}os_{\mathcal{V}al!}(s) = \mathcal{P}os_{\mathcal{V}al!}(t)$. Let 1 and 4 be representatives of $\{1, 2, 3, 7.2\}$ and $\{4, 5, 6\}$. Then, we have $\mu_X = \{x \mapsto 0, x' \mapsto 0, y \mapsto y, y' \mapsto y\}$ and $\mu_Y = \{x \mapsto x, x' \mapsto x, y \mapsto 10, z \mapsto 0\}$. We also have $\varphi\mu_X = ((0 = 0) \wedge (0 = 0) \wedge (y = y))$ and $\psi\mu_Y = ((x \leqslant x) \wedge (x \leqslant x) \wedge (0 = 0) \wedge (10 = (0 + 2) \times 5))$. The remaining key is the correspondence between the sets $\hat{X} \cap X = \{y\}$ and $\hat{Y} \cap Y = \{z\}$.

Lemma 6.10. *Let $\Pi X.\ s\ [\exists \vec{x}.\ \varphi]$ be a satisfiable existentially constrained term, and μ_X a representative substitution of $\Pi X.\ s\ [\exists \vec{x}.\ \varphi]$. Then, $\models_{\mathcal{M}} (\exists \vec{x}.\ \varphi) \Rightarrow (z = \mu_X(z))$ for any variable $z \in X$.*

Let $\theta \subseteq X \times Y$ be a binary relation, and $\tilde{X} \subseteq X$, and $\tilde{Y} \subseteq Y$. Then, $\theta|_{\tilde{X}} = \{\langle x, y \rangle \in \theta \mid x \in \tilde{X}\}$ is denoted by $\theta|_{\tilde{X}} : \tilde{X} \rightarrow \tilde{Y}$ and used as a function if it is a function from $\tilde{X}$ to $\tilde{Y}$, i.e., for any $x \in \tilde{X}$ there exists a unique $y \in \tilde{Y}$ such that $\langle x, y \rangle \in \theta$. Note that if $\tilde{X} \subseteq \mathcal{V}$ and $\tilde{Y} \subseteq \mathcal{T}(\mathcal{F}, \mathcal{V})$, then $\theta|_{\tilde{X}}$ is a substitution.

We now present key properties required to establish our general characterization.

Lemma 6.11. *Let* $\Pi X.\ s\ [\exists \vec{x}.\ \varphi], \Pi Y.\ t\ [\exists \vec{y}.\ \psi]$ *be satisfiable existentially constrained terms such that* $\Pi X.\ s\ [\exists \vec{x}.\ \varphi] \sim \Pi Y.\ t\ [\exists \vec{y}.\ \psi]$. *Let* $\mathsf{Pos}_{X \cup \mathcal{V}\mathsf{al}}(s) = \mathsf{Pos}_{Y \cup \mathcal{V}\mathsf{al}}(t) = \{p_1, \ldots, p_n\}$. *Then, all of the following statements hold:*

(1) for any $i, j \in \{1, \ldots, n\}$, $\mathcal{M} \models (\exists \vec{x}.\ \varphi) \Rightarrow (s|_{p_i} = s|_{p_j})$ *if and only if* $\mathcal{M} \models (\exists \vec{y}.\ \psi) \Rightarrow (t|_{p_i} = t|_{p_j})$,

(2) for any $i \in \{1, \ldots, n\}$ *and* $v \in \mathcal{V}\mathsf{al}$, $\mathcal{M} \models (\exists \vec{x}.\ \varphi) \Rightarrow (s|_{p_i} = v)$ *if and only if* $\mathcal{M} \models (\exists \vec{y}.\ \psi) \Rightarrow (t|_{p_i} = v)$, *and*

(3) $\mathcal{M} \models (\exists \vec{x}.\ \varphi)\mu_X \theta \Leftrightarrow (\exists \vec{y}.\ \psi)\mu_Y$, *let* $\sim\ =\ \sim_{\mathcal{P}\mathsf{os}_{X \cup \mathcal{V}\mathsf{al}}(s)}\ =\ \sim_{\mathcal{P}\mathsf{os}_{X \cup \mathcal{V}\mathsf{al}}(t)}$, *and* μ_X, μ_Y *be representative substitutions of* $\Pi X.\ s\ [\exists \vec{x}.\ \varphi]$ *and* $\Pi Y.\ t\ [\exists \vec{y}.\ \psi]$, *respectively, based on the same representative for each equivalence class* $[p_i]_\sim$ $(1 \leqslant i \leqslant n)$, *and we have* $\models_{\mathcal{M}} (\exists \vec{x}.\ \varphi)\mu_X \theta|_{\tilde{X}} \Leftrightarrow (\exists \vec{y}.\ \psi)\mu_Y$ *with a renaming* $\theta|_{\tilde{X}} : \tilde{X} \to \tilde{Y}$, *where* $\theta = \{\langle s|_{p_i}, t|_{p_i} \rangle \mid 1 \leqslant i \leqslant n\}$, $\tilde{X} = \hat{X} \cap X$, *and* $\tilde{Y} = \hat{Y} \cap Y$.

Proof. Let $\mathrm{PG}(\Pi X.\ s\ [\exists \vec{x}.\ \varphi]) = (\Pi W.\ s[w_1, \ldots, w_n]_{p_1, \ldots, p_n}\ [\exists \vec{x}'.\ \varphi'])$ and $\mathrm{PG}(\Pi Y.\ t\ [\exists \vec{y}.\ \psi]) = (\Pi W'.\ t[w_1', \ldots, w_n']_{p_1, \ldots, p_n}\ [\exists \vec{y}'.\ \psi'])$, where we let $W = \{w_1, \ldots, w_n\}$, $\{\vec{x}'\} = \{\vec{x}\} \cup X$, $\varphi' = (\varphi \wedge \bigwedge_{i=1}^{n} (w_i = s|_{p_i}))$, $W' = \{w_1', \ldots, w_n'\}$, $\{\vec{y}'\} = \{\vec{y}\} \cup Y$, and $\psi' = (\psi \wedge \bigwedge_{i=1}^{n} (w_i' = t|_{p_i}))$. Then, by our assumption and Theorem 5.6, we have

$$(\Pi W.\ s[w_1, \ldots, w_n]_{p_1, \ldots, p_n}\ [\exists \vec{x}'.\ \varphi']) \sim (\Pi W.\ t[w_1', \ldots, w_n']_{p_1, \ldots, p_n}\ [\exists \vec{y}'.\ \psi']).$$

By Theorem 5.11, there is a renaming δ such that $s[w_1, \ldots, w_n]\delta = t[w_1', \ldots, w_n']$ and $\models_{\mathcal{M}} (\exists \vec{x}'.\ \varphi')\delta \Leftrightarrow \exists \vec{y}'.\ \psi'$. Thus, $\delta(w_i) = w_i'$. Then, using Lemma 5.8 (1),

$$
\begin{aligned}
\models_{\mathcal{M}} (\exists \vec{x}.\ \varphi) \Rightarrow (s|_{p_i} = s|_{p_j}) &\iff\ \models_{\mathcal{M}} (\exists \vec{x}'.\ \varphi') \Rightarrow (w_i = w_j) \\
&\iff\ \models_{\mathcal{M}} (\exists \vec{x}'.\ \varphi')\delta \Rightarrow (w_i \delta = w_j \delta) \\
&\iff\ \models_{\mathcal{M}} (\exists \vec{y}'.\ \psi') \Rightarrow (w_i' = w_j') \\
&\iff\ \models_{\mathcal{M}} (\exists \vec{y}.\ \psi) \Rightarrow (t|_{p_i} = t|_{p_j})
\end{aligned}
$$

This proves (1). (2) follows similarly, by using Lemma 5.8 (2). In order to show (3), take $\theta = \{\langle s|_{p_i}, t|_{p_i} \rangle \mid 1 \leqslant i \leqslant n\}$. Then, by (1), (2), and our assumption, we have

- $\mu_X(s|_{p_i}) \in \mathcal{V}\mathsf{al}$ if and only if $\mu_Y(t|_{p_i}) \in \mathcal{V}\mathsf{al}$, and moreover,
- $s|_{p_i} \in \tilde{X}$ if and only if p_i is a representative of an equivalence class $[p_i]$ if and only if $t|_{p_i} \in \tilde{Y}$.

Thus, $\{\langle s|_{p_i}, t|_{p_i} \rangle \mid p_i$ is a representative of an equivalence class $[p_i]$ such that $\mu_X(s|_{p_i}) \notin \mathcal{V}\mathsf{al}\} = \theta|_{\tilde{X}}$ is a renaming from $\tilde{X}$ to $\tilde{Y}$. Take an arbitrary but fixed function $\theta' : X \to Y$ such that $\theta'(s|_{p_i}) \in \{t|_{p_j} \mid p_i \sim p_j\}$. Then (i) $\theta|_{\tilde{X}}(\mu_X(s|_{p_i})) = \theta|_{\tilde{X}}(s|_{\hat{p}_i})) = t|_{\hat{p}_i} = \mu_Y(t|_{p_j}) = \mu_Y(\theta'(s|_{p_i}))$. Let $\sigma = \{w_1 \mapsto s|_{p_1}, \ldots, w_n \mapsto s|_{p_n}\}$ and $\sigma' = \{w_1' \mapsto t|_{p_1}, \ldots, w_n' \mapsto t|_{p_n}\}$. Then, we have (ii) $\mu_Y(\theta'(\sigma(w_i))) = \mu_Y(\theta'(s|_{p_i})) = \mu_Y(t|_{p_j}) = t|_{\hat{p}_i} = \mu_Y(t|_{p_i}) = \mu_Y(\sigma'(w_i')) = \mu_Y(\sigma'(\delta(w_i)))$. Thus, for any valuation ρ,

$$
\begin{aligned}
\models_{\mathcal{M}, \rho} (\exists \vec{x}.\ \varphi)\mu_X \theta|_{\tilde{X}} &\iff\ \models_{\mathcal{M}, \rho} (\exists \vec{x}'.\ \varphi')\sigma \mu_X \theta|_{\tilde{X}} && \text{by Lemma 5.7} \\
&\iff\ \models_{\mathcal{M}, \rho} (\exists \vec{x}'.\ \varphi')\sigma \theta' \mu_Y && \text{by (i)} \\
&\iff\ \models_{\mathcal{M}, \rho} (\exists \vec{x}'.\ \varphi')\delta \sigma' \mu_Y && \text{by (ii)} \\
&\iff\ \models_{\mathcal{M}, \rho} (\exists \vec{y}'.\ \psi')\sigma' \mu_Y && \text{by Lemma 5.7} \\
&\iff\ \models_{\mathcal{M}, \rho} (\exists \vec{y}.\ \psi)\mu_Y
\end{aligned}
$$

Thus, $\vDash_{\mathcal{M}} (\exists \vec{x}.\ \varphi)\mu_X \theta|_{\tilde{X}} \Leftrightarrow (\exists \vec{y}.\ \psi)\mu_Y.$ $\qquad\qquad$ □

We finally arrive at a general characterization of equivalence.

Theorem 6.12. *Let* $\Pi X.\ s\ [\exists \vec{x}.\ \varphi], \Pi Y.\ t\ [\exists \vec{y}.\ \psi]$ *be satisfiable existentially constrained terms, and* $\mathcal{P}os_{X \cup \mathcal{V}al}(s) = \{p_1, \dots, p_n\}$. *Then,* $\Pi X.\ s\ [\exists \vec{x}.\ \varphi] \sim \Pi Y.\ t\ [\exists \vec{y}.\ \psi]$ *if and only if the following statements hold:*

(1) $\mathcal{P}os_{X \cup \mathcal{V}al}(s) = \mathcal{P}os_{Y \cup \mathcal{V}al}(t),$

(2) *there exists a renaming* $\rho \colon \mathcal{V}ar(s) \setminus X \to \mathcal{V}ar(t) \setminus Y$ *such that* $\rho(s[\,]_{p_1,\dots,p_n}) = t[\,]_{p_1,\dots,p_n},$

(3) *for any* $i, j \in \{1, \dots, n\}$, $\vDash_{\mathcal{M}} (\exists \vec{x}.\ \varphi) \Rightarrow (s|_{p_i} = s|_{p_j})$ *if and only if* $\vDash_{\mathcal{M}} (\exists \vec{y}.\ \psi) \Rightarrow (t|_{p_i} = t|_{p_j}),$

(4) *for any* $i \in \{1, \dots, n\}$ *and* $v \in \mathcal{V}al$, $\vDash_{\mathcal{M}} (\exists \vec{x}.\ \varphi) \Rightarrow (s|_{p_i} = v)$ *if and only if* $\vDash_{\mathcal{M}} (\exists \vec{y}.\ \psi) \Rightarrow (t|_{p_i} = v)$, *and*

(5) *let* $\sim\ =\ \sim_{\mathcal{P}os_{X \cup \mathcal{V}al}(s)}\ =\ \sim_{\mathcal{P}os_{X \cup \mathcal{V}al}(t)}$, *and* μ_X, μ_Y *be representative substitutions of* $\Pi X.\ s\ [\exists \vec{x}.\ \varphi]$ *and* $\Pi Y.\ t\ [\exists \vec{y}.\ \psi]$, *respectively, based on the same representative for each equivalence class* $[p_i]_\sim$ *(*$1 \leqslant i \leqslant n$*), and we have* $\vDash_{\mathcal{M}} (\exists \vec{x}.\ \varphi)\mu_X \theta|_{\tilde{X}} \Leftrightarrow (\exists \vec{y}.\ \psi)\mu_Y$ *with a renaming* $\theta|_{\tilde{X}} \colon \tilde{X} \to \tilde{Y}$, *where* $\theta = \{\langle s|_{p_i}, t|_{p_i}\rangle \mid 1 \leqslant i \leqslant n\}$, $\tilde{X} = \hat{X} \cap X$, *and* $\tilde{Y} = \hat{Y} \cap Y$.

Proof (Sketch). The *only-if* part follows Lemma 5.9 and Lemma 6.11. The *if* part is shown by applying the PG-transformation to $\Pi X.\ s\ [\exists \vec{x}.\ \varphi]$ and $\Pi Y.\ t\ [\exists \vec{y}.\ \psi]$, and using Theorem 5.11. For this Lemma 6.10 and Lemma 6.11 are needed. $\quad$ □

7   Conclusion

In this paper, we introduced the notion of existentially constrained terms and provided characterizations of their equivalence. We showed that original formalization of constrained terms can be embedded into existentially constrained terms, and that equivalence between constrained terms coincides with the equivalence of their embedded counterparts.

We first presented a characterization of equivalent existentially constrained terms in the case where the term part of one is a renaming of the other. Then, we introduced pattern-general existentially constrained terms and the PG-transformation, demonstrating that the PG-transformation maps each existentially constrained term to an equivalent pattern-general one.

We have shown a characterization of equivalent pattern-general existentially constrained terms, which in turn yields a sound and complete characterization of equivalent existentially constrained terms via the PG-transformation. Finally, we also established a sound and complete characterization of equivalence for existentially constrained terms in general, independent of the notion of pattern-general existentially constrained terms.

Our future work is to apply our results on existentially constrained terms to other areas of the LCTRS formalism. This includes investigating their benefits for automated reasoning by LCTRS tools.

References

1. Aoto, T., Nishida, N., Schöpf, J.: Equational theories and validity for logically constrained term rewriting. In: Rehof, J. (ed.) Proceedings of the 9th FSCD. LIPIcs, vol. 299, pp. 31:1–31:21 (2024). https://doi.org/10.4230/LIPIcs.FSCD.2024.31
2. Baader, F., Nipkow, T.: Term Rewriting and All That. Cambridge University Press, Cambridge (1998). https://doi.org/10.1145/505863.505888
3. Fuhs, C., Kop, C., Nishida, N.: Verifying procedural programs via constrained rewriting induction. ACM Trans. Comput. Log. **18**(2), 14:1–14:50 (2017). https://doi.org/10.1145/3060143
4. Kojima, M., Nishida, N.: On representations of waiting queues for semaphores in logically constrained term rewrite systems with constant destinations. J. Inf. Process. (2024). to appear
5. Kop, C.: Termination of LCTRSs. CoRR **abs/1601.03206** (2016). https://doi.org/10.48550/ARXIV.1601.03206
6. Kop, C.: Quasi-reductivity of logically constrained term rewriting systems. CoRR **abs/1702.02397** (2017). http://arxiv.org/abs/1702.02397
7. Kop, C., Nishida, N.: Term rewriting with logical constraints. In: Fontaine, P., Ringeissen, C., Schmidt, R.A. (eds.) FroCoS 2013. LNCS (LNAI), vol. 8152, pp. 343–358. Springer, Heidelberg (2013). https://doi.org/10.1007/978-3-642-40885-4_24
8. Kop, C., Nishida, N.: Automatic constrained rewriting induction towards verifying procedural programs. In: Garrigue, J. (ed.) APLAS 2014. LNCS, vol. 8858, pp. 334–353. Springer, Cham (2014). https://doi.org/10.1007/978-3-319-12736-1_18
9. Nishida, N., Winkler, S.: Loop detection by logically constrained term rewriting. In: Piskac, R., Rümmer, P. (eds.) VSTTE 2018. LNCS, vol. 11294, pp. 309–321. Springer, Cham (2018). https://doi.org/10.1007/978-3-030-03592-1_18
10. Ohlebusch, E.: Advanced Topics in Term Rewriting. Springer, Cham (2002). https://doi.org/10.1007/978-1-4757-3661-8
11. Schöpf, J., Middeldorp, A.: Confluence criteria for logically constrained rewrite systems. In: Pientka, B., Tinelli, C. (eds.) Automated Deduction – CADE 29. CADE 2023. LNCS, vol. 14132, pp. 474–490. Springer, Cham (2023). https://doi.org/10.1007/978-3-031-38499-8_27
12. Schöpf, J., Mitterwallner, F., Middeldorp, A.: Confluence of logically constrained rewrite systems revisited. In: Benzmüller, C., Heule, M.J., Schmidt, R.A. (eds.) Automated Reasoning. IJCAR 2024. LNCS, vol. 14740, pp. 298–316. Springer, Cham (2024). https://doi.org/10.1007/978-3-031-63501-4_16
13. Takahata, K., Schöpf, J., Nishida, N., Aoto, T.: Characterizing equivalence of logically constrained terms via existentially constrained terms. CoRR **abs/2505.21986**, 1–29 (2025). https://doi.org/10.48550/arXiv.2505.21986
14. Takahata, K., Schöpf, J., Nishida, N., Aoto, T.: Recovering commutation of logically constrained rewriting and equivalence transformations. In: Proceedings of the 27th International Symposium on Principles and Practice of Declarative Programming. ACM (2025). to appear
15. Winkler, S., Middeldorp, A.: Completion for logically constrained rewriting. In: Kirchner, H. (ed.) Proceedings of the 3rd FSCD. LIPIcs, vol. 108, pp. 30:1–30:18 (2018). https://doi.org/10.4230/LIPIcs.FSCD.2018.30
16. Winkler, S., Moser, G.: Runtime complexity analysis of logically constrained rewriting. In: LOPSTR 2020. LNCS, vol. 12561, pp. 37–55. Springer, Cham (2021). https://doi.org/10.1007/978-3-030-68446-4_2

Focusing Recursive LLM Descents with Plans Expressed as Logic Programs

Paul Tarau$^{(\boxtimes)}$ (iD)

University of North Texas, Denton, USA
`paul.tarau@unt.edu`

Abstract. We propose an approach where human-designed logic programs guide the systematic exploration of concepts and statements using Large Language Models (LLMs).

Undefined facts within these programs, (seen as *abducibles*), are expanded into Prolog clauses by extracting symbolic knowledge stored within an LLM's internal representations.

This collaborative framework combining human expertise and LLM-generated insights allows thorough exploration of the assumptions and potential consequences that support or challenge specific viewpoints or decisions.

We demonstrate the effectiveness of this methodology by analyzing scientific theories, emerging technologies, and key policy decisions.

Keywords: constructive reasoning · Horn and Dual Horn logic · LLM-based falsifiable theory construction · LLM-driven theory verification and falsification · human-guided LLM-based generation of logic programs · symbolic guidance techniques for Generative AI

1   Introduction

Given a controversial scientific theory, a disruptive emerging technology or a highly debated policy decision process, LLMs encapsulate significant knowledge about it in their parametric memory. In fact, an LLM acts, when queried, as an unusually crisp indexing mechanism, that (contrary to its traditional counterparts) also states its results in coherent and well articulated natural language. By concentrating this elegantly indexed knowledge into a single declarative interface, Generative AI can replace with simple LLM API calls complex, labor-intensive software functionality.

Reasoning about the merits of a technology disruptor, a research direction or a policy decision involves *verifying* their details in goal oriented recursive processes that can be expressed as AND/OR trees, and consequently as *theories* implemented as Horn clause programs. Reasoning against such a theory can be seen as a *falsification* process, while exploring recursively its consequences. In fact, falsifying a theory boils down to reasoning backward from its unwanted consequences. In both cases, it makes sense for this process to focus on discovering the key statements and concepts and their inferential connections, without the (possibly hallucinatory) verbosity of the typical LLM dialog.

S. Escobar and L. Titolo (Eds.): LOPSTR 2025, LNCS 16117, pp. 196–211, 2026.
https://doi.org/10.1007/978-3-032-04848-6_13

This brings us to the set of tools we will use to express these Generative and Symbolic AI collaboration techniques, combining our logic programming tools with techniques eliciting structured knowledge from LLMs.

The paper is organized as follows. Section 2 overviews reasoning with Dual Horn clauses. Section 3 describes combining Horn Clauses and Dual Horn clauses in the embedded language SymLP. Section 4 introduces techniques for guiding LLMs with plans expressed as Natlog programs. Section 5 describes reasoning techniques with LLM-generated SymLP programs. Section 6 introduces applications exploring merits and shortcomings of scientific theories, emerging technologies and key policy decisions. Section 7 overviews related work and Sect. 8 concludes the paper.

2 Overview on Reasoning with Duals

We start with an informal overview of Dual Horn Clause programs and the SymLP embedded logic language [14] as a unified set of tools used to validate or falsify the theories involved in reasoning about a given theory, expressed as a logic program.

We will overview here, following [14] only the implicational view of Horn and Dual Horn clauses and their reasoning mechanisms.

A *literal* is assumed here to be a positive (unnegated) Prolog term. A *Horn clause* is an inverse implication between a literal (head) and a conjunction of literals (body). The literal true represents an empty body and the literal false represents an empty head. A Horn clause is *definite* if its head is not empty. Horn clauses with empty heads are called *Horn integrity constraints* [4].

A *Dual Horn clause* is an implication between a literal (head) and a disjunction of literals (body). Definite Dual Horn clauses have non-empty heads (i.e., not marked with the true symbol). Dual Horn clauses with empty heads are called *Dual Horn integrity constraints*.

Horn

$$p_0 \leftarrow p_1 \wedge \ldots \wedge p_n. \tag{1}$$

DualHorn

$$p_0 \rightarrow p_1 \vee \ldots \vee p_n. \tag{2}$$

Thus, while extending Definite Horn clauses with integrity constraints (see (3)), means asserting that at least one p_i must be false, for their duals (see (4)), it means asserting that at least one p_i must be true.

Horn

$$false \leftarrow p_1 \wedge \ldots \wedge p_n. \tag{3}$$

Dual Horn

$$true \rightarrow p_1 \vee \ldots \vee p_n. \tag{4}$$

Satisfiability of propositional Horn clause and Dual Horn clause formulas with or without integrity constraints is P-complete. This follows from Schaefer's dichotomy theorem classifying propositional formulas [10] in P-complete vs. NP-complete types. Note that finding a renaming that might turn a set of clauses into a set of Horn or Dual Horn clauses is also polynomial [2]. This is particularly significant as very large propositional logic programs can be generated by an LLM, when increasing the cut-off limit of the recursive descent.

We will assume here the proof-theoretical semantics [7] of Horn clause Logic in implicational form, that has been known to be compatible also with its reading in Intuitionistic Logic.

Example 1. *We start with a small Dual Definite program, adopting Prolog-like syntax, with $\rightarrow$ represented as "=>" and $\vee$ represented as ";".*

```
p => q ; r.
q => r ; s.
r => false.
s => false.
```

Note also that "s => false" represents a negated fact, the same way as "s :- true" would represent a positive fact. Let's proceed with p as our goal, similarly as if we would evaluate a Horn clause program. Assuming that p were true, we would infer that at least one of q, r and s should be true. Thus at least one of r and s should be true, but both r and s implies false. The falsity of s and r then backpropagates and falsifies the initial goal p. Note that this reasoning is also intuitionistically valid, similarly to its Horn clause counterpart.

We conclude from this example that we have a goal oriented *falsification* process for Dual Horn programs that mimics the *verification* in Horn programs via SLD-resolution. It is easy to see that programs with variable bindings generated via unification will work also in a similar way.

Note that the falsification process relies on the fact that the relations (5) and (6) hold both classically and intuitionistically.

$$(p_0 \leftarrow p_1 \wedge \ldots \wedge p_n) \wedge p_1 \wedge \ldots \wedge p_n \rightarrow p_0 \tag{5}$$

$$(p_0 \rightarrow p_1 \vee \ldots \vee p_n) \wedge \neg p_1 \wedge \ldots \neg p_n \rightarrow \neg p_0 \tag{6}$$

Thus, based on (6), to falsify p_0 we need to falsify all the disjuncts p_i that are consequences of p_0, the essence of a goal-driven falsification process, operationally similar to the SLD-resolution proof procedure on Horn clause programs as illustrated by the need to verify all conjuncts in the body of the clause in (5). Note that inference using (5) reduces to applying *modus ponens* and inference using (6) reduces to applying *modus tollens*.

3   Symmetric Logic Programming (SymLP): Combining Horn and Dual Horn Clauses

Working together with Horn and Dual Horn clause leads to our SymLP language, implemented as an embedded language in SWI-Prolog.

To embed the SymLP language that combines Horn clauses and Dual Horn clauses into Prolog, we will need a few operators. We use "+" to mark facts that are true and "-" to mark facts that are false. We will use "=>" to represent implication and "<=" to represent inverse implication. Note also that -p can be seen as a shortcut for p=>false and that similarly, +p can be seen as a shortcut for p<=true. We will borrow from Prolog the usual notation for conjunction "," and disjunction ";".

In [14] a compilation scheme from Dual Horn programs to Horn Programs is implemented via a simple term expansion mechanism, relying on the similarity between proving a goal by backward reasoning in Horn Clause programs and falsifying a claim via forward reasoning about its consequences in Dual Horn programs.

The compilation mechanism maps a Dual Horn clause $p_0 \rightarrow p_1 \vee \ldots \vee p_n$ into a Horn Clause $p_0 \leftarrow p_1 \wedge \ldots \wedge p_n$ and places the result into the module "false".

The compilation leaves Horn clauses invariant, but moves them into a module "true".

Example 2. *The following SymLP fragment*

```
p => q ; r.
q => r ; s.
-r.
-s.

u <= v,w.
+v.
+w.
```

will become, the Horn Clause Prolog program:

```
% in module false
p :-q ,r.
q :-r ,s.
r.
s.

% in module true
u :-v,w.
v.
w.
```

Then, querying it with

```
?- false:p.
true
```

confirms that p *is indeed falsifiable, while querying with*

```
?- true:u.
true
```

confirms that u *is verifiable.*

4 Eliciting the Horn Clause and Dual Horn Clause Representations Encapsulated in the LLMs Knowledge Store

We customize the recursive descent algorithm of [13] to generate positive and negative views of a given concept, statement or decision process. At the same time, we customize the knowledge stream generated by the LLM to be guided by a planner, along human-specified directions. We will next describe the main components and execution steps of our new algorithm.

4.1 Prompting the LLM to Verify or Falsify

We need a bit of "prompt engineering" to convince an LLM (gpt-4o in our case) to generate supporting alternatives (OR-nodes) as well as details (AND-nodes) when expanding a newly created clause head, while also ensuring that verbose, unfocused and possibly hallucinatory output is avoided. The resulting Horn clause program will be placed in module true.

```
verifier_prompter = dict(
        name='verification_of_a_decision_via_supporting_reasons',
  and_p="""We strongly support and want to achieve the positive
  results of: "$context".
        To help with this task, generate 1-2 noun phrases of 2-4 words
        with each alternative detailing the steps needed to achieve
        the results of "$g".
        Itemize your answer, one result step of "$g" per line.""",
  or_p="""We strongly support and want to achieve the positive
    results of: "$context".
        Generate 1-2 noun phrases of 2-4 words that describe
        alternative ways to achieve "$g".
        Itemize your answer, one noun phrase per line."""
)
```

Similarly, when we want to falsify a given statement we will ask the LLM to find reasons to disaprove it by finding its negative (i.e., unreasonable, undesirable, wasteful, harmful etc.,) consequences. This results into a Dual Horn clause program, that we will actually turn on the fly into its Horn clause dual to be placed in module false.

```
falsifier_prompter = dict(
    name='falsification_of_a_decision_via_negative_consequences',
  or_p="""We strongly disaprove and need to refute that: "$context".
    To help with this task, generate 1-2 noun phrases of 2-4 words
    with each alternative detailing undesirable consequences of "$g".
    Itemize your answer, one consequence of "$g" per line.""",
  and_p="""We strongly disapprove and need to refute that: "$context".
    Generate 1-2 noun phrases of 2-4 words that together are
    undesirable consequences "$g".
    Itemize your answer, one noun phrase per line."""
)
```

Note that the patterns $context (representing the history of interaction) and $g (representing to initiator of the recursive descent) are expanded into appropriate values at each clause head and clause body creation step.

4.2   Outlining the Top Initiator Concept for More Precise LLM Generation

We use human-made Horn or Dual Horn clause program to obtain an LLM output that prioritizes top-level alternatives and elaborations of the topic we want to explore. This can be seen as outlining a plan constraining the main subconcepts to be explored. In this program, we consider facts that are undefined as abducibles that can be verified or falsified using DeepLLM's recursive expansion to a given depth [13]. The LLM generated Prolog programs will then complement the human-made outliner program that plans the big lines of the expansions process.

Example 3. *We will describe this process on an artificial small example. Given the human-made plan:*

```
p :-q,r.
p :-s.
s :-r.
```

q and r will be considered abducibles and passed to the LLM for expansion. Assuming the LLM expands them (at recursion limit 1) into:

```
q :-a,b,c.
r :-b,d.
```

the resulting program will be the union of the two sets of clauses, to be interpreted either as a program to be verified (with its corresponding model computed by the DeepLLM system) or as a Horn program representation "compiled on the fly" (see [13]) of the Dual Horn program to be falsified.

4.3   Generating the Verifier and Falsifier Horn Clause Programs with Natlog

The Natlog Code and Its Python Companion. We use Natlog[1] (see [11] for implementation of user interaction details). Natlog is a simplified syntax Prolog system written in Python (with clauses represented as nested tuples) that seamlessly interfaces with the Python DeepLLM Horn clause code generator.

The Python program imports the necessary code from DeepLLM and Natlog.

```
from deepllm.recursors import run_explorer
from deepllm.prompters import verifier_prompter,falsifier_prompter
from Natlog import Natlog, natprogs
```

```
def run_natlog(natprog="symplan.nat"):
  n = Natlog(
    file_name=natprog,
    with_lib=natprogs() + "lib.nat",
    callables=globals())

  next(n.solve('decide_on_EVs.'))
```

```
def verify(goal,lim):
  run_explorer(prompter=verifier_prompter, goal=goal, lim=lim)

def falsify(goal,lim):
  run_explorer(prompter=falsifier_prompter, goal=goal, lim=lim)

if __name__=="__main__":
  run_natlog()
```

The Natlog program defines the user's toplevel fragment of the resolution tree and triggers the LLMs exploration via the verifier and its falsifier counterpart. Note that, following Natlog's convention, we mark Python functions that do not return a value with the "#" symbol, as in this case we only care about the generated Prolog files as output.

```
limit 1.

verify X : limit L, #verify X L.

falsify X : limit L, #falsify X L.
```

```
buy_ev : % decision on buying an EV
  verify 'EVs_are_ecological',
  verify 'EVS_are_low_maintenance',
  verify 'EVs_cost_less_over_time'.
```

---

[1] Available from https://github.com/ptarau/natlog, online app at https://natlog.streamlit.app/.

```
avoid_ev:
  falsify 'EVs_are_ecological',
  falsify 'EVS_are_low_maintenance',
  falsify 'EVs_cost_less_over_time'.

decide_on_EVs: buy_ev, avoid_ev.
```

The verify and falsify predicates trigger corresponding LLM recursive descent up to given limit. Once the limit is reached, facts at that level will be considered positively marked for verify and negatively marked for falsify. This can be further refined by letting the "human-in-the-loop" edit them out if judged too unrelated to the original goal. Alternatively, DeepLLM's oracles [13] can be used to validate them.

A Verifier's LLM-Generated Prolog Code

We show here the expansion of the leaf: EVs_are_ecological, a step in evaluating the pros and cons of electrical vehicles. We omit the similar expansion for the other two leaves, but the full code is made available online at: https://github.com/ptarau/output_samples/tree/main/symplan.

Note that we generate the verifier Prolog clauses as Horn clauses. Thus the following code will be part of module true.

```
% CLAUSES in module true:
'EVs_are_ecological' :-
  'Renewable energy integration'.
'EVs_are_ecological' :-
  'Sustainable battery production'.
```

```
'Renewable energy integration' :-
  'Solar panel installation',
  'Wind turbine deployment',
  'Grid modernization',
  'Energy storage systems'.
'Sustainable battery production' :-
  'Renewable energy sourcing',
  'Efficient recycling systems',
  'Ethical raw material sourcing',
  'Advanced battery technology'.
'Solar panel installation'.
 'Wind turbine deployment'.
'Grid modernization'.
'Energy storage systems'.
'Renewable energy sourcing'.
'Efficient recycling systems'.
'Ethical raw material sourcing'.
 'Advanced battery technology'.
```

A Falsifier LLM-Generated Prolog Code. Note that we perform the compilation step from Dual Horn clauses to Prolog at clause generation time. Thus the following code will be part of module false.

```
% CLAUSES in module false:
'EVs_are_ecological' :-
  'Battery production emissions'.
'EVs_are_ecological' :-
  'Resource-intensive mining'.
'EVs_are_ecological' :-
  'Limited recycling infrastructure'.
'EVs_are_ecological' :-
  'Energy-intensive manufacturing'.
'EVs_are_ecological' :-
  'Grid dependency increase'.
```

```
'Battery production emissions' :-
  'Resource-intensive mining',
  'Toxic waste generation'.
'Resource-intensive mining' :-
   'Environmental degradation',
   'Habitat destruction'.
'Limited recycling infrastructure' :-
   'Increased landfill waste',
   'Resource extraction demand'.
 'Energy-intensive manufacturing' :-
   'Increased carbon emissions',
   'Resource depletion'.
```

```
'Grid dependency increase' :-
   'Fossil fuel reliance',
   'Infrastructure strain'.
   'Toxic waste generation'.
   'Environmental degradation'.
   'Habitat destruction'.
  'Increased landfill waste'.
   'Resource extraction demand'.
   'Increased carbon emissions'.
   'Resource depletion'.
   'Fossil fuel reliance'.
   'Infrastructure strain'.
```

4.4 Generating the Verifier and Falsifier Fragments Directly

As the human-made plan is assumed to be a hierarchical propositional program, we can simply collect its *leaf nodes*, corresponding to abducible facts, to be handed over to the LLM, followed by an integration step merging the result in a single program. Depending on the prompts used, the program can then be used as a verifier or falsifier. Alternatively, customized verifier plans and falsifier plans can be submitted independently. We will use Natlog syntax (and invoke its parser) for the initiator plan. The generated code will be exported in Horn Clause Prolog form, Natlog form as well as in portable JSON format, ready to be integrated in applications.

When generating positive or negative arguments for an abducible, the LLM will need to be aware of the steps leading from the toplevel initiator (by convention the first clause head in the Natlog program) to the abducible to be explored. We collect this path algorithmically for the Natlog plan clauses. When the control is passed to the LLM, we add to the path the clause heads dynamically created during AND-node and OR-node expansion. Once flattened into a text string, this path will bind the $context pattern in our verifier and falsifier prompt templates described in Subsect. 4.1, while the current goal (part of the Natlog plan or abducible leaf) will bind the pattern variable $g.

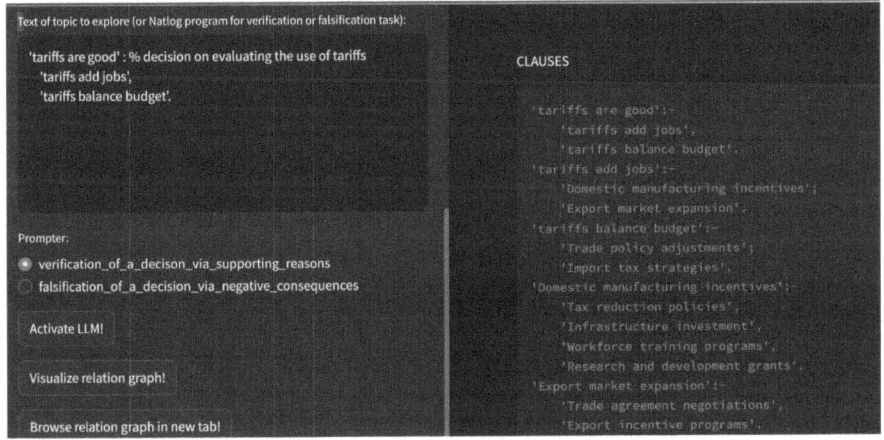

Fig. 1. Support arguments for "tariffs are good"

Figure 1 uses as input a small Natlog program that sets-up the toplevel plan guiding the exploration of the statement "tariffs are good", this time with focus on supporting arguments.

Figure 2 uses the same Natlog program as toplevel plan for exploring falsification of the "theory" that "tariffs are good".

5   Reasoning with LLM-Generated SymLP Programs

Let's start by emphasizing that LLM-induced reasoning is intuitionistic: falsification of p does not result in assuming its negation. In fact, as opposite opinions coexist in the datasets used for the LLMs' training, LLMs can be directed to support or falsify statements independently.

LLM-generated SymLP programs allow for systematic reasoning through explicitly structured logical pathways. Utilizing both Horn and Dual Horn clauses enables

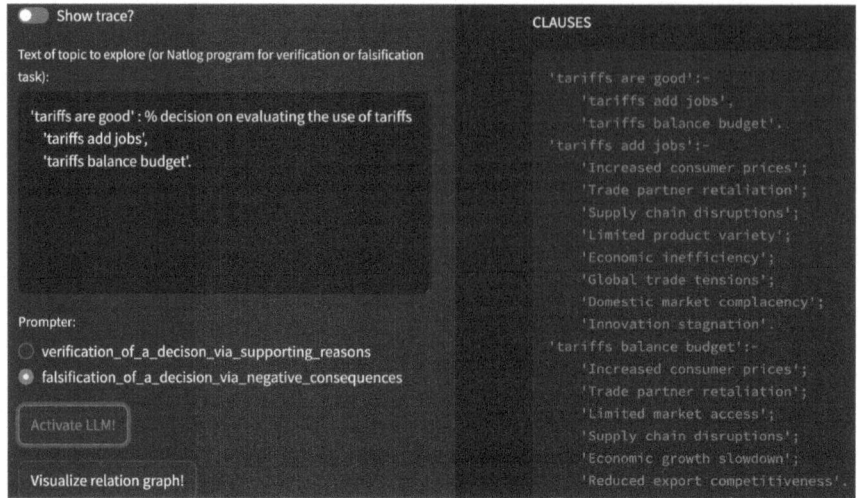

Fig. 2. Falsification of "tariffs are good"

nuanced handling of verification and falsification scenarios. Through recursive exploration guided by human-defined logic, these programs can rigorously assess the validity of statements by deriving clear logical implications or contradictions. The structured approach provided by SymLP significantly mitigates common issues associated with traditional LLM-generated dialogues, such as verbosity and hallucinatory digressions, resulting in precise, verifiable, and falsifiable outcomes. This structured reasoning framework thus represents a robust mechanism for critically evaluating complex concepts and their implications, offering substantial improvements over traditional approaches to logic reasoning with generative AI.

In the context of a multi-agent system, we have also experimented by replacing the human planner by a high quality reasoning LLM (e.g., GPT 4.5 Research Overview), while a locally running small LLM (e.g., llama 3.3) filled out the expansion of the abducibles to deeper levels for free.

The reader is invited to experiment with our system online at https://symplanapp. streamlit.app/.

6   Applications

We will sketch here a few application examples that all benefit from the succinct Horn and Dual Horn representation of successive concept refinements, by contrast to the conventional LLM dialog threads prone to hyperbolae and often hallucinatory digressive elaborations.

6.1   A Controversial Policy Decision

Given a widely discussed policy decision like the one about the arguments for and against imposing tariffs (see Figs. 1 and 2), the training process of the LLMs had the opportunity to encapsulate in its parametric memory often unobvious details of its impacts and consequences. Note that the falsification process expands neutrally or positively stated planning nodes into negative consequences that if successfully proven, will make them succeed in module `false` resulting in their successful falsification. Additionally, the structured exploration offered by SymLP facilitates identification of implicit biases and overlooked scenarios, promoting a balanced and comprehensive assessment of policy decisions. The ability to explicitly represent and systematically explore both supportive and critical perspectives ensures a deeper understanding of their implications, thereby significantly enhancing the quality of policy analysis and debate.

6.2 An "open" Scientific Theory

We picked the belief that "the universe is a computer simulation" as our "open" scientific theory to support (see Fig. 3) or falsify (see Fig. 4). Note in this case the comparative strength of the falsification clauses versus its support clauses, with focus this time on observable consequences easy to disagree with.

Our approach of helps revealing hidden assumptions and potential contradictions within such speculative theories. By clearly delineating logical implications and their consequences, the two sides of SymLP support a more rigorous examination and debate of complex hypotheses. This method can thus foster productive scientific discourse by explicitly outlining verifiable and falsifiable elements of theories that are traditionally challenging to empirically evaluate.

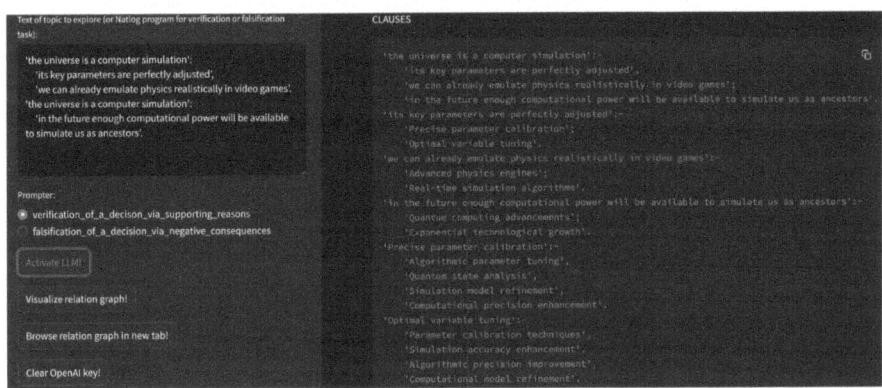

Fig. 3. Support arguments for "the universe is a computer simulation"

6.3 An Emerging Disruptive Technology

We selected "artificial general intelligence" (AGI) as an emerging disruptive technology to examine through SymLP (see Fig. 5 and Fig. 6). The supportive arguments outlined in Fig. 5 emphasize potential breakthroughs in efficiency, human-computer collaboration, and transformative societal impacts. In contrast, Fig. 6 identifies significant

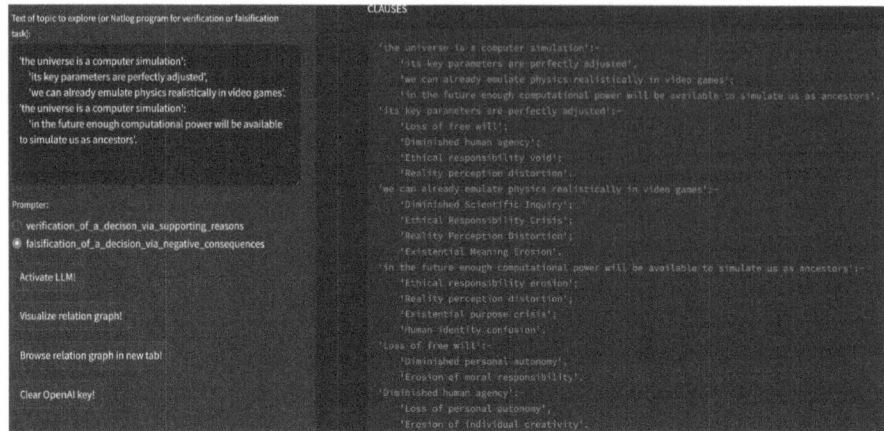

Fig. 4. Falsification of "the universe is a computer simulation"

concerns such as ethical dilemmas, employment disruptions, and potential existential risks associated with AGI. SymLP's structured exploration effectively delineates these perspectives, facilitating clear and rigorous examination of AGI's complex and multifaceted implications. This approach provides valuable insights that aid policymakers, researchers, and stakeholders in understanding and addressing both the optimistic and cautionary viewpoints associated with advanced artificial intelligence developments.

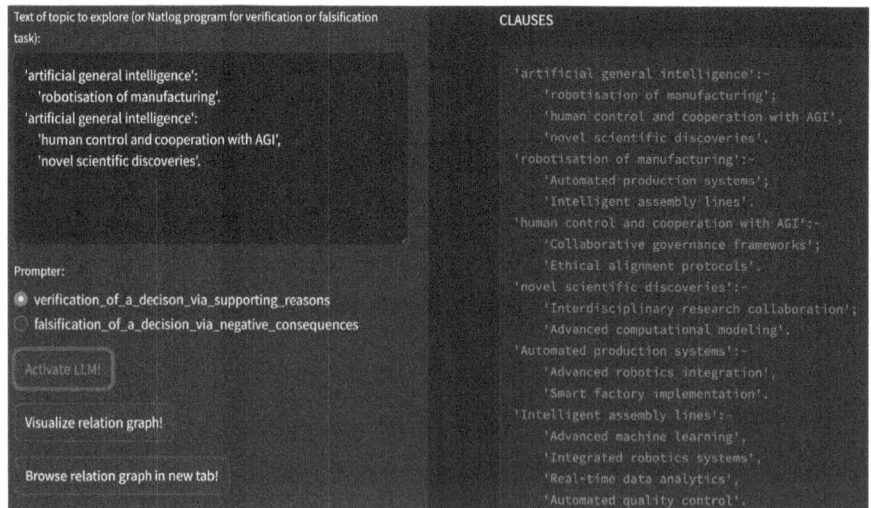

Fig. 5. Support arguments for "artificial general intelligence"

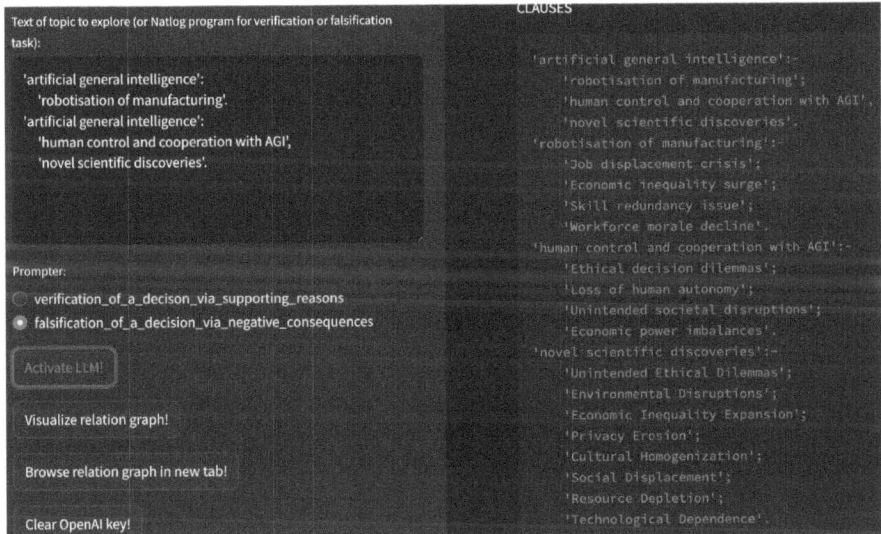

Fig. 6. Arguments against "artificial general intelligence"

7   Related Work

The recursive descent algorithm of [13], adopted here in a customized form, shares the goal of extracting more accurate information from the LLM interaction with work on "Chain of Thought" prompting of LLMs [6,16] and with step by step [5] refinement of the dialog threads. Recursively calling LLMs has been used for different purposes in several recent papers. In [15] a recursive summarization algorithm is described as a way to enhance long-term dialog ability of LLMs, prone to incorrectly recall information from past interactions. In [1] a chain-of-feedback mechanism is used to recursively revise the initially incorrect response by breaking down each in- correct reasoning step into smaller individual problems. Among several papers describing efforts to improve LLM output using logical reasoning we mention [8], where a compositional translation mechanism of logical dependency structures is used in combination with a SAT solver.

By contrast to "neuro-symbolic" AI [9], where the neural architecture is closely intermixed with symbolic steps, in our approach the neural processing encapsulated in the LLMs is guided by a symbolic planner program. This reduces the semantic gap between the neural and symbolic sides as their communication happens at a much higher, fully automated and directly explainable level. Moreover, our output consists of generated Prolog and Natlog programs, ready to be integrated in Prolog applications.

Our refinements to the DeepLLM system described in [13] include the falsification mechanism for LLM-generated Dual Horn clause programs, the Natlog-based planner logic program guiding the LLM, and the new Streamlit app specialized for generating the verifier Horn clause program and the falsifier Dual Horn clause program, both initiated by the same human-designed planner.

Horn clause formulas and Dual Horn clause formulas (called weakly negative and, respectively, weakly positive in [10]) are proven in his "dichotomy theorem" to be among the classes of propositional formulas that are in P. A graph-based linear algorithm exists for Horn clause formulas, described in [3] and given the linear renaming algorithm of propositional variables in [2], the same applies to Dual Horn formulas. Our Python implementation uses this bottom-up fixpoint algorithm to compute models for both the verifier and the falsifier logic programs. We refer to [12] for details of this model computation algorithm.

To some extent, the utility of Dual Horn program relies on the assumption that full knowledge of positive and negative facts can be acquired given their encapsulation in LLMs or traditional knowledge bases. This leaves open the possibility of unknown facts (e.g., those reached at the DeepLLM recursion depth limit) that can be seen as *abducibles*, i.e., verifiable if passing integrity constraints on the Horn clause side or falsifiable if passing the corresponding constraints on the Dual Horn side.

8 Conclusion and Future Work

In this paper, we presented a novel approach combining logic programming with the knowledge encapsulated in large language models (LLMs) to rigorously guide exploration and reasoning tasks. By utilizing Horn clauses for verification and Dual Horn clauses for falsification, our SymLP language enables precise and structured exploration of complex topics, including controversial policy decisions, scientific theories, and emerging disruptive technologies. This approach reduces the verbosity and potential inaccuracies characteristic of conventional LLM interactions, focusing instead on succinct, well-defined logical pathways.

Our experimental results illustrate the practical advantages of this hybrid methodology. It facilitates deeper understanding and clearer articulation of both supporting arguments and potential counterarguments, making it particularly useful for decision-making scenarios.

Looking ahead, there are several promising directions for future research. Exploring the application of these methods to real-time decision-making scenarios presents opportunities for extending our current framework. Lastly, investigating user-centric enhancements that leverage interactive editing or validation steps could significantly enhance usability and alignment with user intentions, further bridging the gap between symbolic reasoning and generative AI technologies.

Acknowledgment. We thank the reviewers of LOPSTR'2025 for their constructive comments and suggestions. The paper's experiments have benefited from OpenAI's high quality LLM models and the flexibility of their API.

References

1. Ahn, J., Shin, K.: Recursive chain-of-feedback prevents performance degradation from redundant prompting (2024). https://arxiv.org/abs/2402.02648

2. Chandru, V., Coullard, C.R., Hammer, P.L., Montañez, M., Sun, X.: On renamable Horn and generalized Horn functions. Ann. Math. Artif. Intell. **1**(1-4), 33–47 (1990). https://doi.org/10.1007/BF01531069

3. Dowling, W.F., Gallier, J.H.: Linear-time algorithms for testing the satisfiability of propositional horn formulae. J. Log. Program. **1**(3), 267–284 (1984). https://doi.org/10.1016/0743-1066(84)90014-1

4. Eshghi, K., Kowalski, R.A.: Abduction compared with negation by failure. In: Levi, G., Martelli, M. (eds.) Logic Programming, Proceedings of the Sixth International Conference, Lisbon, Portugal, 19–23 June 1989, pp. 234–254. MIT Press (1989)

5. Lightman, H., et al.: Let's Verify Step by Step (2023). https://arxiv.org/abs/2305.20050

6. Ling, Z., et al.: Deductive verification of chain-of-thought reasoning (2023). https://doi.org/10.48550/arXiv:2306.03872v3, https://arxiv.org/abs/2306.03872

7. Miller, D.: A survey of the proof-theoretic foundations of logic programming. CoRR **abs/2109.01483** (2021), https://arxiv.org/abs/2109.01483

8. Ryu, H., Kim, G., Lee, H.S., Yang, E.: Divide and translate: compositional first-order logic translation and verification for complex logical reasoning (2025). https://arxiv.org/abs/2410.08047

9. Sarker, M.K., Zhou, L., Eberhart, A., Hitzler, P.: Neuro-symbolic artificial intelligence: current trends (2021). https://doi.org/10.48550/ARXIV.2105.05330, https://arxiv.org/abs/2105.05330

10. Schaefer, T.J.: The complexity of satisfiability problems. In: Proceedings of the Tenth Annual ACM Symposium on Theory of Computing, pp. 216–226. STOC '78, Association for Computing Machinery, New York, NY, USA (1978). https://doi.org/10.1145/800133.804350, https://doi.org/10.1145/800133.804350

11. Tarau, P.: Natlog: embedding logic programming into the python deep-learning ecosystem. In: Pontelli, E., et al. (eds.) Proceedings 39th International Conference on Logic Programming, Imperial College London, UK, 9th July 2023 – 15th July 2023. Electronic Proceedings in Theoretical Computer Science, vol. 385, pp. 141–154. Open Publishing Association (2023). https://doi.org/10.4204/EPTCS.385.15

12. Tarau, P.: On LLM-generated logic programs and their inference execution methods. In: Proceedings 40th International Conference on Logic Programming (ICLP 2024), Electronic Proceedings in Theoretical Computer Science, pp. 1–14 (2024)

13. Tarau, P.: System Description: DeepLLM, Casting Dialog Threads into Logic Programs. In: Gibbons, J., Miller, D. (eds.) Functional and Logic Programming, pp. 117–134. Springer, Singapore (2024). https://doi.org/10.1007/978-981-97-2300-3_7

14. Tarau, P.: Leveraging LLM reasoning with dual horn programs. In: Erdem, E., Vidal, G. (eds.) Practical Aspects of Declarative Languages - 27th International Symposium, PADL 2025, Denver, CO, USA, 20–21 January 2025, Proceedings. LNCS, vol. 15537, pp. 163–178. Springer, Cham (2025). https://doi.org/10.1007/978-3-031-84924-4_11, https://doi.org/10.1007/978-3-031-84924-4_11

15. Wang, Q., Fu, Y., Cao, Y., Wang, S., Tian, Z., Ding, L.: Recursively summarizing enables long-term dialogue memory in large language models (2025). https://arxiv.org/abs/2308.15022

16. Wei, J., et al.: Chain of thought prompting elicits reasoning in large language models. CoRR **abs/2201.11903** (2022). https://doi.org/10.48550/arXiv.2201.11903, https://arxiv.org/abs/2201.11903

Author Index

S. Escobar and L. Titolo (Eds.): LOPSTR 2025, LNCS 16117, p. 213, 2026.
https://doi.org/10.1007/978-3-032-04848-6

The manufacturer's authorised representative in the EU is Springer
Nature Customer Service Centre GmbH, Europaplatz 3, 69115 Heidelberg,
Germany. If you have any concerns regarding our products, please
contact ProductSafety@springernature.com

Printed and bound by CPI Group (UK) Ltd, Croydon, CR0 4YY

29/04/2026

02099461-0008